ARAB NATIONALISM

Also by Bassam Tibi

DER ISLAM UND DAS PROBLEM DER KULTURELLEN
BEWAELTIGUNG SOZIALEN WANDELS

DIE ARABISCHE LINKE

INTERNATIONALE POLITIK UND
ENTWICKLUNGSLÄNDER-FORSCHUNG

ISLAM AND THE CULTURAL ACCOMMODATION OF
SOCIAL CHANGE

KONFLIKTREGION NAHER OSTEN

MILITÄR UND SOZIALISMUS IN DER DRITTEN WELT

NATIONALISMUS IN DER DRITTEN WELT AM ARAB.
BEISPIEL

THE CRISIS OF MODERN ISLAM

UNTERENTWICKLUNG

ZUR SOZIOLOGIE DER DEKOLONISATION IN AFRIKA

ARAB NATIONALISM
A Critical Enquiry

Bassam Tibi

Edited and translated by
Marion Farouk-Sluglett and Peter Sluglett

Second Edition

St. Martin's Press   New York

© 1971 by Suhrkamp-Verlag, Frankfurt/Main
English translation © The Macmillan Press 1981, 1990
English Introduction to the Second Edition © The Macmillan Press 1990

First published in the United States of America in 1990

Printed in Hong Kong

ISBN 0–312–04234–5

Library of Congress Cataloging-in-Publication Data

Tibi, Bassam.
    [Nationalismus in der Dritten Welt am arabischen Beispiel. English]
Arab nationalism: a critical enquiry/Bassam Tibi: edited and
translated by Marion Farouk-Sluglett and Peter Sluglett.—2nd ed.
    p. cm.
Translation of: Nationalismus in der Dritten Welt am arabischen
Beispiel.
Includes bibliographical references (p.   )
ISBN 0–312–04234–5
1. Nationalism—Arab countries.   2. Husrī, Abū Khaldūn Sāti',
1981–1968.   3. Arab countries—Politics and government.   I. Farouk-
Sluglett, Marion.   II. Sluglett, Peter.   III. Title.
DS63.6.T513   1990
320.5'4'09174927—dc20   89–24392
                                                                CIP

Contents

Preface to the Second Edition

This book on Arab nationalism is a critical inquiry into this socio-political phenomenon aimed at explaining it within a world-historical framework as well as placing it into the context of the modern international system of nation-states. The structure and the scope of this inquiry are outlined in the lengthy new introductory chapter completed for this second enlarged edition. Thus there is no need to reiterate here the basic aim of this book. However, it seems to me important to re-emphasise at the outset two issues.

In the first place, this book is not exclusively for readers concerned with the Middle East, nor for scholars of a certain specific discipline. Rather, this inquiry, as well as my research in general as documented in my other books, is aimed at bridging empirical area studies and theory-oriented, conceptual approaches in social sciences and history. In other words, this book addresses social scientists who have insight into the fact that ahistorical and abstract theories and concepts that are developed independent of a study of history lack substance. It also addresses historians who reject the descriptive narrative style of writing history without any conceptual effort.

In the second place, it is important to draw the reader's attention to the fact that the new introductory chapter added to the second edition renders the book a new quality. The new chapter includes new historical material and data. It refers to more recent approaches in social science and history to discuss them in the light of the analysis provided in the earlier version of this book. Furthermore, this new chapter attempts to shed light on the topical debate pertaining to the imputed 'End of Pan-Arabism' while providing an assessment of the political revival of Islam – and its meaning as an alternative option both to the secular ideology of Arab nationalism and the secular reality of the nation-state in the Middle East, a region embedded into the overall international system of nation-states.

The research for this new chapter was first conducted at the University of Michigan, Ann Arbor during the winter term 1988 with a grant from the Rockefeller Foundation. It was continued at Harvard's Center for Middle Eastern Studies in the course of the fall term 1988. The final version, which grew from the many Michigan and Harvard drafts, was completed at my home university, the Georgia Augusta in Göttingen, West Germany.

Bassam Tibi
Harvard University
Cambridge, MA
May 1989

Foreword to the English Translation

> When one considers the enormous amount of writing on nationalism, it comes as a surprise to discover how thin the theoretical literature is on the subject. . . . One reason for this neglect may be that until a short time ago most of the investigators of the subject have been historians, who as a group tend to be more interested in description than in explanation.[1]

This quotation, from Gale Stokes' review of *Theories of Nationalism*, by Anthony Smith,[2] is generally applicable to very many of the works on Arab nationalism that have appeared in European languages. Histories of Arab nationalism have indeed tended to be descriptive: general surveys either adopt the form of narrative history, following the classic work of George Antonius,[3] or intellectual history, most notably the outstanding work of Albert Hourani.[4] Nevertheless, works in European languages are our only reliable source of information on Arab nationalism: apart from primary source materials, such as the works of Sati' al-Husri, Arabic works on the subject are only of limited value for academic purposes. They are not based on an examination of the original sources and their style often resembles that of a literary or polemical pamphlet. The works of al-Duri, al-Fakiki and al-Maghzub may be cited as examples of this tendency.[5] However, these authors can perhaps be forgiven since they do not have the research facilities at their disposal which are available to European and American scholars. Apart from the American University of Beirut, few Arab universities have complete or systematically organised libraries, with comprehensive collections of primary and secondary source material on Arab nationalism. It is therefore not surprising that scholarly monographs on Arab nationalism by Arab authors have generally been written at European or North American universities.[6] The present work, for example, could not have been written

xi

in the Middle East, precisely because of the lack of such facilities. It originated as a doctoral thesis presented to Johann Wolfgang von Goethe University in Frankfurt, and necessitated a number of journeys to the Middle East, especially to Beirut, in order to study Arabic source materials, particularly the works of Sati' al-Husri. The arduous task of translation into English has been undertaken by Dr Marion Farouk-Sluglett and Dr Peter Sluglett, to whom I am deeply grateful.

This study has three principal aims. In the first place, I have attempted to discuss theories of nationalism in the context of the non-Western societies of the 'Third World' and to attempt a definition of nationalism from the point of view of the social sciences. I have made a survey of the emergence of nationalism in Europe and of the theoretical literature on nationalism in the 'Third World'. On this basis I have tried to develop a framework within which to review the historical material on Arab nationalism.

Secondly, I have given an outline of the history of Arab nationalism. I have identified three distinct stages: first, the Arabic literary and linguistic renaissance,[7] during which Westernised Arab intellectuals arrived at a form of national consciousness (the *Nahdha*); secondly, the politicisation of this literary renaissance, and the transformation of cultural into political nationalism; and finally, the narrowing down of this political nationalism into the demand for a unified Arab national state.

Thirdly, I have described the development of what I have called 'Arab germanophilia', that is, the changeover from liberal anglophone and francophone nationalism to a form of nationalism modelled on that of the nineteenth-century German Romantics, which is a characteristic feature of the voluminous works of Sati' al-Husri. al-Husri's works, which show strong traces of the influence of the German idea of the nation as formulated by Herder, Fichte and Arndt, document this Arab germanophilia, which first found expression in literature. The Arab nation was now seen as a cultural community, united by a common language.[8]

After the publication of the German edition (Frankfurt/Main, 1971), I decided to investigate the general problem of the intervention of the military in politics in the 'Third World', particularly in the Arab countries. Thus in 1973 I published my habilitation dissertation. *Militär und Sozialismus in der Dritten Welt* (Socialism and the Military in the Third World).[9] Since the military regimes in the Arab world have combined nationalism with a socialist ideology of social justice as a means of legitimating their rule, it will be understood that Arab nationalism continues to be a central concern of my more recent research. In what follows I shall confine myself to a short discussion of two substantial works on the subject which have appeared in recent years.

The Making of an Arab Nationalist, by William Cleveland,[10] which is a study of Sati' al-Husri, the spiritual father of Arab nationalism, is of particular interest. While I have tried to discuss al-Husri's concept of nationalism within the general context of the history of Arab nationalism, and also to analyse the phenomenon of nationalism in the 'Third World', Cleveland has confined himself to a study of al-Husri's life and work. He is chiefly concerned to analyse 'the transition from Ottomanism to Arabism as exemplified in the life and thought of Sati' al-Husri' (Cleveland, p. ix). As I suggested in my review of Cleveland in 1972 (reprinted in a recent collection of essays),[11] his insistence on the notion of 'the transition from Ottomanism to Arabism' makes him overlook the fundamental change of direction within Arab nationalism from francophilia to germanophilia. Cleveland acknowledges that 'fluent in French and more familiar with European writers than with his own Islamic heritage, [al-Husri] was intellectually a European' (p. 30). Furthermore, he also notes correctly that al-Husri 'himself was largely a man of French culture and outlook. His ideas on nationalism, however, stemmed more from the German romantic nationalists' (p. 85). However, Cleveland cannot explain the significance of the transition from francophilia to germanophilia, which was not peculiar to al-Husri, but also took place in the minds of other Arab nationalists, because of his own excessive pre-occupation with Ottomanism-Arabism. This transition is the central concern of Part III of the present work, and I hope that I have succeeded in explaining it adequately.

The second work which I should like to mention is *La Nation Arabe*, by the Egyptian social scientist and economist Samir Amin, published in Paris in 1976, and in English in London in 1978.[12] Amin attempts a Marxist analysis, and he interprets the history of the Arab nation in terms of economic and social history. While many authors have been primarily concerned to write the intellectual history of Arab nationalism, Amin confines himself to the socio-economic sphere. It seems to me that neither of these approaches should exclude the other; expertise on the ideology of Arab nationalism must be complemented by an analysis of the social structures in which this ideology has emerged and now exists. Amin has not thought it necessary to concern himself with the literary products of Arab nationalism, and has confined himself to a class analysis, which I consider to be a serious weakness in an otherwise stimulating approach.

In the Postscript to this book I have tried to show how the ideology of Arab nationalism has penetrated the political process in the contemporary Middle East, and how politicians and political parties have tried to make use of it. I imply that there are signs that Arab nationalism is being superseded as a political doctrine. In fact, a process of self-criticism did begin among Arab intellectuals after the defeat of the Six Days' War of 1967, which I have called 'From Self-Glorification to Self-Criticism' in an essay in 1972 in which I examined some of the relevant literature.[13] One of the most important contributors to this discussion has been the American-educated Syrian philosopher Sadiq Jalal al-Azm.[14]

However, this phase of self-criticism, which found expression in the works of a number of Arab intellectuals, seems to have come to an end. Following the Syrian occupation of Lebanon there is now no Arab country without censorship, in which intellectuals are able to express themselves freely. Pan-Arab nationalism, whose secularism seemed to have gained the victory over Islam, has also lost much of its influence. In Egypt, the leading Arab country, intellectuals supported by the Sadat regime plead for a rewriting of their history, in which Egyptians will no longer appear as Arabs but as Egyptian patriots. This is the central concern, for example, of the Cairo history professor Nu'mat Fu'ad.[15] A kind of local patriotism, which is no longer secular, is being combined with Islam to serve as the vehicle for the re-Islamisation of Egypt.[16] The reappearance of Islam as a political ideology is not confined to Egypt, but is a phenomenon observable throughout the Arab and Islamic Middle East.[17]

I hope that this study will illuminate a wider canvas than the history of nationalism and of Islam as ideologies in the contemporary Middle East. Its central concern is with the social and political context in which the various ideologies developed. These ideologies contain both indigenous (Oriental) and foreign (European) elements, and are therefore the products of acculturation. It is difficult to arrive at a true understanding of political processes in the contemporary Middle East without some comprehension of the nature of these ideologies.

Here I must thank Marion Farouk-Sluglett and Peter Sluglett once again for having made it possible for this study to be brought to an English audience. It is no secret that the Germans are somewhat provincial, and have little acquaintance with non-European cultures: furthermore, they rarely seem inclined to overcome or remedy this deficiency. The promotion of Middle Eastern and African studies in the Federal Republic of Germany is a rather daunting undertaking. My colleague Professor Dr Gerhard Grohs, who teaches sociology at the University of Mainz, and who is one of the leading German Africanists, once remarked, with some justice 'To publish in German is a form of concealment'. The publication of *Zur Soziologie der Dekolonisation in Afrika* by Professor Grohs and myself and a number of German Africanists was a good illustration of this assertion.[18]

I am grateful to the translators for having enabled my book to reach a wider audience. I would also like to thank the Macmillan Press and Mr John Winckler for their interest in having undertaken the publication.

March 1979

Bassam Tibi

Department of Political Science
University of Göttingen.

Notes to the Foreword

1. Gale Stokes, 'The Undeveloped Theory of Nationalism', *World Politics*, XXI (1978) No. 1, 150–60; here p. 150.
2. Anthony D. Smith, *Theories of Nationalism* (New York, 1972).
3. George Antonius, *The Arab Awakening, The Story of the Arab National Movement*, 4th ed. (New York, 1965).
4. Albert Hourani, *Arabic Thought in the Liberal Age 1798–1939* (London, 1962).
5. 'Abd al-'Aziz al-Duri, *al-Judhur al-Tarikhiyya li'-Qawmiyya al-'Arabiyya* (The Historical Roots of Arab Nationalism) (Beirut, 1960); 'Abd al-Hadi al-Fakiki, *al-Shu'ubiyya wa'l-Qawmiyya al-'Arabiyya* (Xenophilia and Arab Nationalism) (Beirut, n.d., [ca. 1962]); Muhammad al-Maghzub, *al-Qawmiyya al-'Arabiyya* (Arab Nationalism) (Beirut, 1960).
6. For instance H. Z. Nuseibeh, *The Ideas of Arab Nationalism*, 2nd ed. (Ithaca, 1959), and Hasan Saab, *The Arab Federalists of the Ottoman Empire* (Amsterdam, 1958).
7. I have discussed this in connection with Arabic in an essay on socio-linguistics; see B. Tibi, 'Sprachentwicklung und sozialer Wandel. Die Diskussion über

Sprache und Kultur im arabischen Orient', *Die Dritte Welt*, I (1972) No. 4, 518–48.

8. See Joshua A. Fishman, *Language and Nationalism* (Rowley, Mass., 1972).

9. B. Tibi, *Militär und Sozialismus in der Dritten Welt. Allgemeine Theorien und Regionalstudien über arabische Länder* (Frankfurt/Main, 1973).

10. William L. Cleveland, *The Making of an Arab Nationalist: Ottomanism and Arabism in the Life of Sati' al-Husri* (Princeton, 1971).

11. 'Der arabische Nationalismus als Forschungsgegenstand', *Verfassung und Recht in Übersee*, V (1972) 218–21, reprinted in B. Tibi, *Internationale Politik und Entwicklungsländerforschung* (Frankfurt/Main, 1979).

12. Samir Amin, *La Nation Arabe* (Paris, 1976); Eng. transl. *The Arab Nation* (London, 1978).

13. B. Tibi, 'Von der Selbstverherrlichung zur Selbstkritik. Zur Kritik des politischen Schrifttums der zeitgenössischen arabischen Intelligenz', *Die Dritte Welt*, I (1972) No. 2, 158–84.

14. See Sadiq Jalal al-Azm, *al-Naqd al-Dhati ba'd al-Hazima* (Self-criticism after the Defeat) (Beirut, 1968), and *idem.*, *Naqd al-Fikr al-Dini* (Critique of Religious Thought) (Beirut, 1969).

15. Nu'mat A. Fu'ad, *A'idu Kitabat al-Tarikh* (Rewrite the History Books!) (Cairo, 1974).

16. B. Tibi, 'Die Wiederentdeckung des ägyptisch-nationalen, kulturellen Identität. Ägyptens Loslösung vom Panarabismus unter Sadat', *Die Dritte Welt*, VI (1978) No. 2, 253–65.

17. See B. Tibi, 'Der Islam als politische Ideologie', *Die Neue Gesellschaft*, XXVI (1979) No. 3, 212–17.

18. See Gerhard Grohs and Bassam Tibi (eds), *Zur Soziologie der Dekolonisation in Afrika* (Frankfurt/Main, 1973).

A Note on Sources, Quotations and Transliteration

1. SOURCES

The material on nationalism is now so extensive that it is almost impossible for a single scholar to cover it. It has become clear in the course of writing this book that the increasingly specialised nature of research into nationalism cannot lead to viable analytical conclusions unless the various individual studies are considered as part of a general investigation of the phenomenon of nationalism. In other words, the specific must be presented within the context of the whole. This study has made intensive and detailed use of existing monographs on the Arab national movement, which are mostly in German and English. A strictly selective approach has been applied to specialised studies of nationalism in Europe and in the various parts of the 'Third World', and also to theoretical works on the subject. The criteria for this selection were the impact of such a work on the study of nationalism as a whole as well as its inherent quality.

I have omitted any discussion of Sati' al/Husri's strictly educational writings as well as his archaeological and other non-political contributions (see the Bibliography, section 4). As far as the primary source material is concerned, I have generally made direct use of the Arabic originals, and have only consulted secondary works or translations if the originals have not been available. I have listed translations of the Arabic material, where such exist, for the assistance of readers who may not know Arabic.

2. QUOTATIONS

In the notes, the titles of al-Husri's works are not cited, but simply indicated by Roman numerals, which are listed in the bibliography with full reference details. Each Chapter has its own numerical series of notes. All works cited, apart from reviews and short notices, are listed in the bibliography. [Quotations from Arabic sources have been translated into German by the author from the original, and then into English from the German by the translators. Where the author has used German translations of works in other European languages, or German works for which English translations exist, the translators have used either the original English, or standard translations where available and appropriate. The references have been adjusted accordingly, and full details of the translations have been added to the bibliography].

3. TRANSLITERATION
[The translators have adopted a simplified form of Arabic transliteration, in which no diacritical marks have been used. *Hamza* has been omitted, except where final, and ' has been used for *'ain*. Names of Arab authors who have written in languages other than Arabic are spelt as they themselves have spelt them. Titles of works in Arabic appear first in transliteration and then in English translation in brackets.]

Introduction to the Second Edition: Arab Nationalism Revisited

An Interpretative-Historical and Socio-Political Reassessment

This book is a monograph on Arab nationalism. Since Arab nationalism is not an isolated phenomenon, and because this author wants to explain, rather than simply describe or provide a narrative of, events, the idea behind this book is to place the historical phenomenon of Arab nationalism in the overall context in which it belongs.[1] Nation, nationalism and nation-states are phenomena strange to Islamic history.[2] However, since the Europeans have conquered the world, with the ensuing Europeanisation of world order, the Arab and Islamic Middle East has become a part of this modern world, structured as an international system and subdivided into basic units organised as nation-states.[3] Nationalism was originally a European phenomenon related to the emergence of the modern nation-state in Europe.[4] With the globalisation of the initially European international system of nation-states to encompass in this context the entire world,[5] non-Western peoples have come to claim that they also, in each case, constitute a nation. Thus, in the course of the twentieth century, nationalism and decolonisation have become inextricably interrelated.[6] Only if organised as a nation-state can a community of people be a member of the international system.

In a recent collection of essays Ernest Gellner alludes to the fact that by the early 1960s 'decolonization was more or less completed';[7] he adds, however, that nationalism is still 'plainly a major force in the modern world'.[8] There is a vast literature on nationalism in which scholars deal with this phenomenon.[9] Given the enormous amount of writing on nationalism, it strikes one as surprising to find how few works there are dealing with theories. Gale Stokes suggests that 'one reason for this neglect may be that

1

until a short time ago most of the investigators of the subject have been historians, who as a group tend to be more interested in description than in explanation'.[10] In his valuable report on the state of the art in research on nationalism, completed as an introductory part to a useful bibliography, Anthony Smith, too, complains: 'Research in the field has been conducted mainly by historians, concerned largely with description ... There is therefore a pressing need for comparative studies and sociological explanations of this phenomenon.'[11] I would add, there is also a need for further efforts in the discipline of international relations, to which this author belongs, to contribute to a much firmer theory than has hitherto been offered of the nation-state as an institutional and 'legal transplant'[12] in the non-Western world where the bulk of nation-states lack the very substance of the nation. We are talking about artificial nations compounded of divergent groups, and about nominal nation-states whose boundaries have been drawn by colonial powers. In many parts of the Third World nation-states are, more or less, administrative units.

The observation concerning the preponderance of narrative historians might be understood by this group of scholars as a reproach. They also might, and in fact they do, respond by turning the tables on their critics. Historians criticise the fact that social scientists conceptualise history without being familiar with it, and thus – with some justice – they speak with contempt about abstract models of nation-building and nationalism.[13] Both, historians and social science theorists, have a point in their arguments. Currently, historical sociologists seem to close the gap and to do justice to both in combining the study of history with efforts at conceptualisations along the avenues of comparative history and historical sociology.[14] In as far as historical sociologists substantially refer to the international and world-historical contexts of their particular subjects of study, be it revolution or the nation-state, they also combine history, sociology and international relations in an interdisciplinary way. This is the approach also employed in this book. I do not view Arab nationalism as an isolated historical phenomenon, nor do I discuss it within the confines of a national history reduced to an intellectual history. In my view, without referring to the dimension of 'world time'[15] recently outlined by Theda Skocpol with an emphasis on the structures of history one renders oneself unable to understand adequately any aspect of Arab or any other

Third World nationalism chosen as a subject of enquiry.

The kind of criticism of the literature on nationalism offered in these introductory remarks on general grounds applies in particular to the literature on Arab nationalism.[16] To remedy this, it seems to me imperative to broaden the case-study of Arab nationalism to an enquiry into comparative history, and furthermore to venture up the avenues of historically grounded conceptualisation and fruitful theorising. In that sense, this is an ambitious book which attempts to combine the structural study of history with the relevant history of ideas and with international relations, also to integrate these approaches into a frame of reference for studying and explaining Arab nationalism. I simultaneously try – with the sensitivity of the historian – to grasp the specific and unique elements of this variety of nationalism, as well as to interpret – as a social scientist – and find out regularities which occur in this historical case. To me, Arab nationalism is a case in point in the study of nationalism in non-Western societies. In this venture, I, of course, am aware of possible scholarly risks as well as of my own limitations. Nevertheless, the book has been received by the academic community most favourably, thus encouraging me to believe that I am doing the right work. The distinguished scholar and former president of the Middle East Studies Association of North America (MESA), Professor Michael Hudson, wrote in 1985, four years after the publication of the first English translation of this book in 1981: 'It is fortunate that, 10 years after its original publication in German, there is now an English edition of Bassam Tibi's impressive study of Arab nationalism . . . for it fills a need that has not been met thus far in the English literature'.[17] This and other, similar, judgments contributed to wide critical acclaim for this book and have resulted in this second printing with its new introduction.[18]

I

Arab nationalism is a topical subject for both politically and academically interested readers. For students of the Middle East and Islam the conflict that arises from the tensions between the universalism of Islam and the particularities of Arab nationalism/ pan-Arabism has been a major focus of interest.[19] The Iranian revolution accompanied by the claim of Khomaynism to export a non-Arab variety of Islam into the entire 'abode of Islam', including the neighbouring Arab countries, has further contributed to topicality of the conflict between nationalism and Islam,[20] dealt with in this new introduction.

One of the major areas of my enquiry has been highlighted by Professor Michael Hudson, who is a great international authority in Middle East Studies. Professor Hudson holds that this book 'ably combines the insights of the historian of ideas with those of the social scientist ... it also places these writings (of Arab nationalism) in their sociopolitical context juxtaposing them against the historical development of the nationalist movement and also against competing theories and ideologies'.[21] Professor Hudson also commends the contribution of this study to comparative research in as far as one of the four areas of its enquiry focusses on a comparison of European and Third World nationalism. With regard to this, my contribution is very much close and congenial to the approaches of the modern school of historical sociology alluded to earlier. This school places political and socio-historical developments into a world-time context. According to this concept, modern history is characterised by a dimension of 'world time' revealed by some aspects of 'modernisation' which 'have been unique processes affecting the world as a whole'.[22] Viewed from this angle, nationalism, in the Third World and the Arab East alike, as an ideology of nation-building and citizenship is related to this world time. A distinguished Princeton scholar, Professor Carl Brown, touches on this fact, namely that nationalism in the Middle East is a 'virus'[23] coming from the West. It is true that the modern concepts of nation and citizenship[24] are borrowed from Europe or, in the description of a leading Muslim fundamentalist (Yusuf Qurdawi), are 'imported solutions' (*hulul mustawrada*).[25] However, nationalism is not simply an ideology. Without subscribing to an economically globalist as well as reductionist concept of structure, such as the one developed by Wallerstein,[26] the research approach of historical sociology, employed here as well as represented by Skocpol, holds 'that nation-states are, more fundamentally, organizations geared to maintain control of home territories and populations and to undertake actual or potential military competition with the other states in the international system'.[27] Thus, nationalism as an ideology of the nation-state is not simply a transmitted idea, let alone a 'virus', but rather is embodied in existing institutional, both economic and military, state structures on a global scale. Skocpol, as well as this author, is aware that the emphasis on the nation-state (the real one or the one aimed at – more will be said about this below) should not distract from two different sorts of transnational context of this basic unit of analysis, namely, 'on the one hand . . . the structures of world capitalist economy and the international states system . . . And on the other hand . . . changes and transmissions in world time which affect . . . the overall world contexts'.[28]

It is inappropriate and wrong to deal with the reappraisal of political Islam as an ideological challenge to the existing nation-states in the 'abode of Islam' as transplants from non-Muslims, without taking these structural contexts into consideration. As Philip Khoury has plainly shown, this ideological challenge is underlaid by a structural crisis of the secular state in the Arab Middle East.[29] In terms of ideology, however, it is true that with the reappraisal of political Islam, and with the concomitant ideological revival of Islam's universalism, another ideology had tentatively to recede. Since the 1970s, Arab nationalism has had to give way to a wide range of varieties of Islamic fundamentalism and neo-fundamentalism[30] which, despite their differences, mostly share the view that Islam is incompatible with nationalism. For some of the fierce Muslim revivalists, like Garisha and Zaybaq, 'the hidden hand' was behind the abolition of the Islamic caliphate while aiming at 'achieving the separation between religion and the state in employing the means of nationalism'.[31] These authors view this separation between religion and state which is consequential to the adoption of nationalism as an expression of an anti-Islamic spirit that can be traced back to 'the crusaders and also indirectly to Zionism'.[32] Looked at from this point of view, 'the dissemination of Arab nationalism is the achievement of the British spy Lawrence'.[33] Garisha and Zaybaq published their fundamentalist indictment against Arab nationalism prior to the Iranian revolution. Khomayni's claim to export this revolution to the neighbouring Arab states,[34] the ensuing Gulf war, as well as the spill-over effects of this revolution[35] were the source of new constraints put on the ideological demands of universalism included in the Arab variety of political Islam. A need has emerged to modify Arab–Islamic views on nationalism. Indicative of this new need was the great Arab congress held by the Beirut-based Institute for Arab Unity Studies, on 'Islam and Arab Nationalism'. The papers delivered there supported the observation that most pan-Arab nationalists have given up on their secular views – however, without abandoning Arabism.[36] Nonetheless, we cannot reduce the newly emphasised link between Arabism and Islam to an Arab response to the Iranian revolution. Prior to the Iranian threat the Saudi Professor Ahmad Muhammad Jamal contended that the Arabs' familiarity with *'asabiyya*, allegedly an authentic pattern of nationalism, supports the view that the Arabs knew nationalism long before the historical phenomenon related to this ideology took place in Europe.[37] On these grounds, Jamal states that God has honoured the Arabs in choosing one of them to be his messenger to humanity for the revelation of Islam. Thus, 'the Arabs are the guides of the world and the leaders of the peoples and the successors of the prophet. This virtue of the Arabs and their glory are inexorably related to Islam.'[38] With this interpretation Islam acquires an Arabo-centric face while being reconciled with Arab nationalism.

There is no doubt that scholars must discern the ways in which the concerned peoples, here the Arabs, perceive themselves. We have to study the ideologies expressed in the published literature[39] revealing these attitudes and images of the self. Nonetheless, I want to draw on further methods. The reassessment of Arab nationalism offered in this introduction and supported by the findings of this book rests on the historically grounded knowledge that the nation-state is the political form for organising political entities in the contemporary international system of states. As Giddens has put it, 'From the state system that was once one of the peculiarities of Europe there has developed a system of nation-states covering the globe in a network of national communities . . . Two processes have, above all, been responsible for producing these extraordinary changes, the global consolidation of industrial capitalism and the global ascendancy of the nation-state.'[40] Thus, the ideology of nationalism related to this structural framework along the lines of which our world is organised is not an idea that simply can be adopted or rejected on an ideological level. The ideology of nationalism rests on the idea of sovereignty as the organisational principle for the nation-state. The internationalisation of this principle on the grounds of real existing structures in the international system implies – as Hinsley reminds us – 'the recognition that in the normal circumstances of relations between . . . states the sovereignty of a state in theory is a necessary condition of its membership of the international system in practice.'[41]

In this new introduction I propose to take these structural contexts into consideration while assessing the revival of political Islam and reassessing the decay of Arab nationalism. In so doing we are obliged to contest many of the hitherto prevailing views on this subject. In scholarly presentations as well as in the popular literature, Arab nationalism has been viewed in a variety of ways. Some of its authors focus on a partial aspect and overlook the overall context, while others impose a ready-made preoccupation. Eric Davis draws our attention to some of these examples and comments, 'It is obvious that writings on Arab nationalism have been affected by the tendency to view ideology in terms of social pathology. Arab ideologies are seen as irrational and distortive, having transformed Arab history into myth and having twisted the true meaning of Islamic doctrine.'[42] Contrary to this approach, the present book suggests that we study ideologies in their structural, i.e. social-historical, context. When I had completed this book I published further methodologically oriented works on ideologies in Islam and the Arab Middle East[43] upon which this introduction draws.

It is not my concern here to review critically the literature on Arab nationalism, nor to reduce the ways of viewing Arab nationalism documented in this literature to a specific *Weltanschauung*, be it Orientalism, ethnocentrism or whatever. I do not have the least inclination to be involved in the polemic of the Orientalism debate.[44] Even if I were willing to be so, then I would have to restrain myself from it since in that case, just for the sake of objectivity, I would be obliged to include Middle Eastern writers in my criticism. Since by applying the notion of Orientalism we mean distorted ways of looking at Arab nationalism, many Middle Eastern authors are Orientalists in reverse. The Damascene philosophy professor Sadiq Jalal al-'Azm thinks that this notion of Orientalism in reverse (*al-istishraq ma'kusan*) also applies to the *rector spiritus* of the debate on Orientalism, to Edward Said himself.[45]

Touching on these ways of viewing Arab nationalism in this introductory section should not be misunderstood to imply that my focus will be on a critical presentation of the published literature on Arab nationalism, Western and Arab alike. On the contrary, I want at the very beginning to suggest that we leave the bulk of this literature aside to find new ways of exploring Arab nationalism. Whether Arab nationalism has been a modernising ideology, as Western scholars usually argue,[46] and whether or not the Arab nation is much older than all European nations are, as Arab authors suggest,[47] seem to me of little interest for an analysis aiming to explain the phenomenon at issue. Current scholarly standards oblige us to leave this aside and to explore new ground.

II

The frame of reference for dealing with Arab nationalism that I employ in this book and that I develop further in this introduction is based on a combined interdisciplinary approach of history and social science. I propose to overcome the dichotomy of the two notions of *social action* and *social structure* in the study of history and society.[48] I argue that social action always takes place in particular structures and that we cannot reduce the one to the other, nor can we arbitrarily focus on one to the detriment of the other.[49] In other words, we cannot interpret history adequately merely by studying the actions of great men or by exclusively analysing the existing structures. Nor can we derive the deeds of great men from the prevailing structures or, in a reversed way, view historical processes as the achievement of great men. History is always an interplay between the actions of men and the existing structures which form their constraints. To take an example from European history, Napoleon was not simply a 'Weltgeist zu Pferde' (spirit of the age on horseback). His actions could not have been performed by anyone else, but neither could he have performed his deeds in a structurally different environment. Structures constrain the actions of man, but do not determine them. There is always a certain scope for different options of action. In this sense, the history of Arab nationalism is a history of the interplay between the actors, be they writers, politicians or soldiers, and the social structures in which they were acting. Social theory should view societal change as based on such an interplay between the actions of man and structural changes. In the footsteps of the great work of Norbert Elias, *Der Prozess der Zivilisation*,[50] I further propose to get away from abstract formalising models and get closer to real history, not to narrate it, however, but to study it with an effort at conceptualisation. Unfortunately, and despite the fact that Elias' work is available in an English translation, it is still not well known among English readers, not even among historical-sociologists who could learn a lot from him. Elias bridges history and social sciences and provides an exemplary study in which he combines the *analysis of action* of man with the *analysis of structures* as discussed earlier.[51] From the point of view of concept-oriented study of history, quantitative and formalising models lack substance and are empty. The alternative to them cannot be the prevailing method in the scholarly literature on Arab nationalism and the Middle East, i.e. the narrative-descriptive approach.[52] Social theory should be historicised and history should be conceptualised. This is the alternative we ultimately need. In my view, the efforts of the new school of 'historical sociology' referred to earlier contribute to fulfilling this urgently needed requirement in research.[53] To the achievements of this school belongs Tilly's pioneering *The Formation of Nation States in Western Europe*.[54] Tilly and the other authors of that volume greatly improve our knowledge about the emergence and the unfolding of the first nation-states in history. The current international system of nation-states grew from the European nucleus.[55]

In subscribing to this combined history–social science approach in this introduction I want to review the emergence of Arab nationalism conceptually anew, as a historical phenomenon revealing the actions of men striving for a new order in a rapidly and constantly changing structural environment. We first need to clarify the terms that we are using. To be precise, the term 'nationalism' is an expression of an ideology. In taking this into consideration, we are confronted with two questions. First, are we going to restrict our endeavour to a study of political literature in Arabic documenting the ideology of nationalism? Second, is this study of ideologies essentially a history of ideas, or should it be extended to a social history and, if so, in what ways?

If we accept the assumption included in the first question and thus restrict our enquiry to the study of each idea in its own terms, then we will end up where we started. Western scholars argue that the idea of nation was exported from Europe to the 'abode of Islam'. Those who have adopted it are viewed as modernisers, whereas those who reject it are considered to be traditionalists.[56] Arab authors, for their part, contest the notion that nationalism was imported and insist on the authenticity of their own nationalism. We are familiar with these sentiments from the political poetry of Michel Aflaq, who tells us that the Arab nation is an *umma sarmadiyya* (eternal nation), as old as history itself.[57] These contradictory views reflect the attitudes of the Orientalists and of their opponents.

Currently we are witnessing some Middle Easterners acting as Orientalists in reverse, who unwittingly join the Western Orientalists in arguing that the idea of nation is a Western export to the 'abode of Islam'. They reject these *al-hulul al-mustawradah* (imported solutions) in favour of *al-hall al-Islami* (Islamic solution; see note 25). Just to draw a historical comparison: we are familiar with the racist notions about black being ugly. 'Anti-racist racists' (J.-P. Sartre) reverse this scheme, saying that black is more beautiful than white, instead of arguing that human beings are equals. In a similar manner, Islamic Orientalists in reverse do not contest the artificial notion of *homo islamicus*[58] as much as they reverse the names they have been called. Here we find ourselves in the terrain more of polemics than of scholarship. Polemic is not an adequate response to cultural prejudices. It is entirely preferable to move toward more promising avenues.

I have treated the second question at length in an earlier article published in *IJMES* (see note 39); I would propose a new framework to study political ideas in their social context. This conceptual framework, which is essentially the one employed in this book, suggests relating the ideas of Arab nationalism to overall history instead of reducing them to the 'impact of the West', as to a continuation of a traditional Arab *'asabiyya*. The history that we are dealing with is not merely a local history. It is rather a world history to which the history of Arab nationalism specifically belongs. To state this is not to subscribe to a crude structural globalism such as the one put forward in the work of Wallerstein. To be aware of the world-historical structures is not tantamount to overlooking local structures and their specific features. I want to draw here on the great work of Norbert Elias, *The Civilizing Process/Der Prozess der Zivilisation*, in which he views modern history as a globalisation of the historical processes that took place in Europe and which then started to encompass the entire world in the course of the European conquests. Again, the charge of Orientalism may arise. Orientalism and Orientalism in reverse are attitudes. We are not dealing here with attitudes but with real history, structures and actions alike.

In his pioneering *The Civilizing Process* Norbert Elias is aware of the fact that many non-Western civilisations – for instance Islam – were able to spread far beyond their own boundaries. It is, however, only the European process of civilisation which has been able to comprise the entire globe. It is this European conquest of the entire world and its tentative Europeanisation which have created the context of modern world history.[59] The world has become a consistent whole in which each part is affected by the others. To Norbert Elias, this worldwide process of civilisation first generated by Europe and dominated by its standards has been *action-based* as well as *structural*. In the wording of Elias himself, this process encompassed both a *socio-genesis* and a *psycho-genesis*. In ever-changing structures, men and women were acting towards more complexity and more globality.[60] The result of this process which has covered the entire world is the industrial, scientific and technological civilisation that prevails in the present international system, as Hedley Bull among many other eminent scholars has shown in his work.[61] In my book *Crisis of Modern Islam*, in which I draw on Norbert Elias, I interpret Islam as a *pre-industrial culture in the scientific technological age.*[62]

These methodological remarks about the world-historical context of Arab nationalism are central. The argument – earlier stressed – that Arab nationalism is not a unique or discrete historical phenomenon – supports this view. I would further argue that Arab nationalism cannot be properly understood apart from the respective world-historical context I have been touching on. Nationalism is not merely an ideology, as we have seen. It is rather an articulation related to the real setting of the modern international system. Nationalism refers to the nation-state as an organisational unit of this international system. The Peace of Westphalia in 1648 was the historical beginning of this system of sovereign states. With the emergence of the nation-state after the French Revolution and its spread, as a completely new historical phenomenon, these sovereign states were gradually redefined, as well as re-structured as nation-states. The French nation-state provided the model.[63]

Charles Tilly tells us in his book *The Formation of National States in Western Europe*: 'Over the next three hundred years (after the Peace of Westphalia 1648; BT) the Europeans and their descendants managed to impose that system on the entire world.

The recent wave of decolonization has almost completed the mapping of the globe into that system.'[64] No nationalism can be studied apart from this world-historical process. Arab nationalism is part and parcel of this world-historical process. Moreover, the idea of an 'eternal Arab nation' (*al-umma al'Arabiyya al-sarmadiyya*) related to Islam as a religion for the Arabs is an ideological reading of modernity into the Islamic notion of *umma* (community). The late scholar Hamid Enayat ironically points out: 'In defining its relationship with Islam, Arab nationalism often ends where it started: with the glorification of Arabism as a commanding value in Islam.'[65] For this reason it is justified to argue that confining the analysis in studying Arab nationalism to the study of ideologies is like barking up the wrong tree.

III

The birth of Arab nationalism under the Ottoman Empire in the second half of the nineteenth century was closely related to the globalisation of the international system.[66] This process was largely responsible for the crisis of the Islamic caliphate under the Turks[67] and for the disintegration of this universal empire, as well as for the later emergence of the current Arab nation-states.

Prior to the French Revolution the Ottoman Empire lost its military superiority over Europe. Humiliating military defeats were the historical consequence. The treaties of Carlowitz (1699) and Passarowitz (1718) had given these Ottoman defeats 'formal expression and recognition',[68] as Bernard Lewis argues. Military reforms based on a European model became imperative. It is, however, inconceivable that a traditional military organisation could be reformed without certain non-military innovations as byproducts. The early efforts to open the Empire to European know-how[69] (1721–1730) were interrupted under the pressure of traditional forces. They were, however, resumed after the French Revolution which ever afterwards became the major source of determining 'world time', discussed earlier. The military defeats made military reforms inevitable and these led to the spread of modern education and training in the Empire.[70] The consequence of the defeats was the weakening of the Empire and the repercussion of the political and cultural impact of the French

Revolution was the crisis of the legitimacy of the Empire. The Ottoman history of the reform movements 'in the nineteenth and early twentieth centuries is largely concerned with the attempt by Western educated intellectuals to impose a Western pattern of secular political classification and organization on the religious community of Islam'.[71] This Western pattern is based on the concept of the nation; it was not simply an idea emanating from the French Revolution. Since 1789 and since the ensuing wars of revolution[72] the new international system of states, which has existed ever since the Peace of Westphalia, has been transformed into a nation-state system now posing a threat to the dynastic Ottoman Empire legitimised by Islamic universalism but for which there is no place in modern history. This is the world-historical and regional context of Arab nationalism. I can hardly imagine any feature of Arab nationalism that is not linked to the world-historical process outlined here. The result of that process is our present world of nation-states, including the Arab part of the dissolved Ottoman Empire. The fact that this system originated in Europe should not detract from the other fact that this system is today the real organisational principle of the entire world.

The dissolution of the Ottoman Empire did not magically result in the emergence of modern nation-states in that area. The former Arab provinces of the Ottoman Empire went through a period of colonial rule by Western powers. There were a variety of decolonisation processes which resulted in the creation of numerous Arab nation-states, but not in the desired pan-Arab nation-state. It is true that the Arab part of the international system, unlike many parts of Asia and Africa, is characterised by homogeneity in terms of widely shared cultural and religious values as well as in linguistic terms. However, the social mobilisation processes which underlay the emergence of modern nation-states in Europe are still lacking in the Arab East. As Michael Hudson has put it: 'In a political culture noted for effectivity and the persisting salience of . . . primordial identifications, Arabism must coexist or compete with certain other parochial but intensely held corporate identifications . . . It is too easy to assume that modernization is performing an assimilation-ist melting pot function in the area'.[73] The objective set-up of the international system of nation-states imposed on the former parts of the Ottoman Empire has been an external structure.

Domestically the basic requirements of nation-state are still lacking. To state this is not tantamount to revoking the basic argument of this introduction, namely that Arab nationalism is more than simply an ideology. We cannot fail to acknowledge that the domestic requirements of a pan-Arab nation-state are still lacking. On the one hand, Arab nationalism is related to the global structure of the system of nation-states; on the other, this ideology is domestically confronted with pre-national parochialisms and primordial cultural identifications. In this regard we are confronted with attitudes and actions of two contending groups. We can observe this in the Arab region as elsewhere. The opponents are the integrationists and the disintegrationists. The first group seeks to go beyond the existing boundaries of nation-state. The latter rejects being a part of an existing nation-state and aims at separating from it. Pan-Arab nationalists belong to the first group whereas ethnic minorities[74] such as the Kurds in Iraq and Syria and the Dinka in the Sudan belong to the second group. It is striking to the observer to see that both groups share the very same salient feature. As Hedley Bull has put it, integrationists and disintegrationists 'are alike intellectually imprisoned by the theory of the state system, and are in most cases as committed to it as the agents of sovereign states.'[75] Even those Islamic revivalists who view the emergence of the ideology of nationalism based on the principle of nation-state as 'a conspiracy against Islam' (see Garisha and Zaybaq referred to in note 31) are imprisoned by this theory of nation-states. It is unfortunate that James Piscatori[76] fails to grasp this issue in his work on Islam and the state since he does not draw a distinction between the *medieval state* and the *modern nation-state* based on sovereignty.

Following this preliminary conceptual integration of my topic into its overall context I reach the well-grounded first two conclusions. *First,* nationalism is a recent phenomenon inexorably linked with the globalisation of the originally European system of states which has extended to a worldwide international system. Prior to the nineteenth century there never existed such an Arab nationalism. The projections of Arab nationalism into the past, as in the Iraqis' propagandist references to the seventh century as the historical beginning of the conflict between Arab and Iranian nationalism, are based on reading modern history into the past. These projections and references provide ground for propaganda, but there is hardly any evidence to support this view. Prior to the adoption of the European idea of nation, Arabness was an ethnic rather than a national bond. The tensions between the Arabs and the *Mawali*, i.e. non-Arab Muslims, were ethnic – not national – conflicts.

My *second* preliminary conclusion is that Arab nationalists are simultaneously adherents of and opponents of the idea of nation-state, in as much as they both aim to establish a pan-Arab state and resent the existing boundaries of nation-states. They are integrationists in Hedley Bull's sense of the word.

Before moving on to review, discuss and assess some major historical elements of Arab nationalism, I want to sum up, and again emphasise that nationalism is not simply an idea that has invaded the East and intruded upon its culture. The idea of nation is rather the legitimacy of all current states which are, at least in theory, internally and externally sovereign states. Only sovereign states can act in the existing political world order organised as a system of nation-states. The spread of the idea was linked to the globalisation of the European international system of sovereign states.[77]

IV

The crisis of the Ottoman Empire, as well as the crisis of modern Islam,[78] is clearly related to this globalisation process. The crisis of the Ottoman Empire can be dealt with on both an external and an internal level of analysis. Externally the Ottoman Empire could not meet the challenge of the European scientific, industrial and technological civilisation. This is the historical background of the 'Eastern Question' dealt with by Carl Brown in an interesting monograph.[79] Internally, the Ottoman Empire had to get through the historical process underlying the choice 'kings or people'. This is the title of the stimulating book by Reinhard Bendix[80] in which he clearly shows how the sovereignty of the kings and sultans had to give way to the sovereignty of the nation which is interpreted as the expression of the will of the people.[81] The sovereignty of the nation superseded the divine sovereignty of kings. Bendix deals in his book primarily with the British and French models, including, however, chapters on Islam and Arab nationalism which reveal that the East has been no exception with regard to the globalisation of the historical alternative 'kings or people', i.e. divine order versus nation-state.[82] The idea of nation had been adopted by educated Arabs prior to the complete disintegration of the Ottoman Empire. The spread of the idea supported by the globally existing structure was an anticipation of the future realities on a domestic level.

One of the major features of our modern world, 'the shrinking of the globe', as Bull puts it, may explain the speedy dissemination of the idea of nationhood in the Arab East. This shrinking 'has brought societies to a degree of mutual awareness and interaction that they have not had before.'[83] Further, it has contributed simultaneously to structurally unifying and culturally fragmenting the people living in this new order. The Europeans invaded most of the Arab territories of the Ottoman Empire and subjected it to their colonial rule. This colonisation was a prelude to the birth of a variety of nation-states in the former Ottoman provinces. It is not the adoption of the European idea of nation concomitant with the restructuring of the world that has brought Europeans and Arabs together, but the shrinking of the world in the above-cited sense of structural unity and cultural fragmentation that produced this result, as revealed by the political literature published in Arabic. There we find the view that European colonialism is a modern variety of the medieval crusades.[84] Prior to the colonial conquests in the Middle East the Arabs were very enthusiastic about Europe and its culture.[85] While the mapping of the globe into the European system of states was taking place, the growth of worldwide communication contributed to an Arab awareness of the idea of nation. The age of *nahda* (renaissance) marked cultural activities[86] mounted in an Arab cultural nationalism mostly articulated by Christian Arabs (see Chapter 5 of this book). Paralleling Christian Arabs, Muslim Arab officers of the Ottoman army with Western training, were establishing the first secret societies and organisations, so marking the politicisation of early Arab cultural nationalism.[87]

The height of this period of early Arab nationalism was the 1913 congress held by Arab nationalists in Paris. Arab nationalists were at that time still Ottomanists. They were not yet mature enough, nor politically strong enough, to stretch their disintegrationism to the extent of asking for separation from the Ottoman Empire. The demands of pre-1913 Arab nationalists did not go beyond the call for local and cultural autonomy within the confines of Ottomanism. Meanwhile the idea of nationalism was spreading among the Turks themselves. The Young Turks, on whom Arab nationalisms counted, turned out to be uncompromising Turanistic nationalists aiming at Turkicising the non-Turkish parts of the Empire. The split between Ottoman Arab nationalists and the Young Turks[88] encouraged the Arabs to turn their backs on the Empire. The Arab revolt of 1916 during the First World War could be interpreted as the consequence of this split.

V

In modern Arabic the French term *la nation* is translated as *umma*. This is a source of great confusion, since the meaning of this Arabic term goes back to the revelations of the *Qur'an*. The prophet Mohammad united the rival Arab tribes within the framework of an Islamic *umma* which was not restricted to the Arabs. Watt considers the federation of Arab tribes in one *umma* to be the greatest achievement of Islam.[89] The aim of Islam, as fixed in the *Qur'an*, is to disseminate Islam and make it the religion of all humanity. In this sense Islam is a universalism and the very term *umma* does not refer to a specific community. Every Muslim belongs to the Islamic *umma* regardless of his or her ethnicity or location. *Umma* is the universal community of believers and not a civic community related to a particular society in the modern sense, the latter being a projection by some modern Muslim thinkers back into Islam.[90]

In applying the concept of *la nation* to Arabic-speaking Muslims and in translating the very same term with *umma*, Arab nationalists introduced a new understanding into their own culture. Since some of the prime early advocates of the political idea of an Arab nation were Christian Arabs, the new concept of *al-umma al-'Arabiyya* (the Arab Nation) incorporated Christian and Muslim Arabs into the new nation, whereas non-Arab Muslims, primarily the Turks and the Iranians, were perceived to be merely co-believers but no longer members of the same community. The height of this secular perception is the formula developed in the 1920s by Sati' al-Husri, dealt with at great length in this book:[91] *al-din li-Allah wa al watan li-al-jami'* ('Religion is a matter between the individual and God while the fatherland is the concern of all'). The Islamic term *umma* now included in the concept of *al-umma al-'Arabiyya* marked new wine in old bottles. This is virtually the case of the social production of meaning alluded to by Clifford Geertz in his cultural anthropology.[92] Old symbols remain the same to people. They believe in them while they fill them with a new socially produced meaning, without being aware of what they are doing. It is not an exaggeration to say that even many prominent Arab nationalists were virtually secularists without being aware of their secularism.[93] To subdivide the Islamic *umma* into ethnic groups and to relate them to a real nation-state or to a state aimed at (e.g. an Arab state) is virtually a secular position in as much as it abandons the precept of the universal divine order.

Christian Arabs were always very conscious of the secular meaning of their concepts. This statement should not be misunderstood as a biased or partisan one. This author, being of an Arab Sunni Muslim origin, believes himself to be free of such bias. Arab Christians were not willing to be second-class members of the Muslim community as *dhimmi*, i.e. protected minority. The concept of a secular *umma* would provide them with the equal status of a *Citoyen*, of full citizens.

During this period in which Arab nationalism was the prevailing ideology (the 1920s through to the decisive year of 1967) it was not risky to subscribe publicly to a secularist approach. There had been great confusion in Arabic writings between *secularisation* as a social process of functional differentiation and *secularism* as an ideology. *Al-'ilmaniyya* (secularism) was the dominant formula.[94] Until recently there had been no distinction between *al-'almanah* (secularisation) and *al-'ilmaniyya* (secularism).[95] The reappraisal of political Islam in the early 1970s was connected with the emergence of hostility towards secular views. Even the newly coined term *al-'almanah* was dismissed. The sociological meaning of the term 'secularisation' refers to the social by-products of social change which contribute to a functional differentiation of the existing social structure. The term 'secularism' refers merely to the political ideology of the separation between state and religion.

My attempt to discuss, from a social science perspective, the interplay between Islam, as a cultural system, and the real social processes of secularisation, in a paper presented at the First Islamic Philosophy Conference on Islam and Civilization, held in

Cairo in November 1979, was received with hostility.[96] Secularism is no longer a topical issue in Arab political thought as we shall see later; it is merely a domain of writing for Arab Christians.[97] Currently, Arab nationalists have either switched to neo-fundamentalism or they are making an effort at reviving the Arabo-centric perception of Islam to come to terms with it.

In the course of the current process of re-politicisation of Islam, Arab nationalists are developing this new understanding of a link between Islam and Arab nationalism. Within this context the well-known Beirut-based Institute of Arab Unity Studies organised a major congress on 'Islam and Arab Nationalism'. The proceedings were published in a 780-page book already in its second printing.[98] It does not surprise me that the topic 'Arab Nationalism and Secularism' was assigned at that conference to a prominent Christian Lebanese writer, Joseph Mughaizel. The Discussion following that paper, also published in the proceedings, clearly reveals that only the Christian Arabs attending the conference were in favour of secularism. Mughaizel was either attacked by some participants or he was provided with the verbal consolation that a life under the banner of Islam is the best option for Arab Christians.

It is noteworthy that the secularism–divine order dichotomy of the Ottoman Empire did not occur in the contemporary history of the Maghreb, with the exception, of course, of Tunisia. The Ottoman provinces of the Maghreb had been lost to French colonial power. For two reasons a retreat from Islam was not a compelling issue. North Africa does not have Christian minorities. The Jewish minorities of Tunisia and Morocco did not involve themselves in politics as did the Christian Arabs of Syria and Lebanon. To the Maghrebi Arabs the Ottoman Empire was not an enemy as was the case in Greater Syria. In the Maghreb, Islam – and not Arab nationalism – was the basic element of the ideology of decolonisation.[99] Egypt, too, was no longer a part of the Ottoman Empire. Egyptian Christians either aimed at an Egyptian national state or they were committed to social thought, as the famous Salamah Musa was.[100] For this reason Egyptian nationalism was – as is shown in Chapter 9 below – a local nationalism, at times mixed with Islam in a very loose way, as in the writings of Mustafa Kamil, and at other times secular in orientation as in the political thought of Lutfi al-Sayyid. Pre-1913 Arab nationalism was exclusively restricted to the Arab part of

Asia. The Lebanese writer Nagib Azoury provided the definition of the Arab nation already in the title of his well-known book *La Nation Arabe dans L'Asie Turque* published in Paris 1905. This early Arab nationalism was secular in orientation. It was not Islamically driven in its mainstream, as Ernest Dawn contends in his work (see note 16 above). It is also wrong to relate this Arab nationalism to the Palestine issue, as Porath does in his most recent book on Arab unity.[101] Porath, furthermore, links Arabism to Islam and interprets the actions of the Pan-Islamist al-Maraghi as nationalist in character. In doing so he overlooks Maraghi's statements against Arab nationalism discussed in this book.[102] Early Arab nationalism was clearly a predominantly secular ideology. In its unfolding period it was related to an Arab awareness primarily articulated, for the reasons mentioned above, by Christian Arabs. The politicisation of this cultural nationalism took place within the context of the disintegration of the Ottoman Empire as well as in the framework of the structurally supported spread of the idea of nationalism in the Arab part of the Empire. Early Arab nationalists aimed at establishing their own nation-state restricted to Arabs, in Asia Minor. Their actions cannot only be explained by the Palestine-issue, and it is completely wrong to reduce Arab nationalism, as Porath does, to a response to Zionism. It is for this reason that I deliberately kept the Palestine-issue related to Palestinian nationalism out the scope of my book on Arab nationalism. I wanted to distinguish between two different historical processes which were not related to one another in the early period of both of them. Moreover, the history of Arab nationalism is much older than the Palestine-issue.

VI

Given the secular mainstream of early Arab nationalism and also the Christian component of it, it must seem a sheer historical peculiarity that the Arab nationalist movement assigned the leadership of the Arab Revolt of 1916 to a parochial tribal personality, Sharif Hussain of Mecca. Hussain himself had always aimed at becoming the Arab Caliph, or at least the king of the Arabs. Anis al-Sayigh's outstanding book about the Hashemites[103] provides us with strong evidence revealing these attitudes and the traits of that dishonourable leadership. In fact, Hussain's son Abdullah declared his father a caliph through a *bay'a* (vow of allegiance) in 1924 shortly after the abilution of the Caliphate in Turkey. This Arab caliphate was, however, abortive. The Saudis, seeking to establish their own kingdom, ousted Hussain from Hijaz in the same year.

The Arab revolt of 1916 was the first organised political action by Arab nationalists. The history of this revolt was, however, a tragi-comedy. This was due not only to the ridiculousness of its leader Sharif Hussain of Mecca, but was in many ways a historical expression of the philosophical concept of *the simultaneity of the unsimultaneous*: the backwards-oriented utopia of an Arab Caliphate coexisting with the aspirations of a modern nation building along the lines of the French model. In terms of the analysis of ideologies the First World War was conducive to a shift in Arab nationalism *from franco- and anglophilia to germanophilia*. Disenchantment with the unfulfilled promises of the Arab nationalists' British allies, paired with the need to provide evidence for the existence of an Arab nation despite the lack of an Arab nation-state, contributed to the emergence of *Arab germanophilia* after the war. In the light of the French idea of nation, a nation is inconceivable without a state: *nation et état*. Contrary to this is the German perception of a nation as a cultural community, *Gemeinschaft*, based on common history and language. [104] After the First World War Arab nationalists could no longer refer to the French idea, since their dream of an Arab nation-state did not come true. The German model of an under-developed nation, i.e. *a nation without a state*, seemed to apply to them and, thus, was much closer to their case. This is the subject of Part III of this book in which I deal with the resort of Arab nationalists to the German idea of nation as a *Gemeinshaft* rather than a *sociéte* related to a *nation état*. As did their German counterparts the Arabs conceived the Arab nation as an organic entity and not as a political community based on free will, *nationalité élective*. This changeover from liberal anglophone and francophone nationalism to a form of nationalism modelled on that of the nineteenth-century German Romantics is one of the characteristic features of the voluminous works of Sati' al-Husri. To avoid looking at this shift as a changeover in terms of history of ideas or ideologies we have to take a look at the altered structural constraints. The pan-Arab nation-state hoped for did

not come about. There existed no such state backing the claim of
an Arab nation. In resorting to the German concept of the nation
as a *Kulturgemeinschaft*, i.e. cultural community united by a
common language and collective historical memories (see Chapter 6 below) Arab nationalists were now able to disentangle the
claim of being a nation from the hitherto attached requirement of
building a nation-state.

Politically, the history of Arab nationalism in the period 1920
to 1952 was a royal history of kings struggling for larger entities to
sustain their power. The classical documentation of this aspect is
provided in the book by Patrick Seale, *The Struggle for Syria*.[105]
Most recently the Israeli historian Porath has covered this period
in his informative monograph *In Search of Arab Unity 1930–
1945*.[106] In a way, that period reveals a second Middle Eastern
variety of the world-historical choice 'kings or people' dealt with
in the work of Reinhard Bendix cited earlier. The first variety
was, as we have already seen, the one that took place under
Ottoman rule.

VII

The *coup d'état* of the Free Officers in Egypt on 23 July 1952 was
a turning point in the history of Arab nationalism. Arab writers
refer to this coup as a revolution; it put an end to the local Egyptian
nationalism on the one hand,[107] and to the pan-Arabism of the
kings, on the other. The year 1952 was the beginning of *pan-Arab
populism*, a new period in the history of Arab nationalism. The
people themselves, and no longer the kings, were now declared to
have the sovereignty of the nation. Populist nationalism was,
however, the shortest period in the history of Arab nationalism.
It was terminated through the de-legitimisation process engen-
dered by the crushing defeat of the June War 1967.[108] Nasserism,
as a populist variety of pan-Arab nationalism, was not only an
expression of the shift from 'kings to people' as a focus of
legitimacy. Nasserism was also a model of development. In his
outstanding research John Waterbury informs us that it is wrong
to view the June defeat as the source of the failure of Nasserism.
The Nasserite experiment in development failed for two reasons:
structural constraints and inadequate performance and planning.[109] Even though this failure happened prior to the Six-Day

War, the June defeat was a turning point. In the years 1967–1970 Arabs went through the pains of anguished self-criticism.[110] This short-lived period was terminated by the rise of political Islam[111] superseding the ideology of pan-Arabism. In thoroughly ordering the historical material into the real structures of the international system and in taking the actions of the peoples concerned into consideration we cannot separate what happens in the Middle East from the respective international environment. What does the popular metaphor of 'The End of Panarabism'[112] used by Ajami really mean in this context?

It is true that the former territory of the Ottoman Empire has been split into nation-states. With a few exceptions, such as Egypt and Morocco, most of these newly established nation-states lack historical legitimacy and thus are historically questionable although they are not as artificial and based on *nominal sovereignty* as most sub-Saharan African states are. In addition to this, the structural standards of the respective Arab societies are so different that the notion of one Arab society *al-mujtama' al-'Arabi*, is believed by the prevailing realities. The sociological term 'society' cannot be applied to the different Arab entities without losing its sharp meaning. The Arab states rather constitute *a regional subsystem*[113] but not a structurally consistent society. Pan-Arabism has been a rhetoric based on the reality of the Arabs' common traditional cultural heritage projected into the modern model of nation-state. The crushing defeat of June 1967 has been devastating to this rhetoric. A myth could be dismantled by enlightenment. The famous book by the American-educated Damascene Professor Sadiq Jalal al-'Azm: *al-Naqd al-Dhati ba'd al-hazima* (Self-criticism after the Defeat) first published in Beirut in 1968, contributed to a certain extent to this end. In his book al-'Azm asks the Arabs to stop viewing criticism as a disparagement (*dham* or *hija'*) and to learn how to look at themselves critically instead of imputing their own flaws and shortcomings to enemies and outside powers.[114] In the long run, the pan-Arab myth had to be replaced after having been devastated. It was hoped, as the postscript on 'Pan-Arab Nationalism as an Aspect of Contemporary Politics of Arab States' (see pp. 199–207 below) reveals, that pan-Arab nationalist rhetoric would be replaced by an enlightened new outlook. This postscript was written in such a spirit. However, *the myth of an Arab nation has been replaced by another one*: it is the myth of Islamic universal-

ism whose claims are incompatible with the structural realities of
the present world of nation-states. This new myth is based on the
revived idea of worldwide Islamic community *al-umma al-
Islamiyya* combined with the concept *din wa dawla* (the divine
state order).

This again revives the classical separation of the world into a
Muslim and a non-Muslim part, a separation which lacks any real
counterpart in the modern world of nation-states. The political
alternatives of Islamic revivalism are more fragile than any
romantic political concept of Arab nationalism ever was. The
options provided by political Islam document great illusions. The
abode of Islam consists of forty states incorporated into the
international system. These states are diverse on all levels and by
all definitions. Their populations have nothing more in common
than the belief in Islam. However, Islam is not a homogeneous
entity, in as much as religion is always a cultural system. Looked
at as a 'cultural system' in the Geertzian sense, Islam consists of a
multitude of cultural systems, since the social production of
meaning underlying any cultural system, as Clifford Geertz has
shown clearly, is always local.[115] In this sense Islam is not a unity
but rather a variety of cultural systems each with its own locally
produced social patterns of meaning. Islamism does not seem to
me to be a real alternative to pan-Arab nationalism. However,
pan-Arabism in its old pre-1967 form is dead. A future option of
Arabism is likely to be one similar to the model of the European
Community, i.e. a system of regional cooperation based on the
national sovereignty of the participating states. At the present
time, security concerns seem to be perceived as more important
than the urgently needed economic cooperation. The Gulf
Cooperation Council is an example of this preoccupation with
security.[116] The idea of a great comprehensive Arab state stretching from the Atlantic to the Gulf, a dream articulated in an
Arabic song I once learned at school in Damascus as a young boy,
is just a political utopia. Even those who, with a great deal of
noise, pay lip service to this dream do not really want it and have
never honestly desired it. In a world of nation-states, this dream
is, however, less illusory than the one of a universal Islamic
unity. Nevertheless, the real obstacles based on structural constraints as well as the lack of a real political action programme to
bring it about make the realisation of this dream very unlikely.

This critical re-assessment refers to *Arab nationalism with the specific meaning of pan-Arabism*, i.e. the concept of building up an overall state comprising all Arabs in a unified political structure. This criticism does not touch on the fact that the Arabs perceive themselves as one cultural entity, despite our reservations outlined above against the notion of an overall culture. The spread of mass media and modern means of transportation have greatly contributed to an intensification of various patterns of interaction among Arabs on different levels. This intensification supports the image of oneself as a single entity. In terms of the spoken and printed language (modern Arabic) as well as in terms of region-wide mobility (e.g. labour migration) the different Arab peoples have never been closer to one another than they are today. This cannot, however, be viewed as an achievement of Arab nationalisms. It is simply a product of that shrinking of the world alluded to earlier in this chapter. In this case the shrinking, supported by modern mass media and transportation, is not linked to cultural fragmentation as is the case on the global level. This observation does not, however, imply that the intensification of interaction among the Arab peoples is free of conflict. One should be reminded of the non-political, somewhat cultural tensions among the Arabs themselves arising from intensified mobility (migration without integration). In the future, the pan-Arab link is likely to occur in various forms of regional and sub-regional cooperation while maintaining the sovereignty of the participating state. The Gulf Cooperation Council (GCC) is an example of this. Another example is the spread of non-political functional sub-organisations[117] of the Arab League, such as ALECSO, parallel to the loss of the pan-Arab political meaning of this regional organisation.

In re-assessing Arab nationalism, we can conclude that this ideology has proved to be a myth in as much as it was oriented toward the utopia of a United Arab State. Technically, this utopia is feasible since it is based on the idea of an overall Arab nation-state which is compatible with the contemporary world order of nation-states. Ideologically, however, this dream has been replaced currently by the illusion of political Islam which lacks all structural requirements for its achievement.

This illusion of a greater Islamic state in our age of the globalised international system of nation-states is based on assumptions that no longer exist in the modern world. Dreams, much less illusions, have never been a source of change in world history. The dream of Arab unity articulated in the ideology of Arab nationalism may survive political Islam, despite the fact that a single Arab state still lies far beyond the horizon. In comparison to pan-Arabism, political Islam is not an indication of an awareness of an existing homogeneous and unique entity, but rather a sign of crisis,[118] and thus, definitely a passing phenomenon. Looked at from the structural point of view subscribed to in this introduction and in this book as well, this ideological shift from myths to illusions is a sign of sadness. It is the sadness of peoples who culturally fail to cope with the existing global structures determining the content of 'world time'. Thus, these peoples render themselves unable to transform their outlook and self-awareness and especially their world view.[119] Viewed from this angle, the challenge to Islam related to the nation-state in modern history is *not* a problem of a 'tension between political conformists and nonconformists', as Piscatori argues.[120] It is rather the problem of *cultural accommodation of social change*.[121] In other words: the problem is not centred on how 'Muslims have responded to the prevailing political reality of our time – the territorial state, or, simply, the nation state',[122] as Piscatori states the problem in terms of conformism and non-conformism. To Piscatori, Muslim conformists are those who submit to the reality of the nation-states whereas non-conformists are those Muslims who reject this reality. Piscatori infers that it is 'wrong ... to conclude that most Muslims today are nonconformists in the specific sense of rejecting the reality of the nation-state'.[123] To adjust oneself – in terms of behaviour and within the limits of expediences – to existing realities, i.e. to be a conformist, is something different from a cultural accommodation of socio-economically and politically changed realities to one's own cultural system in transforming the respective prevailing world view. To draw a comparison: the legal evasion of the Islamic prohibition of interest through legal devices (*hiyal*)[124] is not more a cultural accommodation of change in a society moving towards greater complexity than an Islamic conformist behaviour in a world structured and organised as a system of nation-states. An Islamic cultural understanding of the nation-state and a corresponding new world view of Muslims is still lacking. This is the major source of political tensions among Muslims and only on the surface can it be viewed as a conflict between conformists and non-conformists.

Part I An Attempt to Distinguish Third World from European Varieties of Nationalism

1 The Origins of Nation Formation and Nationalism in Europe

According to Pollard, ancient history is essentially that of the city state, and medieval history that of the universal world state. He sees modern history as the history of national states whose most 'prominent characteristic' is nationality.[1] The analysis of the national state as a modern phenomenon is a major concern of both history and the social sciences,[2] although there is considerable confusion over its origins. Classical political philosophers have mystified the phenomenon, either by trying to trace back the origins of modern states to differences of climate or geography (Montesquieu) or to language communities (Herder, Fichte), or to what is made out to be a common history and culture, or even to the 'Will of God' (Burke, Mazzini). More modern authors, such as Treitschke, Maurras and Le Bon, have tried to explain the state in terms of biological and racial categories.[3] None of these authors, however, is able to explain why it was not until the eighteenth century that the nation became the dominant political form in Europe, although linguistic, cultural and supposedly racial differences had come into existence long before. This study will not concern itself with speculative and unproductive interpretations,[4] and the analysis of the European nation state and of the development of nationalism in Europe will be based upon those few authors who have succeeded in making a precise historical definition of the matter under discussion. An outline of the development of nationalism and of the European nation state will serve as a background for a discussion of similar developments in colonial and semi-colonial countries, and it will also assist in differentiating these developments from the European experience. Thus what follows is essentially a general account, since detailed case studies are more the province of specialised monographs.

29

Ziegler discusses the process of nation formation in Europe in terms of what he calls the 'political constellation'. In the Middle Ages, the power of the papacy and the empire, which embodied feudalism, was the institutional core of the 'political constellation'. Gradually, Christian universalism, which had legitimised the feudal system, receded in the face of dynastic sovereignty, which legitimised the kingdom, the new 'political constellation'.[5] Christian universalism was initially followed not by the appearance of nations but by a variety of dynastic state forms, all of which tended towards centralisation of power. Although the centralist dynastic state created 'the pre-conditions for the universal validation of the nation, it cannot be interpreted as an embodiment of proto-nationalist politics'.[6] However, the dynastic state, or more accurately medieval kingship, was an important stage in the development of nationalities.

Hans Kohn comes to a similar conclusion in his description of the gradual decay of the universalist world order of the Middle Ages. He asserts that its breakdown during the Renaissance encouraged the formation of states, although 'étatism, not nationalism, emerged from the disintegration of medieval universalism'.[7] Engels sees kingship as a progressive force in the early modern period, the institution which was to make national unity possible: 'it symbolised order among disorder, the emergent nation in contrast to the fragmentation of rebellious vassal states'.[8] Under kingship, the capitalist mode of production had already begun to develop. It was the signal for the release of a number of processes of cultural assimilation and political integration, in the course of which various ethnic, cultural and linguistic groupings became subsumed into larger units, out of which nationalities were ultimately to emerge. The rising middle class in France, in alliance with the monarchy against the papacy, contributed importantly to the consolidation of dynastic sovereignty. Thus, at the meeting of the States General in 1614, the Third Estate proposed that the sovereignty of the Crown should form the basis of the constitution, and this was accepted by the *parlement* of Paris, the highest legal authority.[9] One significant feature of nation formation in the course of the transition to the modern period was the development and refining of national languages: even more striking was the writing of national historiography.[10]

The change in the meaning of the word '*patria*' throws light on the formation of nationality during the period of kingship. In the

Middle Ages, '*patria*' meant 'the City of God'; Augustine used '*patria*' in the sense of heaven, which for him was the 'fatherland' of all Christians. In the fifteenth century the word '*patrie*' (and the adjective '*patriote*') was introduced into the French language, and humanists like Étienne Dolet and Rabelais were already using '*patrie*' in the sense of 'fatherland'.[11] 'The new intellectual climate, in which the notions of "*patrie*" and "*patriotism*" changed their meaning and became generally accepted, undermined the traditional bases of the absolute monarchy.'[12] But this gradual change in meaning, which continued until the mid-eighteenth century, had, according to Kohn, still 'little to do with nationalism. The emphasis was less upon the unity of the nation than upon the liberty of the citizen.'[13] The patriot is the free citizen, in contradistinction to the subject: the vital criterion was bourgeois property.[14]

Under medieval kingship, the city economy encroached gradually onto the territory of the state. It is this phenomenon that Habermas considers to be the point of departure for the organization of the nation.[15] However, before the French Revolution, the state was not yet a national state; it could not form the basis of the legitimation of the rule of the middle class at a time when that class had not come to political power. The dynastic state could thus hold its own until bourgeois society, which had developed within its womb, grew up and overtook it. Only then, 'as a consequence of the revolutionary impetus of the theory of democracy being turned towards a radical overthrow of the state, did the "nation" become the all-embracing focus of political thought and discussion'.[16]

The principles of Natural Law propounded by early bourgeois liberal theoreticians were not intended to be a substitute for existing political power structures. Embedded in their postulates were concepts of general human rights and the notion of an unregulated sphere of activity, into which the state would not intrude, where trade, arts and sciences could develop freely. Marx equated this field with the sphere of commodity exchange. What was at stake for the early middle class 'was not so much the creation of a new form of sovereignty as that of a limitation of the existing one; not so much the creation of a new form of legitimacy and of a new political constellation as the counter-balancing of existing authority'.[17] The postulate of the sovereignty of the nation was not yet a matter of immediate concern to the early bourgeoisie,[18] as the writings of Locke reveal. Euchner has shown that Locke considers it the permanent duty of the state to secure the social reproduction of the

foundations of the capitalist infrastructure.[19] The state is thus
always limited by the rights of individual property-holders,[20] and it
is its duty to remove the risks attendant upon the process of social
reproduction. The weakness of Locke's theory is that the property
rights which it proclaims are antecedent to the formation of the
state;[21] these rights are in fact part of a *pre-state* system of organised
commodity exchange.[22] Only when dynastic sovereignty is superseded by national sovereignty can individual liberties, which are
actually equivalent to property rights in a commodity-producing
society, become part of the foundations of the (national) state.
Locke leaves unresolved the question of how individual liberties are
to become institutionalised in bourgeois society, because in his
liberal concept of Natural Law, the laws of the pre-state system of
commodity exchange are retained as the basic liberties of the
political order. Proceeding from the inapplicability of Locke's
concept of Natural Law to developed bourgeois society,[23] Rousseau
arrived at the notion of *volonté générale*.[24] Habermas has pointed
out the main differences between the two concepts: 'compared to the
liberal construction of human rights, the material automatism of a
Natural Law fulfilled by the Natural Laws of society is replaced by
the formal automatic operation of the general will, which, because
of its own nature, can violate the interests of society just as little as
the freedom of even one individual'.[25] Hence in Rousseau's
postulate of an ordered total integration of state and society,
individual liberties become equivalent to human rights.

Ziegler shows that individual liberties cannot of themselves form
'the basis of an independently constituted system of power. In such a
system the rights of each individual are guaranteed in each political
entity, but no separate political entity is thereby created. Within
democratic systems, this function is fulfilled by a second principle,
that of popular sovereignty.'[26] Historically, popular sovereignty is
realised in the idea of the nation. In Rousseau's view, the General
Will was objectively achieved in the (national) state. National
sovereignty replaced dynastic sovereignty as the legitimation of the
new political order,[27] though this did not take place before the
French Revolution. It was only then that the idea of the nation
gained currency, and the national state became the guiding principle
of bourgeois society. Thus Kohn says 'Nationalism is inconceivable
without the ideas of popular sovereignty preceding—without a
complete revision of the position of ruler and ruled, of classes and
castes',[28] although he was discussing the nationalism of revolution-

aries, which was fused with the democratic concept of liberty.

Ziegler correctly perceives that the idea of the nation forms the philosophical foundation for the legitimation of bourgeois society. '[It] guarantees . . . the legitimacy of modern structures of government. It implies the consent of the masses to the new state, and is one of the basic factors governing the process whereby the masses are incorporated into the political constellation.'[29] The historical phenomenon of the nation and the concept of nationality which underlies it cannot be adequately defined in terms of static categories such as 'common language and culture' or even 'common origins' or 'territorial unity'. The existence of nationalities is not an expression of the fact that peoples with 'common features' and 'common national characteristics'[30] have in some way come to their senses. It is rather that the development of the capitalist mode of production set in motion a number of processes of social mobilisation, and that by means of cultural assimilation and political integration, diverse cultural, ethnic and linguistic groupings came to form nationalities.[31] These nationalities were transformed into nations with the advent of the French Revolution. Weber notes: 'If the concept of "nation" can in any way be defined unambiguously, it certainly cannot be stated in terms of empirical qualities common to those who count as members of the nation.'[32]

The young Marx hails the formation of nations as a progressive act on the part of the bourgeoisie:

The bourgeoisie keeps more and more doing away with the scattered state of the population, of the means of production, and of property. It has agglomerated population, centralised means of production, and has concentrated property in a few hands. The necessary consequence of this was political centralisation. Independent, or but loosely connected provinces, with separate interests, laws, governments and systems of taxation, became lumped together into *one* nation, with *one* government, *one* code of laws, *one* national class interest, and *one* customs tariff.[33]

In fact, the formation of the nation was an expression of the increasing emancipation of the bourgeoisie. Pre-national and supra-national forms of association—clerical, tribal, and so forth—were dissolved into a new form of social commitment: national commitment.[34] An important feature of this process of emancipation was secularisation, without which the national state would have been inconceivable:[35] the Church was deprived of its power by the nationalisation of politics, and became fragmented into a number of neutralised national churches.[36] A famous pamphlet by the Abbé Sieyès demonstrates that the organisation of the European peoples into nations was a result of this process of bourgeois emancipation. Sieyès, a true representative of his class, answers the question 'What is the Third Estate?' (which is also the title of the pamphlet) with an emphatic 'Everything'. Thus the Third Estate is declared to be the same as the nation; hence 'it contains everything which pertains to the whole nation, while nobody outside the Third Estate can be considered as part of the nation'.[37] Sieyès excludes the nobility and the higher clergy from the nation; for him it is not sufficient 'to have shown that the privileged, far from being useful to the nation, can only weaken and injure it; we must prove further that the nobility is not a part of our society at all: it may be a *burden* for the nation, but it cannot be a part of it'.[38] As Marx was to deplore in the nineteenth century, the bourgeoisie sees its own emancipation as a class as the emancipation of the whole nation, and even as the emancipation of all mankind.

Unlike the dynastic state, the *national state* which emerged after the French Revolution was not absolutist. Its organisation corresponded to the political principles of bourgeois society.[39] The philosophical combination of human rights and civil liberties embraces the liberal freedoms. It is thus incorrect to declare[40] that Rousseau's theory of popular sovereignty as the philosophical premise of the national state is the source of a new authoritarianism in the form of 'modern state absolutism', or even to label Rousseau as the spiritual ancestor of modern totalitarianism.[41] Even in its early phase, the national state was a liberal constitutional state. Compared with the dynastic state, its organisation was progressive, in the same way as the dynastic state was itself a progressive development in comparison with the feudal particularism which preceded it.

At first, the *nationalism* which sprang from the French Revolution was also progressive, acknowledging the granting of human rights which had been proclaimed during the Revolution. Nationalism and liberalism stood together in opposition to feudalism and the Church. Albert Sorel emphasised that the French 'considered the combination of love of France and love of the Revolution to be part of the natural order of things'.[42] The nationalists of the Revolutionary period saw their goal as the struggle for freedom against tyranny, and could thus be both patriots and cosmopolitans at the same time. They considered it their mission to assist peoples suffering under the yoke of feudalism to achieve their emancipation, and to help them to constitute themselves as a nation. This attitude had been anticipated by pre-Revolutionary French political philosophers. In her study of the thought of this period, Eva Hoffmann-Linke states that these philosophers were characterised by a certain blend of 'patriotism civilised by cosmopolitanism, which considered that the right of self-determination was confined to one's own nation, and which upheld the duty of self-restraint as a necessary correlative'.[43]

Subsequently, of course, the virtual enforcement of the right of national self-determination became a basic principle of the foreign policy of the Revolution, the rationale for the revolutionary wars, and later for the Napoleonic expansion. Although Napoleon was neither a patriot nor even a nationalist,[44] he sought ideological justification for his campaign of conquests in national terms, and proclaimed that he was fighting for the rights of peoples to obtain their self-determination. Although the Napoleonic wars led to the nationalisation of politics all over Europe, brought some nations into being and hastened the disintegration of states of mixed national composition such as Russia, Austria and the Ottoman Empire, they did little to translate the liberties proclaimed by the French Revolution into reality. In terms of foreign policy, the result of the Revolution was 'not so much the restriction of despotism, or the securing of individual liberties in the face of the absolutism of the political centre but a radical nationalisation of power'.[45] In world historical terms, Napoleon appears as the liberator of the Europe of his day, in the sense that he shattered the structures of feudalism. In their fight against him, the forces of reaction used the same weapon with which Napoleon himself justified his foreign policy: the right of national self-determination. Thus German, Spanish and Russian nationalism were basically the fruits of a challenge emanating from the spirit of the French Revolution and the Napoleonic Wars. As Engels appositely writes: 'Napoleon was not that arbitrary despot to Germany which he is said to have been by his enemies . . . Napoleon was in Germany the representative of the revolution, the propagator of its principles, the destroyer of the old feudal society.'[46] The 'reign of terror' which Napoleon brought to other countries with his wars 'was sadly wanted in Germany. Napoleon dissolved the Holy Roman Empire, and reduced the number of little states in Germany by forming large ones. He brought his code of laws with himself into the conquered countries, a code infinitely superior to all existing ones, and recognising equality in principle.'[47] To oppose Napoleon in those days was to be against the Revolution and its achievements. Thus the hatred which was mobilised in the form of German or Russian nationalism was generally reactionary and retrogressive. Hayes is thus correct in referring to a 'counter-nationalism',[48] which turned against the ideals and achievements of the Revolution. This, however, is only one aspect of counter-nationalism in Europe. Although in world historical terms Napoleon had paved the way for progress in Germany by overturning the feudal system there, he appears, in a national perspective, as the founder of foreign rule, which became the focus of the struggle for national liberation. These two features of the retrogressive German nationalism of the Napoleonic period will be discussed in greater detail in Chapter 6.

The German nationalism which instigated the opposition to Napoleon in the so-called wars of liberation before the Restoration was romantic, irrational and anti-liberal. It repudiated the ideals of the Enlightenment, and condemned them for being imported. German nationalism took refuge in the past, which was glorified and invested with a metaphysical aura. This counter-nationalism was of course the ideological expression of the socio-economic and political backwardness of Germany at that time, an irrational response to a rational challenge. In such circumstances, the development of an ideological synthesis of nationalism, liberalism and democracy such as took place in France as a consequence of the Revolution was not possible in Germany. One of the distinguishing features of German nationalism was that it exalted 'Germanness' above other 'nationhoods'. It expressed itself in xenophobia, particularly in Francophobia,[49] an emphasis which diverted attention from the extreme backwardness of conditions in Germany—which occasioned sharp criticism from Marx.[50] It is no coincidence that Arab nationalists since the 1930s, especially al-Husri, have been harking back to nineteenth-century German romantic nationalism. Although the two ideologies, German nationalism and Arab nationalism, developed in markedly different historical circumstances, it is important to consider the common ground they share. In the analysis which follows these structural similarities will be investigated, in an attempt to show that Arab nationalism is essentially representative of all 'Third World' nationalisms.

When the European bourgeoisie had succeeded in establishing itself politically, it began to assume certain reactionary features. At the same time, the ideological justification for its class domination underwent a partial transformation. The concepts of democracy and nation, which had been identical in the French Revolution, were no longer indissolubly linked to each other. Even in France, Napoleon III was able to legitimise himself nationally as a plebiscite monarch.[51] In Germany, on the other hand, the formation of the nation did not of course take place within a liberal-democratic framework. 'It was not a free people that founded the German national state, but a league of princes.'[52] The same is true of Italy.

After the bourgeoisie had consolidated its domination, the patriot was no longer simply equivalent to the free and responsible citizen. Patriots now became those who mobilised primitive feelings and prejudices against other, apparently inferior, peoples. The integral nationalism of Charles Maurras demonstrates how the idea of the nation, which was closely linked to the idea of *mankind* during the period of the French Revolution, now began to imply separation from the rest of mankind. To the question 'If events say: fatherland *or* mankind, what is one to do in that case?', Maurras answers unhesitatingly: 'Those who say . . ."France first" are patriots, those who say "France, but . . ." are apostles of humanity.'[53] Here the striking difference between integral and Jacobin nationalism becomes clear. In this connection Nolte has emphasised that 'the new nationalism would not become complete, "integral" until it dissociated itself entirely from the ideas of the French Revolution . . . only a monarchistic nationalism therefore, would be an integral, that is, anti-revolutionary, nationalism . . .'.[54]

Thus nationalism came to provide an ideology for expansionist wars and finally the legitimation for imperialism. However, in the face of imperialist expansion, the national state began to seem an anachronism; European domination over non-European peoples was justified in nationalist terms. In so far as nationalism denied rights of self-determination to colonial peoples, it had completely broken away both from its liberal origins and from the idea of the national state that had once been inherent in it.[55] Nolte believes that the fascist-oriented nationalism of the twentieth century was already philosophically anticipated in Maurras' dissociation of the terms 'fatherland' and 'mankind'.[56]

In the discussion so far it has only been possible to hint at the basic prerequisites for the structural transformation of nationalism in

Europe into the ideology of the bourgeoisie. This transformation became socially necessary with the development of a society of commodity exchange, in the course of which the bourgeoisie became transformed from a revolutionary into an *arriviste* class.

2 Social Science Interpretations of Nationalism and of Nation Formation in the 'Third World'[1]

Kohn has come to the conclusion after years of research that while nationalism at the time of the French Revolution was an expression of aspirations towards individual liberty and democracy, it has developed in advanced bourgeois society into a notion which not only seeks to restrict liberty but even claims superiority over it. 'It is different in "underdeveloped" countries, where nationalism still contains elements of human progress, as it once did in the West.'[2] This thesis is accepted by numerous social scientists and historians. Emerson, an expert on national movements in colonial countries, agrees that 'in the large, nationalism in Asia and Africa, as at least in its initial phases in Europe and America, is a forward looking and not a reactionary force, a spur to revolution and not a bulwark of the status quo'.[3] As the present discussion will show, this thesis needs modification to the extent that while nationalism in the 'Third World' does indeed express the desire of oppressed people for emancipation, it cannot of itself bring about emancipation. Furthermore, nationalism in colonial and semi-colonial countries is not *sui generis* connected with the process of nation formation, since nationalism is not always based on a clearly defined notion of nationality.

In this chapter, contemporary theories of nationalism will be discussed, before examining the role of nationalism as an ideological phenomenon in the process of colonial emancipation in Chapter 3. The present discussion attempts to illuminate aspects of the relationship between nationalism and nation formation in the underdeveloped world. Here the terminology employed will be as set out in Chapter 1, note 29. The term *people* or *nationality* is used to signify a homogeneous extended social group; the *nation* is the legitimate sovereignty of the national state; *nation formation* is the establishment of homogeneous extended social groups within either evolutionary or artificially stimulated processes of integration. These processes may take place at the same time as the stages of state formation, but need not necessarily do so.

If the term *nation* is used in the sense of *nationality* (that is, a homogeneous extended social group), and not in the sense of the legitimate sovereignty of the national state, this usage will occur in the discussion of the works of authors who do not follow the definitions outlined above. It is clear however that these definitions must themselves be regarded as tentative, and simply as a means of assisting towards an analysis of the process of nation formation. In the course of the investigation of the historical material, concrete examples will be given, from which it will become clear that the terms *nation, people, nationality* and *national state* cannot strictly be considered synonymous.

(a) Marxist Analyses of the Problem of the Subject and Colonised Peoples[4]

The national question and the future of the subject peoples were matters of major concern to the Second International, which took place against a background of the disintegration of states of mixed national composition.[5] It also raised the colonial question within the framework of theories of imperialism. In both cases it was debated whether oppressed and colonised peoples actually had the right to a separate national existence, that is, to form nations. This controversy, whose practical significance was to become apparent in the course of the First World War, eventually led to the dissolution of the Second International.

Marx and Engels had already considered the national question to be of central importance. Marx used to test continental socialists by their attitude to the Polish question, and English socialists by their attitude to the Irish question. In 1870 he wrote to Engels about the Russian socialist Lopatine: 'Weak point—Poland. With regard to Poland he speaks exactly like an Englishman—say an English chartist of the old school—speaks of Ireland.'[6] Marx firmly rejects the notion, which had been put about by the Free Traders, of an international fraternity of peoples organised under capitalism. For him any unification of peoples must presuppose that they have common interests, and in addition 'existing property relations must be done away with, since these property relations involve the exploitation of some nations by others'.[7] The fraternity advocated by the Free Traders passed over the question of oppressed peoples, and it also ignored the differences between social classes. It was merely 'cosmopolitan exploitation'.[8] Fraternisation of peoples can only come about on the basis of an absence of domination, and such a relationship between an oppressing and an oppressed people was unthinkable. For Marx, this problem is the core of the national question.

Those who do not address themselves to the national question are accused by Marx of chauvinism. Thus he writes to Engels in 1866:

Yesterday there was a discussion in the International Council . . . The discussion wound up, as was to be expected, with 'the question of nationality'. . . . Moreover the representative of 'Young France' came out with the announcement that all nationalities and even nations were antiquated prejudices. . . . The English laughed very much when I began my speech by saying that our friend Lafargue, etc., who had done away with nationalities, had spoken 'French' to us, i.e. a language which nine-tenths of the audience did not understand. I also suggested that by the negation of nationalities he appeared, quite unconsciously, to understand their absorption into the model French nation.[9]

This extract shows the fundamental difference between Marx' internationalism and cosmopolitanism. Internationalism is only possible between free peoples: it remains simply an ideology so long as it serves to mask relations of international exploitation.[10] Marx sympathised with the Irish national emancipation movement, stood up for the right of the Irish to form their own nation and supported Fenianism.[11] In a letter to Engels in 1869 he writes 'it is in the direct interest of the English Working Class to get rid of their present connexion with Ireland. And this is my most complete conviction . . . the English Working Class will never accomplish anything before it has got rid of Ireland. . . . English reaction in England had its roots in the subjugation of Ireland.'[12]

Engels emphasises the same principle in his *plaidoyer* for Poland. 'A nation cannot at the same time obtain its freedom and continue to subjugate other nations.'[13] And again: 'As long as Russian soldiers remain in Poland, the Russian people cannot free itself, either politically or socially.'[14] However, Engels modifies his point of view considerably by saying that his recognition of and sympathy for national aspirations was confined to 'the "great" and precisely defined nations of Europe'.[15] Thus he differentiates between the 'rights of the "great" European nations to an autonomous and independent existence' and the 'principle of nationality', which he rejects,[16] using these terms in the sense of their current meaning in the nineteenth century. He sees the nation not in the sense of a form of political domination which only became established with the national state, but rather more vaguely as a cultural community. Engels uses *people* and *nation* synonymously. Nationalities are not groups of people who have reached a certain degree of cohesion as a result of certain processes of social and economic development and who are therefore capable of forming nations. On the contrary, he considers nationalities to be 'small nations' or 'remnants of peoples' who have no right to form their own national states, but who must instead integrate themselves into groupings designated as 'great historic nations', especially as 'there is no country in Europe where different nationalities cannot be found under a single government . . . but no-one would describe these remnants of conquered peoples as nations'.[17]

Engels considers that the map of Europe of his own day is final. Border changes

> if they are to be permanent, must generally aim at securing true and natural frontiers, determined by language and sympathies, for the 'great' and more viable European states. At the same time the remnants of peoples which continue to exist here and there, and which are no longer capable of an independent national existence, remain incorporated in the structures of 'great' nations, and are either absorbed by them or survive merely as ethnographic curiosities with no political significance.[18]

Marx does not make this distinction between historic nations and remnants of peoples with no history.

As early as 1907, Engels' discredited 'peoples with no history' had been rehabilitated by Otto Bauer. They still have 'no history', but the interpretation is different: they have been oppressed by the so-called 'great' nations, and have thus not been able to play an active role in history. Hence the national question is now interpreted in terms of 'the awakening of nations with no history'.[19] The hatred expressed by oppressed nations towards their oppressors is defined by Bauer as class hatred,[20] or a primitive level of class conscious-ness, which the workers of the oppressing countries counter with a naive cosmopolitanism. The naive nationalism of the oppressed, and the naive cosmopolitanism of the proletariat of the oppressing nations can both only be overcome through proletarian inter-nationalism and mature class consciousness.[21] Neither Engels nor Bauer recognises that oppressed nations have the right to form their own national states. Bauer considers that fraternisation takes place on the level of the national and cultural autonomy of peoples within the framework of states containing several nationalities.[22]

Karl Kautsky accuses Bauer of having neglected the fact that the formation of states was an immanent tendency of capitalism.[23] Lenin endorses this criticism and develops from it his theory of the right to national self-determination. Like Marx and Engels, Lenin defines peoples as nations even if they have not yet so constituted themselves, but in contrast to Engels, he calls for the right to self-determination of all peoples. He was the first to bring colonies into the discussion, and he asserts that the right of colonised peoples to self-determination is a basic principle of socialist foreign policy. He rejects as a 'reactionary notion' Bauer's equation of self-determination with cultural autonomy,[24] and claims that the right of nations to self-determination means 'their political separation from alien national bodies and the formation of an independent national state'.[25] At that time, the right to national self-determination could have no other meaning,[26] since it was clear that 'capitalism, having awakened Asia, has called forth national movements everywhere in that continent too, and that the tendency of these movements is towards the creation of national states in Asia'.[27] Lenin considers that the national question in the West has been solved, since there the national state has already become the basis for the organisation of bourgeois society.[28] On the other hand, colonies and states with several nationalities have not yet reached that stage. Hence socialists in the oppressor nations have a duty to call for the rights of the oppressed peoples to their national existence, and in this way to come closer to their own eman-cipation.[29] Here Lenin alludes to Marx' attitude to the Irish national emancipation movement, which he presents as an 'example of the highest importance', since Marx was held to have shown the way in which the proletariat of the oppressor nations should behave towards national independence movements.[30]

In the same way as Marx and Engels take the question of the national emancipation of Poland and Ireland to be a touchstone for socialists, Lenin considers the attitude adopted by socialists towards the right to self-determination of peoples to be the criterion of their socialism.

> Imperialism consists of the striving of nations oppressing a number of other nations to widen and strengthen that oppression. . . . This is why the question of self-determination of nations pivots, in our time, on the conduct of the Socialists of the *oppressing* nations. A Socialist of any of the oppressing nations . . . who does not recognise and does not struggle for the right of oppressed nations to self-determination . . . is, in reality, not a Socialist but a chauvinist . . . if all the Socialists of the 'great' powers, i.e. the powers that perpetrate great robberies, do not defend this right as far as the colonies are concerned, it is solely because in fact they are imperialists, not Socialists.[31]

Although Lenin constantly demands that oppressed and colonial peoples should be able to form their own nations, he condemns their nationalism, while acknowledging that it has 'a general democratic content' in contrast to that of the oppressors.[32]

Lenin is primarily concerned to make available to every oppressed and colonised people the right to self-determination without further investigation of the extent to which each people possesses the prerequisites for nation formation. Instead, he emphasises the political impact which their separate national existence will have on both the oppressed and the oppressing nations: it will be a first step towards the fraternisation of all peoples on a level of equality. According to Lenin, internationalism will remain an empty phrase as long as the proletariat of the developed world takes no stand on the issue of the political emancipation of the colonies.[33] 'In the same way as mankind can arrive at the abolition of classes only through a transition period of the dictatorship of the oppressed class, it can arrive at the inevitable integration of nations only through a transition period of the complete emancipation of all oppressed nations, i.e. their freedom to secede.'[34] Of course, whether such integration is actually 'inevitable' is open to question.

This right to self-determination for the oppressed and colonised peoples, proclaimed by Lenin following Marx and in the spirit of the French Revolution, was rejected by both the left[35] and the right wings[36] of the Second International, although for different reasons. This led to the currency of the attitude of 'defence of the fatherland' during the First World War and ultimately to the dissolution of the Second International.

(b) Nationalism in the 'Third World' as an Anti-Colonial 'Modernisation Ideology'[37]

American political scientists tend to make use of modernisation theory to interpret processes of development in colonial and semi-colonial countries.[38] According to this theory the problems faced by these countries have their origins in the transition from traditional, that is underdeveloped, to modern, that is industrial, societies.[39] Nationalism in socio-economically less-developed countries thus becomes the ideology of delayed industrialisation,[40] and is justified and accepted as an important factor in the service of modernisation.[41]

John H. Kautsky has provided a representative interpretation of nationalism in less developed countries within this theoretical framework.[42] He argues that the various nationalisms of eighteenth and nineteenth-century Europe each rested on a clearly definable nationality, that is, a linguistically and culturally cohesive group which had developed organically over the centuries alongside the gradual growth of the 'industrial' mode of production. In contrast, nationalism in colonial countries was apparently not based on nationality. This Kautsky takes as a crucial argument for his thesis that 'Third World' nationalism cannot be discussed in terms of categories taken from European history.[43] He considers the frontiers which have resulted from decolonisation to form national states in a legal sense but not nationalities.[44] Nationalism in such states, whose frontiers have been created by colonialism, is according to W. Sulzbach's formulation, an 'administrative national-ism'.[45] R. Emerson on the other hand maintains that there are nationalists, but no nations, in the post-colonial states; nations in the 'Third World' are still 'in the making'.[46] Since the nationalism

which has appeared universally in the period of decolonisation has
no historical tradition, Kautsky suggests that it should be defined as
a form of anti-colonialism, but 'anti-colonialism must here be
understood as opposition not merely to colonialism narrowly
defined, but also to a colonial economic status'.[47] Consequently,
this form of nationalism insists not on decolonisation alone but also
on modernisation, in the sense of the industrialisation of the
country.

Kautsky and the modernisation theorists identify the Western-
educated colonial intellectuals as the carriers of ideas of nationalism;[48] they have absorbed the national intellectual property of
modern Western culture which they then apply to their own colonial
situation. They express their nationalism in their aspirations to
modernise the pre-industrial social structures of their own countries.
The fact that the philosophical origins of colonial nationalism lie in
the West, and that its carriers are educated there, is an 'essential
aspect' of this type of nationalism.[49]

For Kautsky there is one crucial difference between the historical
roles of European and colonial intellectuals. While liberalism was
conceived as a capitalist ideology by the bourgeois intelligentsia,
'industrialisation itself was accomplished by industrial capitalists. In
underdeveloped countries, the intellectuals, in effect, play the roles
of both groups'.[50] Without actually referring to Karl Mannheim's
notion of a socially free-floating intelligentsia, Kautsky in fact takes
up a similar position.[51] Thus the colonial intellectual somehow
stands above classes and has taken upon himself a historic mission,
whose aim is modernisation and whose expression is nationalism.
Only the Western-educated colonial élite can instigate the process of
modernisation,[52] since existing social classes and structures are not
nationally oriented and cannot by definition perform a modernising
role. The indigenous 'aristocracy' and bourgeoisie, described as the
anti-nationalist classes,[53] form an alliance on the basis of the
involvement of their interests with the colonial system, and this
alliance attempts to perpetuate the traditional social structure.

Kautsky does make one modification to this model, though he
does not consider it particularly important. The colonial world is
ruled by a 'dialectic' whose thesis is that the system tries to prevent
modernisation, and will therefore ally itself with pre-technical and
anti-industrial indigenous forces—the 'aristocracy'. The antithesis
is that the colonialism also implies the modernisation of the
colonies, particularly as it has itself sprung from modern industrial

society, whose methods it made use of during the process of colonisation. Because of the latter tendency, the colonial system is supposed to drive the traditional forces into the national camp against their will. 'The national movement unites both those who oppose colonialism because they feel that it introduces modernisation too rapidly, and those who oppose it because in their view it delays and obstructs modernisation.'[54] In these countries the first group are labelled the traditionalist wing of nationalism, and the second the modernist wing. However, in this way Kautsky greatly restricts the modernist features of nationalism which he has previously singled out, but he continues to define nationalism as an anti-colonialist modernisation ideology because the only true nationalists are Western-educated intellectuals. He deprecates the nationalist position of the traditionalist social forces as simply a reaction of defiance, and does not concern himself with them adequately in his model.

For Kautsky it is the nationalism of the colonial intellectual that has made possible the national integration of diverse ethnic, cultural and linguistic groupings in a newly independent colonial country. An important prerequisite for the process of modernisation has thus been created, namely the necessary mobilisation that has been triggered off by national integration. But Kautsky cannot ignore the fact that national mobilisation does not always have a modernising effect upon the former colony, but often serves to mask its absence by directing national energies against a foreign enemy.[55] He does not explain why the nationalism he hails as an ideology of modernisation in the underdeveloped countries does not always fulfil its mission, which means that in practice the model is irrelevant.

This weakness, which is a common feature of the theory of modernisation, derives from the use of abstract categories to describe concrete historical processes. Thus modernisation is considered primarily equivalent to industrialisation, while the particular historical circumstances under which social production has become industrialised, that is, capitalism, are taken for granted in all cases. Modernisation theory does not take into account the objective prerequisites of any particular process of industrialisation, even within the framework which is considered to be the only possibility, the capitalist mode of production. Hence the absence of industrialisation or modernisation in underdeveloped countries appears to be an expression of subjective inadequacy on the part of

the 'ideologists of modernisation'—that is, the Western-educated
colonial intellectuals. In this context another important question
that remains unanswered is in whose interests this modernisation,
and more particularly the industrialisation, of the underdeveloped
country concerned, in fact takes place. Only a class analysis, based
on the actual relations of production in each country, can provide a
satisfactory answer to this question. Modernisation theory excludes
both these explanations from the outset.[55a]

(c) Nationalism in the 'Third World' as a Result of the Process of Acculturation

The interpretation of the phenomenon of nationalism in the 'Third
World' provided by acculturation theory is very similar to that
provided by modernisation theory, in that it also lays stress on the
fact that the Western-educated colonial intellectual is the carrier of
nationalism. In this theory, however, the issue of modernisation is
only marginal. Richard F. Behrendt has attempted an analysis of
nationalism in colonial countries on the basis of acculturation
theory, which will be discussed in this section.

Behrendt considers that underdeveloped countries are currently
experiencing a period of 'discontinuous dynamic cultural transformation' whose creative impulse originates outside rather than
inside them; in other words, their cultural transformation is based
on processes of acculturation,[56] of which Behrendt distinguishes
two models. The first, *'passive-imitative acculturation'*, is an
'unreserved passive adaptation to a culture felt to be superior' which
remains largely superficial and 'cannot in fact dislodge the values
and norms of the indigenous culture which have been instilled since
childhood'.[57] In contrast, *'active-syncretic acculturation'* consists of
'the selection and active application of suitable extraneous cultural
elements . . . taking into consideration their relevance to the needs
and potential of the developing country, together with those
autochthonous cultural elements that are still effective and viable'.[58]
Behrendt considers that both these processes lead to cultural
synthesis, since both contain elements of the autochthonous and the
received culture: however the second process differs from the first in
the sense that there a *conscious* synthesis is taking place.

Within this theoretical framework Behrendt proceeds to interpret nationalism in the 'Third World' as the product of 'a process of imitative adaptation' on the part of the colonial peoples. He describes them as 'marginal peoples', in contradistinction to those in the West, who are 'nuclear peoples'.[59] The 'marginal' intellectuals absorb the Western idea of the nation, since they view nationalism as a means of compensating for and overcoming the collective inferiority complexes caused by colonial rule. The loss of identity as a consequence of the weakening of traditional social structures may also result in promoting nationalism as a substitute identity. The national state to which they aspire is considered by the 'marginal peoples' to be a 'universal mechanism' for achieving a policy of social and economic development.[60]

Behrendt sees nationalism in colonial countries as simply the idea of the nation acquired from the West which 'originates as a protest against the dependence of dynamic marginal peoples on dynamic nuclear peoples in their aspirations for development'.[61] He does not analyse these relations of dependence, but he considers his thesis proved by the fact that these nationalists are usually educated in the West—although they themselves would not consider their nationalism to be a product of acculturation. What is being expressed is 'an internal contradiction between imitation and self-assertion, acculturation and nationalism'.[62] This contradiction shows itself most clearly in the disharmonies occurring in the process of cultural transformation triggered off by acculturation.[63] A by-product of this disharmonious cultural transformation is the alienation of the colonial intellectuals. They are at one and the same time nationalists and opponents of everything autochthonous. 'The nationally conscious and the nationalists in developing countries are not bearers of an independent cultural heritage, but those who are most influenced by ideas borrowed from the West. The élites who speak and act in the name . . . and in the interest of the "nation" are probably the most "alienated", that is, Westernised, and they are most deeply hostile to traditional social structures.'[64]

This definition of 'Third World' nationalism as the product of an imitative adaptation of Western culture corresponds to this model of acculturation. Its acceptance remains superficial and autochthonous features do not disappear, which means that no conscious synthesis is produced. 'The national idea . . . is injected by the new élites into autochthonous traditions which are completely different, in an attempt to extract "indigenous" national myths.'[65] Hence acculturation is seen not for what it really is, but as the 'resuscitation and renaissance of the former but forgotten values and achievements of a people'.[66]

Behrendt is prepared to concede a certain justification for nationalism in underdeveloped countries. He accepts that traditional social bonds such as kinship, tribe, caste or hierarchy cannot provide a sufficient basis for mobilisation to overcome underdevelopment. Traditional forms of social commitment 'do not create new social structures which attract emotional support. Only national consciousness and nationalism can lead a broad movement directed towards mass emotional mobilisation and to integration in more extended social structures.'[67] In political terms the national state to which nationalism in the colonial countries aspires is a form of emancipation. Colonial emancipation is not a 'vertical protest movement of different strata' but a 'horizontal emancipation movement' on the basis of international relations, because the rulers of the underdeveloped regions do not represent autochthonous forces.[68] In the course of the process of emancipation the national state may function as a 'conceptual and geographical unity' while at the same time taking responsibility for carrying out planning and development policies.[69] Although Behrendt initially endorses national integration as a spur towards the adoption of policies of development, he finds it ultimately paradoxical. On the one hand national integration has the necessary function of providing an education for life in relatively extended institutions and frames of reference, while on the other the frontiers of the national state which are also the results of national integration act as an impediment to development.[70] Behrendt particularly emphasises this latter aspect of the post-colonial national state. The national state is an alien form of organisation for the colonial world, since it does not rest on any historical foundations. 'If essentially alien terms such as the nation are to be adopted, which bear no relation to the realities of the situation, every large tribe and language group could declare itself to be a "nation". . . . Thus the adoption of the idea of the nation as a principle of social integration in most developing countries is a potentially anarchic element.'[71] Behrendt also believes that in the present stage of human development the national state has outlived its usefulness.[72]

Behrendt finally comes to the conclusion that the national state must be rejected as a transitional form of organisation as a step towards the emancipation of colonial peoples, since it is unable to fulfil its true purpose. The nationalism which it promotes serves only as a 'device which is always ready to divert the attention of the masses from unsolved problems and the failures and set-backs of their governments'.[73] Furthermore, 'Third World' nationalism is increasingly moving towards a form of 'nativism' which tends to extol local traditions and particularities in a chauvinistic fashion.[74] This chauvinism, which has its origins in nationalism, cannot even be regarded as a primitive form of anti-colonialism since it is directed not only against the colonial rulers but also against neighbouring colonial peoples.[75]

Hence Behrendt's analysis stops exactly at the point where he would have been required to explain why the national state has in fact failed in socially and economically backward countries. If it is claimed that the national state today is the necessary historical alternative for the underdeveloped countries, in that it can mobilise national forces for development and total emancipation, even though it can only be considered as a transitional stage, it must then be measured against the historical realities of the 'Third World' and be subjected to critical examination. Behrendt notes a discrepancy in his analysis between the claims and realities of the national state in the 'Third World', but because he does not investigate the historical reasons for the differences between what 'is' and what 'should be', he makes it impossible for himself to work out a practical strategy for overcoming problems of development and underdevelopment, and is thus preaching a form of national nihilism. Acculturation theory generally takes the foundation of nation states in the 'Third World' to be the result of the adaptation of foreign ideas to indigenous circumstances. This one-sided approach immediately makes it impossible to investigate actual social conditions properly, and to discover the resulting class structures onto which the idea of the national state is fused, and which promote such fusion.

Behrendt's definition of nationalism as it is supposed to exist in the 'Third World' has very limited validity. Since it attempts to explain social phenomena in the 'Third World' as originating from processes of acculturation, it is irrelevant to political realities. Behrendt claims that the process of acculturation, during which 'marginal peoples' adopt the national idea from 'nuclear peoples', does not create national consciousness. Instead of creating 'non-aggressive collective feelings and relations of solidarity directed towards the nation'[76] the process leads to a particular form of nationalism which is defined as 'disassociative collective emotions and modes of behaviour expressed towards peoples and social structures which are considered alien and antagonistic, fuelled by feelings of separateness and resentment'.[77] Such a subjective definition of 'Third World' nationalism makes the problem appear a purely psychological one, for which Behrendt offers no practical solution.

(d) Nation Formation in the Colonies in the Context of Decolonisation Achieved by Armed Struggle

Fanon has provided a general analysis of the phenomenon of nationalism and the process of nation formation in the 'Third World' as part of an anti-colonial revolutionary theory. He considers the formation of nations to be a necessary consequence of decolonisation.

Fanon begins his analysis with the colonial reality. The colonial world is characterised by feudal and pre-feudal structures. The prevailing forces of social commitment are tribe and kinship.[78] He sees the nation as the medium through which these social realities can be changed: the nation unites the people, and mobilises them for the task of national reconstruction. But it can only come into existence after the abolition of *qa'ids*, chiefs, witch-doctors and their institutions.[79] However, the colonial system tends to strengthen sub-national structures and to ally itself with pre and anti-national social forces. 'By its very structure colonialism is separatist and regionalist; it does not simply state the existence of tribes, but also reinforces and separates them.'[80] It has often strengthened or established its domination by 'organising the petrification of the country districts. . . . Encircled by marabouts, witch-doctors and customary chieftains, the majority of the country dwellers are still living in the feudal manner. The full power of the medieval structure of this society is maintained by the military and administrative officials of the colonial system.'[81] Fanon considers such a policy, which systematically prevents the emergence of nations in the colonies, as a basic prerequisite for the continuation of colonial domination.

Fanon proceeds from the assumption that 'truth is that which hurries on the break-up of the colonialist regime, and which promotes the emergence of the nation'.[82] Here, truth means that which is reasonable. The armed struggle of the colonised peoples for their independence is reasonable, because it is only this struggle that has so far been able to dissolve colonial structures and to lead to the emergence of new nations.[83]

The social and political mobilisation of the people, which makes possible the formation of the nation after victory, has already been accomplished in the course of the struggle against colonial rule. It introduces 'into each man's consciousness the ideas of a common cause, of a national destiny and of a collective history'.[84] Hence even the early spontaneous peasant risings derive from a single idea; 'to act in such a way that the nation may live'.[85] In the first phase of emancipation, national unity is group solidarity in the anti-colonial struggle.[86] National consciousness develops gradually in the course of armed action on the part of individuals declaring their solidarity with one another. 'Each man or woman brings the nation to life by his or her action, and is pledged to ensure its triumph in their locality . . . if the nation is everywhere, then it is also here.'[87]

Fanon points out that, in contrast to the situation in Europe, where nationalities grew organically within the womb of feudalism, nationalities in the colonies have developed in the course of revolutionary struggles against the colonial system. While the integration and cohesion necessary for the development of a nationality was supported in Europe by the growth of trade and industry, the integration and cohesion of the various social groups in the colonies was achieved by anti-colonial violence, 'since violence . . . in action is all-inclusive and national'.[88] Decolonisation achieved in this way makes possible the emergence of the nation without nation-worship. As long as the creation of the nation is being undertaken by the people engaged in the struggle, they themselves are forewarned of 'all attempts at mystification, vaccinated against all national anthems'.[89]

It is an essential feature of this kind of nationalism that its carriers, the colonial intellectuals, are aware of their autochthonous pre-colonial culture, that their nationalism should be accompanied by respect for their cultural heritage. This concern for the pre-colonial culture needs further explanation, since the intellectual nationalist will most likely have received a Western education, and will have been particularly influenced by Western culture.

This passionate search for a national culture which existed before the colonial era can be traced to the desire of the native intellectuals to draw back from that Western culture in which they all risk being swamped. Because they realise they are in danger of losing their identities and thus becoming lost to their people, these men, hot-headed and with anger in their hearts, are relentlessly determined to renew contact with the oldest and most authentic pre-colonial springs of life of their people.[90]

This 'tearing away, painful and difficult though it may be', from European culture means a loss of identity for which they try to compensate by a return to their autochthonous pre-colonial culture. Without this, which provides the promise of a new identity, 'there will be serious psycho-affective injuries and the result will be individuals without an anchor, without a horizon, colourless, stateless, rootless—a race of angels'.[91]

Fanon justifies his definition of this nationalism as 'an emotional though illogical antithesis of that insult which the white man flung at his humanity',[92] by explaining that 'colonialism is not satisfied merely with holding a people in its grip and emptying the natives' brains of all form and content. By a kind of perverse logic, it turns to the past of the oppressed, and distorts, disfigures and destroys it.'[93] The positive function of this kind of nationalism is that it gives the colonial intellectual a psycho-affective balance, although this should not obscure its ideological character. Nationalism's pledge to rehabilitate the colonial peoples by emphasising the superiority of their previous culture over that of Europe remains unredeemed. This rehabilitation only takes place superficially, because 'you will never make colonialism blush for shame by spreading out little-known cultural treasures before its eyes. At the very moment when the native intellectual is anxiously trying to create a cultural world, he fails to realise that he is using techniques and language which are borrowed from the stranger in his country. He contents himself with stamping them with a hall-mark which he wishes to be national, but which is strangely reminiscent of exoticism.'[94] The fact that this nationalism is a helpless protest, unable of itself to lead to the ending of colonial rule, is most clearly evident in his art. 'The artist who decides to illustrate the truth of the nation turns paradoxically towards the past and away from current events.'[95] His nationalism is thus almost anachronistic.

Fanon's analysis shows that the nationalism of the colonial intellectual does not provide a guide to political action capable of changing the colonial situation. Its main feature, recourse to the autochthonous pre-colonial culture, 'obeys the law of inertia. There is no taking of the offensive, and no redefining of relationships. There is simply a concentration on a hard core of culture which is becoming more and more shrivelled up, inert and empty.'[96] He feels that the strongest expression of a culture is the conscious and organised struggle of the colonised to achieve their national sovereignty.[97] The assertion of the nation in the face of the colonial system and the re-establishment of indigenous history are the imperatives of the hour. Under colonialism, the colonised participate in an alien history. The material values which their work creates do not contribute to the development of their own country, but to that of other countries. The immobility to which the native is condemned can only be called in question if he decides to put an end to the 'history of colonisation—the history of pillage—and to bring into existence the history of the nation—the history of decolonisation'.[98]

After the re-establishment of his own history, after independence has been won, the undifferentiated nationalism which the colonial intellectual has carried to his people begins to lose its impact. The apparent social harmony which has prevailed during the anti-colonial struggle gives way to a variety of antagonistic social realities. 'Not every negro or Muslim is issued automatically with a hall-mark of genuineness.'[99] Class contradictions become transparent. As the result of the imperialist domination of the world, the indigenous colonial bourgeoisie, unlike their counterparts in early European history, are not in a position to carry out the tasks which history has set for them. Their domination proves a constraint on development, and their policies do not aim at overcoming underdevelopment. The national solidarity created in the course of the anti-colonial struggle was mainly of a political nature, not based on social and economic integration and cohesion. After independence has been won, political solidarity based on anti-colonialism will disintegrate if it is not supported by a genuine development policy. Under the rule of the national bourgeoisie,

national consciousness, instead of being the all-embracing crystallisation of the innermost aspirations of the whole people, instead of being the immediate and most obvious result of their mobilisation, will be only an empty shell, a crude and fragile travesty of what it might have been. Its faults are quite sufficient explanations of the facility with which, when dealing with young and independent nations, the nation is passed over for the race and the tribe is preferred to the state . . . this traditional weakness, which is almost congenital to the national consciousness of underdeveloped countries, is not solely the result of the mutilation of the colonised people by the colonial regime. It is also the result of the intellectual laziness of the national middle class, and of its spiritual penury. . .[100]

In the post-colonial period, nationalism, once simply anti-colonialist, now becomes the integrative ideology of the ruling national bourgeoisie. But this does not aim at the mobilisation of social classes for development. Rather, it serves to divert attention from unachieved aspirations and unaccomplished tasks. Like Behrendt, Fanon observes that in these states it is not national consciousness but ethno-centric nationalism that emerges. Fanon, however, attempts an explanation of the phenomenon. He attributes the failure of the national state in the developing countries to the rule of the national bourgeoisie, although he continues to regard the national state as a viable transitional phase. 'A bourgeoisie that provides nationalism alone as food for the masses fails in its mission and gets caught up in a whole series of mishaps.'[101] These 'mishaps', which he has analysed exhaustively, show that in underdeveloped countries nationalism is almost in conflict with the idea of the nation. The national bourgeoisie takes nationalism to mean the transfer to themselves of the privileges formerly enjoyed by the colonisers.[102] They confiscate the plantations of the colonial rulers in the name of 'the nation' and thus extend their domination over the whole country.[103] Still employing the terminology of nationalism, the national bourgeoisie adopt an anti-industrial position. 'Long speeches will be made about the artisan class. Since the middle class finds it impossible to set up factories that would be more viable both for themselves and for the country as a whole, they will surround the artisan class with a chauvinistic tenderness . . .'.[104] The idealisation of pre-colonial culture, which could in some ways contribute effectively towards the struggle against colonial rule, now becomes the incarnation of irrational anti-industrialisation. Senghor's notion of '*négritude*', which preaches a pre-technical ideology, is only a variation on this theme.[105] Nationalism is now not only directed against imperialist nations, but also against neighbouring states facing similar problems, and thus aspirations towards emancipation turn into chauvinism. 'From nationalism we have crossed over to ultra-nationalism, to chauvinism and finally to racism. The foreigners are called to leave; their shops are burned, their street stalls are wrecked, they are being lynched . . . '.[106] Fanon considers the fact that the national bourgeoisie 'turns more and more towards racism' as a regression to sub- and pre-national social structures,[107] because 'from the chauvinism of the Senegalese to the tribalism of the Wolofs is not a big step'.[108] Under such conditions, the national front

> which has forced colonialism to withdraw, . . . cracks up, and wastes the victory it has gained. The merciless fight engaged upon by races and tribes and the aggressive anxiety to occupy the posts left vacant by the departure of the foreigners, will also give rise to religious rivalries. In the countryside and the bush, minor confraternities, local religious and maraboutic cults will show a new vitality and will once more take up their round of excommunications. In the big towns, on the level of the administrative classes, we will observe the confrontation of the two great religions, Islam and Catholicism.[109]

The revival of pre-national structures and normative systems provides fertile soil for semi-fascist military dictatorship. Fanon considers that this 'narrow-gauge fascism is the dialectic product of semi-colonial states in their independence period'.[110]

In comparison with that of Behrendt and Kautsky, Fanon's analysis attempts to work out a strategy for nation formation differing from those already applied, which have resulted in 'mishaps'. Kautsky does not analyse these failings adequately, and Behrendt simply uses them to preach a kind of national nihilism. Fanon, however, arrives at the important conclusion that under the rule of the national bourgeoisie in socially and economically underdeveloped countries there can be no development of a national consciousness aspiring to overcome underdevelopment for the benefit of all social classes. 'The bourgeois leaders of under-developed countries imprison national consciousness in sterile formalism. It is only when men and women are included on a vast scale in enlightened and fruitful work that form and body are given to that consciousness.'[111]

Fanon follows Marx' theory that internationalism is only possible among free peoples, and that cosmopolitanism based on national nihilism only serves to mask the relationships between exploiters and exploited on an international level.[112] He ends his analysis with a polemic against 'certain pharisees. . . . National claims, it is here and there stated, are a phase that humanity has left behind. It is the day of great concerted actions, and retarded nationalists ought in consequence to set their mistakes aright. We, however, consider that the mistake, which may have very serious consequences, lies in wishing to skip the national period.'[113] Behind this polemic lies the discovery that 'the consciousness of self is not the closing of the door to communication. Philosophical thought teaches us, on the contrary, that it is its guarantee. National consciousness, which is not nationalism, is the only thing that will give us an international dimension.'[114]

3 The Role of Nationalism and Nation Formation in the Process of Emancipation of the Peoples of the 'Third World'

The indigenous social structures of 'Third World' countries, devastated by colonialism, are now experiencing a comprehensive process of transformation triggered off from outside.[1] However the disintegration of these structures has not led to the overcoming of social and economic backwardness,which were both consolidated under colonial rule.

The colonial peoples' desire for emancipation is evident in the emergence of anti-colonial movements which are the bearers of social change.[2] These movements have the dual task of achieving emancipation both from authoritarian institutions and from unfavourable natural conditions.[3] The emancipation of these countries will not of itself be achieved by the abolition of the institutions of colonial rule,[4] nor can these countries simply return to the point in their history at which colonialism burst in. The departure of the colonial troops does not of itself mean emancipation; material needs and hardships must be overcome in the course of a long period of arduous work.

The discussion of nationalism and the national state in these countries can only be meaningful if this historical background is taken into account. Instead of starting off with abstract models, the true potential for change must be investigated. In the following section some preliminary and provisional theoretical points will be made, to serve as the basis for an analysis of the Arab national

movement, which has been chosen as an example of the phenomenon of nationalism in the 'Third World'.

The points made in Chapter 2 may now be usefully recapitulated.
The Marxist discussion of the national question is dominated by the
theme of aspirations for emancipation, although apart from Poland
and Ireland, Lenin gave little consideration to the rights of small
nations to form their own states as a step towards emancipation.
The main finding of this discussion is that it was at the time of the
emergence of capitalism that the formation of national states
became a dominant feature of international relations. Hence a
nihilistic approach can only serve to mask the fact that strong
national states dominate weaker ones. Due to the way in which their
economic affairs are entangled, the relations between national
states are as much based upon subjection and domination as those of
classes within a single society. Hence the emancipation of oppressed
peoples, even if they are already organised into states, must take
place within a primarily national framework.[5]

Supporters of modernisation theory have a different approach to
the subject. They consider it important to pinpoint the role of
nationalists in the transformation processes in colonial and semi-
colonial countries, and therefore concentrate on subjective factors
of social change in the 'Third World'. They come to the conclusion
that the nationalists are mostly Western-educated intellectuals. This
socially free-floating élite, rather than a specific social class, is
supposed to be the bearer of social change.

Supporters of acculturation theory also confine their analysis to
subjective factors in the transformation process. Examples taken
from the work of Behrendt underline the inadequacy of this
approach, which generally ascribes the changes that have taken
place in these countries to Western influences. Failures in their
development are usually explained on the grounds that the innovations which have taken place have been brought about through a
diffusion of European cultural influences, which were bound to fail
because of the absence of the necessary historical infrastructure.

Although Frantz Fanon's analysis of the phenomenon tends to be
emotionally charged (a fact of which he himself was aware),[6] he
nevertheless penetrates to the heart of the problem. He stresses the
importance of the role played by the national question in the process
of colonial emancipation, but also shows that here nation formation
is achieved not in an evolutionary manner, but by force, powered by
the development of a national consciousness which focusses politi-

cal action. But he also shows in detail the 'mishaps of national consciousness' and clearly shows the dangers for emancipation inherent in pursuing a chauvinistic form of nationalism.

Any analysis of this problem must make a strict distinction between the nation, or more accurately the national state, defined as a total social institution, and the nation, defined as the internal and external legitimation of any political authority.[7] A further distinction must be made between the two stages of nationalism. In the beginning, nationalism manifests itself as a cultural defence mechanism[8] while later it becomes an expression of the aspirations for a national state. At this stage it has become political.

The categories used here have been borrowed from the development of European capitalism, and refer to actual historical processes which have taken place in Europe. Here Mühlmann, like Behrendt, correctly emphasises that 'nationalism could be "exported" from Europe to Asia and Africa as an ideology, and there form superstructures over populations whose national integration was insignificant'.[9] Furthermore, this ideology was 'imported' by the Westernised 'upper and middle classes'.[10] However, Mühlmann is on less sure ground when he insists, without sufficient empirical evidence, that nationalism in these countries can only 'exist as a purely ideological superstructure without the real sociological substratum implied in the word "nation"'.[11] Nationalism, he argues, can be imported, but not 'the history that has not taken place'.[12] Elsewhere he concedes that the 'ideological nationalism' of the Westernised intellectual can build up a form of infrastructure by a synthesis with 'nativism' which 'in a sense provides the permanent and popular basis of nationalism'.[13] Mühlmann applies the term 'nativist' to 'collective movements in colonised societies': ' "nativism" is the form of self-expression of the "native inhabitants" '.[14] He considers the romantic attempts to re-establish pre-colonial structures to be 'nativist' rather than nationalist, and tries to explain such attempts: 'Because the native thinks in mythical categories, the product of his mind tends to become a new manifestation of the creative 'dawn of history', accompanied by the return of his saviours and forefathers. In this way the concept of a happy future becomes identical with the "dawn of history", and beginning and end become one . . .'.[15] The desire of the colonised people for their emancipation and their aspirations towards equality are denounced by Mühlmann as 'cargo complexes' on the part of those who 'have not made it, who now believe that they will finally get what is due to them by means of simple processes of "redistribution" '.[16] In spite of their claims to the contrary, such interpretations can add little to the discussion of nation formation; they completely ignore the prevailing social conditions in the colonial and semi-colonial countries and operate within strongly ideological categories such as 'nativism' and similar loaded terms which themselves require critical evaluation.

Behrendt and Mühlmann seem unaware that the processes of nation formation in the 'Third World' are neither the result of the diffusion of Western institutions nor an imitative and hence futile replay of a 'history that has not taken place'. In fact, in each case, a process is taking place under precise historical circumstances, conditioned by both subjective and objective internal factors, as well as by the national state structure of the international system.[17] Behrendt's critique of the national state in the 'Third World'[18] as such is only meaningful as a critique of the historical quality of these states. This critique misses the point, because it considers their 'failure' to be absolute, and simply reduces this to the absence of any local historical infrastructure.[19] Both Behrendt and Mühlmann take state formation in European history as their model. They seem to consider this model to be universally applicable, which prevents them from understanding other historical forms of state formation.[20] C. J. Friedrich has pointed out correctly that the European model is irrelevant for underdeveloped countries, where nation formation must be understood in terms of the creation of group cohesion and group loyalty.[21] In the colonial and semi-colonial countries which are struggling to obtain their emancipation, the problem is not how to overcome foreign domination as such, especially as they are underdeveloped in every way, but first to create a form of authority which will mobilise all forces for the struggle to overcome underdevelopment. It is only in this way that authority can obtain any rational legitimacy. The only alternative provided by history for achieving the emancipation of these countries is the nation as a means of giving internal and external political legitimacy, and the national state as the institutional framework within which the organisation of development policies can take place.[22] Clearly, this alternative can only provide a temporary solution, and it is vital to define the quality of each of these alternatives in concrete terms. But the discussion of whether the national state *as such* provides a suitable framework of organisation for socially and economically backward countries is a-historical, and is thus irrelevant in practice.

C. B. Macpherson also considers nation formation to be an indispensable component of development. He points out that it is necessary 'to create a pervasive loyalty towards the nation rather than the tribe, the ethnic community, or the local community. A pre-political and pre-national people has to be brought to a political and national consciousness.'[23] Here he emphasises the importance of Rousseau's *volonté générale* for the colonial countries in their attempts to reach the level of cohesion both necessary for and conditioned by policies of industrialisation. He even claims to detect echoes of Rousseau in the theoretical declarations of the leaders of the underdeveloped countries.[24]

The frontiers of colonial countries which have obtained political independence may demarcate a national state, but they do not demarcate a nationality.[25] This lack of homogeneity acts as a brake upon the processes of social mobilisation necessary to overcome natural obstacles. However, if the assertion of the nation as the legitimate sovereign authority is accompanied by a meaningful development policy, it may then be possible to overcome pre-national forms of social commitment, and thereby to reach a level of cohesion capable of setting mobilisation processes in motion. In the colonial countries, therefore, nation formation is not identical with state formation, which is merely the achievement of political independence. Nation formation can only come about when the tribal, ethnic, linguistic and cultural differences within a single national structure have been dissolved. In these countries nation formation has not grown organically out of the past, as in Europe, but depends on an integrative policy as part of an overall development strategy. This particularly complex historical situation requires detailed theoretical analysis based upon empirical research which will provide a frame of reference within which these problems can be properly understood. It will now be clear that the theory that the national state is doomed to failure in non-Western societies, because it is alleged to be the result of cultural diffusion and has no historical infrastructure, is both speculative and pointless. The success or failure of nation formation in these states depends primarily on the political structures within which the process takes place.

Karl W. Deutsch has developed a model which shows the components required for successful nation formation.[26] According to this model, two processes need to be investigated: the extent of social mobilisation, and the degree of national homogeneity. The extent to which a heterogeneous people can develop into a homogeneous structure brought about through integrative policies as part of the process of nation formation can be measured according to two criteria; the rate of assimilation and the rate of mobilisation. Here success will depend upon the identity of the 'nation-builders', the bearers of social change, who also hold political power.[27]

Deutsch considers the processes of nation formation in these countries to be necessary, and does not accept attitudes of national nihilism, which misunderstand the nature of the international system, and are generally the product of wishful thinking. '*Not before inequality and insecurity have become less extreme, not before the vast poverty of Asia and Africa will have been reduced substantially by industrialisation, and by gains in living standards and in education—not before then will the age of nationalism and national diversity see the beginning of its end.*'[28] And he adds that 'Even the growth of national consciousness may under certain circumstances contribute to this end',[29] although he remains critical of nationalism and underlines its dangers for the emancipation of colonial peoples.[30] These dangers are inherent in anti-colonial nationalism, because it has an exclusively national perspective. It cannot solve the long-range problems which will arise after the departure of the colonial troops. Nationalism, once a progressive force, becomes transformed in the post-colonial era into an ideology stabilising the élitist domination of those social elements who have fought the war of independence, and who now attempt to take over the positions of privilege which the colonists have vacated.[31]

As soon as they have become ends in themselves, the farcical character of the nation as a means of legitimation, and of the national state as an organisational principle becomes clear. They are only valid as vehicles for development policies during periods of transition. Having arrived at this conclusion, it becomes important to identify those who exercise political power. As Fanon has shown, the indigenous bourgeoisie in these countries, which has developed within the context of the colonial economy, cannot, in the context of the international constellation of forces, carry out the bourgeois revolution which history has assigned to it. Taking India as an example in her discussions with Lenin, Rosa Luxemburg forecast that the national bourgeoisie which would come to power after decolonisation would simply take over the same exploitative role as the colonialists.[32] Fanon has again shown that the nation as a means of legitimising the rule of the indigenous bourgeoisie is equivalent to the rebirth of tribalism under the guise of nationalism—whereby the nation is in fact reduced to the tribe[33]—since the integration of tribes into a cohesive group which might have been achieved through industrialisation does not take place. History shows that if the colonial bourgeoisie inherits political power it is incapable of overcoming backward social structures. Hence a simplistic application of the Western liberal democratic model of government is bound to fail, since it does not take account of local historical circumstances.[34] As a model of government for developing countries, the dictatorship of the proletariat in the name of the nation is equally inadequate, since the industrial proletariat is usually either tiny or non-existent. Trotsky's thesis that the colonial proletariat can play the leading role in spite of its small size is based on the situation in Russia in 1917 and is thus somewhat speculative in the context of the colonial circumstances of the 'Third World'.[35]

A possible structure of authority for underdeveloped countries, which would follow the criteria set out in this analysis, seems to be that of the vanguard party, which unites in itself the conscious, progressive Europeanised elements, and fulfils Macpherson's requirements of internal party democracy and a mass base. The power of this party must be rooted in the people, and the vanguard acts in the name of the *volonté générale*. Such a one-party system, whose philosophical foundations are close to the political philosophy of Rousseau, can in Macpherson's view claim to be democratic.[36] The vanguard party actually functions as the nation, in that it is the carrier of the legitimacy of power, but it must see its hegemony as only a temporary solution. Under its leadership, emancipation from physical backwardness must be achieved through industrialisation, which will generally serve as a base for political emancipation. Inner party democracy and the accountability of the party to all its members will prevent political power becoming an independent entity and facilitate the creation of a mass base. According to Habermas the social reality must include communication as well as instrumentality.[37]

Bonapartist regimes such as that of Nasser and similar military dictatorships cannot be compared with this model. They are not vanguard movements, and do not have a democratic mass base. Fanon's category of 'narrow-gauge fascism' is a more appropriate description of these regimes.[38] The 'Bonapartist nationalism',[39] stirred up by the 'narrow-gauge' fascism of the coup d'état, is generally an institutionalised variant of the nationalism of the anti-colonial period, in a politically independent but still semi-colonial state.

While nationalism in Europe was the ideological expression of social processes of nation formation, in the countries of the 'Third World', where it has an acculturative character, it is the philosophical anticipation of social transformations that are yet to come.[40] Here nationalism develops even before the nation has formed and before a formal-juridical expression of nationality has been articulated. Hence in what follows the phenomenon of nationalism will be treated separately from the question of the national state and nation formation. Furthermore, in investigating the conditions necessary for the development of national movements in colonial countries, it is important to distinguish between areas whose populations are homogeneous, and areas which contain ethnically and culturally diverse populations. In countries with homogeneous populations, the anti-colonial national movement which developed within the womb of colonial rule can refer to a pre-colonial culture in which to find its identity, which will facilitate and legitimate the struggle against colonialism, and give the colonised a psychological backbone. This is not possible among heterogeneous populations, where the national movements tend to construct a common pre-colonial culture in order to derive an identity from it. An example of the first is the Arab cultural nationalism of the nineteenth century, which revived classical Arabic literature. An example of the second is the ideology of *négritude* which Africanised the conservative European critique of civilisations and thereby arrived at the notion of an 'African nature'. However, in spite of their differences, the two forms of nationalism exhibit the same features and have developed in the same way. Both are ideologies of revivalist movements,[41] which aim at re-establishing 'ethnic dignity' and legitimating the solidarity of nationalist or pan-movements.[42] In so far as they question the *status quo*, these movements are objectively revolutionary.[43] In their beginnings they are purely cultural, but in the course of their development explicitly political demands, such as national sovereignty, begin to be made. These national movements are usually of a chiliastic nature and they view the pre-colonial period as a golden age of liberty. It must however be emphasised that such movements are by no means primitivist, as widespread prejudice would allege. Hobsbawm has clearly shown that chiliasm must not be identified with primitivism, and that all revolutionary movements exhibit strongly chiliastic tendencies.[44] Furthermore, these revitalisation movements, which seem to the outside observer to be the expression of an indigenous restorative revivalism, are in fact supported more by the Europeanised intellectuals than by the traditionally educated. This is true both of Arab cultural nationalism[45] and of the *négritude* movement,[46] which are both typical of movements of their kind. In both cases, Western-educated intellectuals reactivate indigenous cultural elements through the medium of the European methodology which they have acquired. The utopias which they formulate and which they project into pre-colonial times reveal pronounced European bourgeois features. The fact that these utopias are located in the past does not mean that 'the natives think in mythical categories, so that the product of their minds tends to become a new manifestation of the "creative dawn of history"'[47] as Mühlmann and other ideologues of colonialism have claimed. On the contrary, the Western-educated colonial intellectuals, for whom colonialism made questionable everything that was indigenous, returned to their own pre-colonial history, since after their Europeanisation they were neither accepted as 'complete human beings' by the colonial system, nor considered as 'belonging' by the traditional authorities of their own people. They had lost their identity. Hence these backward-looking utopias expressing a form of cultural nationalism were in fact an attempt to overcome cultural alienation and to find a new identity.[48] The revolutionary core of these revivalist movements is clear. Although they may appear to be traditional on the surface, they are directed against the *status quo* and towards 'modernisation'. They oppose not only the European colonial powers, but also the traditional elements in their own societies, although in doing so they make use of a language that may seem to be traditional. For instance: 'African nationalism always takes on a doubly defensive aspect: against Europe and against traditional Africa.'[49] The politicisation of the later stages of cultural nationalism can mean its development towards étatism. Under colonial rule, the Western-educated intellectuals invest the extended groups from which they originate with national cultural properties, in order to distinguish their own from other national groups, and above all from the supporters of colonial rule. This extended group then claims that it is a culturally autonomous unit with its own national framework, or its own national state.[50]

These historical processes, which took place in most colonial countries, with some variations of detail, suggest a comparison with late nineteenth-century Europe, when the smaller European peoples, who have at times been considered as national minorities,[51] or somewhat condescendingly described as 'remnants of peoples with no history' (Engels) began to emancipate themselves. The Prague historian Miroslav Hroch suggests describing them as 'not fully eligible ethnic groups' and 'smaller modern nations who have not yet fully emerged' or 'oppressed peoples'.[52] In the beginning their attempts at emancipation were confined to the cultural level, in that they began to revive their suppressed national culture. Like the colonial peoples, however, these nations were exposed to Western, bourgeois, influences.[53] In the course of their national awakening, and encouraged by world political developments, their cultural nationalism assumed an explicitly political nature and began to claim the rights of national statehood for oppressed national minorities.[54] It is of course clear that the colonial situation is a completely different one,[55] although there are certain similarities in the 'mechanisms' which come into existence in the course of the emancipation of oppressed peoples and ethnic groupings. However, the historical point of departure of colonial nationalism is completely different. This nationalism is progressive in a certain phase, in that it is the articulation of the desire for emancipation, but it also has a certain retarding effect, even under colonial rule. Fanon has shown that the nationalism of the colonial intellectual is obstructive, in that it is not aware of any alternatives to colonialism except that of a return to the pre-colonial past, which is not particularly significant except in terms of social psychology. As Fanon puts it, the rejection of the colonial reality which this kind of nationalism preaches tends to obey 'the law of inertia. There is no taking of the offensive, and no redefining of relationships. There is simply a concentration on a hard core of culture, which is becoming more and more shrivelled up, inert and empty.'[56]

In spite of its schizophrenic character, this nationalism may have a role to play during the period of decolonisation. After political independence, however, its role becomes purely obstructive. Its anti-technological and anti-industrial characteristics now tend to act as a brake upon development, and it begins to resemble European populist nationalism in its glorification of pre-technical values. There are striking similarities between the language of anti-colonial nationalism, which always insists upon its originality, and that of European populist nationalism, as will become clear from the consideration of Arab nationalism which follows. Like the populist in Europe, the anti-colonial nationalist glorifies the past and illuminates it in a metaphysical fashion. Thus the society of the future is only conceivable in terms of a utopia set in the past. Just as the populist nationalist declared enlightenment to be heretical and rationalism to be imported, anti-colonial nationalists reject European rationalism and industrialisation simply because they are alien. Thus Senghor, the African nationalist, is suspicious of agricultural modernisation projects in his country 'because they are based on science, and not on the graves of our ancestors, and because they are brought to life by the rhythm of the trumpet and not by that of the traditional tom-tom'.[57] According to Senghor, the African is a peasant by nature, and Africans 'know that science and technology are white, and that nature, which is what it is all about, has become the field of research for the technologist, rather than the field of work of the peasants'.[58] For Senghor 'the acknowledgement of *négritude* means turning one's back on western values, that is on technology, science and reason'.[59] Gandhi[60] and many other colonial nationalists display similar attitudes.

However, colonial nationalism is not always populist and anti-European. Another feature is liberal nationalism, which has European bourgeois-democratic characteristics, a fact which its supporters do not deny. They take Europe as their example and distinguish between the emancipating and the colonising aspects of European culture. This variant of nationalism is particularly common in the early phases of 'Third World' national movements, such as the first generation of West African nationalists,[61] the early Arab nationalists,[62] and the Vietnamese nationalists.[63] This nationalism usually fails for a number of reasons, probably the most important being that a bourgeois liberal nationalism cannot realise its aim in a society which still has a pre-capitalist structure. Furthermore, their disappointment in reformist tendencies in Europe has led many of these liberal nationalists to turn towards populist and generally anti-Western nationalism, although they continue to express themselves in European terms. It is however often difficult to distinguish between liberal and populist variants of 'Third World' nationalism, since they frequently converge.

The anti-industrial character of colonial nationalism in the post-colonial era actually implies a return to tribalism, which prevents the integration of groups which are ethnically, linguistically and culturally heterogeneous.[64] In this respect Behrendt's distinction between nationalism and national consciousness in the underdeveloped countries seems justified.[65] However, this nationalism, whose apogee is chauvinistic apologetics and the idolisation of an alleged originality is not, as has been pointed out earlier, adequately explained in Behrendt's 'emotions of separateness and resentment'. Nothing is said about its social function. If nationalism in the period of decolonisation is exclusively cultural and political, and has no social perspective, it will become a chauvinistic ideology in the post-colonial era. This is socially necessary in that it masks the rule of the forces which have led the independence struggle—an élitist faction which has now acceded to the positions of political power vacated by the colonialists. Their real interests lie not in mobilising the population for the achievement of common goals, nor in the creation of a national consciousness, but in the perpetuation of their own rule, and for this nationalism is a useful vehicle. With the help of this kind of populist nationalism, the population is distracted from internal conflicts and is mobilised against a foreign enemy, however fictitious.

In view of this, interpretations which see the nationalism of the colonial intellectual as an 'ideology of modernisation' and as progressive are inadequate. Particularly in the post-colonial era, as Schuhler states, this nationalism is 'a fundamental hindrance to socio-economic development, in that it stabilises or even increases the social contradictions whose termination is part and parcel of the process of development'.[66] Schuhler then suggests that 'this "regressive-irrational" function of nationalism, which is merely the ideology of a political power clique . . . must be transformed into an "objectively progressive tendency"'.[67] However the present analysis will show that this transformation is by no means inherent in the nationalism of colonial and semi-colonial countries.

An important variant of anti-colonial nationalism is the Pan-ideology, which is found in a number of 'Third World' national movements, especially in Africa (Pan-Africanism) and the Middle East (Pan-Arabism). The leaders of regional national movements became *Pan*-ideologues when they realised that the national state for which they were fighting could only be a transitional form of organisation. Thus Julius Nyerere sees the creation of a national consciousness based on the national state as the first step towards the realisation of an all-African national state. For Nyerere nationalism is 'all-African', which is itself based on Pan-Africanism.[68] Transcending the borders between countries does not mean that national states thereby become obsolete: on the contrary, it will lead to the formation of an extended national state. Furthermore, the attempts of the anti-colonialist *Pan*-movements to abolish the national state have tended to become bogged down in irredentism in the same way as their counterparts in Europe in the nineteenth and twentieth centuries. The supporters of Pan-Africanism and Pan-Arabism consider these movements to be further developments of nationalism. The Senegalese politician Doudou Thiam distinguishes between micro and macro-nationalism, the latter being Pan-Africanism,[69] which is simply the projection of micro-nationalism onto the larger geographical area in which the 'race' allegedly lives. The assumed racial or cultural common interests of a certain area come to be taken as the basis for aspirations for a political entity.

Part II The Emergence and Development of Nationalism in the Arab World before the Second World War

4 The Historical Background of Arab Nationalism

Social change[1] in the Middle East may be explained in terms of acculturation theory, to the extent that the archaic-chiliastic and secular-nationalist variants of the literary and political renaissance which took place in the Arab provinces of the Ottoman Empire in the early nineteenth century were generated by forces from outside the area. However, this theory cannot be particularly fruitful if it implies a Euro-centric approach. Thus Behrendt devalues his otherwise useful explanation by claiming, as a European, that the 'underdeveloped nations' imitate all the achievements of Europe in a negative fashion[2] from a position of psychological weakness. von Grunebaum's more sophisticated attempts to interpret Westernisation in the Islamic world are equally questionable. He sees it as a process which can only be understood in psychological terms: in other words 'cultural change' is seen in terms of psychologically-based American cultural anthropology.[3]

In this attempt to trace the historical roots of Arab nationalism in the early nineteenth century, acculturation theory will be utilised where it seems to be relevant. It is clear that Arab nationalism and the movements which preceded it have largely developed under the influence of Europe. However, such an approach cannot by itself lead to a real understanding of the phenomenon. Here Walther Braune says aptly that 'to declare that its [sc. Arab Nationalism's] origins can be traced back to European influences is the equivalent of carrying dates to Basra. Naturally, in this and almost every other way in modern times, the Arab Orient has been influenced by Western history. But *foreign influences can only take effect when conditions for their reception and subsequent transformation exist.*'[4] It is therefore necessary to describe the social structure of the Ottoman Empire at this time, and also the social changes that took place in

Egypt at the time of Muhammad 'Ali, when it had become more or less independent. This will be followed by a discussion of pre-nationalist religious movements, both 'archaic' and modernist. In Chapter 5 there will be a study of Arab nationalism itself, which was formed in European and American mission schools in the Tanzimat period, against a background of military innovation in the Ottoman army. It is only in this context that it is possible to define the role of Sati 'al-Husri as the expression of a new direction in the history of the Arab national movement since the First World war.

(a) The Middle East under the Ottomans: the Social Structure and Legitimacy of Ottoman Rule

Early capitalist relations of production emerged at the time of the 'Abbasids (750–1258), generally considered the socio-economic apogee of the medieval Muslim East. The researches of Goitein and Sellheim on this period show the self-awareness of the emerging middle class, which, through its enhanced economic position, was able to compete for social status with the bureaucracy of the court.[5] The potential for the development of a bourgeois society within the structure of the 'Abbasid Empire was limited largely by the fact that the key positions in the state apparatus were occupied by non-Arab soldiers, with the result that the military element in an over-powerful state apparatus itself became over-powerful. These mercenaries belonged to the highest echelons of 'Abbasid society and they had vested interests in land and in the army. Thus, as K. Steinhaus points out, 'their interests were diametrically opposed to the economic, cultural and ideological structures within the Islamic cities of Western Asia and North Africa, in which trading and manufacture dominated'.[6] Subsequently the Mongol invasion, which brought about the downfall of the 'Abbasids, encouraged a return to agriculture and to feudal relationships. C. H. Becker also saw the 'beginnings of developments which were similar to those in the West', but he claims that the reason that no further progress was possible was that 'ultimately, things in the East were animated by a different spirit from that in Europe'.[7] This attempt to explain the non-emergence of a bourgeois society in the Middle East in 'racial-psychological terms'[8] and not in terms of social history, is of course simply mystification. More recent research on the relations between Islam and capitalism further refutes such theories.[9]

In the course of the disintegration of the 'Abbasid Empire the formation of smaller states in the Arab East which had already begun in the tenth century, accelerated. The Mamlukes, the former slave soldiers of the caliphate, had already started to become more and more independent before the end of the Empire in 1258. They formed a state of their own in Egypt, and although they nominated one of the surviving 'Abbasids as their caliph, this in no way limited their authority.

The political geography of the whole area changed at the beginning of the fourteenth century, when Turkish warrior tribes, who were also agriculturalists, founded the Ottoman Empire. The new empire was first confined to Asia Minor but quickly expanded into Europe and Asia. By the sixteenth century the Ottomans controlled the entire Arabic-speaking areas of Asia and North Africa (except Morocco), as well as most of South-Eastern Europe. As the Ottomans were essentially tribesmen whose social reproduction was in waging war and agriculture, they were never particularly interested in using and developing the productive forces indigenous to the areas which they conquered.[10] They tended to leave trade and commerce to European traders and to the non-Muslim ethnic minorities (such as Greeks, Armenians and Jews) who were however completely at the mercy of the despotic power of the Ottoman State. These middle-class non-Muslims formed an 'unarmed minority' outside the community of the state. They could not hope to obtain political power over their economic position within society.[11] The Muslim subjects of the Empire rarely engaged in trade and commerce as they were largely taken up with military duties from which the 'unbelieving' minorities were exempt.[12] The eighteenth-century French traveller Volney reported the same ethnic division of labour in the Arab provinces of the Ottoman Empire which form the subject of this study.[13]

In general, the Ottoman Empire was a feudal state organised along the lines of a military bureaucracy. The state was the sole feudal proprietor, owning all the land and leasing it in the form of fiefs to the *sipahis* (knights) on whom the Ottoman army was originally based. In return, the *sipahis* had to supply feudal troops for the military undertakings of the Empire,[14] but they gradually became more and more independent with the passage of time. 'The Turkish upper classes—the leaders of the army, the military bureaucracy and the '*ulama*'—tended to reproduce themselves through groundrents and eventually by forcible expropriation.'[15]

Hence new conquests were always an important feature of the economic reproduction of the Empire.

War is fed on war—and for no state are these words more appropriate than for the state of the sultan-caliph. And that is not all. Here, war fed the whole political and social system. As the material yields of external expansion became indispensable for the maintenance and improvement of the territorial *status quo*, military superiority in return was a basic condition for the continuation of the processess of social reproduction in their existing form.[16]

However, due to the success of the bourgeois revolutions of the eighteenth century, Europe managed to restrict Ottoman expansion, and thus dealt a body blow to the Empire. But the tax farms which were introduced to compensate for the new limitations on expansion tended to promote further disintegration rather than stability,[17] since they encouraged local particularism.

Feudalism in the Ottoman Empire was very different from that in Europe. The Ottoman fief-holders were not autonomous rulers, but only functioned in their exploitation of the peasantry as representatives of the authority of the state, the Sublime Porte. 'The cycle of Eastern feudalism, oppression and plunder was closed by another characteristic; landlord absenteeism. . . . The landowner, who resided in town and sometimes even abroad, made no real attempt to improve the land he rented out or to assist the peasants who groaned under the burden of taxes and debts: he was only concerned with squeezing as much as possible out of them.'[18]

The Ottomans gave legitimacy to their despotic system of government and their military expansion by recourse to Islam and the *shari'a*.[19] Islamic universalism gave ideological sanction to the supra-national character of the Empire.[20] The Ottoman court historians made their contribution here by declaring the sultans to be the legitimate heirs to the caliphate. The last 'Abbasid Caliph al-Mutawakkil is supposed to have handed over his office to Sultan Salim I in 1517, the year in which Cairo fell to the Ottomans. The historians added to this myth by making up genealogies for the sultans, tracing their Arab origin back to the Prophet Muhammad. This falsification of history was essential, since the caliphate, according to Islamic orthodoxy, is reserved to members of the tribe of Quraish, from which Muhammad came.[21] Through this artifice, and also by resisting any form of liberating enlightenment, the Ottomans were able to ensure the loyalty of their Arab subjects on religious grounds.

In socio-economic and cultural terms the Arab East tended to stagnate under Ottoman rule, as is well described by the French traveller Volney at the end of the eighteenth century.[22] The return to agriculture, and hence to feudalism, which began with the end of the 'Abbasid Empire, continued and established new social relations which seemed to have disappeared a long time before. Brockelmann's *History of Arabic Literature* shows the way in which the cultural wealth of the 'Abbasid period, expressed in artistic, literary and scientific form, declined into general cultural stagnation under the Ottomans.[23]

(b) Napoleon's Expedition to Egypt, 1798, and the Seizure of Power by Muhammad 'Ali in 1805: The Beginnings of Externally Generated Social Change in the Middle East

After the conquest of Egypt by Sultan Salim I in 1517, the Mamlukes were made to pay regular taxes to the Sublime Porte, but no attempt was made to end their rule. Under Ottoman suzerainty, as C. H. Becker shows,[24] the Mamlukes, as a military-feudal caste, once more gained 'new scope for manoeuvre'. Egypt was now pillaged by the Ottomans as well as by the Mamlukes. Between 1517 and 1798 Egypt was reduced to the status of an Ottoman province. This was 'a dead period for Egypt: history was taking place elsewhere'.[25] Stanford Shaw divides this period of ultra-military oriental feudalism[26] into three phases, in the course of which a power struggle between two hierarchies was taking place, the 'hierarchy of function', consisting of the representatives of the Ottoman sultan, headed by the *wali*, and the 'hierarchy of power' which was the Mamluke military corps. The object of this struggle was the share of the plunder of Egypt which each hierarchy should have, both parties being aliens in Egypt. The first phase saw the superiority of the Ottomans, the second phase a balance of power, and the third the superiority of the Mamlukes,[27] who had become so strong that they refused to pay tribute to the Sublime Porte, whose occasional military interventions had little success.[28]

When Napoleon's expedition landed in 1798, Egypt was an 'exhausted, paralysed and degenerate country'.[29] The importance of the Napoleonic expedition for the development of the Middle East is apparent from the most cursory look at its history. Historians and social scientists of the Middle East are in agreement in considering 1798 as the year in which the history of the modern Middle East, as well as that of modern Egypt, begins. According to Hans Henle, Napoleon 'woke up the oriental princess from her thousand year sleep'.[30]

Although the expedition's immediate aim was to block Britain's route to India, its impact on political and cultural life in the area was dramatic, and Napoleon cannot in any way be compared to later invaders. He claimed to wish to spread the spirit of the French Revolution throughout the East and he challenged the Islamic-theocratic despotism of the Ottomans and Mamlukes with the principles of liberty and equality. The expedition brought to Egypt and the whole of the Arab Middle East the 'ideas of the French Revolution embodied in a European army',[31] in Albert Hourani's words. This was the beginning of an extensive process of acculturation between East and West, during which modern European culture was absorbed, and the first signs of a national movement emerged in the Middle East, supported in particular by Western-educated Arab intellectuals expressing the desire of the Arabs for liberation from foreign rule.[32]

As well as military units, the Napoleonic expedition[33] also included a number of scientists from various disciplines, a library of modern European literature, a scientific laboratory, and a printing press with Arabic type, which Napoleon had commandeered in Rome on his way to Egypt. It was the first press in the country.[34] The Mamlukes, with their antiquated weapons, were defeated by superior French arms in front of the Pyramids not far from Cairo. The Egyptians, who had been nurtured in a spirit of docility, watched these events as passive spectators, with the same indifference as they had watched the struggle between the Mamlukes and the Ottomans over the preceding centuries. They found it strange that Napoleon should address them as citizens and not as subjects, and that he should proclaim the principles of the French Revolution which were quite alien to their experience, although he used Islamic terminology. He had come, he alleged, not only to abolish the corrupt rule of the Mamlukes and Ottomans but also to revive Islam. His first proclamation was in Arabic, and distributed as a leaflet. It begins, significantly 'In the Name of God, the

Compassionate, the Merciful: there is no God but God.' It then continues

> In the name of the French Republic (*jumhur*), based on foundations of Liberty and Equality, Bonaparte, Commander-in-Chief of the French forces, informs the whole population of Egypt: for many decades those in power have insulted the French nation (*millet*) . . . the Mamlukes, who were brought in from the Caucasus and Georgia, have been corrupting the best region of the whole world. But God, the Omnipotent, the Master of the Universe, has now made the destruction of their state imperative. I came only to rescue your rights from the oppressors. . . . I worship Almighty God and respect his Prophet Muhammad, and the Glorious Qur'an more than the Mamlukes. Tell them also that all people are equal before God.[35]

These empty phrases, borrowed from Islamic theology, cannot conceal the secular, bourgeois implications of the proclamation, which was to have far-reaching consequences for the subsequent development of the Arab world.[36] They certainly illustrate Napoleon's political skill.

Napoleon chose this inflammatory tone, with which the Egyptians were totally unfamiliar, in order to win them over and thus to establish himself in Egypt as conqueror. The *Institut d'Égypte*,[37] which he founded, was the first Western academic institution in the Arab World in modern times. The historiographer al-Jabarti, who described the Napoleonic expedition, remarked with naive frankness, after a visit to this institute: 'They have strange things and objects which show effects which our minds are too small to comprehend'.[38] The Islamic scholar Shaikh Hasan 'Attar, who was a member of Napoleon's entourage, noted 'Our countries must change, and we must take from Europe all the sciences which do not exist here.'[39] 'Attar was sufficiently consistent to abandon his philological and Islamic studies—the only academic fields in the Arab world at the time—for the study of the modern topics introduced by the French. Eventually he sought the introduction of secular studies into al-Azhar, the Islamic university of Cairo.[40] Although he never visited Europe 'Attar is considered the first Arab advocate of modern European science and culture.

In spite of careful preparations, the Napoleonic expedition

encountered great difficulties in Egypt. Naturally, it had to contend with vigorous opposition from Britain, and the '*ulama*' organised a religious revolt, which forced Napoleon to retaliate, thus further incurring the wrath of the religious members of the population against the infidel. By 1801 Napoleon was forced to abandon the expedition, and his troops were eventually brought back to France in British ships under the terms of his agreement with Britain.[41]

In the years between 1801 and 1805, after the departure of the French, there was a power struggle between the Mamlukes, who were themselves divided internally, and the Ottomans, who tried to reassert the claims which had already been substantially limited by the Mamlukes. However, the departure of the French troops by no means simply signalled the end of a short interlude in Egyptian history, during which an isolated province was briefly exposed to European influences. On the contrary, French influence was able to establish itself further, and the Albanian officer Muhammad 'Ali continued the work which Napoleon had begun. Muhammad 'Ali had come to Egypt in 1801 at the head of a detachment of Ottoman troops. He made use of the internecine feuds among the Mamlukes to eliminate them, and to declare himself viceroy of Egypt. From this time Egypt ceased to be a province of the Ottoman Empire.[42]

Like Napoleon, Muhammad 'Ali had hoped to separate Egypt from the rest of the Empire. Although the former's intentions were blatantly colonialist, the expedition was indirectly responsible for initiating a process which ended Egypt's isolation by introducing it to European progress.[43] Muhammad 'Ali's intentions were no less direct: he had great ambitions, and realised that he could only hold his own by underpinning his power with a modern state organisation and a rational economic system, and by securing both with an army trained and equipped on modern lines. Brockelmann's judgement is harsh but accurate: 'If he tried to introduce the blessings of European civilisation, which he certainly valued, this was purely for political ends.'[44] Braune shows that 'even as a young man in Macedonia, . . . Muhammad 'Ali showed a deep respect for what he knew of French culture, and later, in a letter written by him as ruler of Egypt to Louis Philippe in 1840, he assured him of his enduring gratitude to France. In those days, France symbolised Europe for all those aspiring towards a future for the Orient . . .'[45] Braune considers that Muhammad 'Ali was 'more an oriental despot than a ruler inspired by the ideas of France. But he saw that the reason and knowledge which emanated from Europe should be taken as an example.'[46] Thus he was both 'an enlightened ruler imitating Europe, and a despot rooted in ancient traditions'.[47]

Before Muhammad 'Ali could establish his authority and set his plans for modernisation in motion, he had to eliminate the Mamlukes. He did not confine himself to limiting their political influence but also broke their economic power and finally liquidated them physically in the bloodbaths of 1811–14. These appalling massacres were also intended to frighten the '*ulama*' from renewing any active opposition. They had organised a revolt against Muhammad 'Ali in 1809 which was completely crushed.[48]

Muhammad 'Ali built up a modern army and a centralised state administration with French assistance.[49] The *iltizam* or fief system, which had been the basis of military feudalism, was abolished by confiscating agricultural land from the *multazims*, or fief-holders, and declaring all land the property of the state. *Waqf* lands, the property of pious foundations under the control of the '*ulama*' were also taken over by the state. This measure amounted to the deprivation of the political and economic power of the '*ulama*', who had been a part of the ruling feudal caste. All cultivable land was registered and a register kept in each village.[50] At the same time a number of rather unsuccessful attempts at industrialisation were made, largely in connection with Muhammad 'Ali's attempts to build up a strong army.[51] The state, with its industrial and agrarian policies,[52] was the only vehicle for social change.

Although this state monopolist policy certainly inaugurated economic development based on capitalist principles, it did not immediately promote the development of a middle class. Another new social stratum emerged, recruited from the state bureaucracy and the military, whose interests were not based on ownership of the means of production. After the death of Muhammad 'Ali and under his successors 'Abbas and Sa'id the state's monopoly over agriculture and industry was abolished and the bureaucracy made use of its position to obtain land. There was no private sector willing or able to continue Muhammad 'Ali's policies of industrialisation. However, although land returned to private hands, this did not lead to a re-feudalisation of Egyptian society because it had become capitalist in the mean time. The Egyptian peasantry now worked the land as 'free' wage labourers.

Britain had managed to prevent Muhammad 'Ali from fully implementing his plans to extend and modernise the political and social structure of Egypt. She now began systematically to force the

strengthened Egyptian state back to its former perimeters.[53]
Muhammad 'Ali had succeeded in extending his rule northwards as
far as Anatolia, and southwards into both the Arabian peninsula
and the Sudan.[54] During the reigns of his successors, Britain
increased the country's economic dependence, and in 1882 Egypt
proper became a British colony. British policy prevented Egyptian
industrialisation, and the Egyptian middle class, which had emerged
after the abolition of the monopolies, now invested almost exclusively in the agricultural and commercial sectors.

Muhammad 'Ali's efforts to raise Egypt to the economic and
social level of Europe were eventually terminated by British policy
under his successors. Furthermore, as a result of British rule, the
cultural influence of France was gradually either neutralised or
reduced.[55]

(c) Rifa'a Rafi' al-Tahtawi and the first Generation of European-educated Arab Intellectuals: the Beginnings of National Thinking in the Arab World

At the beginning of his reign Muhammad 'Ali began to put his
modernisation plans into practice with the help of French experts
and scientists. Soon after his accession to power, however, he started
to send Egyptian students and officers to be educated and trained in
Europe. He also began to build up a new educational system in
Egypt itself, geared largely to the demands of an efficient modern
army.[56] The influence of the orthodox 'ulama' was suppressed after
the failure of their revolt in 1809,[57] but those 'ulama' who had shown
themselves receptive to the new policies were rewarded by
Muhammad 'Ali with high positions. Among them was Shaikh
'Attar, who had been an enthusiastic supporter of Napoleon,
although he had had to flee after the revolt against him. Under
Muhammad 'Ali, 'Attar became rector of al-Azhar, a post which he
could not have gained without the Viceroy's approval. He was also
given the responsibility for selecting the members of the first
organised group of Egyptian students sent to France for higher
education. One of the imams sent with the scholars was 'Attar's
pupil Rifa'a Rafi' al-Tahtawi.[58] Together with 'Attar himself, al-
Tahtawi had studied the new secular subjects which had just been
introduced at al-Azhar, such as geography and history. Hence when
he arrived in Paris with his group of students in 1826, he was already

acquainted with some aspects of European thought. While in Paris, he developed a strong desire to study, and eventually obtained permission to do so. Between 1826 and 1831 he was a diligent student of the works of the major European thinkers, notably Montesquieu, Rousseau, Voltaire, Racine and Condillac.[59] At the same time, he began to specialise in translation, in order to make European works accessible to his countrymen. Muhammad 'Ali ordered the large-scale publication of the diary al-Tahtawi had kept regularly in Paris, which was made compulsory reading for Egyptian civil servants.[60] This document, which has literary merit as well as historical importance, faithfully reflects the contrast between the static East and the dynamic West. For instance al-Tahtawi describes the table manners of the French, with charming naiveté, contrasting them with those of the Arabs, who use their fingers instead of knives and forks. He was particularly impressed by the cleanliness of the French, the way their women dressed, their ordered lives, and many other aspects of French society.[61]

In the introduction to his diary, al-Tahtawi expresses the hope that the European knowledge described in his book may awaken 'all the peoples of Islam—both Arabs and non-Arabs—from the sleep of indifference'.[62] This is certainly a highly unorthodox venture on the part of an orthodox Muslim addressing his peers, and al-Tahtawi clearly feels the need to justify his undertaking. He contrasts the backwardness of the East with the fact that 'European countries have reached the highest level of mastery in the whole field of mathematics, natural sciences, and metaphysics'.[63] While admitting that the Islamic world of his day needed to borrow from 'foreign countries to obtain from them the things of which it is ignorant',[64] he also draws attention to the fact that at the height of their culture the Arabs were far superior to the Europeans, and even passed on their culture to them. The Europeans 'even admit to us that we have been their teachers in many branches of knowledge, and they acknowledge that we came before them. And it is obvious that the one who is the first to achieve deserves merit.'[65] al-Tahtawi also makes use of this sort of argument to support Muhammad 'Ali who allows 'the representatives of the shining arts and the useful skills' to come to him in streams, 'with the result that in his ignorance the ordinary man in the street in Egypt . . . condemns him severely' without understanding that Muhammad 'Ali only respects the Europeans 'in their capacity as men and because of their knowledge, and not because they are Christians'.[66]

Since contemporary Europe appeared to him merely as culturally and socio-economically superior to the Middle East, and not—as it did to later generations of Arab intellectuals[67]—as a colonial system, his reservations are purely religious. 'Naturally I can only approve of that which is not in contradiction to our Islamic laws . . .',[68] although as will be clear, he does not hesitate to interpret the *shari'a* in a secular manner.

After his return from Paris in 1831 al-Tahtawi worked first as a translator in one of the French educational establishments. At that time, these included Enfantin's institute, greatly influenced by the principles of Saint-Simon,[69] which had a large staff of doctors, engineers and other scientists, and a school run by the Frenchman Clot Bey which was staffed by French experts employed by the Egyptian State. As there was a certain rivalry between the different schools, and as al-Tahtawi was obliged to Muhammad 'Ali, he joined Clot Bey's School. In 1835 he became head of the language school, which translated European works and trained translators.[70] It concentrated on military works, although French philosophy and literature were also translated.[71] Altogether, al-Tahtawi and his pupils translated some two thousand books and pamphlets into Arabic,[72] which enabled Arab intellectuals to absorb European bourgeois ideas. This process of absorption was to continue throughout the succeeding century in the Middle East. Among al-Tahtawi's own translations were those of Voltaire and Montesquieu. His translation of Fénélon's *Télémaque*, in which the author criticises the absolute rule of Louis XIV, is particularly revealing, since he made the translation while in exile in the Sudan at the behest of Muhammad 'Ali's successor 'Abbas.[73] The parallel is striking.

Historically, al-Tahtawi's most important contributions were in the field of translation, but he also wrote a number of influential pamphlets which afford useful insights into the nature of the acculturation process. Albert Hourani sums up his thinking as follows: '[His] ideas about society and the state are neither a mere restatement of a traditional view nor a simple reflection of the ideas he had learnt in Paris. The way in which his ideas are formulated is on the whole traditional: at every point he makes appeal to the example of the Prophet and his Companions, and his conceptions of political authority are within the tradition of Islamic thought. But at points he gives them a new and significant development.'[74] This emerges clearly from his interpretation of the *lex divina*, the Islamic *shari'a*, where he attempts to show that the *shari'a* has a similar structure to the rationalist Natural Law of modern Europe. al-Tahtawi emphasises that the ruler is under the codex of the *shari'a*,[75] following Montesquieu's separation of powers, which means that it is impossible that it should be left to the discretion of the ruler. He encourages the '*ulama*', as pillars of the *shari'a*, to concern themselves with the study of modern knowledge, which is based on reason, in order to reach an up-to-date interpretation of the *shari'a*. Hourani says that al-Tahtawi considered the '*ulama*' to be worldly priests in the Saint-Simonian sense.[76] Hence his interpretation of the '*shari'a* is permeated with European bourgeois values: the Muslim is now no longer a subject but a citizen. He considers that every citizen must participate in the process of government, which is why he insists upon education,[77] and he also pleads for the education of Arab women.[78]

For present purposes, al-Tahtawi's distinction between the religious and the national form of commitment is particularly relevant. For him, the social takes precedence over the religious, and here, for the first time, an Arab is using the word 'nation' in a secular sense. Furthermore, the Egyptians form a nation.[79] In his Arabic translation of the *Marseillaise* al-Tahtawi uses the word *watan* for the French *patrie*: *l'amour de la patrie* becomes *hubb al-watan*. In his translation of Montesquieu's *Considération sur les Causes de la Grandeur des Romains et de leur Decadence*, al-Tahtawi stresses that love of country is one of the prime virtues of civilisation. Where there is no *hubb al-watan*, civilisation must be condemned to perish.[80] The word *watan* does exist in classical Arabic, but only in the sense of the country from which one originates, or in which one lives. al-Tahtawi also uses *watan* in that sense, as in his reminiscences of his home village, Tahta. But it is Egypt, and not Tahta, that is his *patrie*, which is why he must be considered the first Arab national thinker. Patriotism in the modern European bourgeois sense is a permanent leitmotiv of his thought.[81] al-Tahtawi was the founder of a new genre of Arabic literature, patriotic (*wataniyya*) literature, a field in which his works are still of major significance.[82] Patriotism, equality and justice in the liberal-democratic sense are the central themes of his writings, even in his maturer work *The Paths of Egyptian Hearts in the Joys of the Contemporary Arts*.[83]

As Stowasser rightly remarks, al-Tahtawi's life's work, both his translations and his own writings, consists of 'reception and diffusion'.[84] He successfully attempted to modernise the Arabic language in his writings, in order to make it an adequate vehicle to transmit what he had received.[85] His European education is reflected in the systematic manner in which he approached his work, beginning with his Paris diaries. The numerous quotations from the Qur'an and other religious sources which appear throughout his writings seem to have been grafted on in a somewhat incongruous manner, and are clearly designed to prove that the 'new' in fact already existed in the old texts. This coexistence of modern secular and traditional religious dimensions in al-Tahtawi's thought did not appear inconsistent to him,[86] but it was obvious even to the generation immediately following his own, and eventually produced a confrontation. Thus, the literary renaissance which he inaugurated contained elements of both Islamic Modernism and nationalism.[87]

(d) Two Forms of Islamic Revival: the Archaic-Millenarian Wahhabi Movement and the Modernism of al-Afghani and 'Abduh

Long before Napoleon's expedition and the large-scale reforming activities of Muhammad 'Ali had combined to encourage the emergence of a generation of European-educated intellectuals, there had emerged, in the Arabian peninsula, an area never totally subject to Ottoman rule, a movement led by *Arabs* to return to the beginnings of Islam. These potentially nationalist aspirations were directed against Ottoman, and therefore alien, rule. The movement found its political and religious expression in Wahhabism, which originated from the life and teachings of the traditionally educated Muhammad Ibn 'Abd al-Wahhab (1703–91). On his journeys through the Arab regions of the Ottoman Empire, Ibn 'Abd al-Wahhab had observed what he considered to be deviations from true Islam, and believed it his mission to lead Muslims back to true orthodoxy.[88] He himself followed the strictly orthodox school of Hanbalism, and made particular use of the political theology of Ibn Taimiyya and Ibn Qaiyim al-Jauziyya, two prominent fourteenth-century Hanbalis.[89]

Ibn 'Abd al-Wahhab did not object to the despotic autocracy of Ottoman rule as such, but to the corruption and debauchery into which it had fallen. He believed that only the Arabs could bring Islam back to its original pristine purity, and he considered it his life's purpose to mobilise the Muslims for the achievement of this backward-looking utopia. He discounted all the civilising elements in Islam in favour of the norms and ways of life of the nomads. For him, true Islam was that of the generation of the Prophet, which meant that the Arabs alone were the true bearers of the tradition of Islam, and in this way he could challenge the Ottomans' right to rule. In 1924, Hartmann emphasised that

> as a religious movement, Wahhabism can only be properly understood in the context of the fact that social conditions in Arabia have undergone hardly any significant changes since the time of the Prophet. The movement is rooted in the school of Ahmad Ibn Hanbal, the most conservative of the four Sunni rites, and has emerged as a reaction to the adjustment of Islam to more complex cultural conditions, which have themselves resulted in a certain relaxation of the basic tenets of the founder of the religion, together with a degree of Westernisation.[90]

In 1744, Ibn 'Abd al-Wahhab contracted a marriage alliance with the House of Sa'ud, the rulers of the Arabian Peninsula. As a result, his political and theological notions could now form the ideology of a political and religious revivalist movement of an archaic and millenarian kind. Ibn 'Abd al-Wahhab formulated his beliefs in the form of a political creed ('aqida) whose most relevant passage is: 'He who occupies the office of Caliph . . . must be obeyed, and insurrection against him is forbidden; . . . I believe that the modernists have broken their link with the Community and have cut themselves off from it; . . . I declare that every innovation in religious matters is modernism.'[91] Hartmann shows that Ibn 'Abd al-Wahhab's 'aqida only differs slightly from that of Ibn Taimiyya in 1306, and some passages are identical.[92] However, Ibn 'Abd al-Wahhab's 'aqida plays a different historical role; although obedience to the ruler is postulated, opposition to the Ottomans is held to be legitimate. He does not consider the Ottomans to be the rightful representatives of Islam and the Caliphate, and he opposes them as modernists and deviators from true Islam.

Wahhabism continued to flourish after the death of its founder, and until the beginning of the nineteenth century the rulers of the House of Sa'ud continued to bring substantial parts of the Arabian Peninsula under their control. In the regions they conquered they destroyed everything that appeared to them to represent a deviation from true Islam, including whole cities and styles of architecture. The Ottomans were unable to contain the movement, and it was only with the help of Muhammad 'Ali's modern army that the Wahhabi advance was temporarily halted, after a war which lasted from 1811 to 1818.[93]

The other form of Islamic revival, that of Islamic Modernism, was very different from the Wahhabi movement.[94] Although both movements aimed at a revitalisation of Islam, they differed substantially over how this should be achieved. Islamic Modernism has been primarily an intellectual movement in which civilisation was not to be attacked, but to be considered as an element of the renaissance which was being sought. Thus the Modernists did not turn Islam back into an archaic doctrine, but rather tried to increase its chances of survival in the modern world by enriching it with those discoveries of rational European science which would not attack it at its roots.

The Modernist current of the nineteenth-century Islamic revival derives its theoretical foundations from Jamal al-Din al-Afghani (1839–97) and his pupil Muhammad 'Abduh (1849–1905). While al-Tahtawi had unreservedly accepted European bourgeois ideas, and had thus unintentionally undermined the fundamentalist claims of Islam, al-Afghani and 'Abduh now had to face Europe as a colonial power, and their attitudes were hence more uncompromising. In their writings, Islam becomes an anti-colonialist ideology, which calls out for political action against Europe. This aspect of their beliefs has been correctly, if often rather unsubtly, emphasised in the literature.[95] Although al-Afghani and 'Abduh did not hold themselves aloof from Europe, they were only prepared to accept those elements of its civilisation and culture which might strengthen Islam. Both of them were capable of distinguishing between the progressive and the imperialist aspect of Europe, although to different degrees.

al-Afghani, who read Guizot's *Histoire de la Civilisation en Europe* with passionate enthusiasm, and supported its translation into Arabic (Cairo, 1877), considered Islam more of a civilisation than a religion. He agrees with Guizot that the flowering of a civilisation depends on the moral condition of its subjects. Guizot considered that a moral condition can only promote civilisation if actions of people are inspired by reason, and if they have strong feelings of solidarity. al-Afghani accepted this, and saw the revitalisation of Islamic civilisation as his life's work.[96] Influences of

Ibn Khaldun are also apparent. Al-Afghani vigorously opposed the racist notions then current in Europe which claimed that only Europe could produce a culture and civilisation, and ignored all highly developed non-European cultures including Islam. Among the supporters of this point of view was the influential philosopher Ernest Renan, who considered Islam incompatible with science and culture. This thesis so affronted al-Afghani, who was then in Europe, that he decided to challenge Renan's assumptions publicly in the *Journal des Débats*.[97]

al-Afghani was aware that the tendency towards the formation of national states was increasing with the internationalisation of capitalism. He therefore tried to attune Islam to this development, by taking up the European idea of the nation, purifying it of its secular connotations, and declaring that all Muslims were a single nation, disregarding all ethnic, linguistic and cultural differences.[98] The political expression of this adaptation of the European idea of the nation—however modified—is Pan-Islamism. This represents an attempt to strengthen the notion of Islamic universalism,[99] whose functions as a sanction for authority had become somewhat weakened, by providing it with an modern interpretation. The Ottomans, who had always justified their despotic rule in terms of Islamic universalism, were now able to provide themselves with a new and modern form of legitimacy, through a reinterpretation of Pan-Islamism in the form of an irredentist national movement for all Muslims. The Ottoman despot 'Abd al-Hamid II enthusiastically adopted Pan-Islamism as the official ideology of the state and made al-Afghani into the ideologue of his attempts to regenerate the Ottoman Empire. But the latter had different intentions; he had no desire to provide a sanction for despotism, but wished to create a basis for anti-colonialism and for his attempts to revitalise Islam. As Braune indicates, he

never lost sight of his central purpose, to awaken the Islamic peoples to resistance against Europe, and to stir up opposition among them to those of their number who paralysed this resistance . . . 'more forcefully than any of his contemporaries in the Middle East', al-Afghani could conjure up the glorious past, appeal for renewal and awaken passions for a great vision of the future, the unity of all Muslims. Sultan 'Abd al-Hamid was quick to make use of this forceful idea to raise his own person as the symbol of this unity. But the idea was not put forward in order to be misused tactically in this fashion. It was certainly directed against European imperialism, but no less against those representatives of Islam who held their peoples in thrall.[100]

For this reason, al-Afghani totally rejected Sultan 'Abd al-Hamid II's notions of Ottomanism and Pan-Islamism. Subsequently he reduced Pan-Islamism to a form of consciousness which implied the solidarity of all Muslims against colonialism, and completely dropped his idea of a Pan-Islamic state.[101]

Like his teacher al-Afghani, 'Abduh also had to fight on two fronts. On the one hand he had to combat the fossilised version of Islam put forward by the deeply religious '*ulama*', especially those of al-Azhar, according to which all attempts to modernise Islam were heretical, and on the other the rising tide of secular nationalism. He too had become acquainted with bourgeois culture in the course of a stay in Europe. He knew Herbert Spencer personally,[102] and translated his *Education* into Arabic. But unlike al-Afghani, 'Abduh was never a political agitator, nor a people's tribune, and in fact had a certain aversion to practical politics, which became even stronger after his return from exile in France, where he and al-Afghani published the review *al-'Urwa al-Wuthqa* in 1884.[103] He was convinced that Islam could only be revitalised through cultural rather than political activity. His works, notably the famous *Risalat al-Tawhid*, are distinguished for their painstaking scholarship.[104] As Vatikiotis has summarised, 'Abduh intended 'a reformulation of systematic theology and doctrine with gradual reintroduction of historical criticism into the study of tradition'.[105] Like al-Tahtawi, 'Abduh considers the *shari'a*, the kernel of Islamic theology, to be the structural equivalent of European bourgeois natural law.[106] He arrived at a progressive interpretation of the *shari'a* by stressing individual interpretation based on reason and deduction (*ijtihad*) as its source rather than the consensus of the learned (*ijma'*). In this way he was able to go beyond the fossilised Islam of the '*ulama*'.

'Abduh, for whom enlightening education was preferable to political agitation, developed an educational theory which also took account of the national awakening of the Egyptians. He reduced al-Afghani's universal synthesis of Islam with the European bourgeois idea of the nation to the smaller format of Egypt without giving up his opposition to the nationalists, even when their acceptance of Islam was not in doubt. He realised that nationalism, however Islamic it might appear, would have the effect of questioning Islam's claim to be an all-embracing system, a development which was to become particularly prominent in the theories of Mustafa Kamil.[107] For 'Abduh, national education without religion is unthinkable. ' . . . The Egyptian soul is completely consumed by religion in such a way that it can no longer be severed from it. If one seeks to educate and improve the Egyptian nation without religion, it is as if a farmer would try to sow seed in unsuitable soil . . . his efforts will be in vain.'[108]

Walther Braune compares 'Abduh's theories with those of the religious positivists[109] and summarises his work as follows: 'Abduh attempts to locate the alien innovations of the modern world within the revelation of God. In this way all modern science and all technological discovery can be affirmed and accepted by the faithful. If revelation is properly understood, it will be seen that it is not in opposition to modern culture.'[110] Hence modern culture is not contrary to Islam as long as it does not encroach upon the latter's claim to be an all-embracing system.

Considering the obvious dissimilarities between the archaic Wahhabi movement and the modernism of al-Afghani and 'Abduh, it is interesting that both schools should show marked affinities with fourteenth-century Hanbalism, especially, as Hartmann has pointed out, with the ideas of Ibn Taimiyya.[111] It is thus no accident that Rashid Ridha, the pupil and intellectual heir of 'Abduh,[112] should have developed the Hanbalite elements of Islamic Modernism towards Islamic fundamentalism, and should finally have identified himself with the policies of the House of Sa'ud. The latter regained power in the Arabian Peninsula in 1924, and founded the feudal-autocratic state of Sa'udi Arabia, archaic even in its modern form, whose declared ideology is Wahhabism.[113] Ridha's Islamic fundamentalism has been taken up by the Muslim Brethren, a right-wing radical movement founded in 1928, which has ever since been in inexorable opposition to secular nationalism.[114] Another follower of 'Abduh, 'Abd al-Rahman al-Kawakibi, a Syrian like Rashid Ridha, developed 'Abduh's teachings in the opposite direction to that of his fellow-countryman, towards Arab nationalism. al-Kawakibi, who was an orthodox Muslim, developed the notion of al-Afghani and 'Abduh that the Arabs were the only legitimate representatives of Islam in such a way that he can accurately be described as an important pioneer of Arab nationalism.[115]

The rising tide of secular nationalism in the Middle East further

weakened both the Islamic Modernism of al-Afghani and 'Abduh
and the later Pan-Islamic Caliphate movement.[116] 'Religious
commitment was no longer sufficient to sustain a theocratic state',
says Braune. 'The Caliphate became merely the object of a romantic
nostalgia, and the attempt to recreate it brought a reactionary
absolutist state into existence. The romantic notion of a theocracy
crumbled in the face of the now dominant idea of the Nation.'[117] It
is however important to point out that originally, before
Wahhabism and Islamic Modernism became expressions of Muslim
conservatism, they had played something of a progressive role. Both
were revitalisation movements directed against foreign domination,
whether Ottoman or European, and both emphasised the Arab
origins of Islam. Both movements must therefore be considered an
inherent part of the national movement in the Middle East,[118]
although in the minds of their protagonists they were not nationalist
but Muslim.

The fact that the Arab national awakening was based on a form of
secular nationalism which was eventually to destroy the Islamic
revitalisation movement[119] did not mean that its theoreticians had
abandoned Islam entirely. Instead, they denied its claim to be an all-
embracing system, and relegated it to a cultural sphere where it
could only form a *part* of Arab national culture. The nationalisation
of politics on an international level which has taken place since and
through the French Revolution, has had the effect of sustaining
young national movements. In Ziegler's words 'as a regulating
principle of politics, the modern nation . . . has obtained universal
and official recognition, and has become the dominant form of
legitimation in the modern political world'.[120] As early as 1931 he
forecast: 'The transformation of the European political structure
through this principle will lead to the transformation of non-
European political structures in the same fashion.'[121] However the
transformation of political structures in the 'Third World' was not
accompanied by a simultaneous acceptance of the Nation as a
means of sanctioning authority, since this took place as a result of
the expansion of capitalism beyond its natural frontiers. It was
colonialism, which in fact implies a denial of the national existence
of the peoples to whom it is applied, which generated a movement of
resistance to itself. The result was the national awakening of the
colonial world, which set the process of decolonisation in motion.

5 The Genesis of Arab Nationalism

In the early nineteenth century the social structure of Greater Syria, the birthplace of Arab nationalism, was similar to that of Egypt before the reforms of Muhammad 'Ali. The system of tax-farming known as *iltizam* in Egypt was called *muqata'a* in Syria.[1] Although also under Ottoman rule, Syria differed from Egypt in that it had not been governed centrally, but by a number of contending independent local dynasties. Hence it was more difficult to surmount the feudal system in Syria than in Egypt, and the feudal system in fact survived longest in this part of the Ottoman Empire.[2] In Egypt the social structures had undergone an almost complete transformation as a result of the destruction of the feudal system[3] by Muhammad 'Ali after 1805. In the Ottoman heartlands a similar transformation had taken place in the reign of Mahmud II (1808–39), particularly after the dissolution of the *sipahis* and the Janissaries.[4] In Syria, however, social conditions remained virtually unchanged until the 1830s.[5] The continuous internecine struggles between the local dynasties on the one hand and between themselves and the civil and military representatives of the Porte on the other had exhausted the country. Furthermore, outlying cities were regularly pillaged by Bedouin raiders, and, 'the inevitable consequence of this state of affairs was the impoverishment and depopulation of both towns and the countryside'.[6]

An exception to this was the Lebanese coastal area, inhabited mainly by Christian Maronites, who had had contacts with Europe since the sixteenth century. They had maintained regular trading relationships with the Italian merchant republics, and were culturally linked with Rome and later with France, especially after the establishment of French missions in the area. It was here that the first bourgeois strata in Greater Syria developed, partly because the inhabitants were mostly Christians who had no religious loyalties to the Islamic foundation of Ottoman rule, and partly because their changing social status brought them into increasing conflict with the feudal system of Greater Syria.[7] For some time these new social groups were unable to obtain any political power, since, as Christians, they had the status of subjects and were of course excluded from the Muslim *umma*. Even the foreign missions, both French Catholic, and, since 1820, American Presbyterian, who were supposedly protecting the Christians, were unable to work unhindered until the invasion of Syria in 1831 by Muhammad 'Ali's armies under the command of his son Ibrahim Pasha, since the Sublime Porte always contrived to hamper their activities as far as possible. After 1831, however, a new phase in the history of the region began. The innovations and reforms which Ibrahim introduced into Greater Syria, on the lines of those in Egypt, and the emancipation of the Arab Christians which he encouraged, had the effect of promoting the beginnings of the Arab national movement, whose seeds had already been planted.[8]

This section will provide a general outline of the historical development of Greater Syria, as an essential background to the Arab national movement since the First World War, and particularly to provide an understanding of the influence of Sati' al-Husri. A brief outline of the situation of Greater Syria under Muhammad 'Ali between 1831 and 1840 will be given, together with a discussion of the impact of the foreign missions in this period, during which they had complete freedom of action. This will be followed by an examination of the impact of Tanzimat reforms on Greater Syria, and of the emergence of a European-educated Muslim petty bourgeois stratum in addition to the European and American-educated Arab Christians. An attempt will then be made to examine the role of these two wings of the Arab national movement. In the course of this chapter some major questions will be discussed only briefly, since they will be dealt with at greater length later on. These include the differences between Arab and Egyptian nationalism, and the role of Islam and of secularism in these two movements.

(a) Syria under the Rule of Muhammad 'Ali: The Emergence of Secularism, and the Contribution of European and American Christian Missions to the Arab National Literary Renaissance

Due to its geographical location, the Arab Middle East became increasingly important during the early period of the European colonial conquests. France wanted to form an Arab Middle Eastern State, independent of the Ottomans and under her own control, in order to block Britain's route to India, while Britain insisted on the maintenance of a weak and thus unthreatening Ottoman Empire. This divergence of the interests of the two colonial powers is instructive for an understanding both of their attitudes towards Muhammad 'Ali and of the activities of their missionaries. France had already begun to set up missions in the Christian areas of Syria and Lebanon in the eighteenth century, but in addition to her missions, British and American Protestant and Russian Orthodox missions were also active. The restrictive policies of the Ottomans forced the missionaries to concentrate their activities on small groups of Arab Christians, and each mission accommodated itself to the colonial interests of the country from which it originated.

Under the enlightened despotism of Muhammad 'Ali, Egypt, now only formally a part of the Ottoman Empire, had become a modern secular national state, although the *shari'a* still remained the supreme source of legal authority. Muhammad 'Ali saw the weakness of the Ottoman state, and realised that it would not have been able to undermine the Wahhabi movement without his assistance.[9] He understood that the development of the Egyptian economy and the modernisation of its social structure could take place more easily within the framework of a larger oriental state, and his modern army ensured that his expansionist plans could be put into effect. Muhammad 'Ali, who was himself not an Arab but an Albanian, justified his ambitions with reference to the idea of the nation. After his victory over the Wahhabis and his conquests of the Arabian peninsula he occupied the Sudan in 1820, and sought to crown his campaign with the conquest of Syria. He came to the assistance of the Ottoman Sultan in putting down the Greek revolt in 1824 in the hope that he might be made governor of Syria in return. However, the Sultan was not prepared to reward him in this way, and thus Muhammad 'Ali sent his armies to Syria in 1831, having first made sure of the support of France and of the Syrian Christian merchant bourgeoisie who had begun to develop a certain amount of Arab national consciousness. Among the potentially nationalist forces Muhammad 'Ali gained 'particularly faithful and loyal supporters and won over the whole Christian population . . . in may cities [he was] hailed as a saviour and liberator'.[10] His son Ibrahim Pasha appeared ' . . . to the Christian authorities as . . . a victorious lion, a champion and guardian. They accepted and carried out his requests with enthusiasm, and assisted him financially and militarily.'[11] This devotion can be explained by the fact that Ibrahim Pasha had not attempted to justify his campaign against the Ottomans in religious terms, but had claimed to be fighting for the Arabs against the Turks. He considered that the unification of Egypt and Syria would be the beginning of the foundation of a great Arab state,[12] thus presenting the Arab Christians with the possibility of social emancipation, because in a specifically Arab state they would be full citizens, while under the Islamic Ottoman theocracy they were not members of the *umma* and therefore had the status of subjects. And in fact 'among the most important of Ibrahim Pasha's innovations in Syria . . . was the provision of equal status for all religions. Christians were now admitted into the highest ranks, . . . taxes were levied equally on Muslims and Christians alike. Formerly the Christians had had to pay a poll tax, but were exempt from military service. Ibrahim even armed the Christians . . .'.[13] However the political emancipation of the Arab Christians and Jews would have been superficial and ineffectual without a corresponding transformation of the social structure. Ibrahim abolished the former division of the country into pashaliks which had been dominated by local dynasties, and centralised and secularised the system of government and administration.[14] This transformation struck at the roots of the feudal system, whose supporters, the local dynasties,[15] were replaced by civil servants. The administration of justice was taken out of the hands of the '*ulama*', who were a part of the feudal hierarchy, and secularised.[16] The Bedouin raiders who had regularly plundered the urban centres and spread insecurity throughout the country were brought under control by the new Egyptian army. Moshe Ma'oz correctly notes that the Egyptian occupation of Syria put an end to 'a long period of confusion and backwardness, and opened a new era in Syrian history'.[17] For the first time the population of Syria had a greater sense of security on the basis of a unified taxation system. There was greater prosperity because

the public security which was established in the countryside and along the roads made it possible for agriculture and commerce to flourish, and the authorities themselves did much to promote economic development. In agriculture, Egyptian experts introduced new methods and crops; marshes were drained, deserted lands were recultivated, and peasants were given tools, seeds, loans and even tax reductions. Similarly local trade was encouraged not only as a result of greater stability, but also because of the army's need for supplies. In industry too some development took place as new factories (mainly for military purposes) were set up, natural resources exploited and apprentices sent to Egypt to acquire new professions.[18]

The local feudal dynasties which had been deprived of social and political power did not accept these far-reaching changes without resistance. They organised continual peasant revolts against Ibrahim Pasha's regime in alliance with the '*ulama*', in the years between 1831 and 1840. They succeeded in mobilising the religious elements of the Muslim population against the reforms and in arousing them to revolt, particularly because some of the Christians had over-reached themselves and had provoked the Muslims by public wine drinking and by carrying crosses in procession through the streets. Ibrahim relentlessly pursued these misled rebels, and in consequence his rule quickly became unpopular among the Muslim population.[19]

One of the most important instruments of Ibrahim Pasha's policy was the school. During his period of rule the modern school system flourished, which resulted in the emergence of a newly educated social stratum receptive to reform.[19a] With this aspect of education in mind, Ibrahim also permitted the Christian missions to work freely.[20] Hence the American Protestant Mission was able to bring its printing press[21] from Malta to Beirut, and the Jesuits were once more able to open their schools. Smith, an American missionary, even founded a girls' secondary school.

There is no doubt that the emergence of the first generation of Arab nationalists was closely connected with the changes taking place in the contemporary social structure, and the opening up of Syria to European influence. As has been mentioned in the earlier part of this chapter, France sought to create an Arab state in the area which would prevent Britain from securing the route to India for herself. It was therefore clear that France would consider Muhammad 'Ali's successes in Syria as 'her own successes',[22] and she encouraged the Maronite authorities, who were loyal to her, to support him. However, his plan for a great oriental state was in 'grave conflict with Britain, which was to cost him not only Syria, but also subsequently cost his successors their control over Egypt'.[23] As a result of British insistence, Egyptian troops were forced to evacuate Syria in 1840, but the reforms could not be so easily made redundant, and they had, as Ma'oz points out, 'a long term impact on local society'.[24] This was also true of the European and American Christian missions. Although they were in fact the forerunners of colonialism, the missionaries supplied the Arabs with a national consciousness as a result of their own concern with the national language. This was to cause a separation between the Arabs and the Ottomans, whose rule was sanctioned by Islamic tradition, and it also made the Arabs more responsive to missionary activity.[25]

The impact of the three missions—French Jesuits and other Catholics, American Protestants and the Russian Orthodox of Czarist Russia—varied considerably.[26] While the American and Russian missionaries contributed considerably towards the Arab renaissance, the French Catholic missions followed an openly colonialist policy. In the French mission schools, Arab Christians, mostly Maronites, were taught that they could only emancipate themselves under the protection of France, which meant French colonial rule. In the beginning, instruction in the French schools was in French alone, and it was only in the face of competition from the Protestants that they began to use more Arabic, although even then only occasionally. According to Jurgen Brandt, the Maronite clergy 'became the willing accomplices of French Middle Eastern policies'.[27] The missions had the clearly defined task of backing up the economic penetration of the Syrian hinterland, an offensive 'whose main aim was to exploit the emerging independence movement for the colonial ends of the French ruling class'.[28] It is significant that the early Arab nationalists emerged not from the French but from the American Protestant mission schools, whose activities were less directly tied to colonial aims. For its part the United States had no definite colonial interests in the area at the time, since its activities were concentrated to a far greater extent on Latin America.[28a] In addition, since Protestantism situates Christianity firmly within the vernacular, the American missionaries learnt Arabic. The missions also employed Arab scholars on a new evangelical translation of the Bible into Arabic. In addition they encouraged a number of other scholars who were attempting to revitalise the Arabic language, and with their help religious texts were written in Arabic for use in the mission schools. The American missionaries naturally worked in Arabic because this brought greater and more obvious successes. The revitalisation of Arabic also meant the revitalisation of the national culture, and thus the creation of a new national identity, which pushed religious identity, formerly the substance of the Arabs' loyalty to the Ottoman Empire, into the background. The successes achieved by the American missions occasionally forced their competitors to imitate them.[29]

The Russian Orthodox missions played a similarly progressive role. Backed by Czarist policies, they opposed Greek domination of the Eastern church and supported the lower clergy, who were mostly Arab. One of their major achievements was the elevation of an Arab to the patriarchate of Antioch for the first time in 1899, in spite of opposition from the Greek Orthodox hierarchy.[30] Russian politicians even had plans to mobilise the Arabs from the Nile to the Euphrates and the Tigris and the South Slavs in an uprising against the Ottoman Empire, whose weakness was greatly in their interest. As a whole, Russian Orthodox[31] and even more American missionary activity promoted the emergence of an Arab national consciousness among the Christian Arabs, although the literary renaissance cannot be attributed exclusively to the American missions, as American orientalist literature has tended to claim. A. L. Tibawi's research has shown that there were textbooks written in Arabic and an Arabic translation of the Bible before the arrival of the missionaries, as well as a school system. 'The Americans produced merely a different kind of religious literature and a different translation of the Bible.'[32] Tibawi also considers it important that there was no 'evidence that the [sc. American Protestant] press had been an instrument for the reviving of the "largely forgotten" or "rapidly vanishing" Arabic heritage. It was not part of its aim to revive classical Arabic literature, still less other departments of Arab culture.'[33]

The American missionaries only modernised Arabic to have a more suitable means at hand for their religious activities. It was an entirely unintended consequence of their work that the revival of the national language inaugurated a literary renaissance, but this naturally suited the missions in that the movement gradually undermined the loyalty of the Arabs towards the Ottoman Empire.

In its early stages, Arab nationalism was apolitical and it emerged largely out of a concern with Arabic culture and the modernisation of the Arabic language which had been encouraged particularly by the American missions. However, the literary movement was the expression of a political situation, since ' . . . when national consciousness is aroused, the efforts which have been made to reinvigorate the language and the classical literature assume a far-reaching importance. Such was the case in the Arab world . . . the struggle against the alien leads to the rediscovery of one's own heritage.'[34]

The literary renaissance of the nineteenth century was inaugurated by the Christian scholar Nasif al-Yaziji (1800–1871), who mastered the Arabic language in a manner unique for his time in the course of his researches into classical Arabic literature.[35] The American missionaries had engaged al-Yaziji to edit and correct the religious texts which had been written for them in Arabic, and had also asked him to revise their Arabic translation of the Bible. al-Yaziji's work consists mainly of philological writings, but he also wrote *qasidas* (odes) and treatises on logic, medicine and history.[36] Hourani correctly notes that almost all Arab writers of the nineteenth century were his pupils, either directly or indirectly.[37]

Faris-al-Shidyaq (1805–87), a contemporary of al-Yaziji, cooperated more closely with the American missions, and was also one of the first Christian Arab converts to Protestantism.[38] He travelled in Europe and recorded his experiences[39] in a way similar to al-Tahtawi in his Paris Diary, though not so brilliantly. His social criticism,[40] which is partly autobiographical, attacked the Maronite hierarchy which was responsible for the death of his brother, the historian As'ad, after the latter had been converted to Protestantism.[41] al-Shidyaq was the first Arab writer to rebel against the classical literary tradition, and to demand a modernisation of Arabic literature.[42] In order to protect himself from those hostile to his criticisms he took British nationality and thus gained the status and the right to personal protection of a European.[43] Hourani rightly says that there is no sign of any superior political insight in his writing; his concern was primarily with language and only in a more narrow sense with literary criticism.[44]

The most important nineteenth-century Arab national writer was the Syrian scholar Butrus al-Bustani (1819–83), in whose work the revival of Arab culture takes on clearly national overtones.[45] He too worked for the American missions, where he taught the missionaries Arabic, and was himself ultimately converted to Protestantism. Outstanding among his lexicographical works was his pioneering dictionary *Muhit al-muhit* (The Breadth of the Ocean). al-Bustani began work on one of the first Arabic encyclopedias, but only managed to complete the first few volumes before he died, and his descendants finally completed the work in eleven volumes. In a treatise in 1849 he pleaded for the education of girls.[46] As in his other writings, his comparisons between Arab and European practices contain social criticism.[46a] In the course of his attempts to reinvigorate Arab culture, al-Bustani reminds his readers that they had once reached such a high degree of civilisation that all Arabs, both Christians and Muslims, could look back on that period with feelings of national pride. In order to revitalise their indigenous culture al-Bustani considered that his contemporaries should learn from the achievements of contemporary Europe, because European culture, since it was the most advanced, could serve as an example to them. Furthermore al-Bustani considers the national unity of the Arabs of all religions to be a vital prerequisite for the reinvigoration of Arab culture, and this necessitates both religious toleration and the separation of religion from politics.[47]

In 1847, with the assistance of the American missionaries, Butrus al-Bustani and Nasif al-Yaziji founded the first literary society in the Arab world, *Jam'iyyat al-Adab w'al-'Ulum* (The Literary and Scientific Society), whose members were exclusively Syrian Christian and European. In 1857 this society was superseded by *al-Jam'iyya al-'Ilmiyya al-Suriyya* (The Syrian Scientific Society), which included Western-educated Muslims and Druzes as well as Christians among its members. In this Society too al-Bustani played a leading role.[48] He was also the founder of Arab national journalism; during the confessional conflicts in 1860[49] he published *Nafir Suriyya* (Appeal to Syria), a broadsheet which ran into eleven editions. In it al-Bustani called for national solidarity on a supra-religious basis, since he considered that the conflicts were only taking place because the contenders were being incited either by the European powers or by the local dynasties. The magazine *al-Jinan* (The Paradises), which he and his family published between 1870 and 1886, was forced to close down because of the despotism of Sultan 'Abd al-Hamid II. After this the national literary movement and Arab national journalism migrated to Egypt, where unhampered development was possible, since Egypt no longer formed a part of the Ottoman Empire. The motto of *al-Jinan* was 'hubb al-watan min al-iman'—'love of country is an article of faith'. *al-Jinan* and *Nafir Suriyya* were the first organs of Arab cultural nationalism. In addition, al-Bustani had founded *al-Madrasa al-Wataniyya*, the National School, in 1863, the first secular school in Syria, where Nasif al-Yaziji also worked.[50] When the American missionaries founded the Syrian Protestant College in 1866,[51] now the American University of Beirut (AUB), they were able to count on al-Bustani's willing cooperation, and it was from this college that the first generation of liberal Western-educated nationalists emerged.

According to George Antonius, the author of the standard history of Arab nationalism, the first Arab national writer was the linguist and author Ibrahim al-Yaziji (1847–1905), the son of Nasif al-Yaziji. He was the author of the first modern patriotic *qasida*, which he recited at a secret meeting of the Syrian Scientific Society. In this *qasida* Ibrahim al-Yaziji declares that the Arabs are a single independent cultural nation, and condemns the Ottoman yoke. In the first line of the poem he addresses the Arabs: 'Arise, O Arabs and awake!'[52] In praise of the Arabs he says:

> We are the origin of all greatness
> Human kind has drunk from the well of our achievement
> And—ask in the West of our glorious past—
> Its marks are imprinted on the brow of time
> But the memory of the past no longer satisfies us
> Its shackles do not give us shelter
> We shall strive for the heights
> Until they rest upon pillars of substance.'[53]

W. Braune, who quotes these lines, says that 'the echo of these words was to be long awaited'.[54] However, George Antonius claims that this poem was familiar throughout Syria and was recited in literary circles throughout the country.[55]

It is no accident that Arab nationalism in its early phase took the form of a literary renaissance not based on political theories, which was generated exclusively by linguists and men of letters. This was because neither the subjective nor the objective conditions for a political movement existed in the Middle East in the nineteenth century. Thus the early Arab nationalists confined themselves to emphasising the existence of an independent Arab cultural nation without demanding a national state. Either the existence of this 'nation' under Ottoman rule was uncritically accepted as given, or the Ottoman government was criticised for its despotism: in either case there was no questioning of the social organisation. This is equally true of the first political theorist of Arab nationalism, Adib Ishaq (1856–85) a Syrian Christian who gave, in the treatises later collected by his brother known as *al-Durar* (The Pearls),[56] a definition of the nation which transcended literature. Ishaq grew up in a Jesuit mission school and pursued a literary career in Egypt and

Paris, where he produced several publications, including news-papers. For him *watan*, in the liberal-democratic sense, was identical with liberty. 'There is no *terra patria* apart from freedom, and there is no *terra patria* where tyranny prevails', he says, quoting European bourgeois writers with approval.[57] Ishaq considered love of country to be a virtue which could only find expression in freedom. He recognised that the liberalisation which he demanded along the lines of advanced European bourgeois society could not be achieved unless certain social conditions were fulfilled. 'A republic does not work in China, any more than does autocratic monarchy in England. Republicanism, which in essence is government for the people by the people, will not work in a country stricken with ignorance.'[58] Thus Ishaq also criticises those Arabs who became members of the Ottoman Parliament which had been set up by the Reformers, since he considered it to be a sham and unable to function as long as it was not based on true democratic principles.[59] In fact this toy Parliament was to be dissolved without difficulty by Sultan 'Abd al-Hamid II in 1878. However advanced Ishaq's political thinking was for his time, he did not see any contradiction between his own theories and his loyalty to the Ottoman Empire, whose existence as an entity he did not question.[60]

The first secret society whose aims were not simply cultural but political and which put forward separatist demands was founded by students of the Syrian Protestant College in 1875. Its programme shows the logical continuity of the Arab literary renaissance. At first it consisted only of Christians but they were soon joined by Muslims and Druzes, and membership continued to grow. Similar secret societies were soon founded in Syrian cities. The posters which members produced in secret were pasted onto walls at night, demanding an Arab national state in which all Arabs, independent of their religious or other affiliation, should be citizens and no longer subjects.[61] In the early twentieth century, Paris, where Syro-Lebanese Arabs of all confessions were studying, became the centre of Arab nationalist propaganda. The early political national movement was supported by Arabs educated in both Christian missions and European academic institutions, as well as by those who had received a Western education in the Ottoman schools founded during the Tanzimat period. While the former were mainly Arab Christians, the latter were mainly Muslims, as will be discussed in the next section.[62]

(b) The Significance of the Tanzimat Period and of the Emergence of a Stratum of Arab Nationalist Officers and Intellectuals: The Secret Societies and the Politicisation of Nationalism until the anti-Ottoman Revolt of 1916–18

In the year before the evacuation of the Egyptian troops from Syria, a phase of comprehensive structural reorganisation, known as the Tanzimat period,[63] began in the Ottoman Empire. The Tanzimat reforms began with the promulgation of the *Hatt-i Sharif* of Gulhane in 1839, which stressed the necessity 'for a thorough reform and reformation of the old regime'.[64] This decree was supplemented seventeen years later in 1856 by the *Hatt-i Humayun*, which announced that the principal institutions of bourgeois society would be introduced into the Ottoman Empire.[65] Steinhaus considers that the most obvious feature of the Tanzimat period was the 'rapid progress towards the centralisation of state power. The local political power of the "quasi-feudal association of Pashas and tax-collectors of an earlier period" was gradually broken . . . a process of secularisation took place parallel to the centralisation and modernisation of the administration.'[66] European codes of law were introduced, students were sent to Europe to study, and, even more important, officers of the Ottoman Army were trained either in Europe or in the Empire by European instructors. Hence, in the course of the Tanzimat a stratum of Westernised officers of petty bourgeois origin emerged, who had nothing in common with the military caste of the old Ottoman Army. They were to play a decisive political role in the latter decades of the nineteenth century. This officer corps produced the young Turks, and later the Kemalists who actually dissolved the Empire. The Arab nationalist officers, who were to play a central part in the Arab national movement later on, also came from their ranks.[67] Bernard Lewis emphasises correctly that: 'of all the groups in Middle Eastern society, the army officers have had the longest and most intensive exposure to Western influence, and have the most vital professional interest in modernisation and reform. This may help to explain the phenomenon, unusual in other parts of the world, of the professional officer as the spearhead of social change.'[68]

The Tanzimat period, which began at the same time as the restoration of Ottoman rule in Syria, implied for Syria, as Ma'oz has shown,[69] a continuation of the reforms of Muhammad 'Ali and Ibrahim Pasha which had been implemented between 1831 and

1840. The local rulers and '*ulama*' in Syria, who had been deprived of power, hailed the Ottoman restoration as an ideological victory for Islam and sought the re-establishment of their own power. They were of course to be disappointed, and to be forced to the realisation that the Tanzimat too was not to be compatible with a return to the social and political conditions which existed before 1831. In fact it ran contrary to their own particularist interests, though not to the reforms of Muhammad 'Ali and Ibrahim Pasha.[70] The policies of the Tanzimat in Syria were expressed through administrative reforms which centralised the country at the expense of the local dynasties, which had already been weakened over the preceding years, and also submitted them to the stricter administrative control of the Sublime Porte.[71]

The reforms of the Tanzimat came to an end during the reign of Sultan 'Abd al-Hamid II (1878–1909):[72] in 1878 he abrogated the constitution of 1876, and turned the empire *de jure* back from the status of a 'constitutional monarchy' to that of 'unenlightened absolutism'.[73] The enlightened Europeanised forces, who had supported the Tanzimat, were persecuted through an elaborate network of spies and informers.

By the 1860s the Westernised intellectuals whom the Tanzimat had produced had began to express their ideas through the Young Ottoman movement. They firmly believed that the Ottoman Empire could be reinvigorated by absorbing the achievements of contemporary Europe without making major changes in its structure.[74] This movement broke up when 'Abd al-Hamid II came to power. It was succeeded in the 1880s by the Young Turk movement, which consisted of Westernised military officers. From this emerged the *Ittihad ve Terakki Cemiyeti*, or Committee of Union and Progress.[75] Although this organisation was later to be joined by civilians, mainly members of the opposition living in exile in Europe, its nucleus remained the officer corps.[76]

Arab officers of the Ottoman Army were represented in the Committee of Union and Progress. They were mainly of Iraqi origin, but some came from other parts of the Empire. They cooperated against the Hamidian despotism on the basis of a new interpretation of Ottomanism. They were no longer united by the religious bond of Islam, but by the multi-national idea, as Hartmann indicates; the Young Turks tried 'to propagate the idea of the Ottoman state in the same sense, perhaps, as one might speak of an Austrian state in Austria. But as soon as this idea became more closely defined, it was revealed as essentially a vehicle for Ottoman domination. The parallel with Austria is appropriate, though the great difference, which should not be overlooked, is that the other groups of peoples in Turkey had an older culture than the Osmanlis themselves.'[77] It was only after the seizure of power by the young Turks in 1909 that it became clear that Ottomanism, reinterpreted as a multi-national constitutional monarchy, contained the seeds of the legitimation of Turkish supremacy, although no longer in a religious guise. Until then, officers from various different national backgrounds had cooperated smoothly in the Committee of Union and Progress: even the Arab officers were loyal to the idea of the Empire as a multi-national monarchy. They played a decisive role in 1908, when the constitution of 1876, which had been abrogated by 'Abd al-Hamid II in 1878, was restored by force. They also featured prominently in putting down the counter-revolution which 'Abd al-Hamid instigated against the young Turks in 1909. This time however the result was not the introduction of reforms but the dethronement of the Sultan and the seizure of power by the Young Turks.[78]

Two senior Arab officers, the Egyptian 'Aziz 'Ali al-Misri and the more senior Iraqi Mahmud Shaukat led the march on Constantinople aganist the Hamidian counter-revolution in 1909. After the young Turk revolution in 1908, the *Jam'iyyat al-Ikha al-'Amli al-'Uthmani* (Society of Arab-Ottoman Brotherhood) was founded in September of the same year. Its main principle was that although the Arabs should continue to live within the Ottoman Empire, they should have their own rights as a nationality, such as their own administrative and educational system. They also demanded that Arabic should be given parity with Turkish in schools in the regions inhabited by Arabs.[79] After the destruction of 'Abd al-Hamid's network of informers in 1908, and with the beginning of some degree of political freedom, the first secret political and literary societies appeared. In 1908 Western-educated Arab intellectuals living in Constantinople founded *al-Muntada al-Adabi* (The Literary Club), which published a magazine of the same name.[80]

After the young Turks had successfully resisted the Hamidian counter-coup in 1909, with the assistance of the Arab officers, and had taken over power, they revealed their own nationalist ideology, that of Turanianism.[81] Utilising this ideology they tried to restrict the claims of the various peoples of the Ottoman Empire who were now aspiring to emancipation. Braune comments:

Under the pressure of modern national ideas in the Balkans, the young Turks were soon forced to abandon their liberal principles and the unfortunate wars, which resulted in the loss of Tripoli to Italy and the loss of almost all the Ottoman provinces in Europe, drove them towards an authoritarian Turkish nationalism. Obscure theories constructed from the researches of the French historian Leon Cahun made 'Turan' the place of origin of the Turks in Central Asia, and the pre-Islamic Turkish homeland became the focal point of history in the writings of the authoress Halide Edib and the poet-philosopher Ziya Gökalp.[82]

As a result of this change of direction the Society of Arab-Ottoman Brotherhood was dissolved some eight months after its foundation. The Constantinople Literary Club was banned and Arab nationalists, who simply desired a national cultural autonomy within the Ottoman Empire, were restricted and persecuted.[83] This ideological shift followed on a rigorous policy of centralisation which was directed towards the Turkification of the other nationalities, and the systematic suppression of their languages and cultures. The Arab national movement, which had manifested a certain amount of open activity after the overthrow of 'Abd al-Hamid, now returned underground, in order to fight against the new policies of Turkification and Turanianism. They did not however discard their hopes for a transformation of the Ottoman Empire into a constitutional monarchy in which the Arabs would have their own administrative and cultural autonomy.[84]

Among the most important Arab secret societies[85] was the *Jam'iyyat al-'Arabiyya al-Fatat* (The Young Arab Society), founded in Paris in 1911 by Syrian students and graduates. This close-knit organisation worked strictly underground, and although a number of its members became victims of Young Turk persecution the organisation of the society could not be cracked, which was proof of its quality. Its members were almost entirely Muslim.[86] Another organisation, the *Jam'iyyat al-'Ahd* (The Society of the Covenant) was founded in Constantinople in 1913, as a successor to the *Qahtaniyya* Society, founded in 1909, part of whose organisation had been uncovered by treachery. While the *Qahtaniyya* had contained both officers and civilians, the *Jam'iyyat al-'Ahd* was composed entirely of Arab officers, under the command of the high-ranking Egyptian 'Aziz 'Ali al-Misri. As Hartmann has pointed out, 'al-Misri had noticed from his own experience of the Committee of Union and Progress that the army was more capable of effective action than the civilian politicians'.[87] Thus the *Jam'iyyat al-'Ahd* ranked next to *al-Fatat* as the most effective political organisation; in 1914 it contained 315 officers.[88] In addition to these two large secret societies, the *Jam'iyyat al-Islahiyya* (The Reform Society) is also worth mentioning. This was founded in Beirut in 1913 and consisted mainly of Lebanese Christians and Muslims who favoured Ottoman decentralisation. There was also *al-Hizb al-Lamarkaziyya al-Idariyya al-'Uthmaniyya* (The Ottoman Decentralisation Party), founded in Cairo by Syrian exiles in 1912. The proponents of decentralisation in the Party had different political views. For instance, the Syrian Christian Shibli Shumayyil[89] who had Darwinist social-liberal ideas, and pronounced secularist views, was a member. Rashid Ridha,[90] a pupil of 'Abduh, was another: he was later to point Islamic Modernism in a right-wing radical and fundamentalist direction, and became a spokesman for the Wahhabis after their seizure of power in the Arabian Peninsula in 1924.

These secret societies were organised with the support of France, which had been able to maintain good relations with the Arab national movement. An Arab National Congress took place in Paris in 1913, at which political beliefs and aims were articulated. Both Muslims and Christians participated in this Congress, seeing themselves not as members of religious communities, but as Arabs, and, apart from a few francophile Christians from Beirut, still adhered to the ideology of Ottomanism. Their demands did not go beyond a decentralised administration, national cultural autonomy and equality with the Turks within the framework of a multi-national constitutional monarchy.[91] Among the minority which demanded complete severance from the Ottoman Empire was the Syrian K. T. Khairallah,[92] whom Hartmann described as an 'enthusiastic supporter of France', and Najib Azouri. Hartmann believes that 'neither was a supporter of the Arab cause', since they had 'exchanged their own homeland for another, namely France, and were now putting forward strident and transparent propaganda for it'.[93] Azouri in particular was extremely active in Paris where he was able to draw considerable attention to himself, although both Hartmann and Antonius agree that his political influence in the Middle East was negligible.[94] In 1904 Azouri founded the *Ligue de la Patrie Arabe* in Paris: in 1905 he published his *Réveil de la Nation Arabe*, and between 1907 and 1908 published the review *L'Indépendence Arabe*.

All the participants at the conference in Paris in 1913 agreed with Khairallah and Azouri that the 'Arab nation' only included the Arabic-speaking Asiatic portion of the Ottoman Empire. They were not concerned with Egypt or the other Arabic-speaking parts of North Africa. It was only in the writings of Sati' al-Husri that the term 'Arab nation' was later extended to include the whole of the Arabic-speaking world. When Dr Sa'id Kamil, an Egyptian living in Paris, who attended the Congress as an observer, requested permission to contribute to the discussion as an Egyptian, the chairman dismissed him with a curt 'No'.[95] Furthermore the chairman, 'Abd al-Hamid Zahrawi, made it plain in an interview with the Paris newspaper *Le Temps* that the Arab national movement, which the Congress represented, declared itself responsible only for the Ottoman Arabs and was not interested in the Arab regions outside the Empire.[96] The Congress saw itself exclusively as a national gathering, as Zahrawi explained: 'The Congress has no religious character at all . . . hence Christians as well as Muslims are participating.'[97] According to Zahrawi, 'The religious bond has always proved insufficient in any attempt to create political unity.'[98] Ahmad Tabbara, another participant, emphasised 'For us every Arabic speaker (*Natiq b'il-dhadh*) is an Arab: we do not differentiate between Muslims and non-Muslims.'[99] These definitions were more precisely enunciated by the Christian participants, the majority of whom opposed any separatist demands. Alexander 'Ammun acknowledged 'The Arab nation does not desire secession from the Ottoman Empire . . . but merely changes in the existing political system. It should be replaced by one in which all nationalities in the Empire have equal rights. In such a system the primary source of legislation becomes the nation, in which the nationalities are proportionally represented.'[100] 'Ammara stresses the terminological confusion reflected in this quotation, which was representative of the tenor of the Congress as a whole. At one point they referred to the 'Arab nation' (*umma 'arabiyya*), while they also designated the whole Ottoman Empire as a nation (*umma*).[101] However, all the participants were in agreement on the existence of an 'Arab nation' distinct from other nations. 'Abd al-Ghani al-'Arisi asked in his speech:

Are the Arabs a community (*jama'a*)? Communities only deserve this name, in the opinion of political philosophers, if—according to the Germans—they have a common language and a common race; if—according to the Italians—they have a common history and common customs; if—according to the French—they consist of a single political will. If we look at the Arabs from any of these perspectives we see that they have all the features mentioned, so that in the view of all political thinkers without exception they can claim to be a community (*jama'a*), a people (*sha'b*), and a nation (*umma*).[102]

The whole Congress declared itself ready to struggle to bring the 'Arab nation' into being by means of revolution. Although Na'um Mukarzal started cautiously by saying that 'The Revolution must be literary and reformist', he continued more aggressively 'only in the last resort should it be bloody, because the political systems of free nations have been constructed by martyrs and not with printers' ink'.[103]

The most important resolutions of the Congress[104] were a call for the introduction of reforms; the recognition of the Arab people and the claim for its proportionate representation in the central administration of the Empire; decentralised administration for the Ottoman provinces; the recognition of Arabic as an official language of equal status with Turkish, at the very least in Parliament and in the Arab provinces. In the concluding resolution the participants expressed their francophile outlook: 'The Congress thanks the French government with all its heart for its gracious hospitality.'[105] However, the Arab nationalists expressed their reservations. A representative was authorised to inform the French Ministry of Foreign Affairs, under whose auspices the Congress had been held: 'We respect the French but we could never accept then as our superiors. Furthermore, we want to improve our circumstances in cooperation with them, on the condition that we remain Ottomans.'[106]

Although the pre-1914 Arab nationalists asserted, in spite of the policies of the Young Turks, that they only desired national cultural autonomy and equality within the framework of the Empire, their activities, together with those of the Young Turks, had a divisive effect. Helmut Ritter commented in 1924: 'The first practical consequence of the nationalist ideology was the internal disintegration of the old Ottoman Caliphate, which had been based precisely on the idea of a supra-national politico-religious community.'[107] Although the Young Turks were nationalists, they had no wish to sacrifice their non-Turkish territories. The logical result of this was, as Ritter shows, that 'attempts were made to inculcate the non Turkish-speakers with Turkish nationalism by force . . . the highly developed Arab civilisation could not be Turkified at a stroke, and thus relations between the Turkish masters and their non-Turkish subjects gradually became more and more tense'.[108]

As Hartmann indicated, the Paris Congress tended to show 'a certain degree of immaturity and lack of clarity of aim amongst the Arabs'.[109] This 'immaturity' did not go unnoticed by the Young Turks either, who showed themselves inclined to give in to the demands of the Congress. They sent representatives to Paris in order to negotiate with the Arab nationalists, and the result was an agreement.[110] 'As a result of skilful negotiations on the part of the Young Turks', the Arab Congress came to accept 'a rather inadequate settlement'.[111] When it finally came to the point of putting the provisions of the settlement into effect, the Pan-Turanian Young Turks were no longer prepared to recognise the right to Arab self-determination which they had previously agreed upon. The most important members of the Arab national movement were arrested and executed in 1915 and 1916, when Turkey was fighting on the side of the Central Powers. Amongst them were prominent participants in the Paris Congress, including Zahrawi, its chairman. When the Young Turk governor of Syria, Jamal Pasha, who was also Commander-in-Chief of the Fifth Ottoman Army, managed to confiscate documents from the French Consulate in Beirut proving that members of the Arab national movement had had secret contacts with France, he seized the opportunity to conduct an extensive campaign against the movement which claimed numerous victims.[112] It was against this background that the Arab demands for separatism emerged, whose practical expression was the Arab Revolt of 1916. The colonial powers who fought against the Ottoman Empire and its ally Germany gave wide support to the separatist movement: 'Certainly the British side made use of all possible means to incite the Arab nationalists against the Turks, and then used them unscrupulously for their own ends.'[113] This quotation from Hartmann aptly summarises the first Arab national revolt of 1916.

As C. E. Dawn has shown,[114] the Arab national movement was supported not only by Western-educated men of letters and officers from petty bourgeois backgrounds, but also, and particularly after 1914, by large landowners and *grand bourgeois* forces. However the secularism of the Arab national writers, based on the acculturation of Western bourgeois ideas, could hardly have found a social base in the upper reaches of Syrian society. In spite of the reforms of Muhammad 'Ali and Ibrahim Pasha between 1831 and 1840, and the Tanzimat reforms which followed,[115] Syria was by no means a bourgeois society. It was more a semi-feudal society with some incipient bourgeois features. It is therefore not surprising that the undeveloped Syrian bourgeoisie, and the petty bourgeois writers, were unable to lead a revolt against the Ottoman Empire by themselves. They allied with the feudal masters of the Arabian peninsula, the Hashemite dynasty, and left it to them to lead the rising.[116] The head of the dynasty, Sharif Husain of Mecca, who had good relations with Britain, agreed to lead the Arab revolt against the Ottomans within the framework of the McMahon-Husain correspondence. The British assured him that they would support the Revolt and guarantee the 'liberation of the Arabs' within an independent Arab kingdom under Husain's leadership, which was to consist of the Arab part of Asia.[117] This pledge proved to be a tactical manoeuvre, since Britain and France, with the connivance of Czarist Russia, had concluded the Sykes-Picot Agreement in 1916, according to which the two colonial powers were to divide the 'liberated' Arab territories among themselves. Russia was promised freedom of action in the Balkans as a reward for its acquiescence.[118] Sharif Husain had ambitions to proclaim himself caliph after the Arab victory, and to restore the supremacy of Mecca and Medina. According to Rudolf Sellheim, Mecca and Medina, the birthplaces of Islam had 'finally ceased to be the seat of government of the early Islamic Caliphate'[119] after the second Islamic civil war of 680–92, and thenceforward only maintained a purely religious significance. Sharif Husain wished to restore these two cities to their former glory by means of the Arab Revolt and the support of the colonial powers, in order to consolidate the ideological foundations of his rule. While the Syrian Arab nationalists used national revolutionary arguments to justify the uprising, and made the Sharif their leader, the latter interpreted it as an uprising of Islam against the Turkish 'heretics', who had begun to turn their backs on Islam since the time of the Tanzimat.

Dawn, who has examined Sharif Husain's proclamation, comes to the conclusion that 'to him the lawful state is not a national state but a Moslem state, a caliphate, embracing as much of the community of the faithful as possible'.[120] The Sykes-Picot Agreement, which had been drawn up in secrecy, was published by Lenin and declared null and void after the Bolsheviks' seizure of power in Russia. The scandalised Arab nationalists were somehow appeased by France and Britain, and the Allies were able to make their naive associates believe that the published texts were a 'figment of a malicious Bolshevik imagination',[121] although France and Britain themselves continued to maintain the terms of the alliance. By 1918 Turkish troops had been driven from Arab soil, and the nationalists began to believe that they had obtained their national freedom. This was to prove illusory; the Lebanese coast was occupied by French troops as early as 1918,[122] and by 1920 the Arab parts of Asia outside the Arabian Peninsula had become an Anglo-French colony.[123] Faisal, the son of Sharif Husain of Mecca, had made himself King of Syria, but was soon dethroned by French arms. Britain was able to win him over as a partner by bestowing the throne of Iraq upon him just as it had given the crown of Transjordan to his brother 'Abdullah, thereby securing him as an ally. Even after 1920 Sharif Husain continued to wait in vain for the fulfilment of the promises which had been made to him. In 1924, after the success of the Kemalist revolution in Turkey, and the dissolution of the caliphate, he declared himself Caliph of all Muslims, but shortly afterwards, in the same year, was driven out of Mecca by the victorious Wahhabis, and thus obtained the mocking soubriquet of the 'One Day Caliph'.

The story of the Hashemite leadership of the arab revolt of 1916, as well as that of the Revolt itself, is full of betrayals.[124] Anis al-Sayigh has described the Arab national movement to the end of its second phase in 1920, that is, the phase of its politicisation, in the following way:

This national movement was largely a political movement in the narrow sense; it had no social or humanitarian perspectives. It fought merely for formal independence and was unable to achieve real independence . . . secondly, it was a right-wing conservative movement . . . , which had been adjusted to the needs of a particular leadership and was monopolised by traditional politicians who were usually either rich feudalists or their agents. They saw their own interests as being the interests of the homeland and excluded workers, peasants and the middle classes from the power which they were able to gain for themselves for a third of a century . . . thirdly, the movement had no confidence in itself or in the nation; hence it was based more on foreign capital than on the people, and tended to dance to tunes played in foreign capitals . . .[125]

(c) The Development of the Arab National Movement after the First World War: The Role of Sati' al-Husri as a Theoretician of Arab Nationalism

The literary nationalism of the Arab Christians was politicised at the turn of the century. The ideological content of the movement in its first two phases—the literary, in the second half of the nineteenth century, and the liberal-political, which lasted until the end of the First World War—is clear. At first, the nationalists tried to point to the existence of an Arab people who were different from the Turks by referring back to classical Arabic literature. Then equality, and national cultural autonomy within the Ottoman Empire were demanded for this Arab nation. In both cases the advanced bourgeois society of the West was the model. This situation changed with the end of the First World War. The West, under whose colonial rule the Middle East had now fallen, could no longer serve as the model for the Arab national movement; on the contrary, it was now the task of the movement to fight the West in order to free itself from it and to become self-reliant. While Arab nationalism in the pre-colonial period, as formulated by the Syro-Lebanese Western-educated intellectuals, sought the introduction of liberal freedoms and bourgeois democracy on Western lines in the context of a secular Arab state, it developed into an apologetic, reactionary, populist and frequently aggressive ideology under colonial rule.[126] This new variation of Arab nationalism was formulated by Sati' al-Husri and Michel 'Aflaq both in the inter-war period and after the Second World War in a number of influential writings. Both these theoreticians influenced the whole course of Arab political thinking until the beginning of the 1960s in a particularly effective fashion.

Hans Kohn writes: 'Just as formerly French imperialism had roused German nationalism, and Austrian imperialism Italian and Czech nationalism, so, too . . . in the East, imperialism acted as the awakener of nationalism.'[127] In spite of the difficulty of comparing phenomena rooted in different forms of historical experience, and regardless of the fact that the origins of Arab nationalism lie in the pre-colonial period, it can be safely concluded for the moment that Arab nationalism in the colonial period, which persists until the present time, is intellectually related to Italian and German nationalisms, which have been defined by C. J. Hayes as 'counter-nationalism'.[128] This is also evident from the fact that the reception of European liberalism by Arab nationalists in the nineteenth century and until the First World War underwent a change of direction. Arab nationalism, once francophile and partly anglo-phile, changed with the British and French colonisation of the area and became anti-British and anti-French, and germanophile. The germanophilia of Arab nationalism originated partly with the Arab nationalist officers of *al-'Ahd*, who were trained by German instructors,[129] and who shared their germanophilia with the Young Turks. These officers only took part in the pro-British Arab Revolt after considerable hesitation,[130] and the British 'betrayal' of the Arab cause once more strengthened their germanophilia, especially as German policy in the Middle East was always directed against British and French colonial intentions in the area, and was misinterpreted by the Arab officers as 'anti-colonial'. These officers also formed the nucleus of the Iraqi Army which was the first in the area to be nationally conscious.[131] This germanophilia however can also be traced to the influence of the works of Sati 'al-Husri. In fact, as will be shown, the germanophilia of Arab nationalism in the period after the First World War was based on al-Husri's ideas.

The Arab nationalist intellectuals' abandonment of francophilia and anglophilia and their espousal of germanophilia can however not be considered simply as the substitution of one set of ideas for another. It was of course closely connected with the historical circumstances which influenced Arab nationalism, which had undergone a radical change. Furthermore, the germanophilia was narrow and one-sided. The German ideology absorbed by the Arab intellectuals at this time was confined to a set of nationalist ideas which had gained particular currency during the period of the Napoleonic Wars. These ideas carried notions of romantic irration-alism and a hatred of the French to extremes. They excluded from consideration the philosophers influenced by the Enlightenment, such as Lessing, Kant, Hegel and others, on the grounds of what was considered to be their universalism. They were particularly attracted by the notion of the 'People', as defined by German Romanticism, which they proceeded to apply to the 'Arab Nation'.[132] For the nineteenth-century nationalists, such as Adib Ishaq, the liberal national state was simply a means to emancipation; its democratic constitutional character was always taken for granted. The germanophiles of the post-First World War period however saw the national state as the apogee of the 'Arab Nation'—in other words, as an end in itself. It did not matter to them whether the Arab unity which they propagated would come about within the framework of a democratic state or a military dictatorship. In the post-colonial Middle East, this narrow-gauge fascism, already described by Fanon as a characteristic of the semi-independent state, has borrowed most of its ideological apparatus from this form of nationalism.[133] Charles Gallagher, who has also distinguished between the various different phases of Arab nationalism, mentions that an important feature of post-First World War nationalist writings is their narcissistic and ethno-centric character.[134] Although the terminology used is borrowed from Europe, these writings are permeated with an anti-European flavour.[135] The early liberals such as Nasif al-Yaziji and al-Bustani studied classical Arabic literature largely under the influence of European scholarship, in order to discover a cultural identity which would serve to distance them from the Islamically sanctioned rule of the Ottomans and thus provide them with a base to liberate themselves from it. The populist nationalists also studied classical literature in this way, but their position was no longer imbued with the liberal spirit and their idealisation of a mythical past narrowed the perspectives for progress.

It was Sati' al-Husri who began this tradition of populist germanophile Arab nationalism. His nationalism was not mystificatory, fanatic or fascist, but he laid the foundations for the kind of fanatical nationalism formulated by his disciple Michel 'Aflaq, which has found expression in the semi-fascist military dictatorship in Iraq and Syria under the aegis of the Ba'th Party.

al-Husri was born into a Syrian family in Yemen in 1882.[136] His father, Mehmed Hilal Effendi, who had had a traditional Islamic education, was chief Ottoman *qadi* (judge) in the Yemen. al-Husri studied natural sciences at a number of Ottoman higher institutions, and was then given a scholarship to study in Paris. He studied education in Paris, Switzerland and Belgium. While abroad he had contacts with secret Arab national societies and with the Young Turks. He also made use of his time in Paris to study European national ideas more closely, Rousseau and Renan in particular, but also Herder and Fichte whose theories were to be influential in directing his thought. As a young man, according to the literature,[137] al-Husri still supported liberal ideas, in contradistinction to Ziya Gökalp, the guiding spirit of the Young Turks and the Kemalists, with whom he was on friendly terms, who believed in the idea of the organic nation state.[138] In his description of the French idea of the nation, al-Husri admits that he had been attracted to it 'in his earlier days'.[139] It is not entirely clear when the change in the direction of his thinking began, but it probably took place during his stay in Europe, when he began to study the works of the German philosophers. The immediate reason for the growth of his interest in the idea of the organic nation-state seems to have been the occupation of Syria by French colonial troops which he himself experienced and described extensively.[140] Before the French troops marched from the Lebanese coast into Syria, al-Husri, as a representative of Faisal's short-lived kingdom of Syria (1920) met the arabophobe General Gouraud for negotiations. The General aroused in al-Husri a deep hatred for France which he was never able to overcome.[141] However his francophobia never developed into the general xenophobia which often appears as a disguised form of anti-colonialism. He never denied his connections with Europe and always emphatically acknowledged his debt to German, and thus European, sources.[142] A general xenophobia only appears with his successors, especially 'Aflaq, although he too is indebted to European ideas. On the other hand al-Husri was not as unreservedly open-minded towards Europe as the Syrian-Lebanese and Egyptian liberals had been. Thus he criticised Taha Husain, the spokesman of Egyptian nationalism,[143] and Salama Musa, the early Arab socialist,[144] on the grounds that their sympathies for Europe led them to an imitation of everything European, which almost became anti-Arab.

After his return from Paris, al-Husri taught for a time at a number of Ottoman schools and higher institutions. He also held senior administrative posts in the Ottoman Balkan provinces, where he keenly followed the national movements. During the First World War he was appointed Ottoman Director of Education in Syria. There he made contact with the Arab nationalists who were at the time cooperating with Britain and France to organise a Revolt through which the Arab part of Asia might be detached from the Ottoman Empire and become an independent national state. Britain and France supported the Revolt because they hoped it would forestall the total mobilisation of all Muslims that might have taken place in response to an appeal from the Sultan-Caliph for a 'Holy War', since the Ottoman Empire was in alliance with Germany. As has already been mentioned, Britain and France had come to an agreement to divide the Arab provinces, excluding the Holy Places of the Peninsula, between themselves for purposes of colonisation at the same time as they were negotiating with the Arab national-ists.[145] The Arab Revolt, which began in June 1916, under the supervision of British officers, led to the detachment of the Arab provinces from the Ottoman Empire in 1918. Faisal, the son of Sharif Husain of Mecca, and the Arab nationalists in whose name he was negotiating with Britain and France, were forced to recognise that the Sykes-Picot Agreement was a reality and not the 'figment of a malicious Bolshevik imagination' which they had been led to believe. Faisal's attempts to negotiate with the Allies after the war proved fruitless, and as a result, regardless of Allied resolutions, the Arab nationalists declared Syria an independent constitutional monarchy and proclaimed Faisal King on 8 March 1920.[146] al-Husri, who had supported Faisal in his negotiations in Europe, now became one of his advisors and was made Minister of Education. The invasion of Syria by the French on 24 July 1920 and the declaration of the French Mandate over Syria quickly put an end to the Arab national state which had been initially advocated but not in practice supported by the Allies. Faisal and al-Husri immediately set off for Europe for further negotiations with the Allies, and in the same year, 1920, Faisal managed to get himself made King of Iraq under British Mandate. After a brief exile in Egypt al-Husri was appointed to senior posts in Iraq after 1921. He became responsible for Education and Archaeology and was also Dean of the Faculty of Law at the University of Baghdad.[147] In the course of his own teaching, and because of his influence on the educational system in general, al-Husri was able to make national education the focus of the educational and cultural policies of the British Mandate. He was able to do this because Iraq had a certain degree of autonomy in its internal affairs. In his first writings, which were published in the early 1920s, al-Husri transposed the German idea of the nation as formulated by Herder and later by Fichte, to the circumstances of the Arab World. His works were received enthusiastically and helped to create a germanophile Arab nationalist movement. In 1932, a year before the death of King Faisal, Iraq was granted political independence and became a member of the League of Nations. al-Husri continued his activities in independent Iraq, where according to his memoirs his sole aim was to create a higher degree of national consciousness through national education.

Mandatory Iraq, which had had a form of internal autonomy since 1922, became the centre of the Arab national movement after it had gained political independence. Politicians and former Ottoman officers from Syria and Palestine were active in their periods of exile in Iraq. The core of the Iraqi Army in any case consisted of former members of the *al-'Ahd* secret society. In 1940 Iraqi politicians and officers, together with Arab nationalists from neighbouring countries then living in Iraq, joined forces to lay the temporary foundations of an Arab national party.[148] Following the creation of an alliance between the Hashimite dynasty and the Arab national movement there was an another disastrous pact between the secular nationalists and the feudal-religious forces, to whom the leadership of the movement was entrusted, in the person of Hajj Amin al-Husaini, the Mufti of Jerusalem, who had been able to obtain high positions not only in the Arab national party but in the movement as a whole, especially since the 1940s.[149] Under his aegis contacts were made and developed with the Third Reich and his private secretary 'Uthman Kamal Haddad was the contact between Baghdad and Berlin.[150] There is no evidence to suggest that al-Husri collaborated with the group around the Arab national party in Iraq. It is not mentioned in his memoirs, and Haddad himself does not mention al-Husri in any connection with the group in his own memoirs. However, these nationalists certainly knew al-Husri and were influenced by him, since his ideas were widely published in daily newspapers and magazines, though not yet in book form. As no other Arab political writer of the period was familiar with the German idea of the nation, al-Husri's nationalist contemporaries could only have been made aware of these ideas through his work. In April 1941 a group of Iraqi nationalists staged a coup with the aid of the Third Reich and fascist Italy. Rashid 'Ali al-Gailani was appointed Prime Minister of Iraq, which now went over to the side of the Axis.[151]

However, by May 1941 the Regent of Iraq, 'Abd al-Ilah, who had fled after the coup, returned and overthrew the Gailani regime with the help of British troops. Those associated with the regime were either exiled or imprisoned. al-Husri was deprived of his offices and his Iraqi citizenship and deported to Syria.[152] al-Gailani fled to

Germany where he remained until the end of the war. In Syria al-Husri worked as a teacher, and when the country became independent in 1945 he already held important positions in education and continued to play a major role in the formulation of an educational syllabus in which national education once more featured prominently.[153]

In 1947 he went to Egypt, where he worked in the Cultural Department of the Arab League, and ensured that a unified educational policy on the basis of national consciousness was implemented in all Arab countries. At the Arab League he founded the Institute for Advanced Arab Studies in 1953, where postgraduates were given a nationalist education. He himself had the chair of Arab Nationalism at the Institute, and was also its permanent dean. The works which he published in and before his Cairo period were to be among the most influential writings in the Arab world in the years which followed. They became compulsory reading in schools and universities and for members of nationalist parties. al-Husri was hailed as the 'philosopher of Arab nationalism'.[154] Leading political writers even called him 'The Arab Fichte'.[155]

In 1966 al-Husri left Egypt to return to Iraq, where he died on 24 December 1968 at the age of 86. The splendid funeral which he was given, and the period of national mourning which was declared gives some indication of al-Husri's significance for the Arab regimes of his day.

When al-Husri uses the term 'Arab nation' he no longer confines it to the Arab part of Asia, as the early nationalists had done, but extends it to include the whole of Arabic-speaking North Africa. He hoped to create this 'Arab nation' through national education within the school system. It was only with Michel 'Aflaq, the 'Arab Mazzini'[156] who was under al-Husri's spell, that the idea of the Arab nation thus defined became the obligatory and guiding principle of a political organisation, since Rashid 'Ali al-Gailani's early group had had no political programme.

In the following chapters al-Husri's notion of populist Pan-Arab nationalism will be analysed in detail. The intellectual history of the Arab national movement since the First World War, which was deeply influenced by al-Husri's writings, will also be elaborated, and the development of Arab nationalism after al-Husri will be sketched in the Postscript.

Part III Sati' al-Husri's Theory of Populist Pan-Arab Nationalism and its Philosophical Origins

6 The Origins of al-Husri's Definition of the Nation

By the end of the Second World War the process of decolonisation of the Arab countries had begun. This produced a number of independent national states which are, in Sulzbach's terms, administrative nations.[1] Their boundaries were drawn by the colonial administrations, and they correspond to the map on which the powers divided these territories amongst themselves, but they have little or no historical or economic significance. Against this background, a decisive change of direction in the politics of Arab nationalism was to occur, which is documented in al-Husri's works. His political views supersede those of liberal Arab nationalism.

The division of the territory of the Arabic-speaking peoples into different areas, each under the control of a colonial power, out of which politically independent nation states were to emerge, had the effect of bringing the Arab nationalists' idea of a single unitary 'Arab nation' into question. Gallagher has singled out an important feature of post-liberal Arab nationalism in his description of the work of the intellectual founder of this new school as an attempt to prove the existence of a single 'Arab nation' in spite of existing territorial divisions. The point of departure of al-Husri's thinking is the fact that the very existence of the 'Arab nation' is open to question.[2] The attempt to prove its existence required a theoretical basis which could not be derived from the Islamic past, since Islamic history had not experienced the phenomenon of the nation. al-Husri was thus forced to borrow his theoretical tools from European history. The French idea of the nation was unsuitable, since in France, as in other countries which have experienced successful bourgeois-democratic revolutions, the idea of a nation without a national state was politically inconceivable. In the course of these revolutions, the bourgeoisie has been able to legitimise its rule as that of the whole nation. In contrast, in the political thought of the backward European countries, the nation was transfigured into a cultural vision, the incarnation of the spirit of the people, in which the state had no part. Thus Kohn writes:

> Where the third estate became powerful in the eighteenth century—as in Great Britain, in France and in the United States—nationalism found its expression predominantly, but never exclusively, in political and economic changes. Where, on the other hand, the third estate was still weak and only in a budding stage at the beginning of the nineteenth century, as in Germany, Italy, and among the Slavonic peoples, nationalism found its expression predominantly in the cultural field. Among these peoples, at the beginning it was not so much the nation-state as the *Volksgeist* and its manifestations in literature and folklore, in the mother tongue, and in history, which became the centre of the attention of nationalism.[3]

Hence, as Kohn shows, the principal German thinkers have made a basic distinction between *state* and *nation*, where the *nation* is seen in cultural terms.[4] This notion, which originated with Herder, has persisted as a feature of German political philosophy until the present day, as, for example, in the work of Helmut Plessner.[5] In this tradition the *state* is a distinct mechanical and legal construction which is external to the *nation*. The German national thinkers generally consider the *nation* to be something sacred and eternal, with a deeper significance· than the works of man.[6]

One of the reasons for the rising popularity of Germany among Arab nationalists in the period after the First World War was the hostility which they felt towards British and French colonial rule in the region. Until this time they had been predominantly francophile, and their thinking was in the Western tradition of Natural Law and rationalism. By the 1930s, however, they were turning their attention to the Third Reich, which they believed to have no colonialist intentions,[7] and which might free them from British and French colonial rule.

al-Husri is able to provide a theoretical foundation for this emotional germanophilia. He praises German Romanticism, since it had brought into being the idea of the nation as distinct from the state. 'The most important studies and theories of nationalities', he says, 'have emerged in Germany, and it may be observed that leading nationalists from all over Europe have been pupils of the thinkers and authors of the German nation.'[8] al-Husri is particularly impressed by the German national philosophers because they 'have recognised the difference between the nation and the state earlier than the French and the British'.[9] He himself is proud to have been a pupil of this school: 'I say: the two terms *nation* and *state* must be completely separated',[10] especially as the German idea of 'the nation . . . is effectively corroborated by a long chain of historical events'.[11] In the context of this strict distinction between nation and state, al-Husri attempts to provide the theoretical basis for the notion that there was an 'Arab nation' by asserting that the actual non-existence of an all-Arab national state was entirely irrelevant. He draws a historical parallel between divided Germany before 1871 and the fragmented Arab world from the Persian Gulf to the Atlantic Ocean. According to him, the Arabs long for an 'Arab 1871'. How this is to be achieved is a matter of indifference.

In his works al-Husri makes use of the writings of Herder and the later Fichte. He considered von Schönerer's Pan-Germanism[12] to be the logical continuation of the work of these two philosophers, and the poems of Ernst Moritz Arndt as the artistic expression of the German idea of the nation.

Before analysing the main features of al-Husri's contribution to Arab nationalism, it seems appropriate to give an outline of the German idea of the nation, although this will be confined to those sources which al-Husri himself uses. Since his concept of nationalism is also a product of the process of acculturation discussed in Chapter 2, it is thus not simply a reproduction of the German idea of the nation, but also includes its own original features. It takes its central point of reference from the notion of *'asabiyya* formulated by the Arab philosopher Ibn Khaldun, and attempts a synthesis between this and the German idea of the nation. The term *'asabiyya* will be discussed below.

(a) The German Sources: The German Romantics: Herder, Fichte and Arndt

The romantic definition of 'the people' which was of great political importance in the ninehteenth century, goes back to Herder. His continuous influence on the founders of nationalism in the nineteenth century, such as Michelet, Mazzini,[13] Fichte,[14] and the Slav nationalists[15] has already been conclusively proved. However Herder must be exonerated from the charge of populist nationalism, although his explicitly non-political definition of 'the people'[16] contains potential elements of politicisation which could be and were utilised, especially by German nationalists after 1806.[17] Nevertheless, Herder's notion of 'the people' is qualitatively different from that of the populist nationalists of the nineteenth century, especially as it forms a central feature of his humanism, which, as will be shown below, owes much to the ideas of the Enlightenment. It must also not be overlooked that in spite of his polemics against it, especially his 'anti-Enlightenment' broadsheet with the ironic title *Also a Philosophy of History for the Education of Mankind*,[18] Herder stands firmly within the tradition of the Enlightenment, in contradistinction to the populist nationalists. His philosophy of history contains elements which may be considered part of the Enlightenment, as well as elements with which populist nationalists could identify.[19]

Herder believed that a number of separate climatic zones had been formed on earth as a result of processes of natural history. The peoples who have grown up and lived in these different zones are stamped in every respect by their physical environment,[20] so that every man bears upon him 'the imprint of his own strip of the earth and its way of life'.[21] 'The composition of their [sc. mankind's] bodies, their way of life, all happiness, all the activities to which they have been accustomed from childhood onwards, and the whole horizon of their soul, are conditioned by climate.'[22] The particular modes of life which nature has forced upon them become traditional norms of behaviour and customs whose totality determines the culture and national character of a people. 'The particular image of each nation is the more deeply embedded in it because it is its own, related to its sky and its earth. It springs from its way of life, handed down to it from fathers and ancestors.'[23]

The capacity of peoples to differ is thus conditioned by their folk character and cultural heritage, which are a result of the influence of the particular climatic zone in which a particular people happens to reside. Herder was interested in the cultures of peoples, their traditional customs and practices, all of which formed their folk character. He thus firmly rejected any thesis of racial differentiation between peoples. 'Finally I would wish that the categories into which mankind has been divided out of a praiseworthy desire to make a scholarly survey shall not be pushed beyond their limits.'[24] Herder considers the claim that different races exist to be one of the most elementary false distinctions.

The modes of behaviour conditioned by the physical environment become a part of tradition through education, which is founded upon imitation. 'Education . . . can only take place through imitation and practice, that is by the transformation of the concept into action.'[25] Language is the instrument through which tradition is maintained and handed on, and in which mythologies and folk songs find their expression.[26] Taking care of this cultural heritage within the framework of education guarantees its continuity. 'The unknowing child listened with curiosity to the saga . . . which flowed into its soul and nourished it.'[27] This philosophy of history, which is concerned with these traditions, and which sees history as a 'chain of traditions . . . is the true history of mankind'.[28]

A people without a national language cannot exist, since 'a people has no concept for which it does not also have a word. The most brilliant idea remains a dark sensation until the soul finds a distinctive label and embodies it through the word into memory, into recollection, into the mind, yes, finally into the mind of man, into tradition. Pure reason without language remains an earthly utopia.'[29] Thus language is the expression of the intellect of each people 'since the mind and character of a people is imprinted on its language'.[30] But language is not merely a means through which a people expresses itself, but also the 'container and contents' of its form of expression, that is, its literature.[31] 'Every nation has its own storehouse of thoughts, which have become symbols. This is their national language, a reservoir to which they have contributed for centuries.'[32] A language with a script is the prerequisite for the flowering of the arts and sciences which Herder considers to be the manifestation of an active tradition. Hence language is the barometer by which the culture of a people and its level of development may be measured. Hence ' language does not only last as long as the nation lasts, but it also reveals, purifies and consolidates itself in the same way as the nation consolidates and enlightens itself'.[33] In addition he notes most perceptively that language can be a means through which political power can be exercised. When powerful peoples struggle to suppress the languages of the peoples whom they have subjugated they are contributing to the virtual liquidation of the latter's identity. Hence, Greek, Latin and Arabic in classical times, and French and Spanish in modern times, are the means through which national political power has been exercised.[34] In the context of the history of European colonialism, such formulations are particularly apt; Herder's realisation that subjugated peoples were working towards their emancipation in their efforts to revitalise and cherish their national language is still of topical significance even today.[35]

In Herder's philosophy of history, history is interpreted as a succession of national organisms, which are themselves cultural structures.[36] Hence history is entirely apolitical, and politics as such are distasteful.[37] The obviously cultural character of Herder's romantic definition of 'people' protects him from the charge of national arrogance and chauvinism,[38] although others were to give the definition politically reactionary connotations. This development was no part of his purpose, especially as he saw that individual nationalities, in spite of all the differences in their folk character, were all branches from a single trunk: that of human kind, which develops its faculties in the service of man.[39] The individual alone cannot be creative for humanity: every individual deed is a collective act of the nation, an expression of its tradition and a manifestation of its folk character.[40] This vague definition of folk character constitutes the central part of Herder's theory[41] and also that of populist nationalism. His influence persists, however, particularly in the field of cultural anthropology, although, as H. D. Werner has shown,[42] Herder's theories cannot be used for stringent analysis in spite of their scholarly appearance.

Herder's romantic definition of 'the people' was a response to the 'fashion books' of the French Enlightenment. His theories took refuge in the cultural sphere, as his definition of 'the people' indicates, and transcended German middle-class aspirations to emancipation, which were shackled by the socio-economic and political backwardness of Germany. However, his criticism of the more advanced Western countries was not yet xenophobic. His emphasis on the unique nature of the Germans was made within the framework of a pluralist world of peoples, whose overall destiny was the creation of a humane society.[43]

Klaus Epstein has proved that the tradition of German bourgeois conservatism already existed before the French Revolution, and was not as has often been alleged, simply a reaction to it.[44] However, Herder's potentially conservative criticism of the Enlightenment and his Romanticism were not widely shared by the German intellectual middle class, whose sights were already directed towards

France.[45] For most German thinkers the French Revolution had the effect of making their theories assume concrete form, and it was only with the beginning of Napoleon's European campaigns that a trenchant and emotional criticism of the French Revolution developed more widely in Germany. This was to form the basis of Germany nationalism, which was itself first manifested through francophobia. While Herder's cultural nationalism transcended the emancipation that had been awaited in vain, and was an escape from the misery of contemporary conditions in Germany, the nationalism of the so-called Napoleonic wars of liberation, which was the result of the politicisation of the romantic definition of 'the people', became an ideological weapon against foreign rule. As has been noted in Chapter 1, French and Anglo-American nationalism was the philosophical counterpart of the bourgeois-democratic revolution, thus implying liberty and the creation of national, constitutional and liberal institutions on the political level. In contrast neither German nor Slav nationalism was the ideological expression of indigenous historical developments. They emerged as an ideological reaction to an exogenous challenge, first ideological and then military, from a more advanced society. Hence this type of nationalism was directed outwards rather than inwards and it demanded the end of foreign rule and the creation of national independence rather than the establishment of liberal democratic institutions.[46] This important aspect of 'counter-nationalism' in Europe shows why the nationalism of colonial and semi-colonial countries has a formal and philosophical similarity to German and Slav nationalism,[47] and why some of the European-educated nationalists of these countries draw either explicitly or implicitly on the ideological sources of European 'counter-nationalism'.

Hermann Simon is correct in saying that the German nationalist Romanticism of the Napoleonic Wars led to 'the strengthening not only of conservative forces, but also of reactionary and authoritarian-monarchical forces opposed to the Enlightenment and to reason'.[48] This, however, is only one dimension of the political significance of German Romanticism.[49] Although German Romanticism sided with reaction in the final analysis, it had originally put forward a legitimate historical demand, namely liberation from foreign rule. In that it demanded change, it also contained a revolutionary core, but this was bound to disappear as soon as it exhausted itself in revolutionary protest.

It is true that in terms of world history Napoleon led Germany onto the way of progress: in Hegel's vivid phrase, he was 'a world spirit on horseback' (*Weltgeist zu Pferde*). But from a national perspective he appears as the suppressor of the national liberties of other peoples. In this respect the hatred of Napoleon and the francophobia of German Romanticism,[50] was a disguised form of an articulated will for national emancipation, in the same way as the nationalism of the colonial countries was a disguised form of anti-colonialism. However, there is no comparison between the historical significance of the Napoleonic conquest of Germany and the colonial conquest of the non-European world.[51]

The legitimate desire of the German Romantics for national emancipation made them into opponents of the *status quo*. Thus Hans Reiss correctly points out that it is wrong to label them all indiscriminately. 'They demanded radical social change. In fact they were often not conservative but revolutionary, although they did not admit this to themselves. The revolutionary aspect of their thinking explains why they allied themselves so readily with nationalism, which was a truly revolutionary movement. Nationalism completely transformed the traditional social order.'[52] However, German Romanticism was reactionary in the sense that the society which it strove to create was a utopia in the past. The German Romantics considered that the new order ushered in by the French Revolution was 'a system foreign to the German tradition and the German character, likely to destroy the German way of life'.[53] Reiss describes the consequences: 'Fear made many of them lose all sense of proportion and stray into fantasy. At times they did not even accept the social order which existed before 1789, but yearned for a completely utopian society. They created a dream world where considerations of human welfare were often ignored.'[54] This was also true of Arab nationalists, who wanted to restore the 'glorious Arab past' (also, incidentally, a phenomenon of classical Arab history, as Sellheim has pointed out[54a]), and of African nationalists like Senghor, Nyerere and so forth, who lament the passing of 'negro peasant society' and try to conjure up its values. It is also true of the popular Asiatic nationalism of Gandhi or Sun Yat Sen. The later work of Fichte must be considered against this historical background, although the fundamental problems of his political theory must also be examined. As the main concern of this study is not a critical examination of Fichte, but an analysis of his impact on Arab nationalism through the works of Sati' al-Husri, the present discussion will be confined to a single work, the well-known

Reden an die deutsche Nation (Addresses to the German Nation). al-
Husri is evidently only familiar with this one work of Fichte's, to
which he makes frequent reference. However, before examining the
nationalist content of this work,[55] it seems appropriate to make
some general reference to Fichte's later political theories.

Bernard Willms has shown convincingly that the dualism of state
and subjectivity is central to Fichte's whole *oeuvre*.[56] Willms
interprets Fichte's turning towards nationalism as proof that he has
overcome this dualism. According to Willms, his later political
theory derives 'on the one hand, from the concretisation of the
theory of a historical world of states, and on the other as a reaction
to the actual appearance of Napoleon'.[57] This caused a simultaneous change in the content of his theory which Willms describes
as follows: 'Just as in his first phase Fichte thought "the revolution",
in his second phase he thought "the war of liberation against
Napoleon"—both being the self-assertion of his nation. But the
French Revolution was a world historical event, while the war of
liberation was a national one.'[58] Through this change in Fichte's
thought, the nation, which was once the particular in his theory, now
became raised to the level of the general. 'Fichte became the
philosopher of humanity in the nation, and of a "nationalised"
humanity.'[59] However he always spoke of the *German nation*, so
that the later Fichte, as Willms has shown,[60] and as will be seen
later, no longer talks in terms of a pluralism of peoples in the way
that Herder does. 'The tendency to apply the term nation to the
"German nation" is so marked in Fichte . . . that it is hard to find
references to "the nation in general".'[61]

The historical situation of the Germany to which Fichte addresses
his *Reden* was that of a fragmented territory, inhabited by a single
people, whose political homogeneity was decisively enhanced under
the rule of an alien army.[62] 'The general purposes of these speeches
is to bring courage and hope to the vanquished, to proclaim joy to
those in deep mourning . . .'[63] which explains their melancholy
style. Fichte developed a practical political strategy through which
foreign rule might be overcome. 'No nation which has sunk into this
state of dependence can rise out of it by any known or common
means . . . if a nation that has sunk so far is to be able to save itself,
this should be done by completely untried methods, through the
creation of a completely new order of things.'[64] The new 'means of
salvation' that Fichte recommends consists

in the creation of an entirely new national self, which might perhaps have existed among some individuals, but only as an exception, and never as a universal national self. It also consists in the education of a nation whose former life has died out, and which has become the supplement to an alien life, an education directed towards a completely new life which either remains its exclusive possession, or, if it must pass from itself to others, remains whole and undiminished in spite of infinite division. In a word, I propose a total change of the present educational system as the only means of maintaining the existence of the German nation.[65]

This explains why the discussion of national education in general and German national education in particular is the concern of most of the fourteen *Addresses*. According to Binder, the strategy which Fichte advocates against Napoleon does not aim at 'the concentration and mobilisation of popular forces towards political action', but is principally a strategy of political education. Fichte stands out not as a politician but as an educator;[66] his political plan is a plan of national education.[67] It is perhaps no accident that the founders of germanophile Arab nationalism, al-Husri and 'Aflaq, never laid any claim to be politicians, and saw themselves, like Fichte, as educators. In the course of his life al-Husri only accepted posts in the field of political education in Iraq, Syria and Egypt, and always refused to assume any political function. He repeatedly emphasised in his memoirs that he had no wish to concern himself with day-to-day political life.[68] Again 'Aflaq, who was even secretary-general of a political party, the Ba'th Party, strictly refused any political appointments even when his own party was in power. The only political post he ever held was that of Minister of Education.[69]

In his *Addresses* Fichte tries to prove that a 'German Nation' exists, and that the existence of this nation is particularly justified because of its superiority to others. In order to do this, he compares the 'Germans' and the 'other peoples of Germanic origin'. While the Germans remained in the 'original' tribal lands, and held fast to the 'original' tribal language, the other peoples migrated to the neighbouring regions, and took over a different language, which they remodelled in their own fashion.[70] Hence language plays a supremely important role, because it is not man that is speaking, 'but human nature in him, proclaiming himself to his peers. And thus one should say that language is unique and fundamentally necessary.'[71] For Fichte language is a constitutent part of each people. By *people* he understands 'those who are subject to the same externally influenced means of communication, who live together and who progress through the continuous use of their language'.[72] At the same time his approach to language is ahistorical, because 'it remains . . . always the same language'.[73] And as language gives a 'sensory picture of the transcendental', a living 'original' language can only be one which 'has developed continuously out of the genuine common experience of a people, from the moment of its first utterance among them. It contains nothing that is not a part of their genuine experience, and expresses nothing which is at variance with their other views in a comprehensively all-embracing context.'[74] Languages which contain foreign elements are 'dead and incomprehensible' because they transmit only the sensory and not the transcendental, which the language provides as a sensory picture. Such languages thus acquire the 'shallow and dead history of alien civilisation, and by no means that of their own civilisation'.[75] The requirements of an 'original' language are only fulfilled by the German language: hence it is only 'the German who speaks a language whose life force derives from the earliest emanation of the forces of nature. The language of other German tribes stirs only on the surface but is dead at the roots.'[76] And there can be no comparison between them, because German, as it is the 'original' language, embodies the living, and the others embody the dead: 'there is no comparison between life and death, and the former has boundless value in face of the latter. Thus all comparisons between German and the neo-Latin languages are entirely futile . . .'.[77]

Because of his definition of language as a vital constituent of every people, and of the German language as the only 'original' language, Fichte sees the German people as the only 'original people' (*Urvolk*). He dismisses the fact that educated Germans of his day generally had a French education as the result of a 'previous manifestation of "xenophilia"'.[78] This was why the German princes were not particularly German, and were estranged from their people. They isolated themselves from the 'German nation' 'out of "xenophilia" and a passion for distinction and splendour'.[79] He hoped that they would come to their senses and abandon this 'xenophilia'. In his first address he claims to be speaking 'for Germans as such[80] and of Germans as such' and he repeated this emphatically in his final Address: 'O all you Germans, these addresses confirm the place in society which should be yours . . . .'.[81]

Like Herder, Fichte criticised the Enlightenment's definition of the state, which he considered too mechanistic. He emphasised that the nation cannot exist without the state, because people and fatherland are 'the bearers of terrestrial eternity', and thus loom over 'the state . . . and the social order'.[82] Only love for the fatherland can govern the state 'as the highest, ultimate and most independent institution: thus the freedom of the individual must be restricted in various ways . . .'.[83] The man who loves his fatherland, his nation 'must . . . even wish to die that it may live . . .'.[84]

The politicisation of the cultural definition of the people is a further important difference between Herder's theories and those of the nineteenth-century Romantics, as well as the abandonment of the concept of a pluralistic world of peoples on which Herder had insisted. While Herder detested the sphere of politics, and always shunned it, Fichte concentrated his interest entirely on politics, although he always appeared as an educator and not as a politician. According to Fichte, every 'reasonable writer . . . wants to participate in general and public affairs, and form and model them according to his own views'.[85] If a writer wishes to remain politically disengaged, all his talk is empty air, to tickle idle ears:[86] in contrast, he considered that his own *Addresses* should be compulsory reading as a preparation for political practice. Although he came to abandon his earlier ideas, which were influenced by the Enlightenment and the French Revolution, and although he finally became an apostle of chauvinism with his declaration that the Germans were the only 'original' people, his writing never sank to the level of banality of a great number of the nationalist Romantics of nineteenth-century Germany. This is also partially true of Ernst Moritz Arndt, whom al-Husri uses as a source for his theories in addition to Herder and Fichte.

The theoretical framework of Arndt's writing also derives from Herder and Fichte. Like them, Arndt takes *people* and *nation* as synonymous, and sees the *nation* in terms of the *cultural nation*. Language is the central part of the culture of a people, and since only the German language is 'original', only the Germans can be considered an 'original' people. Thus in Arndt as well as in Fichte Herder's notion of a pluralism of peoples gives way to chauvinistic emphasis on German populism.[87] In contrast to Fichte, Arndt appears a people's demagogue. He preaches national hatred against all non-Germans: 'I call for hatred of the French, not just for this

war, I want it to last for a long time, I want it to last for ever . . .'.[88]
This hatred is not directed merely against the French as national
oppressors during the Napoleonic domination of Germany, but
even more against the whole ideological heritage of the French
Revolution and the Enlightenment as well as their practical results.
In his arguments he makes use of a nationally coloured pseudo-
religious form of Christianity.[89]

The superficiality of Arndt's political thought is illustrated in the
following characteristic passage:

> May that which is alien be for ever separated from that which is
> one's own! May the French and the Germans be separated . . . by
> an unsurmountable wall of the burning hatred of the two
> peoples . . . But, O German people, that this radiant hatred may
> be and continue, you must wage war, a hot, bloody and collective
> war of all Germans against the oppressors. Only their blood can
> wash away the shame which stains you: only their blood can
> restore the dignity which you have lost . . .[90]

He does not confine himself to stating that the Germans are an
'original' people because they speak an 'original' language, but also
brings forward racial and biological arguments. In contrast to the
other European peoples, the Germans' are a pure and ancient
people, unmixed and primordial', because they 'have not become
bastardised by foreign peoples and half-breeds'.[91] Of course such
claims were seized upon during the Third Reich and transformed
into guiding principles. The later Fichte and Arndt, and other
German Romantics were hailed as the fathers of German National
Socialism and their nationalist writings enjoyed a widespread
renaissance in the universities,[92] a renaissance which was observed
uncritically in the English-speaking world.

Nineteenth-century Romantic populist nationalism became the
subject of intensive research at German universities, following the
notion that the history of political theory is the anamnesis of social
psychoses.[93] The intention was to show the continuity between
nineteenth-century populist nationalism and fascism,[94] but a discussion of this must lie outside the scope of this study. However, it
should be emphasised that this theory of the origins of fascism,
which developed in British and North American universities during
the Second World War, cannot adequately explain the phenomenon. Like the renaissance of German Romantic nationalism at the

time, such conclusions are largely the product of war. In any case it is clear that the notion that Fichte or even Arndt were in some sense the forerunners of German fascism is one-sided and untenable.

(b) The Arabic Sources: the Social and Historical Philosophy of Ibn Khaldun

In Behrendt's terms,[95] the influence of the German Romantic idea of the nation on al-Husri must be considered as a 'syncretic' rather than a 'passive-imitative' form of acculturation. Although his theory is based on the German concept of the nation, it has also been combined with selected elements from Arab culture, and the synthesis consciously applied to the Arab situation. The most significant indigenous component of al-Husri's concept of nationalism is the social and historical philosophy of Ibn Khaldun.

Ibn Khaldun was a philosopher and statesman of the fourteenth century, whose fame rests largely on his *Muqaddima* (prolegomena, introduction)[96] to his voluminous *History*. This most remarkable work of historical and social philosophy, considered by Rosenthal as 'one of mankind's important triumphs'[97] and somewhat hyperbolically by Arnold Toynbee as 'undoubtedly the greatest work of its kind that has ever yet been created by any mind in any time or place',[98] was only discovered by European orientalists in the nineteenth century, and it has since become the subject of a considerable body of international scholarly writing.[99] al-Husri, who would have become acquainted with it in the course of his Ottoman education,[100] worked on it intensively during the Second World War. He published two lengthy volumes on Ibn Khaldun in 1943 and 1944, in which he gave his own interpretation based on a thorough analysis of the text and an evaluation of the international secondary literature. These volumes provide an estimation of the inherent qualities of the work and also of its contemporary relevance. They were republished in 1961 together with some of al-Husri's hitherto unpublished research on Ibn Khaldun in a 655-page volume which provoked considerable comment.[101] However, his synthesis of the German idea of the nation and Ibn Khaldun's philosophy considerably antedates the publication of these works. In his very first political writing (al-Husri, Vol. III), this synthesis, which will be discussed later, is clearly suggested. The following pages will concentrate on particular points in Ibn Khaldun's philosophy, particularly on his theory of '*asabiyya*, which plays an important role in al-Husri's theory in a modernised form.

Ibn Khaldun's main concern was to provide a theory which would clarify the question of how cohesive human groups, such as tribes, peoples, and so forth, form, the basis of their cohesion, the phases they pass through in the course of history, and the degree of cohesion each of them attains. According to Ibn Khaldun, '*asabiyya* is the bond which makes possible the solidarity of one group vis-à-vis other groups. Each group develops from a state of nomadic society towards civilisation and the formation of states. '*Asabiyya* is particularly pronounced in the nomadic phase: as the process of civilisation continues, its consistency decreases. As its '*asabiyya* withers away, so the group disintegrates, and its place is taken by groups whose '*asabiyya* is younger and therefore stronger. Thus every stage of civilisation is followed by its own downfall, and history is the circulation of social groups and their '*asabiyya*. This implies a view of history in which progress only takes place within the framework of ever-returning cycles, which explains why Ibn Khaldun's philosophy has received considerable attention from conservative European critics of culture and civilisation.

There has been a long and continuing debate amongst social scientists and orientalists on how the term '*asabiyya* should be best rendered in a European language.[102] Baron de Slane, who translated and published the *Muqaddima* between 1863 and 1868, rendered '*asabiyya* as *esprit de corps*, a translation which was generally considered inadequate. Rosenthal,[103] Ritter[104] and Ayad[105] compare '*asabiyya* with Machiavelli's *vertù*, and find considerable similarity between the two terms; hence Ritter equates it with *feeling of solidarity*. H. Simon considers *solidarity* to be the most appropriate translation, because it includes both the instinctive emotional and the conscious spheres, although he prefers to keep the Arabic term and explain it with a paraphrase.[106] As early as 1879, von Kremer had attempted to give a modern interpretation to the term, by rendering it as *concept of nationality*,[107] which was rejected by almost all orientalists. This was repeated by T. Khemiri in an essay in 1936, where '*asabiyya* is interpreted in the framework of a concept of nationalism.[108] However justifiable the resistance of most orientalists to a modern interpretation of Ibn Khaldun's categories may be, this problem must be secondary in the sense that the present interest in Ibn Khaldun is not exegetic; al-Husri quietly took up the modern interpretation and appropriated it into his own theories. For both al-Husri and Ibn Khaldun 'man' is a political animal, and the sociability of men is expressed in a national bond, which is described as *'asabiyya*.

According to Ibn Khaldun, *'asabiyya* takes various forms, corresponding to the historical cycle in which it appears. In primitive nomadic society, it is a form of solidarity based on the belief in blood relationship and common ancestry. However, Ibn Khaldun explicitly states that this form of consciousness has no substance, since *in reality* blood relationship and common ancestry do not exist.[109] But the belief in this bond strengthens the *'asabiyya* and thus by extension the group itself, and hence has a positive effect. In the next cycle *'asabiyya* is based upon relations of alliance and protection within the same group, and in the highest stage of socialisation, urban society, which has its own civilisation and culture, it creates a feeling of community and unity. This is based on 'social intercourse, comradeship, a long period of mutual scrutiny and trial and concern for one another. Furthermore this feeling develops between such people who have been brought up together who share a common destiny.'[110]

A feature of Ibn Khaldun's theory which induced al-Husri and von Kremer before him to project the modern secular idea of the nation on to this *community with a common destiny* was the role of religion in Ibn Khaldun's philosophy of history. For Ibn Khaldun, religion cannot replace *'asabiyya*; the religious bond cannot be the primordial form of social commitment.[111] However, *'asabiyya* finds its highest expression in a synthesis with religion, but in such a synthesis religion takes on the quality of a national religion, to speak in modern terms. As Ritter noted, it is an ideology which strengthens *'asabiyya*.[112] But it remains related to the members of an extended group, who are linked together through *'asabiyya*: it is no longer universal, but has been reduced to a political formula.[113] Von Kremer even goes so far as to say that Ibn Khaldun's theory secularises religion, so that 'in this respect too . . . [he] represents a school of thought which only became important in the West half a millenium later'.[114] Hence religion is only socially relevant to the degree to which it functions as an ideology of 'national' integration. The confusing religious sentences[115] which can be found on almost every page of the *Muqaddima*, are, as many authors have emphasised, a form of camouflage,[116] or, as others have cautiously suggested, simply lie on the surface of Ibn Khaldun's theories without touching their substance,[117] and cannot obscure their essentially secular character.[118] It is thus understandable that Ibn Khaldun has never been and is not, a favourite of Islamic orthodoxy, while he has been much read by Arab nationalists since al-Husri. The latter like to draw the attention of Europeans to Ibn Khaldun, in order to show them that the Arabs have also produced great thinkers as well as commentators on the Greek philosophers.[119]

7 The Foundations of Sati' al-Husri's Political Theory

Even in his earliest writings, al-Husri's main philosophical interests are clear. He takes the Greek myth of Pandora's box to illustrate the political situation which forms the starting point of his theory. The situation of the Arab countries resembles the situation in the world after the opening of Pandora's box: the Arabs are subject to all the evils of the world because they are divided, and are therefore weak and backward.[1] All that is left to them is hope. The focus of al-Husri's political interest is the national unification of the Arabs. He seeks to provide a theoretical foundation for this goal, and a means through which it may be achieved. Thus his political theory is exclusively concerned with the idea of the nation and its emergence and development, and his interest in other matters, such as education, remains confined within this general framework. Hence national education is the only meaningful form of education.

The main tenets of al-Husri's theory, which is a synthesis of the German idea of the nation and Ibn Khaldun's philosophy of history, had already been formulated in essays published in the 1920s, which were reissued in book form in 1944.[2] These early ideas were endlessly reproduced, with no evidence of any further revision or development, in a spate of later writings.[3] al-Husri's extensive and exceedingly influential writings always contain commentaries on and longwinded repetitions of the idea of the nation which he had formulated in the 1920s. The theoretical framework of this idea will now be discussed, and compared with other theories of the nation. Part IV will describe the detailed application of the theory to conditions in the Arab countries.

(a) The General Theoretical Framework

al-Husri considers the nineteenth century to be the age of nationalism, since this was the period in which the disintegration of the multi-national empires—Austria, Czarist Russia, the Ottoman Empire—began, from which independent states were to emerge. A further significant feature of the nineteenth century was the German and Italian irredentist movements, which led to the formation of the greater German or Italian state out of a number of petty states. In a series of lectures given in Cairo in 1948, later published in book form,[4] al-Husri describes the emergence of national states in Central, Eastern and Southern Europe in minute detail. Although providing an informative presentation of the historical material, al-Husri adds nothing to the theoretical definition of the phenomenon of the nation which he had already set out in his first political writings in the 1920s. He emphasised then that 'the idea of the nation has become the most important factor conditioning the formation of national states since the nineteenth century'.[5] The fact that the process of nation formation began in the nineteenth century[6] and not earlier is explained as follows:

> Before the nineteenth century patriotism meant loyalty to king and kingdom . . . each time a territory was annexed to a foreign kingdom . . . the inhabitants of that territory had to change their patriotism . . . they could do this because they believed that kings ruled in the name of God, and that their arbitrariness was the will of God. When this belief was shaken, and finally disappeared completely, a totally new situation was created. The idea of the nation now began to play a supremely important role in the formation of national states.[7]

al-Husri, who does not acknowledge any relationship between socio-economic and historical development, explains the process of nation formation in Europe in ideological and psychological terms. In his opinion, the notion of popular sovereignty, whose historical relativity he does not consider, contributed significantly to the weakening of the belief in the divine right of kings.[8] al-Husri associates this aspect of popular sovereignty with the emergence of the idea of the nation. From then on, power was derived from the people. This led immediately to the question of what was meant by the people, which itself led to the question of each people's claim to national statehood.[9] The kingdom became the substance of state organisation instead of the nation. This does not mean, however, that nationalities only emerged in the nineteenth century: they had existed since time immemorial, but it was only then that they were discovered and consciously perceived.[10]

al-Husri interprets the process of decolonisation and nation formation in Asia and Africa in categories similar to those he applies to nineteenth-century Europe. This was because 'the nineteenth century was the age of nationalism, but nationalism was confined to Europe. Thus the twentieth century is and will be the age of nationalism for all peoples.'[11] Because of its renaissance and achievements, Japan was the Asian country which refuted the Europeans' claim that the peoples of Africa and Asia are not capable of civilisation. 'As a result of this refutation, this claim necessarily became null and void.' Europeans and Americans now became obliged to concede the right of nation formation to all peoples, as illustrated by Woodrow Wilson 'granting' the right of self-determination to all colonial peoples.[12] The pan-movements, which were the carriers of decolonisation, were to be the substitutes for the developments which had already taken place in nineteenth-century Europe. Thus al-Husri turns first to the history of nineteenth-century Europe in order to draw lessons for the Arab national movement. His interpretation is entirely idealistic, seeing the European national movements as manifestations of ideas. He thus analyses the various European ideas of the nation in order to be able to explain history through them.

In his first political writings, al-Husri explains the German idea of the nation, which has been described above. He considers this to be the only correct one, and adopts it accordingly. The French idea of the nation, in the version formulated by Renan, is sketched briefly and found to be inaccurate, and the Marxist interpretation of the state as the product of bourgeois society is similarly dismissed.[13] In a later work he returns to this theme and produces a detailed analysis of the different ideas of the nation, without adding anything significantly new.[14] In this later version he distinguishes between four ideas of the nation: the *German*, which perceives of the nation in terms of the cultural nation, and the national language as the skeleton of national culture; the *French*, which makes the nation inconceivable without the national state, affiliation to which is not pre-determined but is the result of a voluntary act; the *Marxist*, which sees the nation in relation to the rise of capitalism, and finally the *religious*, represented by the Islamic modernists,[15] who equate religious and national affiliation, and who thus attempt to check secular nationalism.

When al-Husri says that these ideas correspond to different political situations, he is hinting at the fact that the difference between the French and German ideas of the nation is not entirely ideological.[16] However this aspect is not followed up, so that he cannot explain why France was able to constitute itself into a nation early on, and why the nation could become the legitimation of the authority of the bourgeois state, while in Germany, which remained divided until 1871, socio-economic and political backwardness was compensated for by a transcendence from the national to the cultural sphere. Since he does not adequately investigate the historical circumstances in which the German and French ideas of the nation developed, he loses sight of his original intentions in the course of the argument. He wants to provide a theoretically convincing foundation for his call for the setting up of a Pan-Arab national state to overcome the national division of the Arabs. However, his writings show that his main concern eventually became to prove that the German idea of the nation was universally applicable, and that the French idea was generally mistaken. In the course of this he falls into an occasionally rapturous germanophilia, with obvious overtones of francophobia.[17]

According to al-Husri, each individual belongs to several different groups which require qualitatively different forms of social commitment.[18] However 'the strongest and most effective tie is the national tie, which derives from a common language and history'.[19] The nation is the institutional expression of this form of social commitment. 'Each nation develops its own moral character, leads its own life, has its own consciousness, and is of a specific kind.'[20] In this way the nation is defined in terms of a national personality. He compares the members of the nation to the cells of an organism, although 'the structure of a biological organism is material, and obeys the laws of matter . . . while the social organism is immaterial and is not governed by the laws of matter'.[21] Language is the decisive bond which holds together the members of the social organism, the nation. 'The life of the nation depends on its language . . . the death of a nation is the loss of its language.'[22] This is because language is the 'soul of the nation and the most important element in it',[23] it is even 'the most important non-material link between the individual and the other members of a social group, because it is the instrument of communication, . . . of thought, . . . and not least, of the heritage of ideas and cultural achievements'.[24] Thus the nation is nothing but a group of people speaking the same language: nations are 'principally distinguished from each other by the fact that they speak different languages, and the separate existence of each one of them is based on this, their own language'.[25] As long as the nation takes care of its language, it will stay alive and have its own personality. If a nation comes under foreign rule, its continued existence will depend entirely on its capacity to maintain and develop its language. If a nation is able to keep its language alive under foreign rule 'it can one day win back its freedom and autonomy, because, due to the fact that it has kept its language, it remains alive and does not lose its existence as a nation, although it may have lost its statehood to foreign rule. A nation, however, which . . . has given up its own language with the passage of time, and has taken up the language of a foreign power, is a dead nation . . .'[26] Such statements suggest a close relationship between the ideas of al-Husri and of Herder, which the former does not disavow. He gives a number of quotations from Herder's writings, and comes to the conclusion that he was a pioneer of the idea of the nation adopted by al-Husri himself.[27] This idea of the nation is a 'corrective' to the French one, which distinguishes between nationality and nation, and only permits the nation to exist within the framework of a national state.[28] However, al-Husri criticises Herder for his non-committal definition of the idea of the nation. It is true that Herder has correctly recognised that people, nation, and nationality are synonymous, describing a group of people with a common language, and a common heritage which constitute a national history. However, Herder has not seen that the cultural nation needs a national state in its territory, without which it is bound to remain weak and divided.[29] al-Husri considers that this weakness has been made good by Herder's successors, who were not satisfied with the establishment of a German cultural nation, but demanded a German national state. 'At the peak of this new generation of German thinkers stand the philosopher Fichte and the poet Arndt.'[30] al-Husri quotes long passages from Fichte's *Addresses* and enriches them with extracts from Arndt's poems. While Fichte gave the German idea of the nation a stringently philosophical character, Arndt gave it a 'fascinating' and 'artistically attractive' form.[31]

The national awakening of an oppressed national community

begins with the revival of language and traditions which have been supplanted by foreign rule. al-Husri considers the language and tradition of a people as its 'common memory'. Thus the efforts of the Slavs Palacki, Safaryk and Kollar to revive the Czech language, inspired by Herder, reflect the awakening of the Czech nation.[32] Taking care of the national language and history will lead to national consciousness.[33] Furthermore, reference to the glorious history of a people has the function of helping it to overcome the misery of the present through the remembrance of the past.[34]

While language is the soul of the nation, its history is its consciousness. 'The nation which keeps its language and forgets its history is like a man who lives in a state of unconsciousness. His life is only invested with meaning when he reawakens and once more regains his buried consciousness.'[35] Therefore, emphasises al-Husri, following Herder, the conquerors will always try to extinguish the language as well as the common memory of the peoples whom they subjugate.[36]

It is well known that Mazzini's definition of the nation goes beyond that of the German Romantics, since he sees the nation not only in terms of an organic cultural entity, but also in terms of a biological entity, due to the common origin of its members.[37] In his discussion of Mazzini's theory, al-Husri criticises racialist notions as such, following Herder and Ibn Khaldun[38] and rejects any common origin of a social group united into a people,[39] although he agrees with Ibn Khaldun that belief in a common descent might at times have a positive effect on the cohesion of a group.[40] Following Ibn Khaldun again, he also rejects the claim that religion can form a basis for social commitment, as religious practice is always carried out in a language, so that the close relationship between language and religion can only allow one possibility, that of a national religion.[41] He tries to bolster his thesis by referring to Fichte's interpretation of the Reformation as a German national movement.[42] The failure of the universal religions (Islam and Christianity) and the success of national religions (Judaism) to construct and consolidate a cohesive community appear to him to provide historical evidence for his position.[43] He uses this argument against the Pan-Islamists, who saw Pan-Islamism as an alternative to secular Pan-Arabism, as will be seen in more detail in Chapter 8.

al-Husri's basic ideas can be precisely summarised in his own words:

A common language and a common history is the basis of nation formation and nationalism. The union of these two spheres leads to a union of emotions and aims, sufferings, hopes, and culture. Thus the members of one group see themselves as members of a unitary nation, which distinguishes itself from others. However neither religion nor the state nor a shared economic life are the basic elements of a nation, and nor is common territory . . . If we want to define the role of language and history for a nation we can say in short that the language is the soul and the life of the nation, but history is its memory and its consciousness.[44]

In order to anticipate his critics, al-Husri immediately takes examples which might be used against his definition of the nation, such as Belgium, Switzerland, and so on. It is not worth entering more deeply into this dispute,[45] especially as al-Husri only repeats his theory in order to conclude that although Switzerland is a state, it is not a nation, and then to claim that the various members of the population of Switzerland feel that they belong to the original nation whose language they speak.[46]

Taking up Fichte's suggestion of a national education to overcome the misery of the German defeat at Jena in 1806,[47] al-Husri discusses the problem of education in general. He considers it to be the best means of initiating the national awakening of oppressed people. He particularly stresses the importance of the teaching of history and calls for nationally orientated historical research, emphasising the 'glorious' past in order to provide a basis for the national awakening.[48] He also sees national education as a means of spreading belief in the nation. 'The struggle for the national awakening requires much more effort and hardship to spread belief in the nation, and all available means must be used to strengthen this belief.'[49] He considers military service a suitable medium for effective national education. 'The barracks are as much institutes for national education as the national schools.'[50] This is because in military life the individual must overcome his egoism and make sacrifices for the fatherland as well as learn to live under rigorous discipline. al-Husri considers these to be the most important objectives of national education, and as an active educationalist he devoted his whole life to bringing them to fruition.[51]

(b) al-Husri's Attack on the French Idea of the Nation: his Critique of Renan

Before discussing al-Husri's critique of the French idea of the nation, in the concise and influential form put forward by Renan, it is useful to give a brief account of Renan's theory.

In a lecture at the Sorbonne in 1882 Renan gave his definition of the nation, which reflected the whole tradition of French and Western European liberal democratic national thought. In this lecture, the famous *Que est-ce qu'une nation?*,[52] Renan shows that a number of forms of socialisation have existed in history up until the present time, none of which have known the phenomenon of the nation. The nation is a product of modern history.[53] He stresses emphatically that nation formation in modern Europe has never been influenced by determinist criteria. Boundary changes and the concentration of the heterogeneous populations of Europe into states under royal dynasties have been primarily the results of conquests. Thus nations are not manifestations of self-contained homogeneous groups of people with constant features of whatever kind; rather they are the historical products of state formation in Europe after the conquests.[54] The heterogeneous populations living in each of these newly emerged entities have adjusted themselves to one another and integrated themselves into homogeneous groups which are usually referred to as nations. The pre-conditions for such integration was that each group *forgot its origin* and identified itself with the new structure. In this way, for instance, the term 'Frenchman' emerged, which expresses affiliation to a certain entity, although the groups which combined to form this entity by no means share common ethnic, cultural etc. origins. Hence Renan considers that detailed historical research is a threat to national consciousness, especially as a return to ancient history may reveal the very different origins of those who now form a single nation. An inaccurately presented past which manages to conceal differences in origins is essential to create a sense of a single national affiliation.[55]

Having defined the nation as a product of modern history,[56] Renan discusses the various different interpretations of the phenomenon. He vigorously rejects the use of ethnographic and anthropological criteria in politics, which may present the nation as a unified race. He even believes that a confusion of the terms nation and race endangers progress and the principle of the nation,[57] since no pure race exists anywhere in the modern world. Even the French nation is a conglomerate of diverse European ethnic groups. To trace nation formation back to racial origins would be a chimera.[58] He goes on to say that the term *race* has developed in two different directions, in the anthropological-physiological sense of blood relationship, and in the philological-historical sense of a cultural community rooted in language and tradition. Renan rejects both these versions,[59] and also denies that language is a constituent of nation formation, since there are peoples speaking the same language who do not form a nation, and others who are united in a nation but do not speak the same language.[60] He rejects the idea of a single linguistically based cultural community, or cultural nation, particularly because it implies a national culture which negates human culture.[61] He stresses that human culture will always be superior to German, French, Italian etc. cultures, and that the great European thinkers were famous as humanists and not as carriers of national characteristics.[62] In the same way, neither religion,[63] common economic interests[64] nor geographical criteria can be the basis of nation formation.[65]

Renan defines the nation as a 'spiritual principle', 'a soul' emerging from the consciousness of a common past. The 'spiritual principle' of the nation is based not only on the sense of a common heritage and of a shared historical memory, but it also implies the wish to live together in the present and to enrich the heritage of the past.[66] Hence the nation is 'a daily plebiscite', in Renan's famous metaphor.[67] It can be enlarged by the absorption of new groups, and it can be reduced by secession. National affiliation cannot be forced upon a group, because that is based on free will (*nationalité élective*) and is in no way predetermined.[68] This definition expresses the fundamental features of the liberal-democratic idea of the nation, and also the most important differences between it and the organic idea of the nation, in which national affiliation is determined by either racial or cultural criteria. Because he believes in this liberal-democratic idea of the nation, in which free will is not allowed to founder, Renan can go beyond national thinking, in, for example, his rejection of the notion of a national culture. Furthermore he defines nations as transient structures, since he sees them as historical products: 'they have beginnings and will have ends'.[69] He does not exclude the possibility that the European nations might dissolve themselves into a single confederacy.[70]

The idea of the nation as defined by Renan does not assist al-Husri in his attempt to prove the existence of a unitary Arab nation.

On the contrary, al-Husri is concerned to show that the Arab people, who now live in a number of independent states, actually belong to a single all-Arab nation, and thus to provide the theoretical foundation for his demand for a Pan-Arab state. However, his attempts to do this are insufficiently consistent: instead of examining the French or German idea of the nation to see how far this or that aspect could be applied to the Arab countries, he tries to adduce a *general* proof that the French idea is false, and that the German is the only correct one. In doing this, he fails to examine the different ideological content of both definitions of the nation, which were conditioned by the different historical development of France and Germany. Turning the facts completely upside-down he even claims that the French idea of the nation developed as a reaction to the German one. This was because expansionist France saw its interests endangered by a definition of the nation as an organic cultural language community, because the territories which she annexed were not French-speaking but primarily·German-speaking.[71] As al-Husri sees it, French philosophers developed their voluntarist ideas of the nation in order to assist the process of annexation in the guise of *nationalité élective*. Accordingly, Renan shows himself in *Que est-ce qu'une nation?* not as a serious thinker but as an apologist for French interests. 'Renan's lecture resembles the speech of a clever lawyer, but not the enquiry of a serious scholar.'[72]

al-Husri considers that the differences between the German and French idea of the nation, as exemplified in Renan's lecture, have their origins in the remote past. In the second part of his series of lectures entitled *The Genesis of the Idea of the Nation*, al-Husri examines this question more thoroughly, under the heading *The Genesis of the Idea of the Nation in Germany, and the Conflict between the German and the French Ideas of the Nation*.[73] He begins his lecture with the characteristic sentence: 'The history of the unification of Germany provides some of the most interesting and most important pages of the history of the last century.'[74] This confident claim which comes at the very beginning, anticipates the tenor of the presentation which follows. He deplores the circumstances in which German thinkers turned away from the nation and gave themselves up to the 'illusion' of cosmopolitanism. He records with satisfaction the downfall of cosmopolitanism in favour of populist nationalism in Germany after the Napoleonic wars: the wars and the occupation of Germany 'produced an energetic reaction among the Germans. It became clear to everyone that the origin of their misery lay in the fact that they had neither unity nor national consciousness. Those thinkers who once paid homage to humanism and were proud to be cosmopolitans, which raised them above the fatherland, now saw the consequences to which this attitude had led . . .'[75] He then describes how German thinkers turned towards nationalism, taking Fichte as an example, and praising Arndt and other German writers who contributed to the creation of a German national consciousness. Finally he discusses the wars of liberation against Napoleon, siding with Germany against France throughout the whole period until the rise of Bismarck. He hails Bismarck as a 'genius' who became 'well-accquainted with the secret intentions of France and the mentality of the French people'[76] during his time as ambassador in Paris, so that he was well prepared for the battle with France. He has a high regard for Bismarck's policies. His presentation ends with the words: 'The unification of Germany was the greatest victory achieved by the idea of the nation in the nineteenth century.'[77] The passages discussed above indicate the prejudice with which al-Husri approaches the French idea of the nation, and his unreserved francophobia and germanophilia. This attitude has had almost unchallenged supremacy in the Middle East, especially as it was incorporated into school textbooks everywhere, with the result that several generations of Arabs grew up in a francophobe, germanophile tradition.

al-Husri explains his contention that 'the conditions and circumstances under which Germany was unified caused the emergence of different ideas of the nation'[78] as follows:

> divergent views came into existence, especially between the thinkers of Germany and France . . . the German thinkers supported the theory that the nation is a living organism which has developed organically through common language and history, which—like all living organisms—is determined by subjective impulses. They also stated that language was the most important element in nation formation, and that it must therefore be a leading factor in state formation. The French rejected this theory, since it could only do them harm, especially as they had expansionist intentions across the Rhine, and because it would support the German theory of the secession of a part of French territory. This was the only reason why they opposed this theory so forcefully, and why they developed a contrary theory of their own, that of *nationalité élective*.[79]

Renan's lecture *Que est-ce qu'une nation?* is seen in the context of the controversy between Fustel de Coulanges and Mommsen[80] on the question of whether Alsace-Lorraine was German or French, during which Mommsen drew on German determinist and de Coulanges on French voluntarist theories to bolster their own arguments. al-Husri first summarises Renan's lecture in detail,[81] and then proceeds to criticise it vehemently. Following Renan's definition of the nation as the result of a plebiscite amounts to saying that national communities have come about as the result of elections. However, elections are not based on the free will of the electors, because they have been influenced by election propaganda beforehand.[82] al-Husri, who tirelessly emphasises the scientific character of his theory, accuses Renan of being unscientific, because he would otherwise have recognised that the will to live together can only emerge in a pre-existing national community, so that the will to belong to a nation is the result of, rather than the pre-condition of, nation formation.[83] Renan himself pointed out that the nations of Europe are not the result of a plebiscite but of contests and arbitrary state formation in various territories.[84]

al-Husri launches a direct attack on Renan's theory that language is not a basic component of nation formation. He refers to the individual structure of each language, and emphasises that the same things cannot be thought in every language. Relying heavily on Fichte, but tacitly discarding his theory of an 'original language', al-Husri agrees with Renan that the European nationalities have been formed as a result of integration. However, this integration has arisen primarily because the inhabitants of a single territory have made the same mother tongue their own, so that language must eventually be recognised as part of the formation of every nation.[85]

al-Husri also rejects later modifications of Renan's notion of *nationalité élective*. He refers to one of the most important, that of Henri Hauser. In an influential study published in 1916,[86] Hauser has stressed that although language is a part of nation formation, it is only so when a homogeneous group speaking the same language agree to live together, as had happened, for instance, among the inhabitants of divided Poland. al-Husri dismisses this synthesis of German and French ideas as tautological,[87] showing once more that he was not primarily concerned to provide a critical analysis of the process of nation formation and the phenomenon of the nation, but to put forward a point of view which would serve his own political ends, and to defend it vigorously. He insists that a unitary Arab nation exists, because the Arab peoples have a common language and live in the same tradition. The organic unity of the Arab nation will find political expression in the same way as Germany in 1871. al-Husri sees resistance to the idea of Arab unity on the part of any of the Arab peoples as evidence of manipulated consciousness; it can in no way put into question the supposedly scientifically proved existence of a unitary Arab nation. This also explains his intransigence towards the French idea of the nation, which allows the individual and small groups the right to self-determination and the choice of national affiliation. As will be discussed below, he takes an equally entrenched view of the Egyptian liberal nationalists, who supported the idea of a sovereign Egyptian nationality.

(c) al-Husri's Criticism of Marxism[88]

Apart from a critique of proletarian internationalism, there is no detailed critique of Marxism in al-Husri's early political writings. This only appears in a series of lectures given in the late 1940s which was published in 1959.

The general concern of al-Husri's early writings is the German idea of the nation as formulated in the age of the Romantics, the features which distinguish it from contemporary Western ideas, and the question of its application to the Arab situation. In this context he only refers to proletarian internationalism because he sees in it a revival of the cosmopolitanism of the Enlightenment, and he vehemently attacks both these currents. He rejects cosmopolitanism, because he claims that although it originally grew out of a desire for perfection it actually leads to passivity. 'Cosmopolitanism is a platonic attitude: it does not prompt the individual to immediate action, and does not expect any sacrifices from him. In contrast patriotism is a realistic attitude . . . To turn away from patriotism to cosmopolitanism is equivalent to turning towards apathy and passivity . . .'[89] In this context al-Husri refers to the controversy between Rousseau and Voltaire. He quotes Rousseau's criticism of the cosmopolitans, where Voltaire is accused of loving the Tatars to make himself exempt from love of fatherland.[90] The dangers of cosmopolitanism become most evident in German history, and here al-Husri's explanations demonstrate the one-sidedness of his germanophilia. The German Jacobins and those cosmopolitans influenced by the Enlightenment are subjected to vigorous polemic. He makes the ideas of these philosophers responsible for the division of Germany and its political subjugation, rather than the socio-economic and political backwardness of the country.[91] It took the defeat of Jena to teach these philosophers a lesson and to make them give up their 'humanistic and cosmopolitan dreams'.[92] From the experience of this defeat he constructs the aphorism: 'We can say that patriotism has emerged whole and victorious from the battle with the idea of cosmopolitanism in all its variations.'[93]

With the spread of Marxism, patriotism was forced to prove itself once again. al-Husri positively defines proletarian internationalism as a new variant of cosmopolitanism, without considering the fact that Marx was one of the severest critics of cosmopolitanism and its national nihilism.[94] This new 'variant' he claims, contains 'far greater dangers' than the original cosmopolitanism. He does not attempt to argue against proletarian internationalism, but simply calls it 'a new and very dangerous enemy'[95] and is content with the conclusion that 'naturally, patriotism has not neglected the struggle with this new enemy. It has mobilised its forces with all steadfastness and great energy for the conflict with proletarian internationalism.'[96] This almost propagandist attack on proletarian internationalism, made in the 1930s, was supplemented further some six years later, although the exact date is not given.[97] Here he documents what he alleges to be the transformation from internationalism to Soviet patriotism in the Soviet Union,[98] and adds with satisfaction: 'Now patriotism has been victorious over internationalism even in Soviet Russia. The Soviet state has gradually abandoned internationalism, until finally the Comintern was dissolved and even gave up the *Internationale* . . .'[99]

Although he was one of the pioneers of Arab nationalist anti-Communism, al-Husri strictly denies the charge of anti-Communism: 'I have no quarrel with those who call for Socialism, not even with those who call for Communism. But I demand from them that they do not confuse their appeals with internationalism, and thus become anti-national.'[100] He argues that internationalism is particularly dangerous in backward countries, where the national idea and national solidarity are still weak, while in the advanced countries, where nationalism has already taken root, internationalism no longer poses a threat. Especially in the Arab countries, internationalism has had devastating effects; its influence upon them and upon national unity has been 'lethal'.[101] It must be stressed that al-Husri does not take backwardness to mean socio-economic underdevelopment, but a state of society in which national awakening has not taken place, and in which national consciousness is weak.

The early al-Husri is satisfied with an understanding of Marxism based on hearsay. In the late 1940s, however, he began to study the Marxist analysis of nationalism more closely and in 1959 he published a more detailed study of Marxism for the first time.[102] However, from another of his publications it becomes clear that what appeared in 1959 consisted in fact of lectures delivered between 1944 and 1947.[103] Thus the claim of Elias Murqus[104] that al-Husri's extensive critique of Marxism was a reaction to the bloody battle of Mosul between Iraqi Communists and Pan-Arab nationalists in 1959 is without foundation.[105] It is possible that the events of Mosul encouraged him to publish these lectures, though this too seems improbable, since the critique of Marxism is not central to the lectures of 1944–7.[106] Furthermore, there is no reference whatever to the events of Mosul in the 1959 book, which only contains theoretical arguments.

In a publication in 1951, al-Husri rounds on all critics of Pan-Arabism, without mentioning any names or groups. They 'consider the differences in the economic interests of each Arab country to be of paramount significance only because they hold to a theory which claims that economic interests are the primary determinants of the course of the world and of history'.[107] The accusation that Pan-Arabism ignores the differences in the mode of production between individual Arab countries is considered irrelevant. He admits that within any national structure—in this case, the Arab countries—different socio-economic formations exist, but these would not break up the nation, but rather hold it together since they are secondary social phenomena. Hence he concludes typically that these objections are invalid 'and cannot stand up to serious investigation or scholarly criticism'.[108] These comments appear in more extended form in the 1959 book which has been referred to above. Here he emphasises that

> all countries have . . . agricultural regions, industrial regions and trading regions, and in some countries we find holiday and recreation regions on the one hand and spas on the other. Certainly, the interests of these regions conflict . . . but a wise government unites the variety of interests within itself and reconciles them with one another in order to pursue a single

common interest . . . we can therefore assert that it is against all reason and logic to claim that economic interests are a necessary component of nation formation.[109]

Two pages later he writes: 'It must be added to all that has been said that utilitarian interests, material considerations, and the economy are not everything in human life; ideological and moral factors also play a decisive role and even influence economic activity.'[110] His comments on the different modes of production in the Arab countries and the last quotation clearly shows his simplistic understanding of Marxism, for which he alone is not responsible, but for which all Arab Communist Parties must share responsibility, since they have been diffusing a form of vulgar Marxism for decades.[111]

al-Husri takes the discoveries of the nineteenth century as proof of his claim that ideas exist independently of the material sphere. He makes a comparison between the allegedly non-materially motivated scientist and those with national aspirations and arrives at the claim that 'national emotions are never connected with utilitarian thought or economic or material interests. They are supra-material passions and emotions which resemble the love of children for their mothers and vice-versa . . .'[112] Finally he brings an example to illustrate his thesis that the economy can in no way be of primary social relevance, and that it has no connection with nation formation. He argues that when a colonial power conquers a country it can immediately take over and control the occupied country's economy but it cannot destroy the national language nor control the historical memory of the population. If the colonial power should ever succeed in this, it could only take place under special conditions and as a result of efforts lasting for generations. 'This fact alone is sufficient to disprove all possible theories which attempt to establish a connection between economy and nation.'[113]

Having made these generalisations, al-Husri begins a more detailed study of the Marxist analysis of nationalism. He is unaware of Marx' position on the national question or the multitude of Marxist writings on this subject.[114] He only knows Stalin's *Marxism and the National Question*, published in 1913, and Lenin's famous article *The Right of Nations to Self-Determination*. He briefly discusses Stalin's contribution, concentrating on his definition of the nation as a 'historically constituted stable community of people, formed on the basis of a common language, territory, economic life and psychological make-up manifested in a common culture'.[115] al-Husri singles out 'historically developed' for particular criticism, since he considers the nation not to be something that has emerged historically, but a structural constant of human history. Furthermore, he vehemently opposes the suggestion that language and economic life are of equal importance for the emergence of nations. Thus Stalin's theory is 'wildly wrong, to such an extent that its falsity is evident, even axiomatic'.[116] In his discussion of Lenin's interpretation of the national question,[117] al-Husri concentrates on the thesis that the national state is a typical product of rising capitalism. al-Husri insists that nationalities in fact already existed before the nineteenth century, but that it was only then that the processes of the formation of national consciousness began, in the course of which nationalities became manifest. Those who claim that national states have only come into existence since capitalism are wrong, in the same way as those who claim that steam did not exist before James Watt.[118]

al-Husri argues in this fashion throughout his writings. It becomes increasingly evident to the reader that he continually emphasises that 'science', 'logic' and not least 'reason' support and verify his theories and refute those of other thinkers. It is only possible to give the merest impression of these tactics, which are not peculiar to al-Husri, but are also found in almost all modern Arab political writing. They have the obvious function of creating the impression in the mind of the Arab reader that the author is making use of modern European science to bolster his arguments, which thus gain increased credibility. In a short glossary of terms in modern Arabic, Kamel Abu Jaber defines the adjective *'ilmi* (scientific) and its synonyms as follows: 'These expressions are normally used to distinguish the more from the less modern. "Scientific" expresses acknowledgement, because it includes the idea of objectivity, lack of prejudice, and that which is practical as against superstition and tradition . . .'.[119] al-Husri's insistence on the scientific nature of his approach must be understood in this sense. It is hardly possible for him to uphold any claim to rigorous scholarship. His work is less important for its philosophical content, or its methodology, than for the extraordinary influence which it has exerted not only on the intellectual climate in the Arab countries, but also on political practice there.

Part IV al-Husri's Theory in Action: Populist Pan-Arab Nationalism in Competition with other Political Currents in the Middle East

8 Pan-Arab Nationalism versus Pan-Islamism: The Role of Islam in al-Husri's Writings

(a) Preliminary Remarks

In the course of a long life (1882–1968) al-Husri was able to ensure that his ideas gained maximum publicity. He published frequently, and also managed to spread his theories in the course of his employment as an educationalist in various Arab countries. The application of his general theory to the specific conditions of the Arab world appeared in the form of painstaking historical works on the genesis of the Arab national movement, as well as in polemics and controversies with representatives of other political currents in the Arab Middle East.

The general framework of the Arab national movement has already been described. Accordingly, this section will concentrate on al-Husri's exposition of the phenomenon, and on his discussions and disagreements with other Arab nationalists, notably the Pan-Islamists, the Egyptian nationalists, and the Syrian Social Nationalist Party.

al-Husri's systematic account of the history of the Arab countries under Ottoman rule[1] is a classic of its kind. He gives a detailed description of the way in which the Arab lands became a part of the Empire[2] and an account of the general stagnation into which the Arab world fell under Ottoman rule,[3] as a result of characteristics inherent in the social structure of the Empire. According to al-Husri, the wave of modernisation during the Tanzimat period[4] particularly affected the Arab countries, because the modernisation of social institutions was accompanied by a more rigorous political centralisation, which included a more systematic and hence more effective

161

Turkification of the Arab provinces. This tendency was given further impetus by the Young Turks, who followed a Turanian nationalism[5] which had the effect of creating a national opposition among the Arab populations whom they dominated. Hitherto, the peoples of the Ottoman Empire had been loyal to Ottoman rule because it appeared to represent the continuity of the Islamic caliphate. However, the rise of Turanianism weakened this loyalty, since Ottoman rule now seemed to have lost its Islamic content. al-Husri considers the Arab Revolt of 1916 to be the high watermark of the political consciousness of the 'Arab nation'. He sees the Arab state of Greater Syria, founded after the 1918 rising, as the 'first modern Arab national state', and devotes considerable attention to it. The invasion of Syria in 1920 by French colonial troops, who had been in occupation of the Lebanese coast since 1918, and who defeated the Syrian army at the battle of Maysalun on 24 July 1920 is the subject of al-Husri's lengthy work, *Yawm Maysalun* (The Day of Maysalun).[6] He believes that this day of defeat was one of the 'most important days in the modern history of the Arab nation'.[7] For al-Husri, who witnessed it, it was significant not only as a biographical detail but also because of its decisive importance for the whole Arab national movement. With the 'Day of Maysalun' a new phase in the movement began, that of francophobia and germanophilia, and this is also apparent in the book, where his animosity towards France is expressed in his description of French colonial rule.

However, al-Husri does not see the emergence of the Arab national movement purely in terms of a reaction against Turkification, which tried to force the Arabs to abandon their cultural heritage entirely: it was also and principally the result of the Arab cultural revival, which had been fostered by the Christian missions.[8] Even the Wahhabi revolt, although essentially an archaic religious movement, has, according to al-Husri, contributed indirectly to the Arab national movement, in that it sought to weaken the Ottoman Empire and to strengthen the Arab element in it.[9] The rise of Muhammad 'Ali also served national aspirations: it 'performed a great service for Arab nationalism . . ., because it made possible the existence of a modern state in an Arab country, where an Arab intellectual and literary renaissance could take place'.[10] However, the most crucial contribution to the Arab renaissance came from the Syro-Lebanese intellectuals, particularly the Christians, in the second half of the nineteenth century. Because of their religious affiliation, they did not feel any particular loyalty towards the Ottoman Empire, and it was thus much easier for them to press for an independent secular Arab state.[11] In contrast, their Muslim contemporaries had to suffer a severe conflict of loyalties before they could free themselves from the Empire and Islamic religious thinking. Hence, in the beginning they sought to harmonise the idea of the nation with Islam by advocating an *Arab* caliphate, as was done for instance by al-Kawakibi,[12] or by confining themselves to demands for national cultural autonomy for the Arabs within an Ottoman Empire sanctioned by Islam.[13] It was not only that the Arab Christians belonged to a religion different from the one which functioned as the state ideology which facilitated their espousal of secular nationalist thought: a further decisive factor was the education they received from the European and American missions. Here al-Husri excludes the French Catholic missions, who at first taught only in French, and who taught the Syro-Lebanese Catholics that they needed the protection of France against the Muslims, and thus actually ensured the loyalty of their pupils to French colonial rule in advance. The Russian Orthodox[14] and the American Protestant missions thought in somewhat longer terms.[15] They addressed themselves to all the Arabs, whom they sought to win over through the revival of Arabic language and culture, and thus to separate them from the Ottoman Empire. In this they eventually became so successful that even the Jesuit missions occasionally taught in Arabic.

The Arab Christian and Muslim nationalists who gathered in Paris in 1913 expressed their desire for national independence, although they were prepared to settle in the short term for the achievement of this autonomy within the framework of the Ottoman Empire. The Young Turks initially accepted these demands, but only to give themselves breathing space, as was to become evident later, when they liquidated the leaders of the Arab national movement who had organised the Congress in Paris.[16]

Apart from the Arabian Peninsula, those parts of the Arab world which became European colonies after the First World War (North Africa having already reached colonial status at various times in the nineteenth century), developed, as al-Husri frequently admits, in a number of different political directions. He accuses those Arabs who have developed a form of nationalism confined to their own region, such as the Egyptian nationalists, of not having grasped the fact that the borders they defend have been drawn by colonialism. '*We rebelled against the English and the French; we rebelled against those*

who conquered our homeland and who tried to subjugate it . . . but
when we had liberated ourselves from them, we began to hallow the
borders which they had drawn in our country . . .'[17] al-Husri reduces
the various political schools which are opposed to Pan-Arabism to
(1) local patriots of all kinds, (2) those who mourn the passing of the
Ottoman Empire, and (3) cosmopolitans and internationalists. He
fights with equal vehemence against all three currents, both in
outright controversies and in writings about Arab culture and
language, which seek to prove, along the lines of the German idea of
the nation, that a unitary Arab nation exists; it only lacks a united
national state.[18]

(b) al-Husri's Interpretation of al-Afghani

Pan-Islamism, founded by al-Afghani as a political and religious
response to colonialism, has already been defined as the ideological
weapon of Islamic modernism. It has also been mentioned that al-
Afghani gave up the notion of Pan-Islamism as a national state as
soon as he realised that 'Abd al-Hamid II was misusing this ideology
to consolidate his own rule against the rising national movements in
the Ottoman Empire. In his later writings he no longer postulated a
Pan-Islamic state as the institutional framework for Islamic society,
and began to see Pan-Islamism as an expression of Muslim anti-
imperialist solidarity. However, al-Afghani did not simply reduce
Pan-Islamism to this formula; at the same time, he began to
recognise the sub-Islamic national structures of the Persians, the
Indian Muslims and the Arabs, although this development in his
thought has been systematically ignored by supporters of Pan-
Islamism. After the collapse of the Ottoman Empire, the Pan-
Islamic Caliphate movement, which united all conservative forces
and accused the Arab national movement of being responsible for
the downfall of the Empire, claimed al-Afghani as its spiritual
father. This claim not only fails to take al-Afghani's later development into account, but also suppresses the fact that his main aim was
to fight against colonialist influence in the Muslim world. The post-
war Caliphate movement, on the other hand, was in overt alliance
with the forces of reaction and imperialism.[19]

al-Husri's argument with Pan-Islamism, which he saw as a
challenge to Pan-Arab nationalism, was conducted on two levels. In
the first place, he refers back to the spiritual sources of Pan-

Islamism. Although he points out the different stages in al-Afghani's political thinking, he misinterprets him in the same manner as the Pan-Islamists. Unlike them, however, he stresses the significance of his later work and glosses over his early Pan-Islamist period. Secondly, al-Husri argues with the Pan-Islamists on a general theoretical level, and as usual quotes his own theories to refute their views.

Before discussing al-Husri's interpretation of al-Afghani, it is useful to examine al-Afghani's political theories in greater detail. According to al-Afghani, mankind consists of various communities, whose existence is vested in the will of God. The individual can only exist in the community. Each community (*umma*) is 'like a living organism, with its own limbs, which are directed by a single soul, so that every community is like a man, who is different from all other men in the stages of his life, his concerns, his fortunes and his misfortunes'.[20] He distinguishes between the two forms of social commitment which hold such organisms together, the national and the religious bond. He gives priority to the religious bond: Islam is more integrative and culturally loaded than any national commitment. 'Muslim history from the rise of Islam to the present day shows that Muslims have acknowledged the bond of religion over and above any racial bond or national group solidarity. This is why the Turks and the Persians have no objection to the rule of the Arabs, and the Indian subordinates himself to the Afghan . . . as long as the ruler follows the *shari'a*.'[21] Hence he does in fact acknowledge the existence of nationalities, although with a different degree of emphasis in each of his writings. But he always stresses that it is only Islam which can be the foundation of nationality for the Muslims, because it has proved itself superior to other forms of association. Hence the pre-Islamic Arabs did not manage to generate major cultural achievements, and were even unable to unite themselves on the basis of a common Arab identity: these primitive tribes lived in constant feud with one another. It was only Islam 'which could, in a short time, raise the Arab nation (*umma*), deeply rooted in savagery (*tawahhush*) and barbarism, to the highest level of wisdom and civilisation'.[22]

These ideas form the general framework of al-Afghani's political thinking, whose substance changed according to the historical situation. In the period when he was co-operating with Abd al-Hamid II[23] al-Afghani postulated a state for the Islamic *umma*, which he considered to have been brought into being in the Ottoman

Empire, and sanctioned by Islam. After his disenchantment with
Abd al-Hamid's despotism, he renounced Ottomanism[24] and
considerably altered his notions of the state framework of the
Islamic *umma*. The believers, whom God has made brothers, should
unite 'to enable them through their unity to create a dam to protect
them from all the floods streaming towards them! But I do not mean
to insist that all Muslims should have a single ruler, since *this would
probably be difficult to achieve*. I demand, however, that their
supreme Lord should be the Qur'an and that religion should be the
basis of their unity.'[25] It is only this unity, within the framework of
an Islam based on the achievements of modern science and
technology, that is, of a modernised Islam, which can protect the
Muslims from the colonial system and ensure them the ultimate
victory over their colonial rulers. 'The colonial powers direct their
gaze towards those countries with rich resources and fertile soils,
whose populations are sunk in ignorance, and have reached such a
state of idleness that they no longer do a hand's turn, and are no
longer prepared to engage in conflict.'[26]

Having turned away from the Ottoman abuse of Pan-Islamism,
and having reduced the Pan-Islamic bond to a primarily anti-
colonial form of consciousness, al-Afghani was now in a position to
address the individual Islamic peoples, and to mobilise their
national feelings against colonialism. Accordingly he supported the
national struggle of the Egyptians against the British colonial
system. 'If the Egyptians united themselves and raised themselves
into a nation (*umma*) which would fight for its independence, and if
they refused to accept anything else, and could endure the repression
which the struggle would bring . . . then one could almost con-
gratulate them on their independence in advance.'[27] He also defends
the Arab cultural heritage against Renan's accusations that the
Arabs, like all Semites, are not a creative people; Arab philosophy,
Renan says, has been developed by Muslims of non-Arab origin.[28]
Clearly, as in his early phase in India, al-Afghani's writings on this
subject inevitably have an air of pragmatism. Nikki Keddie points
out: 'It is within the context of pragmatic anti-imperialist and anti-
foreign goals that one can make sense of Afghani's contradictory
writings on national versus religious ties.'[29] The Egyptian author
'Ammara has wrongly interpreted al-Afghani's later writings on
nationalism as showing 'national maturity'.[30] This explanation in
some sense also contradicts his own more or less correct interpretation of al-Afghani's rejection of Ottoman Pan-Islamism,

which 'Ammara sees not as a rejection of Pan-Islamism as such but of the Ottoman Empire, in order to formulate a theory of anti-colonialism.[31] For al-Afghani, Islam remained the guiding principle throughout his life. In contrast to 'Ammara, Keddie has succeeded in making an accurate and comprehensive assessment of his work. 'His main role was rather to use Islam as an ideology—to strengthen its position as a focus of identity and solidarity against the attacks of the Christian West, and to use it as a rallying point for the repulsion of Western Conquerors.'[32] In short, al-Afghani's political theory is an 'Islamic Response to Imperialism', in the words of the title of Keddie's selection of his writings.

As has already been noted, al-Husri makes no mention of the fact that before he broke with Sultan 'Abd al-Hamid, al-Afghani recognised him as the Caliph of the Muslims and the Ottoman Empire, and the Ottoman Empire as the institutional framework of Pan-Islamism. He begins his exposition of al-Afghani's ideas by quoting extracts from articles which the latter had published in 1884 in the short-lived review *al-'Urwa al-Wuthqa* (The Unbreakable Bond) during his exile in Paris together with his pupil Muhammad Abduh.[33] These articles contain the sentence which has just been quoted, in which al-Afghani emphasises that he does not intend Pan-Islamism to mean that all Muslims should live in a single state under a single ruler. al-Husri uses this quotation as the evidence for his allegation that al-Afghani never demanded a state framework for Pan-Islamism. Indeed he is supposed to have been 'very far away' from this idea.[34] For al-Afghani, Pan-Islamism means 'friendships, solidarity, compromise, and exchange of ambassadors'.[35]

al-Husri refers to a number of passages in al-Afghani's writings in which the latter deals with the difference between national and religious communities. al-Husri correctly states that al-Afghani does not deny the existence of nationalities in general, and points out that he also emphasises that Muslims can do without the national bond because they possess in Islam a superior form of social commitment, which implies that the national bond is in some way in conflict with the principles of the Islamic *shari'a*.[36] al-Husri tries to show that this interpretation changes in the course of al-Afghani's intellectual development. al-Husri quotes passages in which the reader almost hears al-Husri himself speaking, for instance in his description of al-Afghani's definition of language as an integral part of the cohesion of every social group:

We can observe that the populations of many lands which have been conquered by foreigners have maintained their national language in spite of foreign rule. In the course of their history, these peoples have been able to rise and regain their freedom, and unite all those who speak their language. The course of this development is entirely determined by the fate of the language. If these peoples had lost their language, they would have lost their history at the same time, and forgotten their glory, and would have ended in a state of servitude . . .[37]

Such a formulation could easily have come from the quill of either Herder or al-Husri. However, al-Husri uses it for his own purposes and isolates it from the main stream of al-Afghani's thought. It is important to emphasise that al-Afghani was not a political philosopher in a strict sense, but more of a political agitator. His political writings are either in the form of occasional works, dictated to a secretary, or notes of his lectures taken down by his pupils. He never seriously attempted to put down his political ideas in the form of a systematic theory. In spite of this, all his works contain a single common feature: they are *an appeal to the Muslims, as the objects of colonialism, in an attempt to mobilise them against European colonial rule*. This dimension seems to have escaped al-Husri entirely. He confines himself to an imprecise analysis of the texts, only citing passages which would prove his own case. Here al-Husri attaches particular significance to a newly discovered work of al-Afghani's which first appeared in Persian: this was translated into Turkish in 1913, and only became more widely known through a French translation published in 1958.[38] Its precise date cannot be accurately established. In it al-Afghani says that language is the basis of nationality, and that it provides a firmer basis for social commitment than religion. There are many peoples who have changed their religion without having lost their identity, which would not be possible if they had lost their national language.[39] al-Husri tries to prove that since this text was translated into Turkish, al-Afghani must have been considered a pioneer of Turkish nationalism by the Turkish nationalists themselves, while the Arabs know him primarily as Pan-Islamist.[40]

According to al-Husri, al-Afghani's thinking went through three stages of development: first, an overemphasis of religious as against national bonds; second, the recognition of the existence of nationalities as homogeneous structures; third, the recognition of a greater degree of homogeneity of nationalities as cultural communities based on a national language as against the homogeneity of social groups united on the basis of religion. al-Husri accuses al-Afghani of a general inability to distinguish between reality and wishful thinking. For al-Husri, reality is the existence of nationalities; wishful thinking is the notion of a homogeneous Islamic *umma*. He also alleges that al-Afghani's writings are not well reasoned and are full of mistakes,[41] which illustrates his own failure to understand that these writings are primarily demagogic in character.

It has already been made clear that Arab nationalism in the 1920s, which was strongly influenced by al-Husri, has its primary ideological roots in the political theories of the German Romantics. In the discussion of al-Afghani's political ideas it has been shown that neither he nor al-Husri considers the individual as a separate entity, but rather as a member of a community. For al-Afghani, this community is religious, while for al-Husri it is cultural. Due to the affinity between these two definitions, the question must arise whether, in fact, al-Husri's notion of community does not after all contain some Islamic features, and is not a mere reproduction of the German notion of the national spirit. Sylvia Haim, who has done research into the Arab national movement, has produced a study of the notion of community in the works of both al-Afghani and al-Husri. In her view, al-Husri's notion of *umma* can be unambiguously translated as 'nation' in the European sense, while al-Afghani's *umma* cannot be directly translated into modern terminology.[42] She shows that similar ideas already existed in classical Islamic political philosophy. Ibn Taimiyya, who died in 1328, denied the separate entity of the individual, and compared the body of Muslims to an organism which he called the 'Islamic *umma*'.[43] Hence al-Afghani's notion of the *umma* may not be of exclusively European origin, although his thinking shows strong European features. However, these European influences are only accepted by al-Afghani to the extent to which they are compatible with Islam, as has been noted in Chapter 4. In contrast, al-Husri's nationalism can be said to have been little influenced by Islam—if his debt to Ibn Khaldun is excludèd, and in any case, Ibn Khaldun is hardly representative of traditional Islamic thought. Haim correctly stresses that al-Husri's ideas 'are only to be understood in the light of romantic European thought . . . but the Islamic tradition apparent in the extracts from Jamal al-Din and Muhammad 'Abduh is still too strong to allow one

to give ready made European equivalents to the Arabic expressions
which confront the reader.'[44]

A closer comparison of al-Husri's and al-Afghani's definition of
the *umma* shows that Haim has correctly concluded that the most
important difference lies in the fact that al-Husri sees the *umma* as an
autonomous entity while al-Afghani derives it from the Will of
God.[45] A further difference, which is closely connected to this, is
that:

> Traditionally, a Muslim has to be solidary (sic) with the *umma*
> because the Qur'an dictates it and Islam expects it. But Sati' al-
> Husri bases his doctrine on individual feelings. It is the individual
> who feels the call of tradition, it is he who feels that he must
> answer it, it is he who does not feel fulfilment and total realisation
> if he does not lose himself in his nation. *Fichte and not the Qur'an
> inspires Sati' al-Husri.*[46]

It can therefore be asserted that al-Husri's definition of the *umma*
is not a secularisation of the orthodox Islamic concept, as formulated systematically in the political philosophy of Ibn Taimiyya,
and restated in modernised form by al-Afghani. It is a term of
modern origin, which derives from European thought, although its
affinity to the Islamic definition of the *umma*, and especially its
denial of the separate existence of the individual, has greatly
contributed to its applicability to the circumstances of the Arab
world.

(c) al-Husri's Discussion of al-Kawakibi's anti-Ottomanism and 'Abd al-Raziq's Critique of the Caliphate

Long before al-Husri had developed his definition of the *umma* in
the European sense of the nation, 'Abd al-Rahman al-Kawakibi,
(1849–1902), a follower of al-Afghani and 'Abduh, had interpreted
the Islamic notion of the *umma* in a manner which amounted to
secularisation, although this was very far from his intention. al-
Kawakibi claims that as well as the Islamic *umma*, an Arab *umma*
also exists as an independent community. In this way, according to
Sylvia Haim, he 'made more than one step to meeting Western
secularism, and indeed al-Kawakibi worked out an almost racial
theory of nationality while remaining an orthodox Muslim . . .'.[47]

al-Kawakibi,[48] who was born in Aleppo, received a thoroughly orthodox Islamic education in his native city. As a young man he fought against the despotic rule of 'Abd al-Hamid, and suffered under his repression. He eventually fled to Cairo, where he worked in the circle of Muhammad 'Abduh and his disciple Rashid Ridha until his death. He published many of his articles in *al-Manar* (The Minaret), a review edited by Ridha, which was a focus of Islamic modernist revivalism. al-Kawakibi later collected these essays in two volumes, called *Umm al-Qura* (Mother of the Villages)[49] and *Taba'i'al-Istibdad* (Features of Tyranny).[50] In *Umm al-Qura* his criticism of the Ottomans goes as far as to question their capability to uphold the Islamic Caliphate; he pleads for the return of the caliphate to Quraish, the tribe of the Prophet Muhammad.[51] In addition to taking on a national character, al-Kawakibi's version of the caliphate contains other modern features. He suggests, for instance, that the caliph should be elected every three years. His power is to be limited; he is neither allowed an army, nor the opportunity to interfere in the affairs of the prospective autonomous sultanates. For their part, the sultanates would have to recognise the spiritual authority of the caliphate. Haim underlines the secular and national implications of this interpretation of the caliphate: 'A pious Muslim as he no doubt was, he unconsciously adopted the Western fallacies about the temporal and the spiritual powers of the caliph, and carried the distinction so far that he had justified through it the setting up of an Arabian caliphate.'[52] The unintended consequence of this was, as Haim continues, that 'the general weight of all al-Kawakibi's arguments . . . inclines towards a theory of Arab nationalism'.[53]

In the essays in *Taba'i'al-Istibdad*, al-Kawakibi formulates a pointed criticism of despotism, alluding to the Ottoman despotism of 'Abd al-Hamid II. He shows the way in which such rule is destructive to man, although he is opposed to fighting it by force because this will not guarantee the removal of the basis of despotism, which is the ignorance of the subject. Despotic rule can only be ended by education and enlightenment, however long this process may take.[54]

al-Husri eagerly quotes al-Kawakibi's work since he can use it to support his own theories. He can now point to an orthodox Muslim critic of the Ottoman caliphate, and he can even make use of some of al-Kawakibi's arguments to prop up his basic thesis of a unitary Arab nation. In his writings on al-Kawakibi, he stresses that he was 'an Islamic scholar, and that Shaikh Rashid Ridha, the editor of *al-Manar*, publicised and supported his views',[55] although this is clearly questionable, because al-Kawakibi and Ridha developed the ideas of their teacher Muhammad 'Abduh in completely opposite directions.[56]

al-Husri does not limit himself to quoting the orthodox Muslim al-Kawakibi to support his arguments against the Pan-Islamists and his critique of the Ottoman Caliphate. al-Kawakibi, incidentally, certainly contributed a great deal to the development of Arab national thought, but can be regarded more as an Islamic revivalist than a conscious nationalist. al-Husri went one step further by making use of the arguments of an equally orthodox Muslim, 'Ali 'Abd al-Raziq, in order to question the political form of the Caliphate as such.

As has been indicated at the beginning, al-Husri's dispute with the Pan-Islamists takes place on two levels, first on the level of a philological interpretation of al-Afghani's political writings, to prove that al-Afghani never actually postulated a political framework for Pan-Islamism, and secondly on a general theoretical level, in which the main issue is whether a religious community can also be a national one. It is clear that al-Husri has not dealt accurately with his source material. He ignores the early al-Afghani, the state ideologue of the Ottoman Empire under 'Abd al-Hamid II. Hence his theoretical differences with the Pan-Islamists still need to be investigated.

In the discussion of the general theoretical framework of al-Husri's work, it was concluded that, following Ibn Khaldun, religion plays only a secondary role in the formation of nations, and that, following the nineteenth-century German Romantics, it can only be of real significance if it is a national religion. Hence the gist of al-Husri's controversy with the Pan-Islamists, on both theoretical and practical levels, is that Pan-Arabism is easier to put into practice than Pan-Islamism.[57]

al-Husri says that the universal religions of Christianity and Islam have been unable to achieve a political unity of peoples speaking different languages, and if this has taken place, it has done so only for brief historical periods within a very limited framework.[58] From this he concludes that irredentist movements cannot be successful if based on religion, but only if based on a common culture, language and historical heritage. He knows that such secular ideas would be bitterly opposed as heretical by the influential Islamic *'ulama'*, and he therefore makes tactical allowances in order to avoid open conflict with them. He attempts a definition of Pan-Islamism which does not conflict with the political assumptions of his own theory. He explains that he always uses unity in the sense of the unity of the national state; he is only opposed to Muslim unity where it implies a single national state, and he is not opposed to Islamic solidarity and brotherhood as such.[59] He suggests that there should be a strict distinction between Pan-Islamism and Islamic solidarity, and that the first should be given up for the sake of the second, particularly because the creation of an Islamic national state as postulated by Pan-Islamism is impossible.[60] However, he does not seek to force this idea upon the Islamic '*ulama*':

I am aware that my words will displease many Islamic scholars. I know very well that the historical facts which I mention cannot shake the belief of the '*ulama*' because they argue without reference to history or geography. They have never been able to distinguish between the implications of 'religious brotherhood' and 'political bond' and they have even accustomed themselves to confuse the moral category of 'Islamic solidarity' with the political category of Pan-Islamism. I see no reason why I should attempt to convince the '*ulama*' that their belief is wrong, but I do consider it necessary to ask them to apply reason and logic in this matter. As far as I am concerned, they can maintain their belief in Pan-Islamism as long as they grasp that Pan-Arabism must be realised even if only as a step towards the realisation of the Pan-Islamism in which they believe. It is impossible that they should oppose Pan-Arab activities under Pan-Islamic pretexts.[61]

He repeats this argument in his dialogue with the former rector of al-Azhar, Shaikh Muhammad Mustafa Maraghi, who declared, in answer to a question put by al-Husri: 'I have nothing to say about Pan-Arabism . . . I am not concerned about it . . . I am neither for it nor against it.'[62] al-Husri comments ironically on this answer: 'If someone were to convey these words to me, and were to ask me to guess the nationality of the speaker, I would assume that he belonged to one of those nations lying far away from the great Arab world, . . . between Sweden and Transvaal, Tibet and Alaska . . . That these words should come from the mouth of Shaikh Muhammad Mustafa Maraghi, the head of the oldest academic institution in the Arab world, who has the weighty historical task of maintaining Arab culture, astounds me . . .'[63]

Ultimately al-Husri was unable to avoid incurring the hostility of the 'ulama', especially as he made no secret of the fact that he was not well disposed towards them. He considered them a serious obstruction to the maturation process of the Arab national movement. In his view, they had become instruments of the Ottoman Empire in its struggle against the Arab national movement by insisting that nationalism was in contradiction to Islamic teaching, and that every Muslim had the duty of obedience to the Sultan-Caliph.[64]

It is significant that al-Husri either uses arguments inherent in Islam or secular notions derived from Islamic scholars in the course of his controversy with the 'ulama'. He first seeks to prove that Ottoman historians have falsified history by claiming that the last 'Abbasid caliph, al-Mutawakkil, transferred the caliphate to the Ottomans,[65] from which they derived their rights to be its heirs. al-Husri considers that this manipulation of history vitally contributed to their success in securing the loyalty of the Arabs to the Empire, and delayed the rise of the Arab national movement.[66] However, he is not content simply to question the right of the Ottomans to the caliphate, but he also challenges the role of the caliphate as the cornerstone of the Islamic polity. In this context he quotes the work of 'Ali 'Abd al-Raziq, a professor at al-Azhar, who spoke out against the misuse of Islam in the name of the caliphate.

'Abd al-Raziq was one of the most distinguished Islamic scholars of the 1920s. He taught traditional Islamic studies with an infusion of modern European thought, in the tradition of Muhammad 'Abduh, and in contrast to his colleagues was thoroughly familiar with Islamic political philosophy as well as with the Qur'an and the Hadith. In his epoch-making work *Islam wa Usul al-Hukm* (Islam and the Foundations of Rule),[67] which appeared in Cairo in 1925, he complains that the study of politics has always been grievously neglected in Islam. The reason for this has been the fear of rulers of the possible outcome of such studies. 'The study of politics is the most dangerous science for governments, because it reveals the forms, characteristics and systems of power. Hence the rulers have always been opposed to this science and have barred their subjects' access to it.'[68] He saw his own work as an Islamic contribution to the study of politics, which would throw light on the question of the caliphate. The content of his work was so revolutionary for the 'ulama' that they dismissed him from the postgraduate department of al-Azhar, stripped him of all his academic titles and his judicial office and declared him a heretic.[69]

The core of 'Abd al-Raziq's thought is that the caliphate is a form of government. Here he follows Ibn Khaldun, who explains in the *Muqaddima* that every form of government is an expression of domination, and that domination is based on power.[70] 'In Islam the caliphate has always been based on brute force, and except in rare cases, this has been material power. The caliph consolidated his position with the help of spears and swords, a well equipped army and its overall might. He legitimated his rule and obtained security on this basis alone.'[71] 'Abd al-Raziq modifies Ibn Taimiyya's notion that obedience is due to the political ruler, and limits the duty of obedience to the relationship between man and God. Hence 'it is natural that those Muslims who stand by liberty in their thoughts and deeds, and who subordinate themselves only to God will refuse to subordinate themselves to human beings in the way that rulers demand from their subjects . . .'[72] He aims to show that Islam is innocent of the misdeeds of the caliphate, and that those misdeeds which have been committed in the name of religion by the rulers and the powerful cannot be laid at the door of Islam, since 'it is a fact that the caliphate is based on power'.[73]

For 'Abd al-Raziq, the powerful empire which the Muslims constructed in the course of the spread of Islam is the state of the Arabs. They have built this empire, they were its 'rulers and colonisers'.[74] 'The new state which was founded and governed by Arabs was an Arab state. In contrast, Islam in the way I know it, is a religion for all mankind. It is neither Arab nor foreign.'[75] Finally he says: 'In fact, Islam is not responsible for what the Muslims have suffered under the caliphate: it is not responsible for the mis-deeds, the tyranny and the lust for power that went with it.'[76] This view is of course potentially secular. 'Abd al-Raziq reduces Islam to a spiritual formula, to a direct relationship between God and man, without any need for a mediator. However, like al-Kawakibi, who declared the Arabs to be an independent nationality and demanded an Arab-Islamic caliphate for them, 'Abd al-Raziq himself remained an orthodox Muslim. For him secularism is merely the result rather than, as for al-Husri, the aim, of his thinking. al-Husri, who is far removed from 'Abd al-Raziq's politico-theological arguments, and even differs fundamentally from him in his demand for obedience not to God but to the nation, does not hesitate to make use of his ideas and his eminence as an Islamic scholar for his own ends. He declares to the Pan-Islamists who mourn the passing of the Ottoman Empire—following his own and al-Kawakibi's historical research—that the Ottomans had no legitimate claim to the caliphate, since it rightly belonged to the Arabs. He further confronts them with the thesis, derived from 'Abd al-Raziq, that true Islamic orthodoxy does not recognise a caliphate, nor for that matter any religiously sanctioned form of earthly government.[77] However al-Husri by no means fails to appreciate the significance of Islam for the Arabs. He considers that without the Qur'an the Arabic language would have suffered the same fate as Latin, but he also stresses the part played by the Arab Christians in rescuing classical Arabic, since they recite the Bible in Arabic. Fundamentally al-Husri accepts Islam as a part of Arab national culture, but he does not consider that Islam alone constitutes Arab culture. He vehemently attacks the claim of the Pan-Islamists and the Islamic historians that Arab history only began with the rise of Islam, and that before that the Arabs lived in primitive feuding tribes. The highly developed literary form of pre-Islamic poetry proves the contrary:

> It is true that the advent of Islam marked a new and significant period in Arab history, but it is wrong to claim that the Arabs before Islam were an uncivilised or primitive people. Historical research has proved the falsity of this view. But even if we leave aside the results of this research and simply examine the Arabic language of this period more closely, it becomes clear to us that this is not the language of a primitive people . . . on the contrary, it is a language which shows a high capacity for abstraction, which could not have been achieved without the foundation of an intellectual tradition. Thus we must insist that the denial of a pre-Islamic culture and of the existence of a spiritual tradition among the Arabs in no way corresponds to the historical evidence.[78]

It will be evident from this discussion that al-Husri's theory of the nation is secular in the European sense, and that its affinity with Islamic political philosophy is *accidental* and only occasionally formal. But it was precisely this affinity which created a fertile soil for the diffusion of al-Husri's theories in a profoundly Islamic society, together with the pioneering work of the early Syro-Lebanese Christian nationalists, and those orthodox Muslims who unintentionally secularised Islam.

On the basis of this analysis, it is possible to refute the claim that

Pan-Arabism is the historical continuation of Pan-Islamism. There is a great deal of evidence to suggest that Pan-Arabism and Pan-Islamism are two rival political movements.[79] This is also clear from the fierce hostility expressed by the still powerful Muslim Brethren towards the Arab national movement. In spite of all this evidence, the facile thesis that Pan-Arabism is the continuation of Pan-Islamism continues to be aired in the literature, not only in popular writing[80] but also in academic journals.[81]

9 Pan-Arab versus Local Nationalism I: al-Husri and the Egyptian Nationalists

It has already been shown that Arab nationalism first emerged in Greater Syria, and that it was confined to that part of the Middle East in its early years. It originated among Syro-Lebanese intellectuals, who were primarily Christian, and who had been educated in European and American mission schools. For these nationalists, the Arab nation consisted exclusively of Arab 'Asians', a definition already implied in the title of a work by the early Arab nationalist Najib Azouri, *La Réveil de la Nation Arabe dans l'Asie Turque*.[1] The first links between the 'Asian' Arab nationalists and Arab North Africa were established during the period of Muhammad 'Ali's conquest of Syria between 1831 and 1840,[2] although they were disrupted by the intervention of the colonial powers, especially Britain.

(a) Egyptian Nationalism: the History of its Development and Transformation

As in the other parts of Arab North Africa (the Maghrib including Libya), the Arab national movement in Egypt has an entirely different tradition from the rest of the Arab Middle East. After the Napoleonic occupation in 1798 Egypt was virtually severed from the rest of the Ottoman Empire. This continued after the departure of Napoleon's army in 1801, since although Muhammad 'Ali came to power supposedly as Ottoman governor in 1805, he in fact became the sovereign of an autonomous country whose development the Ottomans were no longer able to influence.[3] After Muhammad

178

'Ali's death, Egyptian sovereignty diminished continuously as a result of the interference of the colonial powers and their increasing economic hegemony. The British occupation of Egypt in 1882, after the crushing of 'Urabi's revolt[4] was the beginning of a new phase in Egyptian history.[5]

This historical experience of Egypt accounts for the difference between the Pan-Arab and the Egyptian national movement. The Syro-Lebanese intellectuals desired to free their country from Ottoman rule. They were prepared to collaborate with the European colonial powers for this purpose, since they did not realise the full implications of the phenomenon of colonialism, and could not distinguish between the emancipating features of European culture and European colonial ambitions.[6] In contrast, the focus of opposition for the Egyptian nationalists was not the Ottoman Empire, which no longer wielded any influence in Egypt, but the British colonial system under which they lived. While the Egyptian nationalists condemned the Pan-Arab nationalists for their co-operation with Britain and for their conspiracies against the Ottoman Empire, the Pan-Arab nationalists could not understand the pro-Ottomanism of the Egyptians. They could not understand, as Steppat shows, 'why the Egyptians would rather be subjects of the Ottoman Empire than endure British occupation'.[7] However, the real issue for the Egyptians was not whether or not they wished to be Ottoman subjects, since, as Braune writes, 'in Egypt, where the Sultan is far away, he can be honoured, and Ottoman unity can be used as a tactical weapon. By the same token, the Ottoman Sultan supports nationalism not because of its national content but because he is opposed to Britain. . . . In Egypt Pan-Islamic ideology is still relevant to the struggle, while in Syria its break up has become apparent.'[8]

The controversy between the Egyptian and the Pan-Arab nationalists is also reflected in the literature of Egyptian nationalism, especially in the writings of Mustafa Kamil, the pioneer of the Egyptian national movement.

The tradition of Islamic modernism, or Islamic liberalism, developed in Egypt under the influence of al-Afghani and his pupil Muhammad 'Abduh. Even in the latter's lifetime[9] this tradition had begun to split into two different branches: the nationalist, as exemplified by Mustafa Kamil, and the more fundamentalist, as exemplified by Rashid Ridha.[10] Regardless of their differences with each other, both tendencies were opposed to Arab nationalism. In what follows the Arab nationalist development will be discussed, since the fundamentalist branch belongs more properly to Pan-Islamism, which has already been described.

It was Mustafa Kamil who made the first formulations of Egyptian nationalism. As Steppat has shown, Kamil's loyalty wavered between religion and the nation, and he even believed that a harmonious co-existence between the two was possible. In the long run this view leads to the separation of politics from religion.[11] Although Kamil adhered strictly to Islam, in reality Islam no longer plays an essential role in his theory. It has become secular, in that its terminology expresses a nationalist content. God has been replaced by the nation, and patriotism has become the new religion, although Kamil himself was not aware of the implications of this.[12] It is therefore incorrect to reduce the difference between Pan-Arab and Egyptian nationalism to the formula secular/non-secular, since in fact both are secular, although only the Pan-Arabists see their nationalism this way. The difference must be sought elsewhere: it lies in the different strategic role played by the Ottoman Empire in the early stages of the two movements.

As Steppat has shown,[13] Kamil's religious belief was superficial. In his political theory, Islam loses its claim to be a totality and is subordinated to nationalism,[14] which explains why he refused to co-operate with 'Abduh. Kamil's concern was not to modernise Islam, but to strengthen the Egyptian national movement; the modernisation of Islam was only relevant to the extent to which it was able to contribute to the national movement.[15] In spite of this, Kamil was a supporter of the Ottoman Empire, and detested its critics. Although he did not believe in a racial definition of the nation, and was prepared to accept everyone, regardless of religious affiliation or racial origin, he despised the Syro-Lebanese nationalists, who had been forced to seek refuge in Egypt as a result of persecution for Pan-Arabism in their own country, as 'intruders', and outsiders in the Egyptian nation.[16] He excluded the Pan-Arab nationalists simply because they were opposed to the Ottomans. He saw in the Pan-Islamism which the Pan-Arabs opposed the means of freeing Egypt from British colonial rule.[17] Kamil called himself an 'Ottoman Egyptian', and declared that loyalty to the caliphate was a sacred patriotic duty.[18] 'May God bless the Ottoman Empire, grant its Sultan victory, and uphold his rule so that we may profit from his strength!'[19] A critical study of his work shows that Islam was of practical political significance for Kamil, as will have been already evident from this quotation. The Ottoman Empire was the only power which Europe feared, and it was an ally of the Egyptian national movement to the extent that it was opposed to British colonial rule.[20] This interpretation of Steppat's can be further supported with reference to Mustafa Kamil's view of Pan-Islamism, since he opposed the creation of a universal theocratic Islamic Empire.[21] For Kamil, like the later al-Afghani, Pan-Islamism was more an expression of anti-colonial solidarity than an irredentist movement.

In spite of the Islamic content of his political thought, Kamil was a Europeanised liberal intellectual. Initially he was capable of making a distinction between European colonialism and the occidental civilisation which he admired.[22] Like all liberal Egyptian nationalists, he had particular admiration for France, since French culture had been strongly entrenched in Egypt since the time of Muhammad 'Ali's attempts at modernisation. But he did not retain the capacity to make this distinction, and finally fell victim to the illusion that France would liberate Egypt from British colonial rule; he could not see that France was also a colonial power with similar interests to those of Britain. His disillusionment came only in 1904, when the *Entente Cordiale* was established between Britain and France, under which Britain acknowledged French pre-eminence in Morocco, and France acknowledged British pre-eminence in Egypt in return.[23]

After Kamil's death in 1908, the National Party (*al-Hizb al-Watani*), which he had founded in 1907, was banned, and its leaders imprisoned. The party became illegal, and began to operate abroad, in the Kaiser's Germany, where its new leader, Muhammad Farid, lived until his death.[24]

Thus the National Party in fact died with Kamil, and other nationalist parties now became increasingly able to gain ground, particularly those which had been founded by the British authorities under Cromer's direction[25] in order to provide a counterweight to the National Party. Their supporters included European-educated nationalists, such as Ahmad Lutfi al-Sayyid, Taha Husain, and Muhammad Husain Haikal, most of whom, except for Taha Husain, came either from the higher ranks of the bourgeoisie, or from the landowning classes, or were senior civil servants in the colonial bureaucracy. These new forces supported a less radical nationalism than that of Mustafa Kamil, and only sought to obtain certain concessions within the framework of the colonial system. By this time too all traces of Ottomanism had disappeared. The pioneer of this form of 'moderate' nationalism was Ahmad Lutfi al-Sayyid, whose definition of Egyptian nationalism was far more liberal than Kamil's. The latter can only be considered the 'founder of modern Egyptian nationalism', in Safran's words, 'if we have in mind the nationalist movement; but if we think of the nationalist ideology, the credit must go to Lutfi al-Sayyid'.[26] Although there is much truth in this, Safran's opinion ignores the basic difference between the two nationalists.

Lutfi al-Sayyid[27] began his political career as a follower of Kamil, but broke away after a period in Europe, and helped to found the *Umma* Party in 1907. His break with Kamil was also a break with Ottomanism and an Islamic interpretation of nationalism, and he now headed towards the European liberal-democratic tradition. He sought a constitutional parliamentary democracy for Egypt and the separation of powers on the lines envisaged by Montesquieu.[28] His rejection of Pan-Islamism did not however lead him to support the Pan-Arab nationalism of the Syro-Lebanese intellectuals. Like all adherents of the liberal nationalist tradition in Egypt, he continued to insist on the existence of an 'Egyptian nation'. Liberal nationalism underwent a crisis in Egypt as a result of the inability of the Egyptian bourgeoisie to create a material base for the European bourgeois-liberal ideology which it supported.[29] This failure led in its turn to the promotion of the Muslim Brethren, who followed Rashid Ridha's archaic fundamentalism and whose supporters were even more opposed to Pan-Arabism than the Egyptian nationalists.[30] It was only with the seizure of power by the Pan-Arab nationalist Free Officers under Nasser in 1952 that Pan-Arabism was able to gain a greater hold on Egyptian society. The mentor of the Free Officers was General 'Aziz 'Ali al-Misri, who had been prominent in the Pan-Arab movement. As a young man he had served in the Ottoman Army, and as a member of Committee of Union and Progress had been one of the leaders of the revolutionary march on Constantinople against Sultan 'Abd al-Hamid II in 1909. He had been a member of *al-Qahtaniyya*, a secret Arab nationalist society. In 1914, disappointed with the Turanianism of the Young Turks, he founded *al-'Ahd*, a more effective secret society, which consisted exclusively of Arab officers with modern training, and he fought with these men in the Arab Revolt of 1916. His political and military career led him to the highest posts in the Egyptian Army, that of Inspector-General in 1938 and Chief of General Staff in 1939.

However, in 1940, he was retired from the army as a result of pressure from Britain, which feared his influence.[31] al-Misri was greatly respected by the Free Officers, and was to be an important influence in guiding them away from Egyptian local nationalism towards Pan-Arabism. al-Misri's germanophilia dates from the time of his co-operation with the Young Turks. This also true of the Iraqi officers in the Ottoman Army who were fellow members of *al-'Ahd*, and who formed the core of the Iraqi Army after the fall of the Ottoman Empire. The Free Officers also seem to have absorbed this germanophilia, in the naive belief that Germany would liberate the Arabs from Anglo-French colonial rule, and they made contact with the Third Reich during the Second World War at al-Misri's instigation.[32] When the Pan-Arab nationalist officers seized power in Iraq under the leadership of Rashid 'Ali al-Gailani, following negotiations with the Third Reich,[33] the Free Officers, according to one of their leaders, Anwar al-Sadat, 'watched these events with admiration. This was the beginning of liberation, the first hint of the deliverance of the Arab East . . . For us, al-Gailani's rising was the signal for the struggle for independence, and it was our duty to follow as fast as we could.'[34] However, General al-Misri realised the true nature of British power in Iraq, and accurately forecast al-Gailani's chances of victory. He managed to convince the Free Officers, who were planning a similar coup d'état against British rule in Egypt, that they would have little chance of success. According to al-Sadat 'he anticipated the stab in the back which al-Gailani was to receive'.[35] The Arab defeat in the Palestine war of 1948 deepened the Pan-Arab consciousness of the Free Officers, to such an extent that they were now determined to act. A few years later, on 23 July 1952, they succeeded in taking over in Egypt.

Nasser's early pamphlet, *The Philosophy of the Revolution* (1952) declares that Egypt is a part of three 'circles', the Arab, which has priority, the Islamic, and the African.[36] On 16 January 1956 the Free Officers issued a new constitution whose preamble states for the first time that the Egyptian people 'consciously perceives of its existence as a part of the great Arab whole, and correctly acknowledges its responsibility and duty within the common Arab struggle for the victory and glory of the Arab nation . . .'[37] The first paragraph emphasises that Egypt is an Arab country and that the Egyptians are an Arab people. However natural such a declaration may appear today, it was certainly revolutionary at the time, especially in view of the fact that the modern Egyptian intelligentsia was sufficiently far from the tradition of Arab nationalism to continue to be opposed to it well after 1952.

(b) al-Husri's Discussions with the Liberal Egyptian Nationalists

al-Husri describes 16 January 1956, the date of the proclamation of the new Egyptian constitution as 'a most glorious stage in the history of the development of Arab national thinking in Egypt'.[38] He says that in Syria the content of the passage quoted above from the constitution would be a self-evident truth, because Syria 'is the most traditional of all Arab countries as far as Arab national consciousness is concerned, the most elevated above considerations of local patriotism, and the most ardent for Pan-Arabism'.[39] The significance of the new Egyptian constitution can only be fully appreciated if it is understood that the 'Egyptian view of the national question has been greatly distorted. They waver backwards and forwards between Pharaonism, Egyptian particularist national-ism, Orientalism, and Pan-Islamism. The Arab national idea has been suppressed by these different trends, and has only found its way to consciousness under great difficulties.'[40]

al-Husri visited Egypt for the first time in 1919. At that time he was Minister of Education in Syria, then no longer under Ottoman rule. He went to Egypt on official business, wishing to have a look at Arabic textbooks in order to give himself an idea of the degree to which the language had been modernised. He wanted to make use of the experience he would obtain in Egypt in the Arabisation of education in Syria. As is well-known, the revival of Arabic had already begun in the first half of the nineteenth century, in Egypt with the work of al-Tahtawi,[41] and in Syria with that of al-Yaziji, al-Shidyaq, and al-Bustani.[42] In Egypt the educational system had already been considerably Arabised under Muhammad 'Ali,[42a] but in Syria, particularly after the Ottomans had started to put their Turanian ideology into practice, Turkish remained the sole official language.

al-Husri's journey to Egypt in 1919 coincided with the Egyptian revolt against British rule, and as a result he had to cut the visit short. He returned to Syria with the illusion that 'We must consider the Egyptian revolt as a complementary part of the Arab revolt, which took place a few years ago [i.e. in 1916 against the Ottomans—B.T.].'[43] However, al-Husri realised that this was an illusion when he had to seek political asylum in Egypt in 1921 after Faisal's Kingdom in Syria had collapsed in the face of the invasion of French colonial troops. The Egyptian nationalists accused al-Husri and the other Pan-Arab nationalists of having contributed to the disintegration of the Ottoman Empire, which had been their 'only hope in the struggle against European colonialism'.[44] al-Husri was particularly disappointed that none of the Egyptian nationalist intelligentsia were prepared to join the Arab national movement. It was only later that he realised that opposition to Pan-Arabism in Egypt had its roots in the historical development of the country since the nineteenth century.[45] He took part in discussions between different Egyptian political groups on the question of Egyptian national identity, in the belief that he would eventually be able to convince the Egyptians of the validity of Pan-Arabism. He countered the frequent accusation that he was interfering in the affairs of another country as follows:

I beg you not to accuse me of interfering in Egyptian affairs. I am an Arab in the depths of my being, and I profess the religion of Arabness with all my feelings. I am as interested in Egypt as I am in Syria or Iraq; in fact I shall not exaggerate if I say that I am more interested in Egypt than in Syria or Iraq, because Egypt . . . is the most impressive model for the whole Arab world . . .[46]

In 1936 al-Husri still believed that Egypt could play a leading role in the Arab national movement, although he had often been forced to learn the lesson that no form of Arab nationalism found a ready reception in Egypt and in fact was even vigorously opposed there.

Nature has provided Egypt with all the advantages to enable it to assume a leading role in the revival of Arab nationalism. It is the centre of the Arab world, connecting the Asian with the African parts: it is the most populous member of the Arab nation, which has been split into a number of small states. And this most populous part of the Arab world had the good fortune to be the most extensively exposed to the fruits of the civilisation of the modern world, so that Egypt has become the most important cultural centre in the whole Arab world . . .[47]

In his attack on the Egyptian nationalists, al-Husri deals with each major figure in turn. He accuses Ahmad 'Urabi[48] and Muhammad Farid[49] and other members of the early Egyptian national movement of ignorance and inconsistency. Although they still adhered to Islam, it was to an Islam which had lost much of its original meaning. Muhammad Farid, the leader of the National Party after the death of Mustafa Kamil, denounced as heretics those who criticised the Ottoman Empire, and defined obedience to the Empire as an integral part of Islam. In the face of this fanatical approach, al-Husri points out that the Qur'an makes no reference to obedience to wordly rulers, let alone to obedience to the caliphate, and hence cannot be used to condemn opposition to it.[50] Although both Farid and 'Urabi considered the caliphate to be sacrosanct, they were more Egyptian nationalist than Pan-Islamist in orientation. Here al-Husri argues with some justice that the Ottoman Sultan-Caliph had opposed 'Urabi's revolt and had called for disciplinary punishment for the 'mutineers', while 'Urabi continued to insist that the Sultan-Caliph must be obeyed.[51]

al-Husri considered the outspoken liberal Egyptian nationalists of the school of Lutfi al-Sayyid and Taha Husain a far more serious threat than Farid or 'Urabi. They considered Egypt to be an independent nation, with a culture of its own which was greatly influenced by European models. Lutfi al-Sayyid[52] took the Greeks as an example of a people who had retained their national identity in spite of a long experience of foreign rule. 'In the same way, we Egyptians must hold fast to our Egyptianness, and must not profess allegiance to any other fatherland than the Egypt from which we originate . . .'[53] al-Husri, on the other hand, takes the Greek example as proof of the correctness of his own Pan-Arab view. He compares the divided Arab world with divided Greece after 1830, part of which was under Ottoman rule, and part of which was independent. The Greeks—and here he agrees with Lutfi al-Sayyid—held fast to their nationality, conserved their language and resisted attempts at Turkification. When part of their lands was freed from Ottoman rule in 1830, they considered the part still under the Ottomans as part of their fatherland. The Egyptians on the other hand considered themselves to be an independent nation when they had been separated from the rest of the Arab world through the colonial policy of the Great Powers. After saying this, al-Husri remarks ironically: 'Those who employ arguments drawn from history must listen carefully to its voice and not assign to it things which contradict it.'[54]

It was Taha Husain's approach to nationalism[55] that provoked al-Husri's sharpest criticism. For Husain, Egypt is Pharaonic, and he even disputes its Arab character. As he only assigns a secondary place to language in the process of nation formation, he considers the fact that Arabic is the national language of the Egyptians to be immaterial.[56] Taha Husain rejects Pan-Arabism on the grounds that it contains features of oriental despotism, and traces of absolutist and fundamentalist Islamic thought. He suggests the liberal idea of the nation and the general principles of liberalism as an alternative.[57] al-Husri began a dialogue with Taha Husain in the columns of a journal, where he engaged in vigorous polemic, accusing him of having embezzled 'at least thirteen centuries of Arab history from Egypt'.[58] al-Husri vehemently countered Taha Husain's comment that Pan-Arabism is merely oriental traditionalism in a modern guise by saying that he and his followers resolutely refused to permit the introduction of Islamic thought into politics. This was why they rejected both Pan-Islamism and the Caliphate movement. According to al-Husri, the claim that the Arab national movement smacks of religious fanaticism is of colonialist origin: the colonial powers always gloss over the emancipating character of these secularist movements by such accusations.[59]

Taha Husain set down his political ideas, which can be considered as representative of the bourgeois-liberal Europeanised Egyptian intellectual, in *The Future of Culture in Egypt*, published in 1938.[60] Albert Hourani describes this book as Taha Husain's 'most important work of social thought—one might almost say, his only work of systematic thought'.[61] In it Taha Husain compares the cultures of Europe and of Egypt to demonstrate the extensive similarities between the two.[62] However, when he speaks of the Egyptians he is not talking about the illiterate peasants of Upper Egypt but implicitly about his own class, who are Europeanised and educated. Taha Husain uses the comparison to support his arbitrary conclusion that although Egypt is geographically a part of the Orient, it has nothing in common with it, and is in fact a part of European culture.[63] The bonds of religion (that is, Islam), and of language (that is, Arabic), do not, in his view, play a major social role in Egypt.[64] Since he considered that Egypt belonged to European culture, he also pressed for the introduction of Latin and Greek as compulsory subjects in the Egyptian school and university curriculum.[65]

al-Husri, who had borrowed his own theoretical equipment from

European thinkers, argues that Taha Husain accepts Europe too unreservedly. This is because, al-Husri argues 'if Latin and Greek were to be introduced into our schools we would become like the stupid tailor in the story, who exhausted his talents in making a pair of trousers for a British sailor, by copying an old pair of the man's trousers so faithfully that he even reproduced the patches'.[66] al-Husri's view that nothing should be accepted blindly from Europe gives his theory its specific character: it is the product of an active-syncretic and not of a passive-imitative acculturation.

al-Husri objects to Taha Husain's *Mustaqbal al-Thaqafa fi Misr* (The Future of Culture in Egypt) on the grounds that it lacks system and is not scholarly.[67] The argument is not entirely without foundation: al-Husri can show convincingly that many of Husain's pronouncements are both inconsistent and contradictory. However, al-Husri's concern was not to show whether Taha Husain's work was scholarly or not, but primarily to denounce a political viewpoint which saw Egypt as an independent entity, cut off from the rest of the Arab world, which was of course quite different from the Pan-Arab nationalism which he himself advocated.

In the Arab countries in general, al-Husri distinguished between nationalists and regionalists, or better, local patriots. The latter 'limit their horizons to the borders of the states in which they live, and consider everything beyond as outlandish. The former do not allow themselves to be confined within this narrow space, but look towards the national borders, which reach further than those of the state.'[68] In this perspective the Egyptian nationalists appear simply as regionalists and local patriots, although in al-Husri's view they belong to the Arab nation regardless of their own political consciousness. He put forward the same view in a lecture given in Cairo to the *Jam'iyyat al-Wahda al-'Arabiyya* (Society for Arab Unity) in 1950.[69] He warned his Egyptian audience once again not to mix up or identify the nation with the national state, since the national state is only a political framework, which says nothing about the existence or non-existence of the nation. The nation is a cultural community which speaks a common language and has a common historical memory.[70] He stresses once more the correctness of the German organic theory of the people and dismisses the liberal French notion of *nationalité élective* as an irrelevant theory invented by French writers in order to facilitate French expansion.[71] In spite of this, however, as al-Husri insinuates in the context of the Egyptian nationalists, the French idea of the nation has found an echo in 'many Arab circles'.[72] It is false consciousness on the part of the Egyptian liberal nationalists to believe that they can create an independent Egyptian nation by their own will alone. This is because 'Egypt is undoubtedly a part of the Arab world, as long as it shares its language, its culture and its long history with it . . . The Egyptian people is as Arab as the Iraqi or the Syrian . . .'[73] The notion that he is an Arab who wishes to be one contradicts al-Husri's thesis that national affiliation is pre-determined and is thus not obtained by an act of free will.

> Every Arabic-speaking people is an Arab people. Every individual belonging to one of these Arabic-speaking peoples is an Arab. And if an Arab does not recognise this, and if he is not proud to be an Arab, we must look for the reasons that have made him take this stand. His view may be an expression of ignorance: in that case we must teach him the truth. It may spring from a false consciousness: in that case we must enlighten him and show him the right way. It may be an expression of his egoism: in that case we must limit his egoism. But under no circumstances should we say: 'He is not an Arab as long as he does not wish to be one, and does not accept his Arabness.' He is an Arab whether he wishes to be one or not . . . although perhaps an Arab without feeling, without consciousness and perhaps even without conscience.[74]

This quotation shows once more the authoritarian kernel of al-Husri's thought, but it also demonstrates that the controversy between him and the liberal Egyptian nationalists was not only one between Pan-Arabism and local nationalism, but was primarily a clash between his authoritarian-integrationist position and their liberal-democratic orientation.

In any consideration of Egyptian nationalism as a movement, it is important to remember that although it looked towards progressive European bourgeois society and its liberal democratic institutions, it was a position adopted by Western-educated Egyptian intellectuals, who lacked the corresponding material base of their European counterparts. This explains why the Egyptian middle class and its parties, the Liberal Constitutional Party and the Wafd, lost their democratic liberalism when they began to apply their programme to a semi-feudal colonial society. In the 1920s, when social problems in Egypt cried out for solutions, the Egyptian middle class was no longer able to pass off its own class interest as the interest of the whole nation, and adopted a reactionary stance. The social and economic demands of the lower classes now appeared to the middle class as a threat to its own individual and political liberties.[75] The popular uprising of 1919 caused the liberal nationalist Muhammad Husain Haikal to comment that: 'The talking animal has been released from its fetters.'[76] In the face of the smouldering discontent of most of the population, the colonial system came to occupy a secondary place as the enemy of the Egyptian middle class. As the party of government, the Wafd, in alliance with the feudal landlords, pursued an essentially anti-democratic policy against the emergent social movement and the social reforms which it demanded.[77] The coup d'état of the Pan-Arabist Free Officers in 1952, which terminated the political rule of the Egyptian nationalist bourgeoisie did not take place because the Egyptian middle class was not Pan-Arabist, but was an expression of the dissatisfaction of the lower classes with their social conditions. It is beyond the scope of this study to determine how it was that the national revolutionary petty bourgeoisie which seized power on 23 July 1952 proved unable to solve the social problems of Egypt in spite of all the reforms which it enacted—even though it succeeded not only in uniting Egypt with her neighbours, but also, as al-Husri had always hoped, in assuming the leadership of the Pan-Arab movement.[78]

10 Pan-Arab versus Local Nationalism II: al-Husri's Critique of Antun Sa'ada and his Syrian Social Nationalist Party (SSNP)*

The Egyptian variety of local nationalism provoked al-Husri's criticism on two grounds. In the first place, its regional limitation contradicted his own Pan-Arab views, and in the second place, it derived from bourgeois-liberal individualism, while al-Husri virtually sanctifies the community in his theory of nationalism. The Syrian variant of local nationalism differs from the Egyptian one: it was developed largely by Antun Sa'ada, and found its organisational framework in his Syrian Social Nationalist Party (*al-Hizb al-Qawmi al-Ijtima'i al-Suri*), SSNP.[1] At first sight Sa'ada's germanophile theory of nationalism, which emphasises the notion of the community even more radically than al-Husri's, seems to differ from the latter only in its denial of the existence of an 'Arab' nation, and in its application to the 'Syrian nation' whose Arabness Sa'ada disputes. In fact the difference is more fundamental, as will be shown.

Antun Sa'ada was born into a Greek Orthodox family in the Lebanese village of Shuwair in 1904. His father emigrated to Brazil before the First World War, and settled in São Paulo. In 1920 Antun followed him to Brazil, where father and son began to publish an Arabic literary magazine, *al-Majalla*. In 1929 Antun Sa'ada returned to Lebanon where he gave private German lessons in the evenings at the American University of Beirut (AUB). He had evidently learned German in Brazil. But it seems that he had not

* Or PPS, *Parti Populaire Syrien*

only learned the language but had also developed an admiration for the Germany of his day which he expressed in his nationalist ideas. Although Sa'ada denied that he had been influenced by Western thought in his theory of Pan-Syrian nationalism, it is abundantly clear that his ideas are an agglomeration of different Western theories.[2]

In 1932 Sa'ada formed the first SSNP group with a few AUB students. It was a strictly secret society, and had the cover-name of the Syrian Trading Company (*al-Sharika al-Tijariyya al-Suriyya*). This phase lasted until 1935, when the SSNP was uncovered by the French administration, and Sa'ada was arrested and charged with subersive activities.[3] He remained in prison until 1936. After his release a new phase of underground SSNP activity began. Even before his arrest in1935 he had started on the only systematic one of his many writings[4] in which he attempted to present his theory of Pan-Syrian nationalism. He managed to continue this in prison, and it finally appeared in 1938 under the title of *Nushu' al-Umam* (The Development of Nations). However, this is only a partial presentation of his theory, as the confiscation of his prison notes and his zealous activities combined to prevent him from completing the work. His other writings were either of immediate political relevance, or pithy directives and programmes of political action written by the 'Führer of the Syrian nation' as Sa'ada styled himself. In *Nushu' al-Umam* the Syrian nation incorporates all the population of the Levant including Cyprus. In a second extended edition, which was published in Damascus in 1951 after his death, Mesopotamia, or Iraq, was included in the 'Syrian nation' as 'Eastern Syria'.[5]

Sa'ada's political career came to an end in 1949 when he was condemned to death by the Lebanese government. He was found guilty by a summary court of having plotted an armed uprising aimed at undermining the integrity of Lebanon and at creating a state of Greater Syria. After the failure of the insurrection he had fled to Damascus, where he was briefly protected by the military regime of General Za'im, but for reasons which are still obscure[6] he was then handed over to the Lebanese authorities. The SSNP, which Sa'ada had founded with five students in 1932, managed to survive the death of its leader. It continued to play an important role in the history of Lebanon and made another unsuccessful bid for power in December 1961.[7] The Party was both anti-Communist and anti-Western at the same time, although its anti-Communism was dominant. In times of crisis, the SSNP fought on the side of imperialist forces in Lebanon against the national revolutionary movement. For example, it supported the Baghdad Pact,[8] and President Cham'un,[9] a protégé of the United States whose position was challenged by a popular rising which resulted in the Sixth Fleet landing in Lebanon to preserve the status quo.[10] For some years, particularly since the release of those of its members who participated in the attempted coup of 1961, the party has been producing publications, although these have not met with the same reception as in its earlier period of activity.[11]

It has been shown that al-Husri's germanophilia is expressed in his definition of the nation as the incarnation of culture, as a cultural community, based primarily on the thought of the early nineteenth century German Romantics. In contrast, Sa'ada's germanophilia is based on the kind of vulgar-scientific biological definition of the nation which predominated in the Third Reich. Hence his ideas show marked tendencies towards social-Darwinism. In 1938 Sa'ada travelled in the Third Reich and fascist Italy, and he was suspected by the French colonial authorities in the Lebanon of being an agent of the two states. However, little is known about his visit to Germany and Italy, and its influence on the future course of the SSNP is not quite clear. The Party's official version is that his sole purpose was to visit SSNP cadres in the two countries.[12] Critical followers of the Party such as Labib Yamak confirm that the structure of the SSNP and the principle of the Führer reflect fascist features, but they deny any collaboration between the SSNP and Nazi Germany or fascist Italy.[13]

As Yamak summarises, Sa'ada considers that 'the key components of nation are biology and geography: people and territory'.[14] Thus Sa'ada is primarily concerned with the supposed correlation between the racial origins and the spiritual condition of a people: a 'higher race' is supposed to have a superior spirituality.[15] Yamak quotes Sa'ada's definition of the nation: 'a group of people who share a common life (i.e., have common interests, a common destiny, common psycho-physical characteristics), within a well-defined territory which, through its interaction with them in the process of evolution, imparts to them certain special traits and characteristics that distinguish them from other groups'.[16] Religion, and language and history in particular, are features which he excludes from his definition of the nation.[17] Had he included them they would of course have contradicted his preconception of the existence of a Syrian rather than an Arab nation. While al-Husri tries to give theoretical support to his own preconception of a unitary Arab nation by asserting that common language and history are decisive factors in the definition of the nation, Sa'ada is forced to ignore the Arab character of Greater Syria and thus to consider these two factors immaterial.[18] al-Husri considers that the nation is a cultural community, while for Sa'ada it is a biological community; neither of them accept the separate identity of the individual within either of these communities. Sa'ada explains that 'individuals come and go: they live their lives to the end and then perish like leaves in autumn, but that which is real (or ever-lasting) does not disappear: it continues to live (in the community) . . .!'[19]

Like al-Husri, Sa'ada first formulated a general theory of nationalism, which he then tried to apply to the Syrian situation. He attempts to articulate the 'fact' that the population of Greater Syria constitutes an organic entity inhabiting a single territory in order to bring about a renaissance in Greater Syria: the SSNP was to be the vehicle for an Italian-style Risorgimento.[20] Sa'ada adumbrated the 'general principles of the SSNP' and the 'reforming principles of Syrian Social Nationalism' in *Ta'alim wa Shuruh fi'l-'Aqida al-Qawmiyya al-Suriyya* (Principles and Elucidation of the Doctrine of Syrian Nationalism), which appeared in Damascus in 1950. He lists eight general principles of Party policy:[21]

1. Syria belongs to the Syrians.
2. The Syrian question is an independent national question, which must be solved without reference to other national questions.
3. The Syrian question is the question of the Syrian nation and of the Syrian fatherland.
4. The Syrian question is the unity of the Syrian people, which has been in existence since prehistoric times.
5. The Syrian fatherland is the physical milieu in which the Syrian nation has developed; it includes Greater Syria, Mesopotamia and Sinai: in short, the Fertile Crescent and its star, Cyprus.
6. The Syrian nation is an undivided society.
7. The national and social renaissance of Syria draws its energies from the talents of the Syrian nation and its political and cultural history.
8. The general interest of Syria takes precedence over all other interests.

Sa'ada mentions the following 'reform principles' of Syrian social nationalism:[22]

1. Separation of religion and state.
2. The clergy are forbidden to interfere in politics and the affairs of the judiciary.
3. All barriers between different religions and their sects are to be abolished.
4. The dissolution of feudalism and the organisation of the economy on national lines.
5. The creation of a strong army which can play an effective part in determining the fate of the nation and the fatherland.

With this programme Sa'ada challenges both the Pan-Arabists and the Lebanese nationalists. To the Pan-Arabists, he is a regional nationalist who attempts to sever Syria, the 'centre of Arabism' from the rest of the Arab nation. To the Lebanese nationalists, mainly Maronite Christians with an ideology of a francophone Lebanese nation held together as an 'association des communautés',[23] he is a Pan-Nationalist, who endangers the integrity of Lebanon by his irredentist aspirations and who threatens confessionalism, the basic political and ideological principle of the state.

Sa'ada has decided views on the leadership of the Pan-Syrian national movement and the structure of its organisation, the SSNP, which are reflected in the constitution of the Party. In the preamble it says:

> The SSNP is founded on the basis of a *contract* between the legislator (*al-Shari'*) who originated the idea of Syrian Social Nationalism [meaning Sa'ada—B.T.] and all those who have accepted it, on condition that the formulator of the principles of the Syrian Social Nationalist renaissance shall be the leader of the Party for life, and that all those who believe in its principles and mission shall therefore become members of the Party, defend its cause, and give absolute support and allegiance to the leader, his legislations and constitutional administration.[24]

In addition, members were enjoined to make Party doctrine the guiding principle of their family lives. Party membership was restricted to those under forty, and the para-military SSNP thus drew its strength primarily from the young. 'What was attractive', writes Patrick Seale,

> was the accent on youth, the rigid discipline, the Fascist conception of the role of the leader, as well as the simple thesis that 'natural Syria' was a great nation which had played, and would play once more, a great role in history. Sa'ada was perhaps the first Arab to produce a wholly indigenous version of the youth formations which flourished in Italy and Germany in the 1930s. From the start, the para-military side of the party assumed great importance.[25]

al-Husri followed the development of the SSNP with interest. When he visited Beirut in 1948, the year before Sa'ada's execution, he took the opportunity to arrange a meeting with Sa'ada, which took place, as he writes, in a 'cordial atmosphere, without official character or formality'.[26] al-Husri expected to acquire detailed information on the Pan-Syrian movement. Sa'ada clearly made a deep impression on him, as was generally the case with those with whom he came into contact.[27] At the time al-Husri wrote: 'There is no party in the Arab world which can compete with the SSNP for the quality of its propaganda, which influences reason as well as the emotions, and for the strength of its organisation, which is as efficient on the surface as it is underground.'[28] He was impressed by the discipline of the Party, its anti-clerical viewpoint and its opposition to the isolationist stance of the Lebanese Maronites.[29] Naturally he was critical of the fact that the Party doctrine denied the Arab character of Syria.[30] He also criticised Sa'ada's concept of the nation as a physical rather than a cultural community,[31] and he also disliked his arrogant style of leadership.[32]

With his wide and accurate knowledge of history, al-Husri was able to point to numerous factual errors in Sa'ada's attempt to prove the existence of a homogeneous Syrian nation. Later he made use of Sa'ada's deficient historical knowledge in general and the history of Syria before the Arabs in particular to question his theory as a whole.[33] At first he sought to avoid a break with Sa'ada. He was convinced that his unfamiliarity with Syrian history was due to his having grown up in Brazil, and that careful study would show him that Syria was in fact Arab, and that he would change his views accordingly. He saw his later inclusion of Mesopotamia within the territory of the Syrian nation as a preliminary step in this direction.[34] He would also eventually be forced to give up his rather narrow definition of the Arabs as the Bedouins of the desert, rather than those who speak Arabic.[35] al-Husri explains Sa'ada's rejection of Pan-Arabism in terms of the fact that the Pan-Arabists whom he met were 'usually Muslims, and perhaps also reactionary and confused, with the result that he might well imagine that all Pan-Arabists were confessionalist at heart . . . This is the main reason why Sa'ada deviated from the true path.'[36]

After his meeting with Sa'ada in Beirut in 1948 al-Husri concluded 'It is certain that this man will come over to us before long'[37] as soon as he had developed and seen the error of his ways. After Sa'ada's execution a year later, in 1949, al-Husri published a criticism of his doctrine in the hope that this would 'help Sa'ada's followers to develop and advance in the service of the Arab countries and the renaissance of the Arab nation'.[38] His work *al-'Uruba baina Du'atiha wa Mu'aridhiha* (Arabism for its Followers and its Opponents)[39] contains a matter-of-fact correction of Sa'ada's version of Syrian history, and a critique of his biological definition of the nation and of the principle of the leadership of the SSNP. The unaggressive style of this critique reflected al-Husri's purpose, which was to convert SSNP members to Pan-Arabism. His sudden and extremely violent attack on the SSNP in *al-Difa' 'an al-'Uruba*[40] was promoted, as he himself acknowledged, by an insult later directed at him in the pages of the SSNP official journal, *al-Jil al-Jadid* (The New Generation). A letter was printed in the entertainment part of the paper from a peasant living in the city to his cousin in the country, in which it said '*Arabism for its Followers and its Opponents* is not worth the paper it has been written on'.[41] The paper did not publish al-Husri's letters to the editor, and a further four issues contained defamatory material including a passage which said 'his [al-Husri's—B.T.] childish noises deserve no more than a mention in the entertainment columns'.[42] After this, al-Husri, who did not consider himself 'in the camp of those who opposed the SSNP'[43] began to attack the Party more vigorously, although without sinking to its level of vulgarity. He would refer to Sa'ada's doctrine, which his followers call the 'sacred doctrine of the Führer' as 'mindless nationalism' (*Qawmiyya I'tibatiyya*).[44]

However, the massive attack of such an influential political writer as al-Husri on the SSNP, which had not yet gained a strong foothold, severely damaged its development, and his critique was made use of by all the Party's opponents. The reply by Sami al-

Khuri, one of Sa'ada's pupils,[45] could in no way effectively counter the widespread and favourable reception of al-Husri's two attacks.

Unlike Pan-Arab nationalism, the SSNP, with its ideology of a Syrian nation, was unable to mobilise great numbers of intellectuals towards political activity. This semi-fascist para-military movement was also unable to win over the traditionally-minded majority of Arabs, to whom the idea of a Syrian rather than an Arab nation was unfamiliar. Furthermore, the pro-imperialist stance of the SSNP made it unacceptable to most of the population, who joined the national revolutionary movement under the leadership of the petty bourgeoisie.

Postscript: Pan-Arab Nationalism as an Aspect of the Contemporary Politics of Arab States and Political Parties

The significance of Sati' al-Husri's work lies first of all in the fact that it faithfully reflects an important phase in modern Arab history and the political thought which accompanied it, and secondly in that his writings themselves had a considerable impact on political developments in the Middle East. al-Husri's ideas became part of an obligatory political ideology in those Arab states which were formed out of the process of decolonisation after the Second World War. They were also taken as the guiding principles of the nationalist parties and organisations which represented the Arab national movement in this period. The two most important Pan-Arab political organisations were the Arab Ba'th, or Rebirth, Party, and the organisation of the Arab Nationalist Movement (ANM), (*Haraka al-Qawmiyyin al-'Arab*). The Ba'th Party was founded in the 1940s by a group of Syrian students led by Michel 'Aflaq, all of whom had studied at the Sorbonne. The ANM was founded in the early 1950s by Arab students at the American University of Beirut. Both organisations took al-Husri's notion of populist Pan-Arab nationalism as their starting point. Their only significant departure from al-Husri's theories is their addition of the no less mystical doctrine of 'Arab socialism' to Arab nationalism.

Michel 'Aflaq was born into a Greek Orthodox family in Damascus where he also went to school. Subsequently he went to Paris and studied history at the Sorbonne between 1928 and 1932. After his return to Syria he worked as a teacher. He began to attract a circle of pupils and European-educated nationalists, and out of this group *al-Ba'th al-'Arabi* (The Arab Rebirth) emerged in 1943, seeking, as its name implies, the renaissance of the 'Arab nation'. In 1947 this group joined forces with *al-Ihya' al-'Arabi* (The Arab Revival), which was led by Zaki al-Arsuzi. al-Arsuzi too had been educated in the West, having studied philosophy in Paris. In 1953 they were joined by Akram al-Hawrani's Arab Socialist Party, and the organisation was from then known as the Arab Ba'th Socialist Party.[1]

'Aflaq sought a synthesis between nationalism and socialism, as he understood them, within an all-Arab state stretching from the 'Arab' Gulf in the East to the Atlantic Ocean in the West. He may have found the theoretical basis for this synthesis during his time in Paris in 1937, in Grosclaude's French translation of Alfred Rosenberg's *Der Mythos des zwanzigsten Jahrhunderts* (The Myth of the Twentieth Century).[2] His Syrian party colleagues found 'Aflaq full of enthusiasm for Rosenberg and Hitler. He saw National Socialist Germany as a model for his ideas of a synthesis between nationalism and socialism.[3] After the seizure of power in Iraq by the germanophile Pan-Arab nationalists under Rashid 'Ali, with the collaboration of the Third Reich, 'Aflaq formed a committee which assured al-Gailani's regime of its full support.[4]

After Syria obtained independence in 1945 the military wing of the Ba'th Party took part in most of the coups which have been a feature of modern Syrian history.[5] In the 1960s the military wing of the party became so strong that it organised its own coups and was no longer content simply to participate in the coups of others. Thus Arab nationalism, as formulated by 'Aflaq, became the ideological justification for the military dictatorship in the Middle East, which have been aptly defined by Fanon as narrow-gauge fascism.[6]

'Aflaq's concept of Pan-Arab nationalism differs from al-Husri's, to which it is deeply indebted, only in that it presses it to its logical conclusion. In addition, 'Aflaq adds the social dimension which al-Husri omitted.[7] Like al-Husri, 'Aflaq only accepts the individual as part of the community, of a unitary 'Arab nation'. To be a nationalist means to lead a happy life. 'Imagine a man whose nationalism has not yet been awakened . . . What sort of a person would he be? What would history mean for him? . . . Whenever I think of the situation of such a person, I shiver with fear at the thought of the misery and isolation under which he must suffer.'[8] The good life can only be fulfilled in the context of the nation. The strategy which 'Aflaq has developed for the achievement of this aim, and which is followed by the Ba'th Party under his leadership, is to revive the 'glorious' Arab past, since he can only conceive of the future in terms of the restoration of the past. 'The past for which our nation is longing . . . is the time when the soul of this nation finds realisation. The future . . . which must be struggled for . . . can only be that future in which the Arab soul is reborn.'[9] For 'Aflaq the search for an alternative explanation of the relationship between past and present is a 'fictitious problem'.

The socialism which 'Aflaq seeks to bring into synthesis with nationalism has, as he himself emphasises, a specific character. This 'Arab Socialism' has nothing to do with Marxism. 'When I am asked to give a definition of socialism, I can say that it is not to be found in the works of Marx and Lenin. I say: socialism is the religion of life, and of its victory over death. By giving work to everyone and helping them to develop their talents it keeps the patrimony of life for life, and leaves for death only dried up flesh and scorched bones.'[10] Thus defined, socialism does not claim to be giving directives for the emancipation of the oppressed classes within the nation. 'Aflaq abstracts from the realities of class relationships, and the clashes of interest which result, and still seeks to create a nation where all elements are harmoniously united and justice is done to everyone. He appeals to the Arabs to take care 'not to lose their nationalism nor to confuse it with the felonious notion of class interests',[11] so as not to endanger national unity. 'Aflaq's theory gives some insight into the nature of 'socialism' as applied by the Ba'th Party in Syria and Iraq. Its carriers, the nationalist petty bourgeoisie, see themselves as mediators and arbitrators between the social classes.[12]

al-Husri's works were generally well-known in the Ba'th Party, since they conform to the accepted thinking of the organisation. al-Husri himself pointed out the common ground and the cordial relations that had existed between himself and the Ba'th Party for some time. 'My preference for the Ba'th Party', he confesses in the course of a work in which he also discusses his later controversy with them,

was to a certain extent emotional. The basic principles of the Party conform to everything which I have said in my teaching, lectures, articles and educational directives. Presumably the Party leaders also felt the spiritual bond between us, as they expressed trust and friendship towards me on many occasions. When Michel 'Aflaq took over the Ministry of Education in Syria after the fall of Za'im [1949—B. T.], he sent me a telegram inviting me to Damascus to help him in his work, although I had only met him once before. When Salah al-Din Bitar came to Cairo to conclude a cultural agreement between Egypt and Syria [in 1957—B. T.] the Syrian delegation presented me with the draft of the agreement in order to obtain my advice. Akram al-Hawrani sent me a telegram on the day on which the United Arab Republic of Syria and Egypt was founded which said 'On the morning of this joyful day, when the hope of the union between two Arab regions has become a reality, we salute the illustrious fighters for freedom who have nourished the soul of this generation with national consciousness, and we honour their patriotic spirit. They have carried the nationalist flame without counting the cost to themselves, and to them the thanks of the fatherland are due' . . . [13]

al-Husri's relationship with the Ba'th Party only began to fade when the Pan-Arab movement split into two mutually hostile wings, Nasserism and the Ba'th Party. al-Husri, who had assigned Egypt a central place in the Pan-Arab movement, sided unhesitatingly with Nasserism against the Ba'th Party. He now discovered a number of arguments against the Ba'th Party and challenged its qualifications to be the vanguard of the Pan-Arab movement and the instrument to revive the 'Arab nation'. [14] The struggle for the leadership of the Pan-Arab movement between the individual Arab states, especially between Nasserism and the Ba'th Party has already been researched by Malcolm Kerr, and does not require further discussion here. [15]

Nasserism was able to galvanise the emotions of the mass of the population in the Middle East in a demagogic fashion. In spite of all Nasser's assurances that his regime represented the oppressed masses of Egypt, this was in fact not the case. [16] Nasserism lacked a Pan-Arab organisation. In contrast, except in the Maghrib, the Ba'th Party set up regional organisations in every Arab country, each of which were subordinate to the national Pan-Arab leadership of the party. [17] The organisation of the Arab Nationalist Movement (ANM) seemed to fill this vacuum for Nasserism, especially as its organisational structure was similar to that of the Ba'th Party. It is worth noting that the extremely Nasserist ANM was unable to create a regional organisation in Egypt, and, like the Ba'th Party, it was active mainly in Syria, Lebanon, Iraq and Jordan. The ANM has not been the subject of detailed research, which means that it is difficult to provide reliable and accurate information about it. Again, it has not produced many publications, in contrast to the Ba'th Party, which has issued a seven-volume history of its activities since its foundation,[18] as well as theoretical works by 'Aflaq, Bitar, al-Arsuzi and their pupils.[19] Apart from a few occasional pamphlets and leaflets the ANM has only published one theoretical work which outlines the guiding principles of the movement. The contents of this work will not be discussed in detail, largely because its outlook differs only slightly from al-Husri's. Like 'Aflaq, its two authors Darwaza and Jabburi[20] merely superimpose the doctrine of 'Arab Socialism' onto Arab nationalism. In its early phase in the nineteenth century the Pan-Arab movement had implicitly excluded Egypt and the Maghrib (Libya, Tunisia, Algeria, Morocco). As al-Husri's works illustrate, these countries have been considered part of the 'Arab fatherland' by the Pan-Arabists since the 1920s. In spite of this however the Pan-Arab movement has had only a limited impact in the Maghrib countries. The Egyptians had their own nationalist tradition which tended to isolate them and bring them into opposition to the Pan-Arab movement. Pan-Arab nationalism only gained a foothold in Egypt with Nasser's coup d'état on 23 July 1952. In the Maghrib states, Pan-Arab nationalism was even more alien to the local nationalism than in Egypt. There was a Moroccan,[21] an Algerian,[22] and a Tunisian[23] nationalism, each with its own history, even though each country had been subjected to French colonial rule and had been confronted with similar problems. Maghrib irredentism, or Pan-Maghribism, is a relatively recent growth. The links between the Maghrib and the rest of the Arab world were forged primarily during the Algerian revolution,[24] largely through the generous support of the independent Arab states, particularly Egypt and Syria, the centres of the Pan-Arab movement at the time. In 1958 Tunisia and Morocco joined the Arab League, which had been founded in 1945, and were followed by Algeria as soon as it had gained political independence. Libya had already been a member since 1952.

Since the 1950s, Pan-Arab nationalism has been a more or less obligatory doctrine in most Arab countries, although often expressed more in words than in deeds. This is true of feudal states such as Sa'udi Arabia, pseudo-socialist states such as Egypt, Syria and Iraq, and of pseudo-democratic parliamentary states, such as Lebanon. The Arab League was given the task of propagating the idea in the outside world.

During the process of emancipation from Turkish domination, and later from Anglo-French colonial rule, Arab nationalism played a clearly progressive role. It provided the Westernised intellectuals, who had been alienated from their own societies, with a new identity (see Chapters 3, 4, and 5). However, in the post-colonial period, it has degenerated into an ideology which serves to mask existing social contradictions and deficiencies. It is only possible to give an indication of this function and further research into the basis of this ideology is highly desirable. The development of the social-revolutionary movement since the 1960s illustrates the crisis of the Arab national movement, and indicates that Pan-Arab nationalism is on the wane. Left wings have emerged within such existing nationalist organisations as the Ba'th Party and the ANM, and have severed their connection with the mother organisation. Hence the left wing of the Syrian Ba'th Party founded its own organisation under Yasin al-Hafiz in 1966, *al-Hizb al-'Ummal al-'Arabi al-Thawri* (Arab Revolutionary Workers Party). Part of the founding statement of the Party runs as follows:

> We are an entirely new party and no longer have any ideological, political or organisational link with the Arab Ba'th Socialist Party . . . The Ba'th Party has become incapable of keeping up with the movement of the Arab masses, not only because of its incorrect policies but also because of the traditional ideology which it follows . . . 'Aflaq's ideology is based on the thesis that the aim of the Arabs' present struggle is to restore the past. In 'Aflaq's ideology progress is a backward step into the past. For the Ba'th, the future consists of making contact with the souls of our ancestors. But while we seek to expose 'Aflaq's ideology, we certainly do not wish to cast any doubt on the significance of the Arab past, since this past is an integral part of our national identity. What we want to say is that scientific socialism sees history as a process of advance, and as a transition from lower to higher stages, and not as a re-establishment of the past. Even the word Ba'th [= rebirth—B. T.] is not socialist, but conservative and counter-revolutionary . . .[25]

Yasin al-Hafiz, the theoretician and founder of the Arab Revolutionary Workers Party, makes the following criticisms of Arab nationalism, in which he had formerly believed:

The content of the numerous bourgeois chauvinist terms imported by the Arab petty bourgeoisie are not only alien to the Arab
emancipation movement, but to our time in general. At a time
when the Arab national movement became the expression of the
aspirations of emancipation of a divided and oppressed people,
the Arab nationalist petty bourgeoisie suddenly began to speak in
German. German and Italian nationalist terms became part of the
vocabulary of the Arab nationalist petty bourgeoisie . . . The
Arab nationalist petty bourgeoisie babbled virtually identical
ideas and formulae. Their supporters taught European nationalist ideas and myths, especially those of Germany, to speak
Arabic, and dressed them up in Arab clothes . . . The deep and
all-embracing misery of the present has driven the Arab petty
bourgeoisie to take refuge in a past in which the Arabs were both
united and superior. As the Arab bourgeoisie was and is weak and
incapable of anything, Arab chauvinist nationalism in no way
corresponds to Arab realities. It is merely empty phrases and a
loud hullabaloo.[26]

al-Hafiz then goes on to criticise the Pan-Arab version of socialism:

The Arab petty bourgeoisie denies historical change and sees
history as a static state in which the Arab soul is constant and
unchanging. By dismissing the historical process as an illusion or
a lie, Arab socialism is considered as a crystallised form of the
Arab soul and of Arab nationalism. The Arab petty bourgeoisie
refuses to distinguish between nationalism and socialism, because
it believes that they are one and the same thing . . . by perverting
socialism in this way, it degenerates into a reconciliation of classes
and a petty bourgeois reformist compromise . . . In order for the
movement of the masses to be able to march forwards, it is
necessary to do away with nationalist interpretations of socialist
ideas.[27]

This criticism does not mean that al-Hafiz wishes to abandon the
goal of Arab unity, but he insists that it can only be achieved on a
progressive basis and not within the framework of the nationalist
demagogy of the Arab states. Similar arguments have been put
forward by *Perspectives*, a group of Tunisian intellectuals:

The roads to socialism in our countries must be coordinated and made to lead towards the unity of the Arab peoples, since these peoples have a common language, culture, religion and history. Arab unity is the only alternative to building socialism, in order to create a real independence from imperialism and a common market for our resources and our products as a precondition for our industrialisation. Finally it presents the only method of preventing the possible uneven development of our countries. Although this unity forms the necessary economic, cultural and historical framework for the building of socialism, this does not mean that it must precede the struggle for a socialist society: on the contrary. Experience teaches us every day that Arab unity is only possible within a socialist system . . . if the slogan of Arab unity is not linked to practical steps towards the building of socialism, it remains an empty demagogic rant.[28]

In such an atmosphere critical discussion of al-Husri's Pan-Arab nationalism has a certain topicality. In 1966 the Syrian Marxist Elias Murqus published a long monograph on al-Husri, in which he says

The real popular national movement transforms itself through a continual and natural process of development. But bourgeois-nationalist thought, which always stood to the right of this movement, cannot transform itself . . . The struggle against this tendency in contemporary Arab thought is an urgent task . . . This struggle will take a long time, and necessitates the refutation of the literary and philosophical sources of this school, of German and other Western sources, and it requires the formulation of the theory of a unitary Arab socialist revolution.[29]

The defeat which followed the war of June 1967 dealt a severe blow to Arab nationalism. Reality, which had been concealed from the mass of the population by demagogy, now became more transparent. It was thus an external factor, the defeat of 1967, which sped up the process of the transformation of the Arab national movement which had already begun in the early 1960s.[30] The Ba'thist governments in Syria and Iraq and Nasser's regime[31] reacted to the waves of criticism of the hitherto unchallenged foundations of their rule by an escalation in the use of repressive measures, which clearly demonstrated that these regimes and their ideologies are in fact a barrier to a progressive transformation of the Arab Middle East. Such unpopular measures against their critics robbed the Ba'th Party and Nasserism of the mass base with which their demagogy had always credited them. Even the ultra-nationalists, the ANM, who revered Nasser as the Arab Bismarck, and who built up his image outside Egypt, split into Marxist and nationalist wings. In the course of 1970 the nationalist wing dissolved itself, while the Marxist wing began to build regional organisations in each Arab country. The most important of these is *Munadhdhama al-Ishtirakiyyin al-Lubnaniyyin* (The Organisation of Lebanese Socialists), which has published a critical account of the history of the ANM since its foundation, in which the ANM is portrayed as a nationalist-fascistoid movement.[32]

This brief sketch of contemporary Arab nationalism and its supporters must necessarily remain incomplete, since the movement is profoundly affected by day-to-day political realities. It seemed necessary however, to give a brief outline of the most recent political developments in the Arab Middle East, in order to illustrate that the political theories of Sati' al-Husri, which have formed the central concern of this book, form an integral part of the recent history of the Arab world.

NOTE

This postscript should be read contextually together with the new Introduction, in particular pages 23–4 there. In view of the historical value of this text, I decided to refrain from making any changes in it, though William Cleveland contended in his appreciative review in the *Middle East Journal* (1/1982) that this epilogue 'cries out for an update!' In fact, this postscript is a historical document of the end of the period of pan-Arab populist nationalism. The Introduction (p. 26, notes 208–19) completed for this second edition explains why, instead of the enlightenment hoped for by my generation, political Islam took the place of pan-Arab nationalism. The epilogue, as it stands retains its explanatory value for the history of Arab nationalism until the turning point of June 1967.

B.T.

Notes

Notes to the Introduction to the Second Edition

Acknowledgement: The author acknowledges with great gratitude that the research for this new introduction has been conducted within the framework of a Rockefeller Residency Research Fellowship provided by the Center for Near Eastern and North African Studies, University of Michigan, Ann Arbor in the Winter Term 1988. The research for this chapter was continued at Harvard University Center for Middle Eastern Studies in the Fall Term 1988 within the framework of my affiliation as a research associate. I am grateful to the Center's Director, Professor Roy Mottahedeh for this affiliation. This final version was completed in January 1989 in Göttingen. I am particularly grateful to Michigan Center's director, Dr Ernest McCarus for his critical reading of an early draft of this paper and for his comments. Dr Fatma Müge Göcek of Michigan's Sociology department made valuable comments on this paper which I have considered in the revised version. I am also grateful to Princeton University History Department's Professor Harold James, for having invited me to deliver a draft of this chapter at Princeton's colloquium on Nationalism (with a world-historical focus). The Princeton discussion contributed to sharpening my views and integrating new insights into the paper while revising it.

1. This context is modern world history since the seventeenth century. With regard to this see the impressive comparative study by Reinhard Bendix, *Kings or People. Power and the Mandate to Rule* (Berkeley, 1978). Bendix' book includes a small section on Arab nationalism, pp. 588–99. See also the impressive study on the modern nation-state by Anthony Giddens, *Nation-State and Violence* (Berkeley, 1987) which contributes to a great improvement in our understanding of the nation-state.

2. Thus, I basically disagree with the interpretation of James Piscatori, *Islam in a World of Nation-States* (Cambridge, 1986); see note 76 below.

3. Hedley Bull, *The Anarchical Society. A Study of Order in World Politics* (New York, 1977) in particular pp. 33ff., 38ff. and Chapter 11, pp. 257ff. See also the valuable contributions in the volume by Hedley Bull and Adam Watson (eds.), *The Expansion of International Society*, 3rd printing (Oxford, 1988).

4. See Chapter 4 in Giddens (full reference in note 1 above), in particular pp. 103ff., 116ff.

5. Francis H. Hinsley, *Nationalism and the International System* (London, 1973), pp. 35ff. and also Part II, pp. 67ff.; see also Charles Tilly's book mentioned in note 54 below.

6. Elie Keddourie (ed.), *Nationalism in Asia and Africa* (London, 1970), introduction. A historical comparison of the varieties of nationalism including the French origin and the African and Asian varieties is provided by Louis Snyder, *Varieties of Nationalism. A Comparative Study* (Hinsdale/Illinois, 1976), pp. 75ff., 162ff., 181ff.; see pp. 238ff. on pan-Arabism. The political focus on decolonisation notwithstanding, one must discern the economic constraints; see Peter J. Burnell, *Economic Nationalism in the Third World* (Brighton, 1986), in particular pp. 54–7.

7. Ernest Gellner, *Culture, Identity, and Politics* (Cambridge, 1987), p. 111.

8. *Ibid.*, p. 113.

9. See the bibliography by Karl Deutsch/Richard L. Merritt, *Nationalism and National Development. An Interdisciplinary Bibliography* (Cambridge, Mass., 1970); see also the bibliographies quoted in notes 13 and 16. For an overview of research standards see Michael Palumbo and William Shanahan (eds.), *Nationalism: Essays in Honor of Louis Snyder* Westport/Conn., 1981), in particular the section 'Analytical Essays', pp. 3–84.

10. Gale Stokes, 'The Underdeveloped Theory of Nationalism', *World Politics*, 31 (1978) No. 1, pp. 150–60, here p. 150. This is a review article by Anthony Smith, *Theories of Nationalism* (New York, 1972).

11. Anthony D. Smith, *Nationalism. A Trend Report and Bibliography* (The Hague, 1973) p. 7. See also the interesting articles by Anthony D. Smith, 'Nationalism and Classical Social Theory' in *The British Journal of Sociology*, 34 (1983) No. 1, 19–38 and 'The Diffusion of Nationalism: Some Historical and Sociological Perspectives', *British Journal of Sociology*, 29 (1978) No. 2, 234–48.

12. A. Watson, *Legal Transplants* (Edinburgh, 1974). See also the articles in parts III and IV of Bull and Watson referred to in note 3 above.

13. See however the bibliography of the social science literature on nation-building completed by the late Stein Rokkan *et al.*, *Nation-Building. A Review of Recent Comparative Research and a Select Bibliography* (The Hague, 1971).

14. See the contributions in Theda Skocpol (ed.), *Vision and Method in Historical Sociology*, 4th printing (Cambridge, 1987).

15. Theda Skocpol, *States and Social Revolutions*, 12th printing (Cambridge, 1987), p. 23.

16. An extreme example of this is Ernest C. Dawn, *From Ottomanism to Arabism. Essays on the Origins of Arab Nationalism* (Chicago and Urbana, 1973). Dawn repeats these flaws in his recent article 'The Formation of Pan-Arab Ideology', *International Journal of Middle East Studies*, 20 (1988) No. 1, pp. 67–91. For an overview of the literature on this subject see the bibliography in Frank Clements, *The Emergence of Arab Nationalism from the Nineteenth Century to 1921* (London, 1976).

17. Michael C. Hudson, in a review of the first edition of this book, *International Journal of Middle East Studies*, 17 (1985) No. 2, pp. 292–4.

18. As indicated in the acknowledgement to this introduction, this essay is an original contribution completed in English and is *not* a translation of – nor is it based on – the new introduction to the second edition of the German original of this book now published under the changed title: B. Tibi, *Vom Gottesreich zum Nationalstaat. Islam und panarabischer Nationalismus*

(Frankfurt, 1987), pp. V–XLI.

19. For more details about this see B. Tibi, 'Islam and Arab Nationalism' in Barbara F. Stowasser (ed.), *The Islamic Impulse* (London, 1987) pp. 59–74. Some scholars are still having difficulties in grasping the difference between the universalism of Islam and secular Arab nationalism. Seton-Watson, for instance, argues, 'the driving force behind Panarabism came from traditional Muslim fanaticism'. Hugh Seton-Watson, *Nations and States. An Enquiry into the Origins of Nations and the Politics of Nationalism* (London, 1977), p. 271.

20. See the contributions included in Said A. Arjomand (ed.), *From Nationalism to Revolutionary Islam* (Albany, 1984) and my article referenced in note 34 below, in particular pp. 37ff.

21. Michael C. Hudson, as referenced in note 17 above.

22. Theda Skocpol, *States and Social Revolutions. . .*, referenced in note 15.

23. L. Carl Brown, 'The June 1967 War: A Turning Point?', in Y. Lukacs and A. Battah (eds.), *The Arab Israeli Conflict: Two Decades of Change* (Boulder, Col., 1988), pp. 133–46; see here p. 142, 'The Western imported virus of nationalism spread throughout the Middle East.'

24. On this subject see the fascinating book by Reinhard Bendix, *Nation-Building and Citizenship. Studies of our Changing Order*, New enlarged edition (Berkeley, 1977).

25. Yusuf al-Qurdawi, *al-hulul al-mustawrada wa kaif janat 'ala ummatina* (The Imported Solutions and How they have Hurt our Community), vol. I of a two-volume series: *hatmiyat al-hall al-islami/The Necessity of Islamic Solution*, 2nd printing (Beirut, 1980), pp. 58ff.

26. Immanuel Wallerstein, *The Modern World System*, two volumes (New York, 1974/1980). On Wallerstein's approach see Ch. Ragin and D. Chirot, 'The World System of I. Wallerstein', in Th. Skocpol (ed.), *Vision. . .* (full reference in note 14), pp. 276–312. Wallerstein's economistic reductionism is misleading in as far as in overemphasising the global structure it does not acknowledge the importance of individual nation-states.

27. Skocpol, *States. . .* (note 15), p. 23.

28. *Ibid.*, p. 23.

29. Philip Khoury, 'Islamic Revival and the Crisis of the Secular State in the Arab World: A Historical Reappraisal', in I. Ibrahim (ed.), *Arab Resources. The Transformation of a Society* (London, 1983), pp. 213–36.

30. On this see B. Tibi, 'The Renewed Role of Islam in the Political and Social Development of the Middle East', *Middle East Journal*, 37 (1983) No. 1, pp. 3–13, and B. Tibi, 'Neo-Islamic Fundamentalism', *Development. Journal of The Society of International Development* (Rome) (1987) No. 1, pp. 62–6.

31. 'Ali M. Garisha and Muhammad Sh. Zaybaq, *Asalib al-ghazu al-fikri li al-'alam al-Islami* (Methods of Intellectual Invasion of the Muslim World). 2nd printing (Cairo, 1978), p. 39.

32. *Ibid.*, p. 41.

33. *Ibid.*

34. See B. Tibi, 'The Iranian Revolution and the Arabs', *Arab Studies Quarterly*, 8 (1986) No. 1, pp. 29–44.

35. For more details see R. K. Ramazani, *Revolutionary Iran. Challenge and Response in the Middle East* (Baltimore, 1986), in particular pp. 32ff., 62ff.

On the nature of the Islamic revolution in Iran see Said A. Arjomand, *The Turban for the Crown. The Islamic Revolution in Iran* (New York, 1988), Part Two, pp. 91ff.

36. See note 98 below with a full reference for the published proceedings of this congress and a comment on these contributions.

37. Ahmad Muhammad Jamal, *Muhadarat fi al-thaqafa al-Islamiyya* (Lectures on Islamic Culture), 3rd printing (Cairo, 1975), pp. 273–4.

38. *Ibid.*, pp. 278–9. See the chapter on 'Islam and Nationalism' in Hamid Enayat, *Modern Islamic Political Thought* (Austin, 182), pp. 111–24.

39. B. Tibi, 'Islam and Modern European Ideologies', *International Journal of Middle Eastern Studies*, 18 (1986) No. 1, pp. 15–29.

40. Anthony Giddens, *The Nation-State and Violence*, p. 255.

41. F. H. Hinsley, *Sovereignty*, 2nd ed. (Cambridge, 1986), p. 224. See also Hinsley's other book referenced in note 5 above.

42. Eric Davis-Willard, 'Theory and Method in the Study of Arab Nationalism', *Review of Middle East Studies*, 3 (1978), pp. 18–31, here p. 26; see also Elie Chalala, 'Arab Nationalism. A Bibliographical Essay', in Tawfic E. Farrah (ed.), *Pan-Arabism and Arab Nationalism* (Boulder, Col., 1987), pp. 18–56.

43. See the chapter 'Ideology and Critique of Ideology' in B. Tibi, *Crisis of Modern Islam. A Preindustrial Culture in the Scientific Technological Age*, tr. by Judith von Sivers, Foreword by Peter von Sivers (Salt Lake City, 1988), pp. 34ff.; see also my *IJMES* article quoted above (full reference in note 39).

44. See however the critical survey of B. Tibi, 'Orient und Okzident. Feindschaft oder inter-kulturelle Kommunikation. Anmerkungen zur Orientalismus-Debatte', *Neue Politische Literatur*, 39 (1984) No. 3, pp. 267–86.

45. See Sadiq Jalal al-'Azm, *al-Istishraq wa al-istishraq ma'kusan* (Orientalism and Orientalism in Reverse) (Beirut, 1981) harshly criticising Edward Said, *Orientalism* (New York, 1978). An overview and an assessment of the Orientalism-debate is provided in the lengthy article by B. Tibi, 'Orient und Okzident' (see note 44 above).

46. Manfred Halpern, *The Politics of Social Change in the Middle East and North Africa*, 2nd printing (Princeton, 1965), pp. 196–213.

47. This political poetry can be found among others by Michel Aflaq, *Fi Sabil al-Ba'th*, 3rd ed. (Beirut, 1963), pp. 41ff., 102ff. In a published Cairo Ph.D. Dissertation by Yusuf Khalil Yusuf, *al-Qawmiyya al-'Arabiyya Wa dawr al-Tarbiya* (Arab Nationalism and Education) (Cairo, 1967), the idea that Arab nationalism existed throughout the entire history is criticised. Yusuf – not less confused than Aflaq – depicts 'early Arab nationalism' (of the seventh century) as 'tribal nationalism' (*qawmiyya qabaliyya*); see Yusuf p. 23 and pp. 96–7.

48. On this see the interesting contribution of Anthony Giddens, *Central Problems in Social Theory. Action, Structure and Contradiction in Social Analysis*, 3rd printing (Berkeley, 1986).

49. Unfortunately, Skocpol overemphasised the notion of structure against the action-groups theory of Tilly (see Skocpol, *States...*, note 15 above, pp. 10–11, 16, 26–7). Thus, she overlooks that *structure* and *action* should be

viewed as interrelated concepts. For this reason a non-reductionist linkage-analysis of cultural innovations (actions of the individuals) and their environment seems to me imperative. See my modest contribution to this debate in B. Tibi, 'The Interplay between Social and Cultural Change: The Case of Germany and the Arab Middle East', in George Atiyeh and Ibrahim Oweiss (eds.), *Arab Civilization. Challenge and Responses. Studies in Honor of Constantine Zurayk* (Albany, 1988), pp. 166–82. See also note 48 above. Norbert Elias does not separate human actions from the structures in which they take place. Vol. 1 of Elias' book (see note 50) deals with *History of Manners* (subtitle); vol. 2 deals with *Power and Civility* (subtitle). Despite this subdivision of the subject Elias always systematically relates the change in manners and the social change to one another.

50. Norbert Elias, *Ueber den Prozess der Zivilisation. Soziogenetische und psychogenetische Untersuchungen*, two vols, 6th printing (Frankfurt, 1979). English trans., *The Civilizing Process*, two vols (New York, 1978, 1982). See my comments in note 49 above.

51. In my work I employ the Elias' approach for understanding Islam. See B. Tibi, *Crisis of Modern Islam*, tr. Judith von Sivers (note 43 above), pp. 22–5, also B. Tibi, *Der Islam und das Problem der kulturellen Bewaeltigung sozialen Wandels* (Frankfurt, 1985), reviewed by Barbara Stowasser, *International Journal of Middle East Studies*, 20 (1988) No. 4, pp. 564–8.

52. A representative example of this is P. J. Vatikiotis, *The Modern History of Egypt*, 2nd ed. (London, 1980) and also the work of Ernest C. Dawn (note 16 above).

53. See the following introductory works by the authors of this school: Peter Burke, *Sociology and History*, 2nd printing (London, 1981); Philip Abrams, *Historical Sociology* (Ithaca, 1982); in addition to the books of Skocpol (quoted in notes 14 and 15) and Charles Tilly, *Big Structures, Large Processes, Huge Comparisons* (New York, 1984).

54. Charles Tilly, *The Formation of National States in Western Europe* (Princeton, 1975).

55. See the standard books cited above: Bendix and Giddens (note 1), Bull (note 3), Hinsley (notes 5 and 41), Snyder (note 6); in addition to Karl W. Deutsch, *Nationalism and its Alternatives* (New York, 1969), on Europe pp. 3–36, on Third-World nationalism pp. 67–92; John Breuilly, *Nationalism and the State* (Manchester, 1982), in particular Part II, pp. 221ff., and Kenneth R. Minogue, *Nationalism* (London, 1967).

56. For classical examples of this Western scholarship see Leonard Binder, *The Ideological Revolution in the Middle East* (New York, 1964) and Manfred Halpern, *The Politics of Social Change in the Middle East and North Africa* (reference in note 46).

57. See note 47 above. There are prominent Arab authors who avoid such an ahistorical notion, in as much as they acknowledge that nation and nationalism are phenomena related to modern history. Among these authors is 'Abd al-Rahman al-Bazzaz, *Hadhihi Qawmiyyatuna* (This is our Nationalism), 2nd ed. (Cairo, 1964), pp. 81ff. However, when it comes to the 'Arab nation' al-Bazzaz turns romantic and suddenly states, 'Arab nationalism ... requires a belief in the distinct Arab nation and in its immutable features ... Arab nationalism does not need to be defined...'

(p. 87). On Bazzaz see Hamid Enayat, (referenced in note 38), pp. 112–13.

58. In my view, the best criticism on the concept of *homo islamicus* has been provided by Maxime Rodinson, *Islam et capitalisme* (Paris, 1966). On this issue see B. Tibi, 'Maxime Rodinson, der Islam und die westlichen Islam-Studien', published as a lengthy introduction to the new German edition of Maxime Rodinson, *Islam und Kapitalismus* (Frankfurt, 1986). The notion of *homo islamicus* can be traced back to the work of Max Weber. See Wolfgang Schluchter (ed.), *Max Webers Sicht des Islams* (Frankfurt, 1987) and the review article by B. Tibi, 'Gibt es einem Homo Islamicus?', *Frankfurter Allgemeine Zeitung*, 20 September 1988, issue no. 219, p. 30.

59. See Skocpol, *States...* (note 15), pp. 19–24 and B. Tibi, *Crisis...* (note 43), pp. 9–25.

60. See notes 49 and 50 above.

61. See note 3 above.

62. See note 43 above.

63. Albert Soboul, *Die Grosse Franzoesische Revolution* 4th printing (Darmstadt, 1983), in particular pp. 540ff.; see also the chapter on the formation of the nation-state in France as a model which generated spill-over effects in the book by Bendix, referenced in note 1 above, pp. 321–77.

64. Tilly (see note 54 above), p. 45. See also the stimulating new book by Ch. Tilly, *Big Structures, Large Processes, Huge Comparisons* (note 53 above). This book also includes an assessment of Bendix' book mentioned in notes 1 and 63 above (Tilly pp. 91–4), as well as of Skocpol's work cited in note 15 (Tilly pp. 105–15).

65. Hamid Enayat, *Modern Islamic Political Thought*, p. 114.

66. As regards the general setting (international system), see Francis H. Hinsley, *Nationalism and the International System* (note 5 above), and as regards the meaning of this context to the Ottoman Empire see William W. Haddad and William Ochsenwald (eds.), *Nationalism in a Non-National State. The Dissolution of the Ottoman Empire* (Columbus, 1977), in particular the contributions by Rashid Khalidi (pp. 207–37) and S. Mousa (pp. 241–63) on Arab nationalism.

67. See the relevant chapters in the standard work by Bernard Lewis, *The Emergence of Modern Turkey*, 2nd ed. (London, 1979), II, III and IV. See also Friedemann Büttner, 'Die Krise der islamischen Ordnung. Studien zur Zerstörung des Ordnungsverständnisses im Osmanischen Reich' (Unpublished Ph.D. Dissertation, University of Munich, 1979).

68. Bernard Lewis (Note 67), p. 45. See also Thomas Naff, 'The Ottoman Empire and the European States System' in Watson and Bull (eds.), *The Expansion of International Society* (note 3 above), pp. 143–69.

69. Lewis pp. 45–7. Bernard Lewis also supervised the remarkable new contribution to this subject by Fatma Müge Göcek, *East Encounters West. France and the Ottoman Empire in the Eighteenth Century* (New York and Oxford, 1987) in particular Part III, pp. 97–137.

70. On the impact of modern education and its effects on the crisis of modern Islam see Chapter 7 in B. Tibi, *Crisis of Modern Islam* (referenced in note 43), pp. 95–112.

71. Bernard Lewis (see note 67), p. 55.

72. For more details see Larry H. Addington, *The Patterns of War since the Eighteenth Century* (Bloomington, 1984), pp. 17–38. In his comprehensive survey on war Luard devotes a sub-chapter to 'The Age of Nationalism' in each of the major parts of his book: Evan Luard, *War in International Society* (New Haven, 1986), in particular pp. 52–64. Wars, similar to revolutions, were functionally 'midwives' in the processes of change in history. See also M. Howard, 'The Military Factor in European Expansion' in Bull and Watson (note 3 above) pp. 33–42.

73. Michael C. Hudson, *Arab Politics. The Search for Legitimacy* (New Haven, 1977), p. 56–7.

74. Breuilly coins the terms 'unification nationalism' for the ideology of the *integrationists* and 'separatist nationalism' for that of the *disintegrationists*. John Breuilly, *Nationalism and the State* (full reference in note 55), pp. 65ff., 90ff.

   Separatist nationalism raises the issue of *ethnicity*, which has become a major concern in Middle East studies in particular, as well as in research on nationalism in general. As regards the Middle East, see the new volume by Milton J. Esman and Itamar Rabinovich (eds.), *Ethnicity, Pluralism and the State in the Middle East* (Ithaca, 1988). For a full treatment of the general issue see Anthony Smith, *The Ethnic Origins of Nations* (Oxford, 1986). See also Joane Nagel, 'The Ethnic Revolution: The Emergence of Ethnic Nationalism in Modern States', *Sociology and Social Research*, 68 (1983) No. 4, pp. 417–34. *The Canadian Review on Studies in Nationalism* published some interesting contributions on this disputed issue; see among others Louis Snyder, 'Nationalism and the Flawed Concept of Ethnicity', (10, (1983) No. 4, pp. 253–5) and Mark V. Kauppi, 'The Resurgence of Ethno-Nationalism and Perspectives on State-Society Relations', (11 (1984) No. 1 pp. 119–32). Also, *Nationalism: Essays in Honor of Louis Snyder*, referenced in note 9 above, includes an interesting contribution to this debate by Peter Sugar, 'From Ethnicity to Nationalism and Back Again', pp. 67–84.

75. Hedley Bull (note 3), p. 275.

76. James Piscatori (note 2), pp. 40ff., 76ff., 117ff. With regard to this criticism see also the thoughtful review by John Voll in *MESA Bulletin*, 21 (1987) No. 2, pp. 245–7. Piscatori rejects the views which 'assume that the nation-state is either impossible in theory, or so inherently contradictory to Islamic values' and holds that a 'consensus has emerged which says that the nation-state is, or can be, an Islamic institution' (pp. 149–150). John Voll justifiedly makes the point that Piscatori 'seems to assume that "state" in the medieval context was basically similar to what it meant by "state" in the modern world' (p. 246). Thus, Piscatori fails to see the world-historical context of the modern phenomenon of the *nation-state* he is dealing with.

77. See the overall view of Rupert Emerson, *From Empire to Nation*, 3rd printing (Boston, 1964). See also the analysis by Anthony Giddens on the expansion of industrial capitalism as a basis for the globalisation of the nation-state system. Giddens, referenced in note 1 above, pp. 255ff., 281ff., 287ff; see also the books referenced in note 55 above and the works of Hinsley (notes 5 and 41 above).

78. See B. Tibi, *Crisis of Modern Islam* (note 43 above).
79. L. Carl Brown, *International Politics and the Middle East* (Princeton, 1984).
80. Reinhard Bendix, *Kings or People. Power and the Mandate to Rule* (see note 1 above), pp. 3–18.
81. For an analysis of the intellectual and historical origins of this concept see F. H. Hinsley, *Sovereignty*, 2nd ed. (Cambridge, 1986), pp. 45ff., 126ff.
82. Bendix (see note 1 above), pp. 588–603 and Chapter 8 of this volume, pp. 161–77.
83. Hedley Bull (see note 3 above), p. 273.
84. Examples of this are: From the present, 'Ali M. Garisha and Muhammad Sh. Zaybaq, *Asalib al-ghazu al fikri li al-'Alam al-Islami* (quoted in note 31 above) and the relatively classical work of Muhammad al-Bahi, *al-fikr al-Islami al-hadith wa silatuhu bi al-isti'mar al-gharbi* (Modern Islamic Thought and its Relationship to Western Colonialism), 4th printing (Cairo, no date/1964).
85. al-Tahtawi's diary of his stay in Paris is the classical example of this. See Rifa' al-Tahtawi, *Takhlis al-ibriz ila-talkis Paris* (1834). See the German translation of Karl Stowasser, tr., Rifa'a al-Tahtawi, *Ein Muslim entdeckt Europa. Die Reise eines Ägypters im 19. Jahrhundert nach Paris* (Munich, 1989). See also the section on Tahtawi in this book, pp. 84–8 below.
86. The standard work on this period is still: Albert Hourani, *Arabic Thought in the Liberal Age* (Oxford, 1962; new printing. Cambridge, 1987).
87. The Iraqi practitioners of Arab nationalism are dealt with in the new monograph of Reeva Simon, *Iraq Between the Two World Wars* (New York, 1986). It is an example of this politicisation process.
88. The yet unpublished Harvard Ph.D. dissertation by Hasan Kayali (1988) on this topic updates the interesting work of Ferez Ahmad, *The Young Turks. The Committee of Union and Progress in Turkish Politics 1908–1914* (London, 1969).
89. See W. Montgomery Watt, *Muhammad at Medina*, 6th printing (Oxford, 1977), Chapter IV, 'The Unifying of the Arabs', pp. 78–150; also W. Montgomery Watt, *Islamic Political Thought* (Edinburgh, 1968), pp. 6–9 on 'The Pre-Islamic Tribe and the Medinan State'.
90. Such projections can be found, for example, in Hussain Fawzi, al-Najjar, *al-Islam wa al-siyasa* (Islam and Politics) (Cairo, 1977); see also James Piscatori, *Islam in the World of Nation States*, referenced in note 2 above, and the criticism in note 76 above and note 120 below.
91. See Parts III and IV of this book. On Husri, see also William Cleveland, *The Making of an Arab Nationalist. Ottomanism and Arabism in the Life and Thought of Sati' al-Husri* (Princeton, 1971). While in this book on Arab nationalism, I discuss Husri's concept of nationalism within the general concept of the history of Arab nationalism and also try to analyse this phenomenon in its *world-historical context* ('World Time'), Cleveland has confined himself to a study of al-Husri's life and work, thus providing an exclusively intellectual biography of al-Husri. See my review article of Cleveland's book included in a collection of essays, B. Tibi, *Internationale Politik und Entwicklungslaender-Forschung* (Frankfurt, 1979), pp. 142–50.
92. Clifford Geertz, *The Interpretation of Cultures* (New York, 1973), in particular pp. 87ff. A study of Islam as a cultural system with the Geertzian

concept referred to as a framework is provided in B. Tibi, *Der Islam und das Problem der kulturellen Bewaeltigung sozialen Wandels* (referenced in note 51 above; see also the lengthy review of this book by Barbara Stowasser mentioned in the same note).

93. See the now largely forgotten books by Muhammad al-Mubarak, *al-Umma wa al'awamil al-mukawwina laha* 2nd printing (Damascus, no date) and his *al-Umma al-'Arabiyya fi ma'rakat tahqiq al-dhat* (Damascus, 1959). As a dean of the Shari' a faculty, University of Damascus, during the 1950s, Muhammad al-Mubarak was a leading Islamic authority and simultaneously an Arab nationalist.

94. See 'Conclusions:... The Secularization of Islam' in B. Tibi, *Crisis of Modern Islam* (referenced in note 43), pp. 127–48.

95. B. Tibi, 'Islam and Secularization. Religion and the Functional Differentiation of the Social System', *Archiv fuer Rechts-und Sozialphilosophie*, 66 (1980) No. 2, pp. 207–22.

96. B. Tibi, 'Islam and Secularization', in Mourad Wahba (ed.), *Proceedings of the First Philosophy Conference on Islam and Civilization* (Cairo, 1982), pp. 65–79.

97. See, on the one hand, the book of the Lebanese Christian Joseph Mughaizel, *al-'Uruba was al-'ilmaniyya* (Arabism and Secularism) (Beirut, 1980) and on the other, the anti-secular polemic of 'Imaduldin Khalil, *Tahafut al-'ilmaniyya* (The Refutation of Secularism) (Beirut, 1979).

98. Markaz Dirasat al-Wihda al-'Arabiyya/Center for Arab Unity Studies (ed.), *al-Qaumiyya al-'Arabiyya wa al-Islam* (Arab Nationalism and Islam), 2nd printing (Beirut, 1982). Mughaizel's paper is on pp. 361–84, the discussion on pp. 385–439. That volume also includes a paper of Muhammad 'Ammara (pp. 145–76) who has become one of the current major propounders of the idea of the fusion between Islam and Arabism. This anti-secular, yet, national interpretation of the otherwise universal Islam is further developed in Muhammad 'Ammara *al-Islam wa al-'Uruba wa al-'Ilmaniyya* (Islam, Arabism and Secularism) (Beirut, 1981). 'Ammara is very tough here on those who argue *al-'Uruba Awwalan* (Arabism first), as Husri once did, since to 'Ammara, Arabism is inseparable from Islam. See 'Ammara, pp. 41ff.

99. Ali Mérad, *Le reformisme Musulman en Algérie* (Paris, 1967). David Gordon, *The Passing of French Algeria* (London, 1966), pp. 109–18 deals with the ambivalence in Algerian anti-colonial nationalist ideology towards Islam and describes (p. 111) in this context the 'dichotomy that characterizes the ideological consciousness of independent Algeria'.

100. See the new monograph of Vernon Egger, *A Fabian in Egypt. Salamah Musa and the Rise of the Professional Classes in Egypt* (Lanham, Md, 1986). This was originally a University of Michigan, Ann Arbor, Ph.D.; see also note 107 below.

101. Yehoshua Porath, *In Search of Arab Unity 1930–1945* (London, 1986) believes that the Palestine conflict stands as 'the most important factor which contributes to the growth of pan-Arab ideology', p. 162. If the findings of this book on Arab nationalism in which I do not deal with this 'most important factor' are correct, then Porath must be wrong. See my review of Porath's book in *International Journal of Middle East Studies*, 20

(1988) No. 3, pp. 389–90. In the interpretation of the Palestinian narrative historian Muhammad Y. Muslih, *The Origins of Palestinian Nationalism* (New York, 1988), pp. 214–15, 'The failure of the "universalism" [whatever that might be, BT] of Arab nationalism played a critical role in the emergence of Palestinian nationalism. . . For all the pan-Arab fervor of dominant Syrians and Iraqis, *the Palestinians were not at the top of their agenda*' [italics my own BT]. It is true one can apply Porath's argument to Palestinian nationalism in arguing that Zionism was the 'most important factor' in it; this is, however, wrong when applied to Arab nationalism in general, in particular in its formative years when Palestine was a minor issue for it.

102. See pp. 172–3 below. Ironically Porath quotes my book, however, without a specific page reference. In Porath's account, the pan-Islamist Maraghi turns pan-Arabist.

103. For a lengthy quotation (as well as a reference to this book by Sayigh) reflecting Sayigh's views on the Hashemites, see pp. 115–16 below. As regards Sharif Husain's aspirations to become a Caliph of the Arabs see pp. 237–239 of Sayigh's book.

104. See pp. 127–38 below.

105. Patrick Seale, *The Struggle for Syria. A Study of Post-War Arab Politics*, new edn (New Haven, 1986), with a Foreword by Albert Hourani.

106. For a full reference and an evaluation see note 101 above. Despite the criticism put forward in my book review referenced there, I think that Porath has valuably contributed to documenting the royal period of pan-Arabism when Arab kings were the promoters of Arab natonalism.

107. See pp. 178–90 below and, recently, the interpretation of Ralph M. Coury, 'Who "Invented" Egyptian Arab Nationalism?', in two parts, *International Journal of Middle East Studies*, 14 (1982), pp. 249–81 and pp. 459–79.

108. B. Tibi, 'Structural and Ideological Change in the Arab Subsystem Since the Six-Day-War', in Y. Lukacs and A. Battah, *The Arab Israeli Conflict. Two Decades of Change* (Boulder, 1988), pp. 147–63. See also the works quoted in note 72 concerning the meaning of wars for change in history.

109. John Waterbury, *The Egypt of Nasser and Sadat. The Political Economy of Two Regimes* (Princeton, 1983), p. 99–100.

110. The classic of this period is Sadiq Jalal al-'Azm, *al-Naqd al-Dhati ba'd al-Hazimah* (Self-criticism after the Defeat) (Beirut, 1968; 4th printing, 1970). This period is covered in Fouad Ajami's, *The Arab Predicament. Arab Political Thought and Practices since 1967* (Cambridge, 1981); see in particular pp. 25–40.

111. The writings of political Islam (see notes 31, 37, 90 and 97 above) are as numerous as they are intellectually insignificant. See also Yusuf al-Qurdawi, *Hatmiyyat al-Hall al-Islami* (The Islamic Solution is Determinable), referenced in note 25 above. An interesting interpretation of this subject is provided by Emmanuel Sivan, *Radical Islam* (New Haven, 1985). See also the interpretation by B. Tibi, 'The Renewed Role of Islam in the Political and Social Development of the Middle East', fully referenced in note 30 above.

112. Ajami's famous article 'The End of Panarabism' is reprinted in Tawfic Farah (ed.), *Panarabism and Arab Nationalism* (Boulder, 1987).

113. More details about the applicability of the concept of regional subsystems to the Middle East are included with plenty of references in B. Tibi, 'Structural and Ideological Change in the Arab Subsystem...' referenced in note 108 above. See also the chapter on subsystems in B. Tibi, *Konfliktregion Naher Osten* (Munich, 1989), pp. 26–79.

114. See al-'Azm, *al-Naqd al-dhati...* (referenced in note 110) *passim.*

115. On Geertz, see note 92 above and also B. Tibi, 'Neo-Islamic Fundamentalism' (referenced in note 30), as well as my essay on Geertz' interpretation of Islam included in the German edition of his book, *Islam Observed: Religioese Entwicklung im Islam beobachtet in Marokko und in Indonesien* (Frankfurt, 1988), pp. 185–200.

116. See Ursula Braun, *Der Kooperationsrat arabischer Staaten am Golf* (Baden-Baden, 1986), pp. 57ff.

117. This interpretation of Pan-Arabism as a framework of regional cooperation can be found in the book of 'Ali Eddin Hillal and Jamil Matar, *al-Nizam al-Iqlimi al-Arabi* (The Arab Regional System), 3rd edn (Beirut, 1983), pp. 135ff., 156ff. This book, published by the Beirut-based Center for Arab Unity Studies (see note 98 above) enjoys widespread dissemination (3rd printing) and thus is authoritative.

118. The crisis is societal as well as related to the prevailing cultural system, i.e., Islam. See B. Tibi, *Crisis of Modern Islam* (note 43 above), Part III.

119. The transformation of European societies in the modern age was greatly related to achieved cultural innovations (see note 49 above) which contributed to a new *view of the world* (*Weltbild*). See the classical enquiry on the emergence of this new *Weltbild* by the Frankfurt School sociologist Franz Borkenau, *Der Übergang vom feudalen zum bürgerlichen Weltbild*, new edn, first published in German in Paris 1934 (Darmstadt, 1980). Enlightened Arab authors such as the researchers group of Khair-El-Din Hasib (ed.), *Mustaqbal al-umma al-'Arabiyya* (Beirut, 1988) deal soberly with future prospects of the 'Arab nation', but they conspiciously evade posing the sensitive question of the compatability of the inherited *Arabo-Islamic world-view* with the requirements of our '*world time*', as did European philosophers with regard to their own culture, as Borkenau's classic volume reveals.

120. Piscatori (note 2 above), p. 40.

121. This is the English translation of the title of my book *Kulturelle Bewaeltigung des Wandels* (see note 51 above); an English translation is forthcoming (Boulder, Col., 1990).

122. Piscatori, pp. 41–2. One of the sources of this wrong interpretation by Piscatori is, in my view, his inaccurate handling of the historical development of *the state*, as revealed in his uncertain use of the terminology. In his footnote to the cited statement he adds: 'I am conscious (?) of the debate over the proper terminology here... I will use the terms "state", "territorial state", "sovereign state" and "national state" interchangeably' (Piscatori, p. 168). Students of the historical phenomenon of the state relate the 'territorial state' to the medieval age, the 'sovereign state' to the period after the Peace of Westphalia and the 'nation state' to the epoch following the French Revolution. Thus, these terms cannot be used 'interchangeably'.

123. Piscatori, p. 45. The source of this wrong conclusion is his ahistorical, and thus unspecific, use of the term 'nation-state'. See also the review by John Voll mentioned in note 76 above.

124. Joseph Schacht, *An Introduction to Islamic Law*, 5th printing (Oxford, 1979), p. 78 describes the *hiyal* (legal devices) 'as the use of legal means for extra-legal ends, ends that could not . . . be achieved directly with means provided by the *shari'a*'. Thus the *shari'a*, as much as Islamic universalism, cannot be questioned, but evaded. This is *not* a cultural accommodation of change in terms of altering the prevailing view of the world.

Notes to Chapter 1

1. A. F. Pollard, *Factors in Modern History* (London, 1907) p. 3.

2. Koppel S. Pinson has compiled a comprehensive bibliography to 1935: *A Bibliographical Introduction to Nationalism* (New York, 1935). For later research, see Karl W. Deutsch, *An Interdisciplinary Bibliography on Nationalism 1935–1953* (Cambridge, 1956). Deutsch gives a survey of the literature up to 1965 in the introduction to the second edition of his *Nationalism and Social Communication; An Inquiry into the Foundations of Nationality*, 2nd ed. (Cambridge, Mass., 1966), pp. 7–14. Hannah Vogt has published a selection of texts on nationalism in political philosophy in *Nationalismus gestern und heute* (Opladen, 1967). Details of different interpretations of nationalism are given by Louis L. Snyder, *The Meaning of Nationalism* (New Brunswick, 1954), and Eugen Lemberg, 'Nationalismus: Definition, Tendenzen, Theorien', *Moderne Welt*, VIII (1967) No. 3, pp. 317–33.

3. On this see Boyd C. Shafer, *Nationalism: Myth and Reality* (New York, 1955) pp. 36 f. Shafer classifies the mystification of the nation and of nationalism in political philosophy into 'metaphysical myths', 'physical myths', and 'cultural myths'; see *ibid.*, pp. 13–56.

4. On this see Karl W. Deutsch, *Nationalism and Social Communication*, pp. 15–28, and Shafer, *op. cit.*, *passim*; also Heinz O. Ziegler, *Die moderne Nation: Ein Beitrag zur politischen Soziologie* (Tübingen, 1931) pp. 27–54.

5. Ziegler, *op. cit.*, p. 73.

6. *Ibid.*, p. 75.

7. Hans Kohn, *The Idea of Nationalism: A Study in its Origins and Background* (New York, 1945) p. 188.

8. F. Engels, *Über den Verfall des Feudalismus und das Aufkommen der Bourgeoisie*, in *Marx-Engels-Werke*, vol. XXI (Berlin, 1962) pp. 392 ff, here p. 397. On the relationship between sovereignty and kingship during the course of nation formation in Europe, see Joseph R. Stryer, 'The Historical Experience of Nation-Building in Europe', in Karl W. Deutsch and William J. Foltz (eds), *Nation-Building* (New York, 1963) pp. 17–26. The emergence of nationalities under kingship has been researched by H. Munro Chadwick, *Nationalities in Europe and the Growth of National Ideologies*, 2nd ed. (Cambridge, 1966) Chap. V, pp. 91–113.

9. Ziegler, *op. cit.*, pp. 90 f.

10. See Shafer, *op. cit.*, pp. 92 f.

11. *Ibid.*, pp. 94 f.

12. Kohn, *op. cit.*, p. 206.
13. *Ibid.*, p. 218.
14. *Ibid.*, p. 221.
15. J. Habermas, *Strukturwandel der Öffentlichkeit, Untersuchungen zu einer Kategorie der bürgerlichen Geselleschaft*, 2nd ed. (Berlin-Neuwied, 1965) p. 28.
16. Ziegler, *op. cit.*, p. 96.
17. *Ibid.*, p. 95.
18. *Ibid.*
19. W. Euchner, *Naturrecht und Politik bei John Locke* (Frankfurt/Main, 1969) pp. 198 ff.
20. *Ibid.*, p. 201.
21. J. Habermas, 'Naturrecht und Revolution', in *Theorie und Praxis: Sozialphilosophische Studien* (Berlin, 1963) pp. 52 ff.; here p. 68. Eng. transl. 'Natural Law and Revolution', in *Theory and Practice* (London, 1974) pp. 82–120; here p. 93.
22. *Ibid.*, p. 73. Eng. transl., p. 98.
23. See Euchner, *op. cit.*, pp. 222 f.
24. On the structure of the *volonté générale* see I. Fetscher, *Rousseaus politische Philosophie; zur Geschichte des demokratischen Freiheitsbegriffs* (Berlin, 1960) pp. 111–26.
25. Habermas, 'Naturrecht und Revolution', p. 69. Eng. transl., p. 99.
26. Ziegler, *op. cit.*, p. 97.
27. *Ibid.*, p. 64.
28. Kohn, *op. cit.*, p. 3.
29. Ziegler, *op. cit.*, p. 64. On the question of terminology: following Ziegler, *nation* is seen only in terms of a form of political organisation. *People, nationhood*, or more accurately *nationality* is seen as the formation of a group with a certain cohesion, though not necessarily organised into a national state. W. Sulzbach, 'Zur Definition und Psychologie von "Nation" und Nationalbewußtsein', *Politische Vierteljahresschrift*, III (1962) No. 2, 139–58, discusses the terminological confusion in the literature about nationalism. Sulzbach comments on the inadequacy of the interpretation which explains the nation in terms of common features of language and literature etc. For Sulzbach the state as a power structure is a constituent element of the nation. However, he goes on to interpret the genesis of the nation and of nationalism in entirely subjective terms. 'The ideal of national sovereignty first came into the minds of a few individuals. It then obtained more widespread support. Finally it became common property through education and propaganda.' (p. 154) For a criticism of Sulzbach's interpretation of nationalism, see G. Kress and K. J. Gantzel 'Pseudowissenschaftliches zur Nationalismus- Diskussion', *Neue Politische Literatur*, XV (1970) No. 3, 394–6.
30. Hans D. Werner has shown that *national character* is an inadequate term for scholarly purposes in *Klassenstruktur und Nationalcharakter: Eine soziologische Kritik* (Tübingen, n.d. [1968], reviewed by B. Tibi in *Das Argument*, XII (1970) No 56, 58–60.
31. See Karl W. Deutsch, 'Nation-Building and National Development: Some Issues for Political Research', in Karl W. Deutsch and William J. Foltz (eds), *Nation-Building*, pp. 1–16, especially pp. 6 f.
32. Max Weber, *Wirtschaft und Gesellschaft: Grundriß der verstehenden*

Soziologie, 2 vols (Cologne and Berlin, 1962) vol. II, p. 675. Eng. transl., *Economy and Society*, 3 vols (New York, 1968) vol. II, p. 922. However, Weber sees the nation in purely psychological terms: it exists only in the mind.

33. K. Marx and F. Engels, 'Manifest der kommunistischen Partei', in *Marx-Engels-Werke*, 3rd ed., vol. IV (Berlin, 1964) pp. 459–93, here pp. 466–7; Eng. transl., 'The Communist Manifesto', in L. S. Feuer (ed.), *Karl Marx and Friedrich Engels: Basic Writings on Politics and Philosophy* (London, 1969) pp. 43–82; here p. 53.

34. Cf. Ziegler, *op. cit.*, p. 69: also Shafer, *op. cit.*, p. 106.

35. Cf. Kohn, *op. cit.*, p. 191. Also K. D. Bracher's article 'Der Nationalstaat', in K. D. Bracher and E. Fraenkel (eds), *Das Fischer-Lexicon*, vol. II, *Staat und Politik* (Frankfurt/Main, 1962) pp. 198–204; here p. 198 ff.; also Hermann Lübbe, *Säkularisierung, Geschichte eines ideenpolitischen Begriffs* (Freiburg and Munich, 1965).

36. Pollard, *op. cit.*, p. 9, sees the Reformation as the beginning of the disintegration of Christian universalism. Salo Wittmayer Baron, *Modern Nationalism and Religion* (New York and London, 1947) p. 7, considers that 'Modern nationalism has displaced religion as the chief factor in human group relationships . . . religion, now displaced from its position of primacy, continued to influence profoundly national life both through the various state controlled, state subsidised or even state-separated churches and through their supra-national, non-political ethical teachings.'

37. Emmanuel Sieyès, *Qu'est-ce que le Tiers Etat?*, ed. R. Zapperi (Geneva, 1970) p. 126. Eng. transl., *What is the Third Estate?* (London, 1963) p. 58.

38. *Ibid.*, p. 124; Eng. transl., p. 57.

39. Marx describes the (national) state in bourgeois society as follows:

> By the mere fact that it is a *class* and no longer an *estate*, the bourgeoisie is forced to organise itself no longer locally, but nationally, and to give a general form to its average interests. Through the emancipation of private property from the community, the state has become a separate entity, alongside and outside civil society; but it is nothing more than the form of organisation which the bourgeois are compelled to adopt, both for internal and external purposes, for the mutual guarantee of their property and interests. 'Die deutsche Ideologie', in *Marx-Engels-Werke*, 3rd ed., vol. III (Berlin, 1962) p. 62; Eng. transl., 'The German Ideology', in *Collected Works*, vol. V (London, 1976) p. 90.

40. This is claimed by Ziegler, *op. cit.*, pp. 96,104 and *passim*; for a contrary interpretation, see Fetscher's analysis of Rousseau's interpretation of democratic freedom; Fetscher, *op. cit.*, *passim*.

41. This undiscriminating theory is held by, e.g., J. L. Talmon, *The Origins of Totalitarian Democracy* (London, 1952) pp. 38–49.

42. A. Sorel, quoted by Shafer, *op. cit.*, p. 134.

43. Eva Hoffmann-Linke, *Zwischen Nationalismus und Demokratie, Gestalten der Französischen Vorrevolution* (Munich and Berlin, 1927) p. 3.

44. Hans Kohn has proved convincingly that Napoleon was never a French nationalist in 'Napoleon and the Age of Nationalism', *Journal of Modern History*, XII (1950) No. 1, 21–37.

45. Ziegler, *op. cit.*, pp. 114 f.
46. Friedrich Engels, 'The State of Germany', *The Northern Star*, 25 October 1845; Karl Marx and Friedrich Engels, *Collected Works*, vol. VI (London, 1976) p. 19.
47. *Ibid.*, p. 22.
48. C. J. H. Hayes, *The Historical Evolution of Modern Nationalism* (New York, 1950).
49. Louis L. Snyder has provided a comprehensive analysis of this in *German Nationalism, the Tragedy of a People: Extremism contra Liberalism in Modern German History* (Harrisburg, 1952). The same theme has been discussed by Helga Grebing in 'Nationalismus und Demokratie in Deutschland', in I. Fetscher (ed.), *Rechtsradikalismus*, 2nd ed. (Frankfurt/Main, 1967) pp. 31–66. Further references are given in the notes to Chapter 6.
50. The 'inflated and extravagant national pride' of the Germans, whose lot is 'everywhere . . . merely to look on and be left high and dry' results, according to Marx in 'practical activity of the pettiest kind, worthy of shop-keepers and artisans'. See K. Marx and F. Engels, *Deutsche Ideologie*, p. 458; Eng. transl., p. 470.
51. See Ziegler, *op. cit.*, p. 121.
52. K. O. Freiherr von Aretin, 'Uber die Notwendigkeit kritischer Distanzierung vom Nationsbegriff in Deutschland nach 1945', in H. Bolewski (ed.), *Nation und Nationalismus* (Stuttgart, 1967) pp. 26–45, here p. 29. In 'Das Problem des deutschen Nationalstaates', *Politische Vierteljahresschrift*, III (1962) No. 2, 159–86, W. Sauer shows that the national state in the advanced countries of Europe 'has a clearly democratic emphasis, which is somewhat distorted in the German version' (p. 160). The French and the British national states both sprang out of a bourgeois-democratic revolution: in Germany this revolution failed, 'which is why the European synthesis of nationalism and democracy was never achieved here' (p. 161).
53. C. Maurras, quoted by E. Nolte, *Der Faschismus in seiner Epoche*, 2nd ed. (Munich, 1965) p. 146. Eng. transl., *Three Faces of Fascism* (New York and Toronto, 1969) p. 144. See also William C. Buthman, *The Rise of Integral Nationalism in France, with Special Reference to the Ideas and Activities of Charles Maurras* (New York, 1939). See also Wittmayer Baron, *op. cit.*, pp. 61–68. On the general subject of integral nationalism, see E. Lemberg, *Geschichte des Nationalismus in Europe* (Stuttgart, 1950) pp. 267 ff.
54. Nolte, *op. cit.*, p. 105., Eng. transl., p. 99.
55. Hannah Arendt, *The Origins of Totalitarianism*, revised ed. (London, 1967) pp. 267–302.
56. Nolte, *op. cit.*, p. 146., Eng. transl., p. 144.

Notes to Chapter 2

1. In 'Types of Nationalism', *American Journal of Sociology*, XLI (1936) No. 6, 723–37, L. Wirth has suggested a typology for research into nationalism, giving four ideal types of nationalism: (1) *hegemonic nationalism*, which tends to develop after the unification of several territories, for example, German and Italian nationalism in the nineteenth century; (2) *particularist nationalism*,

which demands the separation of one territory from another and the setting up of a new national sovereignty, such as for instance, Irish nationalism; (3) the marginal nationalism of border peoples; (4) the nationalism of minorities. According to this typology, the first phase of anti-colonial nationalism would be defined as particularist. As this definition in fact says little about the content of nationalism in the 'Third World', its application will not be discussed here. Karl Teodor Schuon has criticised the typology method in 'Typologie und kritische Theorie', *Das Argument*, XI (1969) No. 50 (Special number) 93–124.

2. H. Kohn, *The Idea of Nationalism: A Study in Its Origins and Background*, p. 20.
3. Rupert Emerson, *From Empire to Nation: The Rise of Self-Assertion of Asian and African Peoples*, 3rd ed. (Boston, 1964) p. 206.
4. Fetscher documents the points discussed in this section in *Der Marxismus und seine Geschichte in Dokumenten*, vol. III, *Politik* (Munich, 1965), especially the chapter 'Die Nation', pp. 91–121. See also Solomon Frank Bloom, 'The World of Nations: A Study of the National Implications in the Work of Karl Marx', Unpub. Ph. D. thesis (New York, 1941); Horace B. Davis, *Nationalism and Socialism. Marxist and Labor Theories of Nationalism to 1917* (New York and London, 1967), and a review of this by B. Tibi, 'Marxismus and Nationalismusanalyse', *Neue Politische Literatur*, XIV (1969) 560–1.
5. Karl Kautsky in 'Nationalität und Internationalität', Supplementary Number of *Neue Zeit*, No. 1, 18 January 1908, pp. 17 ff., 23 ff., considers the national state to be 'the form of state which corresponds with modern conditions' (p. 23), while in contrast states of mixed national composition are considered backward.
6. Karl Marx, Letter to Engels, 5 July 1870, in *Marx-Engels-Werke*, vol. XXXII (Berlin, 1965) p. 520. Marx' position on the Polish Question can be surmised from his *Manuskripte über die polnische Frage (1863–1864)*, ed. W. Conze ('sGravenhage, 1961).
7. Karl Marx, 'Rede über Polen', in *Marx-Engels-Werke*, 3rd ed., vol. IV (Berlin, 1964) pp. 416 f.; Eng. transl., 'On Poland', in *Collected Works*, vol. VI (London, 1976) pp. 388–9.
8. Karl Marx, 'Rede über die Frage des Freihandels', in *Marx-Engels-Werke*, 3rd ed., vol. IV (Berlin, 1964) pp. 444–58; Eng. transl., 'Speech on the Question of Free Trade', in *Collected Works*, vol. VI (London, 1976) pp. 450–65; here p. 464.
9. Karl Marx, Letter to Engels, 20 June 1866, in *Marx-Engels-Werke*, vol. XXXI (Berlin, 1965) pp. 228 f.; Eng. transl., in Dona Torr (ed. and transl.), *The Correspondence of Marx and Engels, 1846–1895* (London, 1934) p. 207.
10. See H. B. Davis, *op. cit.*, p. 13. For the theory that proletarian internationalism is only possible among free peoples, and that it does not imply national nihilism, see Friedrich Engels, 'Das Fest der Nationen in London', in *Marx-Engels-Werke*, vol. II (Berlin, 1962) pp. 611–24; Eng. transl. 'The Festival of Nations in London', in *Collected Works*, vol. VI (London, 1976) pp. 3–14. This dimension has been entirely overlooked by the French Communist Party in its colonial policy: see here J. Moneta, *Die Kolonialpolitik der französischen KP* (Hanover, 1968), and my review in *Das Argument*, II (1969) No. 53, 353–6.

11. See K. Marx, 'Die englische Regierung und die eingekerkerten Fenier', in *Marx-Engels-Werke*, vol. XVI (Berlin, 1962) pp. 401–6; *idem.*, 'Entwurf eines Vortrages zur irischen Frage', *ibid.*, pp. 445–59; *idem.*, 'Entwurf einer nicht gehaltenen Rede zur irischen Frage', *ibid.*, pp. 439–46. On the Irish question see Lawrence J. McCaffrey, *The Irish Question 1800–1922* (Lexington, 1968).
12. K. Marx, Letter to Engels, 10 Dec. 1869, in *Marx-Engels-Werke*, vol. XXXII (Berlin, 1965) pp. 414 ff.
13. F. Engels, 'Rede über Polen', in *Marx-Engels-Werke*, 3rd ed., vol IV (Berlin, 1964) pp. 417 f.; here p. 417; Eng. transl., 'Speech on Poland', in K. Marx and F. Engels, *Collected Works*, vol. VI (London, 1976) pp. 389–90; here p. 389.
14. F. Engels, 'Eine polnische Proklamation', in *Marx-Engels-Werke*, 2nd ed., vol. XVIII (Berlin, 1964) pp. 521–7; here p. 527.
15. F. Engels, 'Was hat die Arbeiterklasse mit Polen zu tun?', in *Marx-Engels-Werke*, vol. XVI (Berlin, 1962) pp. 153–63; here p. 157.
16. *Ibid.*
17. *Ibid.*
18. F. Engels, 'Po und Rhein', in *Marx-Engels-Werke*, 2nd ed., vol. XIII (Berlin, 1964) pp. 225–68; here p. 267. The distinction between nations with and without history is now being refuted by structuralism. In *La Pensée Sauvage* (Eng. transl., *The Savage Mind*, (London, 1966)), Lévi-Strauss argues, against Sartre, that the categories *historical* and *having no history* originate from European thought, and that history is thus a European myth. However, in his humanist effort to rehabilitate 'The Savage Mind', Lévi-Strauss contradicts his own structuralist method, which denies the validity of history as such. For a critique of the structuralists' hostility towards history, and particularly that of Lévi-Strauss, cf. Alfred Schmidt (ed.), *Beiträge zur marxistischen Erkenntnistheorie* (Frankfurt/Main, 1969) pp. 194–265.
19. O. Bauer, *Die Nationalitätenfrage und die Sozialdemokratie*, Marx-Studien, vol. II, ed. M. Adler and R. Hilferding, 2nd ed. (Vienna, 1924) Chapter 17, pp. 215 ff. Bauer's definition of the nation as a community with a common fate will not be considered. The earliest critique of Bauer's theory of nationalism is by Karl Kautsky, 'Nationalität und Internationalität', *op. cit.*; see Bauer's reply, 'Bemerkungen zur Nationalitätenfrage', *Die Neue Zeit*, XXVI, pt. 1, (1907–8). Davis, *op. cit.*, pp. 149–57, discusses Bauer's theory and the controversy which has arisen from it, pp. 157–63. For a critique of Bauer, see H. O. Ziegler, *Die moderne Nation* (Tübingen, 1931) pp. 49 ff.; cf. also Karl W. Deutsch, *Nationalism and Social Communication*, 2nd ed. (Cambridge, Mass., 1966) pp. 19 f.
20. Bauer, 'Die Nationalitätenfrage', *op. cit.*, p. 263.
21. *Ibid.*, pp. 304–310.
22. *Ibid.*, p. 319, p. 323, and *passim*.
23. K. Kautsky, *op. cit.*
24. V. I. Lenin, 'Socialism and War', (Eng. transl.) in *Collected Works*, vol. XVIII (London, n.d.) pp. 215–58; here p. 236.
25. V. I. Lenin, 'The Right of Nations to Self-Determination', (Eng. transl.) in *Collected Works*, vol. XX (Moscow and London, 1964) pp. 393–454; here p. 397.
26. *Ibid.*, p. 400.
27. *Ibid.*, p. 399.

28. *Ibid.*, p. 405.
29. *Ibid.*, p. 413.
30. *Ibid.*, p. 264; pp. 255 ff. Lenin also quotes some of the letters from Marx to Engels on Ireland to which reference has been made. He was not familiar with the minor works of Marx, since they had not yet been published (see Note 11 above).
31. V. I. Lenin, 'The Peace Question' (Eng. transl.) in *Collected Works*, vol. XVIII (London, n.d.) pp. 264–8; here p. 267. See also 'Socialism and War', *op. cit.*, pp. 234–5. For a summary of Lenin's position on the national and colonial question, see H. B. Davis, *op. cit.*, pp. 185–210.
32. V. I. Lenin, 'The Right of Nations to Self-Determination', *Collected Works*, pp. 411 ff.
33. V. I. Lenin, 'The Socialist Revolution and the Right of Nations to Self-Determination', (Eng. transl.) in *Collected Works*, vol. XXII (Moscow and London, 1964) pp. 143–56; here p. 148.
34. *Ibid.*, p. 147.
35. Rosa Luxemburg writes: 'The famous "right of self-determination of nations", is nothing but hollow petty-bourgeois phraseology and humbug.' *Die russische Revolution*, ed. O. Flechtheim (Frankfurt/Main, 1963) p. 60; Eng. transl., *The Russian Revolution*, intro. B. D. Wolfe (Ann Arbor, 1961) p. 49.
36. One of the arguments put forward by Bernstein against the right of national self-determination was 'We must get away from the utopian idea which leads to disposing of the colonies. The colonies are here to stay, and we must come to terms with that. Civilised people have to exercise a certain guardianship over uncivilised peoples—even socialists have to recognise this.' E. Bernstein, quoted by Karl Kautsky, *Sozialismus und Kolonialpolitik* (Berlin, 1907) p. 6; Eng. transl., *Socialism and Colonial Policy: An Analysis* (Belfast, 1975) p. 3.
37. The ideological approach followed by modernisation theorists is a popularised form of the 'total ideological approach' put forward by Karl Mannheim and his successors. A quotation from Paul E. Sigmund illustrates what modernisation theorists mean by ideology. Sigmund holds that anticolonial nationalism is 'a sufficiently coherent body of ideas to be called ideology—the ideology of nationalism'. P. E. Sigmund (ed.), *The Ideologies of Developing Nations*, 2nd ed. (New York, 1967) pp. 36 ff. See also David Apter, *The Politics of Modernization* (Chicago, 1965) pp. 330 ff., also pp. 172 ff. For the source of this popular ideology approach, see Karl Mannheim, *Ideologie und Utopie*, 4th ed. (Frankfurt/Main, 1965) pp. 49–94; Eng. transl., *Ideology and Utopia*, 7th ed. (London, 1954) pp. 49–96, where he develops the 'total ideological approach'. On the problem of ideology, see Kurt Lenk (ed.), *Ideologie, Ideologiekritik und Wissenssoziologie: Problemgeschichtliche Einleitung*, 2nd ed. (Berlin, 1964) Ch. 1.
38. Conrad Schuhler provides a brief and critical account of the various versions of modernisation theory; *Zur politischen Ökonomie der Armen Welt* (Munich, 1968) pp. 32–44. 'It is abundantly clear that *a single* historical and cultural example of "modern" society is *idealised* as modern society itself . . . A modernisation theorist sees the problem in terms of the transition from a "traditional" to a "modern" society.' (p. 33)
39. Hence the title of one of the most influential contributions to modernisation

theory in the context of underdevelopment: *The Passing of Traditional Society*, 2nd ed. (Glencoe/Ill., 1962), by Daniel Lerner. In a study by a group of eminent modernisation theorists, to which Lerner also belongs, the question is posed as follows: colonial, semi-colonial and post-colonial societies are seen and described as traditional societies. Under 'the impact of the West', a process of disintegration begins, leading to modernisation. The conflict that arises from the resistance of the traditional forces to modernisation and the demands of those social forces which support modernisation hastens this process. The nationalism of the colonial intellectual tends to serve modernisation. See Max F. Millikan and Donald L. M. Blackmer (eds), *The Emerging Nations* (Boston and Toronto, 1961). The role of nationalism in the process of the disintegration of traditional societies is also discussed by the modernisation theorist Edward Shils in *Political Development in the New States* (The Hague, 1965) pp. 32 f. Shils sees a certain dualism between modernising nationalism and parochialism.

40. See Mary Matossian, 'Ideologies of Delayed Industrialisation: Some Tensions and Ambiguities', *Economic Development and Cultural Change*, VI (1958) No. 3, 217–28. Matossian sees nationalism, communism and fascism as 'ideologies of delayed industrialisation'.

41. K. H. Silvert, 'The Strategy of the Study of Nationalism', in *idem* (ed.), *Expectant Peoples, Nationalism and Development* (New York, 1963) pp. 3–38; here p. 26. Silvert believes that nationalism in the underdeveloped countries is the primary cohesive force and considers it as 'a necessary part of the process of development'. This collection contains case studies on the role of nationalism in the process of modernisation in a number of underdeveloped countries, including Bolivia, Indonesia, and the Arab countries.

42. John H. Kautsky, 'An Essay in the Politics of Development', in *idem* (ed.), *Political Change in Underdeveloped Countries, Nationalism and Communism*, 7th ed. (New York, 1967) pp. 3–119.

43. *Ibid.*, pp. 33 f. For Kautsky, Irish nationalism is an exception, and it resembles the nationalism of the colonial peoples in that it is directed against an advanced country, Britain. See also Note 11 above, also Chapter 2(a).

44. *Ibid.*, p. 35.

45. W. Sulzbach, *Imperialismus und Nationalbewußtsein* (Frankfurt/Main, 1959) pp. 108 f. (On Sulzbach cf. Chapter 1, note 11).

46. Emerson, *op. cit.*, pp. 85, 95.

47. J. H. Kautsky, *op. cit.*, p. 39 f. See also Emerson, *op. cit.*, p. 85 and pp. 89 f.

48. J. H. Kautsky, *op. cit.*, p. 48. Emerson (*op. cit.*, p. 196) writes that all nationalists in the colonial countries are intellectuals 'who had been exposed to a Western Type of Education and Experience . . . in principle, the Nationalists were all men who had become familiar with the West in one or another fashion'. Emerson also emphasises that these nationalists have drawn mainly on the writings on European thinkers, such as Rousseau, Fichte, Burke, Mazzini etc., and that their political models are European nationalists such as Cavour, Garibaldi, Bismarck, etc. (p. 199). This will be more rigorously discussed and illustrated with a case study of Arab nationalism in later chapters. On this see also C. B. Macpherson, *The Real World of Democracy* (Oxford, 1966) pp. 23–34.

49. J. H. Kautsky, *op. cit.*, p. 48.
50. *Ibid.*, p. 49. On the role of the anti-colonial intellectual cf. Edward Shils, 'The Intellectuals in the Political Development of the New States,' in John H. Kautsky (ed.), *op. cit.*, pp. 195–234. The relationship between the colonial intellectual and nationalism has been investigated by Klaus Mehnert, 'The Social and Political Role of the Intelligentsia in the New Countries', in Kurt London (ed.), *New Nations in a Divided World* (New York, 1963) pp. 121–33. Mehnert also believes that nationalism is an expression of the aspirations of the colonial intellectual and of anticolonialism. See pp. 126 ff.
51. See Karl Mannheim, *Ideologie und Utopie*, pp. 134 ff; Eng. transl., pp. 136–45. For a critique cf. A. Neusüss, *Utopisches Bewußtsein und freischwebende Intelligenz; Zur Wissenssoziologie Karl Mannheims* (Meisenheim am Glan, 1968).
52. Jean Ziegler, *Politische Soziologie des neuen Afrika* (Munich, 1966) pp. 16 f., points to authors who, following Pareto, interpret social change in the underdeveloped countries in terms of the circulation of élites. Ziegler considers élite theory to be invalid, and insists on a theory of classes, but believes that it must be newly formulated for Africa (cf. pp. 32 ff.). He thinks that in Africa membership of a certain class cannot simply be defined in terms of the individual's role in the process of production, but also in terms of the social power available to him. The class which controls power rather than the class which controls the means of production is thus supposed to be the ruling class (pp. 37 ff.). For a critique of this thesis, see B. Tibi, 'Zum Verhältnis von Militär und kolonialem Nationalismus am Beispiel der arabischen Länder', *Sozialistische Politik*, I (1969) No. 4, 4–19, especially page 9. T. B. Bottomore believes that in the underdeveloped countries five successive ideal élites take over the leadership of the process of industrialisation, since the majority of the population is not organised. In addition to the nationalist leaders, he mentions a dynastic élite, a middle class, the revolutionary intellectuals and the colonial officials. See T. B. Bottomore, *Elites and Society*, 2nd ed. (London, 1966) pp. 93–111, especially p. 96. See also Harry J. Benda, 'Non-Western Intelligentsias as Political Elites', in J. H. Kautsky (ed.), *op. cit.*, pp. 235–51.
53. J. H. Kautsky, *op. cit.*, pp. 42, 44.
54. *Ibid.*, p. 53.
55. *Ibid.*, p. 39. See also pp. 54 f.
55ª. Lars Clausen's study of industrialisation in an underdeveloped country is rich in material but does not provide a particularly convincing model of development. (*Industrialisierung in Schwarzafrika, eine soziologische Lotstudie zweier Großbetriebe in Sambia* (Bielefeld, 1968)). Like Weber, Clausen no longer wishes to view industrialisation in purely technical terms. He is concerned to see it as part of the transition from 'traditional' to 'purposeful-rational', that is, modern, 'industrially-directed' action. However, it remains unclear for what purpose such action, whether rational or irrational, will appear rational (cf. pp. 159 ff.). While Clausen's work, with its wealth of empirical material, could support Kautsky's interpretation, particularly as both analyses are fundamentally similar, Clausen comes to the conclusion that in Zambia 'industrial orientation' could be enforced to such an extent that 'even a modern or otherwise very strongly non-industrial form of reward, (!) the new nationalism, was forced to retreat' (p. 160). On Clausen's research,

see the review by B. Tibi in *Das Argument*, XII (1970) No. 59, 641–3.

56. Richard F. Behrendt, *Soziale Strategie für Entwicklungsländer, Entwurf einer Entwicklungsstragegie* (Frankfurt/Main, 1965) p. 250.
57. *Ibid.*, p. 250 f.
58. *Ibid.*, p. 251.
59. See *ibid.*, p. 236.
60. See *ibid.*, pp. 331–4.
61. *Ibid.*, p. 336.
62. *Ibid.*, see also note 48 above.
63. *Ibid.*, p. 338.
64. *Ibid.*, p. 343.
65. *Ibid.*, p. 340.
66. *Ibid.*, p. 361.
67. *Ibid.*, p. 331.
68. *Ibid.*, p. 335.
69. *Ibid.*
70. *Ibid.*, p. 371.
71. *Ibid.*, p. 346.
72. *Ibid.*, p. 337.
73. *Ibid.*, pp. 355 f.
74. See *ibid.*, p. 362.
75. *Ibid.*
76. *Ibid.*, p. 355.
77. *Ibid.*
78. Frantz Fanon, *Les Damnés de la Terre* (Paris, 1961); Eng. transl., *The Wretched of the Earth*, 2nd ed. (London, 1967). (Page references in the notes below are to adaptations from the English translation—*Trs.*) For references to secondary literature on Fanon, see Chapter 3, note 48.
79. *Ibid.*, p. 74.
80. *Ibid.*
81. *Ibid.*, p. 87.
82. *Ibid.*, p. 39.
83. *Ibid.*, pp. 50 ff.
84. *Ibid.*, p. 73.
85. *Ibid.*, p. 104.
86. *Ibid.*, p. 106.
87. *Ibid.*, p. 105.
88. *Ibid.*, p. 74.
89. *Ibid.*, p. 118.
90. *Ibid.*, pp. 168–9. An example of this is the attempt of the British educated scholar J. C. de Graft-Johnson to reconstruct pre-colonial African history. See J. C. de Graft-Johnson, *African Glory: The story of Vanished Negro Civilisation*, 2nd ed. (New York, 1966), and the review by B. Tibi in *Der Politologe*, VIII, No. 24 (1967) 44 ff.
91. Fanon, *op. cit.*, p. 175.
92. *Ibid.*, p. 171.
93. *Ibid.*, p. 169.
94. *Ibid.*, p. 179 f. This tendency to exoticism can be found, for example, in the work of L. S. Senghor, a leading African nationalist. He rejects 'European

reason' and replaces it by 'Black reason'. Traditional African society is glorified through the medium of European speech. See L. S. Senghor, *Négritude et Humanisme* (Paris, 1964) *passim*. In contrast, Aimé Césaire, who, like Senghor, seeks to rehabilitate pre-colonial culture, rejects any backward-looking Utopia: 'It is not a dead society that we wish to revive. We leave that to those who go in for exoticism.' *Discours sur le Colonialisme* (Paris, 1955); Eng. transl., *Discourse on Colonialism* (New York and London, 1972) p. 31. For a review of the German translation, see B. Tibi, *Das Argument*, XI (1969) No. 51, 138 ff.

95. Fanon, *op. cit.*, p. 181.
96. *Ibid.*, p. 191.
97. *Ibid.*, pp. 190–9.
98. *Ibid.*, pp. 40 ff.
99. *Ibid.*, pp. 116–17.
100. *Ibid.*, p. 119.
101. *Ibid.*, pp. 164–5.
102. *Ibid.*, p. 122.
103. *Ibid.*, p. 124.
104. *Ibid.*, p. 121.
105. Cf. Senghor, *op. cit.*, *passim*. See also B. Tibi, 'Léopold Senghors "Négritude"', *Das Argument*, IX (1967) No. 45, 422 ff. For further source material see Chapter 3, note 57.
106. Fanon, *op. cit.*, pp. 125 ff.
107. *Ibid.*, p. 125.
108. *Ibid.*, p. 127.
109. *Ibid.*, p. 128.
110. *Ibid.*, p. 138.
111. *Ibid.*, p. 165.
112. On this see Chapter 2 above.
113. Fanon, *op. cit.*, p. 198.
114. *Ibid.*, p. 199.

Notes to Chapter 3

1. Marx assumed that after the enforced disintegration of their social structures under colonial rule, the colonial countries would develop in a capitalist, that is, historically more progressive, direction. Hence he justified colonisation with world historical arguments. See his 'The British Rule in India', *New York Daily Tribune*, 25 June 1853, quoted in L. S. Feuer (ed.), *Karl Marx and Friedrich Engels: Basic Writings on Politics and Philosophy*, *op. cit.*, pp. 511–18. See also H. B. Davis, *Nationalism and Socialism*, *op. cit.*, pp. 59 ff. This thesis has proved untenable. Capitalism in the colonies has not even taken on a strictly capitalist character, but has become an exploitative mechanism which has preserved the local feudal structures in a modernised form. This has been illustrated by Aimé Césaire in *Discours sur le colonialisme*; Eng. transl. pp. 13–15, and by Jean-Paul Sartre in *Colonialisme et Néocolonialisme* (Paris, 1964).

2. Social change is taken to include all forms of change, socio-economic, socio-psychological, political and cultural. Behrendt's definition of cultural change is too subjective to be adequate. For a survey of current theories of social change, see the collection edited by H. P. Dreitzel, *Sozialer Wandel* (Neuwied and Berlin, 1967), which includes both older and more recent interpretations. The latest American theories are documented in W. Zapf (ed.), *Theorien des sozialen Wandels*, 2nd ed. (Cologne and Berlin, 1970), and in P. Heintz (ed.), *Soziologie der Entwicklungsländer* (Cologne and Berlin, 1962).

3. For these two stages of emancipation, see J. Habermas, *Erkenntnis und Interesse* (Frankfurt/Main, 1968) p. 71; Eng. transl., *Knowledge and Human Interests* (London, 1972) p. 53.

4. For the definition of alien and indigenous history see the section above on Fanon (Chapter 2d). For the problem of alien rule and of self-government as an expression of the re-establishment of indigenous history, see John Plamenatz, *On Alien Rule and Self-government* (London, 1960), and Rupert Emerson, *From Empire to Nation*, 3rd ed. (Boston, 1964), (1st ed., Cambridge, Mass., 1960).

5. Although colonial national states are equal in terms of international law, their colonial status has hardly changed as far as the realities of international relations are concerned. G. L. Matus has shown that state formation is not yet equivalent to emancipation; 'Der Status der Nation und das internationale Schichtungssystem', in P. Heintz (ed.), *Soziologie der Entwicklungsländer*, pp. 45–69. Matus asserts that the real status of a 'nation' in the international constellation derives from its economic strength, and the power which derives from that strength.

6. Fanon wrote his main work, *The Wretched of the Earth*, Eng. transl. (London, 1967) under great pressure during his last illness before his death. When he sent the manuscript to his publisher he wrote 'I have the impression that I have been extremely vehement in what I have written. This is probably because at times the whole project seemed to be in jeopardy.' Quoted in Renate Zahar, *Kolonialismus und Entfremdung: Zur politischen Theorie Frantz Fanons* (Frankfurt/Main, 1969) p. 13. For further references, see Zahar's bibliography and note 48 below.

7. See Conrad Schuhler, *Zur politischen Ökonomie der Armen Welt* (Munich, 1968) pp. 107 f.

8. The definitions are from R. König (ed.), *Aspekte der Entwicklungssoziologie* (Cologne and Opladen, 1970) p. 31. They are useful, but König's models will not be applied. In this context it is sufficient to point out that apart from a few unimportant differences, König's explanations are derived from Mühlmann, whose interpretation will be discussed below.

9. W. E. Mühlmann (ed.), *Chiliasmus und Nativismus* (Berlin, 1961) p. 383.

10. *Ibid.*, pp. 385 f.

11. *Ibid.*, p. 386.

12. *Ibid.*, p. 287.

13. W. E. Mühlmann, *Rassen, Ethnien, Kulturen, Moderne Ethnologie* (Neuwied and Berlin, 1964) p. 324.

14. *Ibid.*, p. 323.

15. *Ibid.*

16. W. E. Mühlmann (ed.), *Chiliasmus und Nativismus*, p. 355. For a critique of

Mühlmann, cf. C. Schuhler, *op. cit.*, pp. 109 f.

17. See C. Schuhler, *op. cit.*, pp. 108 f.

18. See R. F. Behrendt, *Soziale Strategie für Entwicklungsländer* (Frankfurt/Main, 1965) pp. 337 ff., and the references in Chapter 2. For a critique of Behrendt, see C. Schuhler, *op. cit.*, pp. 112 f. In the postscript to the second edition of this work (Frankfurt/Main, 1968, pp. 628–54), Behrendt once more emphasises his belief in the unsuitability of the national state as a framework for the development of the economically weaker countries. This postscript shows an obvious deterioration in the quality of Behrendt's argument, and it seems that his disagreements with his reviewers and with the work on the topic that has appeared since 1965 have caused his work to degenerate into polemics and affectation. For example, he accuses Baran of 'absurdity', 'blindness' and 'superficiality'. But his opinions of Fanon, whom he does not seem to have understood properly, are particularly embarrassing. Apart from his pejorative reference to Fanon's 'half-caste' origins, he claims that he was 'basically the Sorel of anti-colonial anarchism, and like him a manufacturer of a social myth' (p. 645). Anyone remotely familiar with Fanon's theories knows that he undertook to write a rejoinder to Sorel, and actually did so. His theory of violence totally contradicts Sorel's both in its claim and in its structure, so that Behrendt's assertion is meaningless. See B. Tibi, 'Fanon's Gewalttheorie und Hegel-Rezeption', *Sozialistische Politik*, I (1969) No. 2, 84–7. See also my comments on Sorel's theory of violence in *Das Argument*, XII (1970) No. 58, 415–19. Behrendt's attempts to stigmatise Fanon are particularly difficult to understand, since Fanon has in no sense produced a myth, but a stringent analysis of nation formation and of nationalism in colonial countries which is more soundly based than Behrendt's researches.

19. See C. Schuhler, *op. cit.*, pp. 112 f.

20. Although Behrendt's writings contain some useful interpretations, while Mühlmann's work is strongly reminiscent of the ideology of colonialism.

21. C. J. Friedrich, 'Nation-Building?', in K. W. Deutsch and W. J. Foltz (eds), *Nation-Building* (New York, 1963) pp. 27–32; here pp. 31 f.

22. See Plamenatz, *op. cit.*, pp. 35 ff., 112 ff; also R. Emerson, *op. cit.*

23. C. B. Macpherson, *The Real World of Democracy*, p. 27.

24. *Ibid.*, p. 29.

25. See W. Sulzbach, *Imperialismus und Nationalbewußtsein* (Frankfurt/Main, 1959) pp. 108 f.

26. K. W. Deutsch, *Nationalism and Social Communication*, 2nd ed. (Cambridge, Mass., 1966). For the American contributions to the theory of nation formation and Deutsch's role in this field see the article by S. Rokkan, 'Die vergleichende Analyse der Staaten-und Nationsbildung: Methoden und Modelle', in W. Zapf (ed.), *op. cit.*, pp. 228–52.

27. Deutsch, *op. cit.*, esp. Ch. 6, pp. 123 ff. Unfortunately, however, Deutsch does not give any analysis of the character of the government under which nation formation takes place. Thus he attributes the failure of processes of nation formation to factors other than the nature of the particular system of government.

28. *Ibid.*, p. 191.

29. *Ibid.*

30. *Ibid.*, p. 192.

31. Heribert Adam, 'Die afrikanische Misere' in *idem.*, *Südafrika, soziologie einer Rassengesellschaft* (Frankfurt/Main, 1969) pp. 110 f., illustrates these political circumstances, and shows that in the post-colonial period the African nationalists did not dismantle the colonial governmental apparatus but instead began to take over the same position with regard to the rest of the population as the colonialists had occupied previously. As proof he shows that the ratio of the average income of an unskilled worker and a civil servant in Germany is 1 : 5, while in some African countries it can be as much as 1 : 40.

32. Rosa Luxemburg, *Die russische Revolution*, p. 84: 'In India nationalism is an expression of the rising indigenous bourgeoisie, which seeks to exploit the country for its own ends rather than to be drained by English capital.'

33. Cf. Chapter 2.

34. The view that the underdeveloped countries are faced with the alternative of 'liberal democracy' or 'totalitarianism' is very prevalent in American writing on the subject: e.g. see Manfred Halpern, *The Politics of Social Change in the Middle East and North Africa* (Princeton, 1963). In contrast, see C. B. Macpherson, *op. cit.*, pp. 24–25.

35. Trotsky believed that 'with the acute agrarian problem and the intolerable national oppression in the colonial countries, their young and relatively small proletariats can come to power on the basis of a *national democratic* revolution sooner than the proletariat of an advanced country'. L. Trotsky, *The Permanent Revolution*, Eng. transl. (London, 1962) p. 130. And later on: 'With regard to the countries with a belated bourgeois development, especially the colonial and semi-colonial countries, the theory of permanent revolution signifies that the complete and genuine solution of their democratic tasks of achieving democracy and emancipation is conceivable only through the dictatorship of the proletariat as the leader of the subjugated nation, and above all of its peasant masses.' *ibid.*, p. 152.

36. C. B. Macpherson, *op. cit.*, pp. 29 ff.

37. Cf. J. Habermas, *Erkenntnis und Interesse*, Eng. transl., Chapter 1, section 3, 43 ff., especially 52 ff.

38. Fanon's definition can be developed further in the framework of a Bonapartist theory. See B. Tibi (ed.), *Die arabische Linke* (Frankfurt/Main, 1969) Ch. III, pp. 87 ff. Régis Debray uses the term 'demo-bourgeois fascism' to describe the same phenomenon. Cf. R. Debray, 'Probleme der revolutionären Strategie in Lateinamerika', in G. Feltrinelli (ed.), *Lateinamerika—ein zweites Vietnam*? (Reinbek, 1968) pp. 133 ff., pp. 157 ff., See also p. 407.

39. For a definition of 'Bonapartist nationalism' see G. Feltrinelli (ed.), *op. cit.*, p. 406; see also B. Tibi, 'Zum Verhältnis von Militär und kolonialem Nationalismus am Beispiel der arabischen Länder', *Sozialistische Politik*, I (1969) No. 4, 4–19.

40. K. Steinhaus illustrates this with the example of Turkish nationalism in *Soziologie der türkischen Revolution, Zum Problem der Entfaltung der bürgerlichen Gesellschaft in sozioökonomisch schwach entwickelten Ländern* (Frankfurt/Main, 1969), see esp. pp. 170 ff.

41. See A. F. C. Wallace, 'Die Revitalisierungsbewegungen', in P. Heintz (ed.), *Soziologie der Entwicklungsländer*, *op. cit.*, pp. 431–54, as well as B. Ryan, 'Die Bedeutung der Revitalisierungsbewegungen für den sozialen Wandel in den Entwicklungsländern', in R. König (ed.), *op. cit.*, pp. 37–65.

42. B. Ryan, *op. cit.*, pp. 55 ff.
43. *Ibid.*, pp. 38 ff.
44. Cf. E. J. Hobsbawm, *Primitive Rebels: Studies in Archaic Forms of Social Movement in the 19th and 20th Centuries* (Manchester, 1959).
45. Cf. Ibrahim AbuLughod, *The Arab Rediscovery of Europe* (Princeton, New Jersey, 1963) and H. Z. Nuseibeh, *The Ideas of Arab Nationalism*, 2nd ed. (Ithaca, 1959): also Albert Hourani, *Arabic Thought in the Liberal Age* (London, 1962). In 'Typische ideologische Reaktionen arabischer Intellektueller auf das Entwicklungsgefälle', in R. König (ed.), *op. cit.*, pp. 136–62, U. Simson shows a striking capacity to generalise without sufficient knowledge of the facts. Simson 'analyses' the reactions of the Arab intellectuals without having anything concrete to consider, since he has no knowledge of the literary work of these intellectuals, which might perhaps be thought important for the success of his enterprise. He only cites journalistic secondary sources which are either out of date or inadequate. Furthermore he is not familiar with the source material quoted here, nor with H. B. Sharabi's competent work 'Die Entstehung einer revolutionären Ideologie in der arabischen Welt', *Bustan*, X (1969) Nos. 2/3, 3–11.
46. Cf. also G. Grohs, *Stufen afrikanischer Emanzipation: Studien zum Selbstverständnis afrikanischer Eliten* (Stuttgart, 1967) pp. 183 ff., and E. Geiss, *Zur Geschichte der Dekolonisation* (Frankfurt/Main, 1968) pp. 237 ff.; for review of both, see B. Tibi in *Sozialistische Politik*, I (1969) No. 4, 129–34.
47. W. E. Mühlmann, *Rassen, Ethnien, Kulturen*, p. 323.
48. The best available analysis of the cultural alienation of Europeanised colonial intellectuals is in Fanon, *The Wretched of the Earth, op. cit.*, and in his earlier work *Black Skin–White Masks, the Experience of a Black Man in a White World* (New York, 1967). There is a recent if rather inadequate study of Fanon's theory of alienation: Renate Zahar, *Kolonialismus und Entfremdung: Zur politischen Theorie Frantz Fanons*; see my review in *Sozialistische Politik*, I (1969) No. 3, 75 f. See also G. Grohs, 'Frantz Fanon, ein Theoretiker der afrikanischen Revolution', *Kölner Zeitschrift für Soziologie und Sozialpsychologie*, XVI (1964) No. 3, 457–80; B. Tibi, 'Fanons Gewalttheorie und Hegel-Rezeption', *op. cit.*, and more recently, P. Geismar 'Frantz Fanon, Evolution of a Revolutionary, A Biographical Sketch', *Monthly Review*, XXI (1969/70) No. 1, 22–30; P. Worsley, 'Revolutionary Theories', *ibid.*, pp. 30–49.
49. C. Zeller, *Elfenbeinküste, Ein Entwicklungsland auf dem Wege zur Nation* (Freiburg/Br., 1969) p. 22.
50. C. Zeller *op. cit.*, pp. 19 ff., divides the process of nation-formation in Africa into three phases: (1) that of colonialism, in which the 'colonial boundaries' are demarcated. This is important because it defines the spatial framework 'within which the future national state is to develop.' (p. 19); (2) the phase of the national movement, which emerges and operates within these borders as an anti-colonialist movement (pp. 21 ff); (3) the phase of state formation in the period after decolonisation, from which a legal entity emerges which acts as an independent body in international relations (pp. 23 ff). For Zeller, state formation is not the same as nation formation, since 'the organisation of the state is not structurally grounded upon a political, economic, and cultural community. It is, in short, a state without a nation.' (p. 24) However, Zeller

emphasises that in the post-colonial phase in these countries a form of national homogeneity can be achieved through comprehensive development policies. Hence the success of a post-colonial regime can be judged according to its ability to create national homogeneity (cf. p. 25).

51. Cf. Erwin Viefhaus, *Die Minderheitsfrage und die Entstehung der Minderheitsschutzverträge auf der Pariser Friedenskonferenz 1919: Eine Studie zur Geschichte des Nationalitätenproblems im 19. und 20. Jahrhundert* (Würzburg, 1960).

52. M. Hroch, *Die Vorkämpfer der nationalen Bewegungen bei den kleinen völkern Europas, eine vergleichende Analyse zur gesellschaftlichen Schichtung der patriotischen Bewegungen* (Prague, 1968) esp. pp. 16 f.

53. E. g. see H. Kohn, *Pan-Slavism: Its History and Ideology* (Notre Dame, 1953), and J. Matl, *Europa und die Slaven* (Wiesbaden, 1964) esp. pp. 209 ff.

54. E. Viefhaus, *op. cit.*, pp. 2 ff.

55. E. Geiss, *op. cit.*, pp. 10 ff., has also compared German and Slav nationalism with similar forms of African nationalism, although he does not seem sufficiently aware of the difference in historical background.

56. Fanon, *The Wretched of the Earth*, p. 191; also Chapter 2, above.

57. L. S. Senghor, *Négritude et Humanisme* (Paris, 1964). On Senghor, see C. Serauky, 'Das philosophisch-literarische System der Négritude bei Senghor', *Mitteilungen des Institutes Für Orient-Forschung*, XV (1969) No. 3, 425–39, and B. Tibi, 'Léopold Senghors "Négritude"' *Das Argument*, IX (1967) No. 45, 422–5, and also my reviews of Grohs and Geiss (see note 46 above). The only study of Senghor, *Léopold S. Senghor, Wegbereiter der Culture Universelle*, by G. Bonn, is too journalistic and uncritical for scholarly consideration. See my review in *Das Argument*, XXII (1970) No. 59, 601–3.

58. L. S. Senghor, *op. cit.*, p. 103.

59. *Ibid.* See B. Tibi, 'Léopold Senghors "Négritude"', *op. cit.*; in this connection it seems surprising that a neo-Marxist author like Marcuse believes that the resistance of the colonial peoples to technology, and the glorification of pre-technological structures are progressive developments. Marcuse poses the question: 'If industrialisation and the introduction of technology to the backward countries are faced with severe resistance on the part of the indigenous and traditional ways of life and work . . ., can this pre-technical tradition itself become the source of progress and industrialisation?' H. Marcuse, *One Dimensional Man* (London, 1964).

60. See M. Gandhi, *Freiheit ohne Gewalt*, ed. K. Klostermaier (Cologne, 1968) pp. 40, 43, 176, and 195 and *passim*; also see my remarks on Gandhi in *Das Argument*, XII (1970) No. 59, 629–35.

61. See G. Grohs, *op. cit.*, pp. 138 ff.

62. See Chapters 4, 5 and 9 below. For references see Chapter 3, note 45.

63. For instance Phan-chu-Trinh, the pioneer of early Vietnamese nationalism, who was deeply influenced by Rousseau and Montesquieu. See J. Chesneaux, *Le Vietnam:Études de Politique et d'Historie* (Paris, 1968). See also B. Tibi, 'Aspekte der vietnamesischen Emanzipations Bewegung', *Neue Politische Literatur*, XV (1970) 396–402.

64. See Chapter 2 above.

65. See Chapter 2 above.

66. C. Schuhler, *op. cit.*, p. 111 f.

67. *Ibid.*, p. 112.
68. Quoted in Paul Trappe, *Die Entwicklungsfunktion des Genossenschaftswesens am Beispiel ostafrikanischer Stämme* (Neuwied and Berlin, 1966) pp. 344 ff.
69. Doudou Thiam, *La Politique Etrangère des Etats Africains. Ses Fondaments Idéologiques. Sa Réalité Présente. Ses Perspectives d'Avenir* (Paris, 1963); Eng. transl., *The Foreign Policy of African States; Ideological Bases, Present Realities, Future Prospects* (London, 1965). For the history of Pan-Africanism, see E. Geiss, *op. cit.*, which includes an extensive bibliography. See also D. Senghaas, 'Politische Innovation, Versuch über den Panafrikanismus', *Zeitschrift für Politik*, XII (1965) No. 4, 333–55.

Notes to Chapter 4

1. See Chapter 3, note 2. For studies of social change in the Middle East based on modernisation theory, see Carl Leiden (ed.), *The Conflict of Traditionalism and Modernity in the Muslim Middle East* (Austin, 1966); see also Daniel Lerner, *The Passing of Traditional Society; Modernising the Middle East* (Glencoe, 1962). On this, and on matters raised in Chapter 5, see Fritz Steppat, 'Die arabische Welt in der Epoche des Nationalismus', which forms the postscript to Franz Taeschner, *Geschichte der arabischen Welt* (Stuttgart, 1964) pp. 178–236. However, the modernisation theorists' notion of the spectrum traditionalism/modernism seems inadequate.
2. See R. F. Behrendt, *Soziale Strategie für Entwicklungsländer* (Frankfurt/Main, 1965) esp. Ch. VI, pp. 331 ff. See also Chapter 2 above, and the critique in Chapter 3. The theory of 'cultural change' is an integral part of Behrendt's thesis. See *ibid.*, pp. 110 f., where development is described as 'directed cultural change'.
3. See for instance G. von Grunebaum, 'The Intellectual Problems of Westernization in the self-view of the Arab world', in *idem., Modern Islam: The Search for Cultural Identity* (Berkeley and Los Angeles, 1962) pp. 128–79, and 'Acculturation as a theme in contemporary Arabic literature', in *ibid.*, pp. 248–88.
4. Walther Braune, 'Die Entwicklung des Nationalismus bei den Arabern', in R. Hartmann (ed.), *BASI* (Leipzig, 1944) pp. 425 ff., and on this p. 247.
5. S. D. Goitein, 'The Rise of the Near-Eastern Bourgeoisie in the Early Islamic Times', *Journal of World History*, III (1957) 583–604, which also contains a number of important references. See also Rudolf Sellheim, 'Neue Materialien zur Biographie des Yaqut', in R. Sellheim *et al.*, *Schriften und Bilder, Drei orientalische Untersuchungen* (Wiesbaden, 1967) pp. 41–72, who discusses these relationships with reference to the life of the eminent Arab geographer Yaqut, who was an active member of the mercantile society of his time.
6. Kurt Steinhaus, *Soziologie der türkischen Revolution, Zum Problem der Entfaltung der bürgerlichen Gesellschaft in sozioökonomisch schwach entwickelten Ländern* (Frankfurt/Main, 1969) p. 19.
7. C. H. Becker, *Islamstudien, Vom Werden und Wesen der islamischen Welt*, 2 vols (Hildesheim, 1967) (first publ. 1924, 1932); here vol. I, p. 247.
8. *Ibid.*
9. See Maxime Rodinson, *Islam and Capitalism* (London, 1974).

10. Steinhaus, *op. cit.*, p. 16: see also Karl Wittfogel, *Oriental Despotism, a Study of Total Power* (New Haven and London, 1964) pp. 181 ff, 284 ff.

11. K. Steinhaus, *op. cit.*, p. 26.

12. *Ibid.*, p. 24.

13. See C. F. Volney, *Voyage en Egypte et en Syrie les années 1783–1785* (repr. Paris, 1959). Eng. transl., *Travels through Syria and Egypt in the years 1783, 1784, and 1785*, 2 vols (London, 1787), facsimile reproduction, Farnborough, 1972. Extracts from the English translation are also in C. Issawi (ed.), *The Economic History of the Middle East, 1800–1914* (Chicago and London, 1966) pp. 213–19. On the division of labour in the Middle East, see p. 218.

14. K. Steinhaus, *op. cit.*, p. 20.

15. *Ibid.*, pp. 20 f.

16. *Ibid.*, p. 29.

17. *Ibid.*, p. 30.

18. Zvi Y. Hershlag, *Introduction to the Modern Economic History of the Middle East* (Leiden, 1964) p. 17.

19. Shari'a = Islamic law; see H. A. R. Gibb, *Mohammedanism, An Historical Survey*, 2nd ed. (London, 1950) pp. 88–106, as well as Majid Khadduri, 'The Nature and Sources of the Shari'a', *George Washington Law Review*, xx (1953) 3–23.

20. On the doctrine of Islamic universalism see W. M. Watt, *Islam and the Integration of Society* (London, 1961) pp. 273 ff. Watt sees Islamic universalism primarily in terms of the claim of Islam to be a universal religion in contrast to other religions; he neglects the political, that is the supra-national, dimension of authority which this universalism has sanctioned in Islamic history.

21. The question of the caliphate will be discussed in Chapter 8. References to the Ottomans' falsification of the history of the caliphate, and the rectification of this, can be found in note 65 below and in Chapter 8, note 19.

22. See F. Volney, *op. cit.* (note 13 above).

23. C. Brockelmann devoted the second volume of his *Geschichte der arabischen Literatur* (international abbreviation *GAL*) (Leiden, 1902), and one of his three Supplementary Volumes (vol. II, Leiden, 1938) to the theme of 'The decline of Islamic Literature'. The second edition of *GAL* has been used here (Leiden, 1949), as well as the two Supplementary Volumes II and III, which are indispensable for a study of this period. Vol. II and Supplementary Vol. II of *GAL* only deal briefly with the literary renaissance since the Napoleonic Expedition in the final chapter, but Supplementary Vol. III (Leiden, 1942), is entirely devoted to modern Arabic literature with much valuable information and bibliographical notes.

24. C. H. Becker, *Islamstudien*, p. 163.

25. *Ibid.*

26. See *ibid.*, p. 179.

27. S. J. Shaw, *The Financial and Administrative Organization and Development of Ottoman Egypt 1517–1798* (Princeton, New Jersey, 1962) pp. 3f. This extensive and copiously documented study gives a detailed picture of Ottoman Egypt. See also H. A. R. Gibb and H. Bowen, *Islamic Society and the West; Part I, Islamic Society in the 18th Century*, 2 vols (London, 1950, 1957) on Egypt, II, pp. 59 ff.

28. Before the Sublime Porte sent troops to Egypt, it asked Cezzar Ahmad Pasha to prepare a report on the situation in Egypt under the Mamlukes in the eighteenth century, which he produced in 1785. Cezzar Ahmad Pasha was a Mamluke in Ottoman service who was governor of Sa'ida and Damascus, residing in Acre. S. J. Shaw has produced an edition of the original Turkish text together with an introduction and English translation: see Shaw (ed.), *Ottoman Egypt in the Eighteenth Century. The Nizāmnāme-i-Misr of Cezzar Ahmad Pasha* (Cambridge, Mass., 1962). In his introduction Shaw says that the Ottomans would have been prepared to allow the Mamlukes to continue to govern Egypt if the latter could have assured them that the country's valuable revenues would be delivered to the treasury in Istanbul. However, the Ottomans' military intervention failed, since their tróops were engaged in Campaigns elsewhere in the Empire and soon had to be withdrawn.

29. See C. H. Becker, *op. cit.*, p. 200. This can also be seen in the stagnation of cultural life. Apart from the relevant sections of Brockelmann's *GAL* which have been cited above, see also the short survey by J. Heyworth-Dunne in 'Arabic Literature in Egypt in the Eighteenth century', *Bulletin of the School of Oriental and African Studies*, IX (1937/39) pp. 675–89.

30. Hans Henle, *Der neue Nahe Osten* (Hamburg, 1966) p. 19. On European influences on the Middle East since 1798 apart from those works cited in the notes below, see e.g. Walther Braune, *Der islamische Orient zwischen Vergangenheit und Zukunft* (Berne and Munich, 1960); Bernard Lewis, *The Middle East and the West*, 2nd ed. (Bloomington, 1965); Carleton S. Coon, 'The Impact of the West on Middle Eastern Social Institutions', *Proceedings of the Academy of Political Science*, XXIV (1952) No. 4, 443–66; Arnold Toynbee, *A Study of History*, VIII *The West and the Islamic World* (London, 1954) pp. 216 ff.; B. Tibi, introduction to *Die arabische Linke* (Frankfurt/Main, 1969) pp. 7–41; Ibraham Abu-Lughod, *The Arab Rediscovery of Europe, A study in Cultural Encounters* (New Jersey, 1963); and finally Philip K. Hitti, 'The Impact of the West on Syria and Lebanon in the Nineteenth Century', *Journal of World History*, II (1955) No. 3, 608–33.

31. Albert Hourani, *Arabic Thought in the Liberal Age* (London, 1962) p. 49.

32. Nationalism is therefore a new phenomeι.on in the Middle East. Hence Richard Hartmann is incorrect in saying, in the first sentence of his *Islam and Nationalismus*, (Berlin, 1948), that the relationship between nationalism and Islam is as old as Islam itself. The thesis that Arab nationalism goes back to the early history of the Arabs is untenable, although some Arab scholars subscribe to it, e.g. H. Z. Nuseibeh, *The Ideas of Arab Nationalism*, 2nd ed. (Ithaca, 1959); H. Saab, *The Arab Federalists of the Ottoman Empire* (Amsterdam, 1959).

33. For details of the Napoleonic Expedition see F. Charles-Roux, *Bonaparte, Gouverneur d'Egypte*, 2nd ed. (Paris, 1946), and more recently, Georges Spillmann, *Napoléon et l'Islam* (Paris, 1969) esp. Part I, pp. 49–149. Further references can be found in Spillmann's bibliography.

34. This press was used in Rome to print religious texts in Arabic for the Syrian Christians. The first printing press was installed in Aleppo in 1702 under the auspices of the Orthodox patriarch al-Dabbas, but was not much used within the Ottoman Empire. The printing of Arabic and Turkish books was generally prohibited except for religious texts. This prohibition was lifted in 1727 on the

occasion of the inauguration of a printing press, but by 1742 the latter had been shut down. It was only in 1784 that non-religious books were produced and since they were in Turkish, they also had a limited circulation in the Arab part of the Ottoman Empire. Apart from the press which Napoleon had confiscated from Rome, the press which the Protestant mission had set up in Malta in 1822 also played a significant role. With Muhammad 'Ali's permission this press was brought to Syria in 1834, which was at that time under his enlightened rule (See Chapter 5, note 21). Even more important were a number of presses which Muhammad 'Ali imported from Europe which were largely used to print contemporary works translated from European languages. See K. Steinhaus, *op. cit.*, p. 32; also Philip K. Hitti, *op. cit.*, *passim*, as well as J. Heyworth-Dunne, 'Printing and Translations under Muhammad 'Ali of Egypt', *Journal of the Royal Asiatic Society* (1940) 325–49.

35. The complete text can be found in Ibrahim Abu-Lughod, *The Arab Rediscovery of Europe, op. cit.*, pp. 13–16, here esp. pp. 13 f.; see also Abu-Lughod note i, p. 13, where he gives details of the production of this leaflet, of which none of the originals have survived. On the general subject of the relations between ruler and ruled in Islamic history see Fritz Steppat, 'Der Muslim und die Obrigkeit', *Zeitschrift für Politik*, XII (1965) No. 4, 319–32, which may help to explain the reception that the leaflet received.

36. For the significance of the Expedition, see Ibrahim Abu-Lughod, *op. cit.*, *passim*; A. Hourani, *op. cit.*, 49 ff.; J. M. Ahmed, *The Intellectual Origins of Egyptian Nationalism* (London, 1960) pp. 1–6; F. Charles-Roux, *op. cit.*; G. Spillmann, *op. cit.*; W. Braune, *op. cit.*; M. Rifaat, *The Awakening of Modern Egypt* (London, 1947) pp. 1–15.

37. See H. Pérès, 'L'Institut d'Egypte et l'oeuvre de Bonaparte jugés par deux historiens arabes contemporains', *Arabica*, IV (1957) pp. 113–30; see also the references in note 36 above, esp. F. Charles-Roux, *op. cit.*, pp. 154 ff.

38. 'Abd al-Rahman al-Jabarti, *'Aja'ib al-Athar fi'l-Tarajim w'al-Akhbar*, 4 vols (Cairo, 1904–05), cited in K. Stowasser, 'al-Tahtawi in Paris', unpublished Ph.D. thesis (Münster, 1966) p. 5. al-Jabarti's four-volume work is the most important historical source for the period of transition from Ottoman and Mamluke to modern Egypt. There is a French translation, *Merveilles biographiques et historiques, ou chroniques du Cheikh Abu El-Rahman El-Djabarti*, 9 vols (Cairo, 1888–96). al-Jabarti was generally opposed to the Europeanisation that began with the Napoleonic Expedition. For the historical significance of his position, see W. Braune, *Der islamische Orient zwischen Vergangenheit und Zukunft*, pp. 38 ff. On al-Jabarti see David Ayalon, 'The Historian al-Jabarti and his Background', *Bulletin of the School of Oriental and African Studies*, XXII (1960) pp. 217–49. Ayalon advises caution in the use of the French translation, which contains grave errors.

39. Quoted in J. M. Ahmed, *op. cit.*, p. 5.

40. For Sheikh 'Attar see J. M. Ahmed, *op. cit.*, pp. 5 f, and J. Shayyal, *Rifa'a R. al-Tahtawi, 1801–1873* (Cairo, 1958) pp. 13–15, as well as C. Brockelmann, *GAL*, II, pp. 623 f. 'Attar fled from the French to Upper Egypt but later returned and cooperated with them. Under Muhammad 'Ali he played an important role as rector of al-Azhar in Cairo, to which reference will be made in part (c) of this section in connection with al-Tahtawi.

41. This was after the British fleet had sunk the French ships in which the

Expedition had been transported. For the Anglo-French conflict over Egypt at this time, see John Marlowe, *Anglo-Egyptian Relations 1800–1953* (London, 1954) pp. 7–29, esp. pp. 15 ff.

42. C. Issawi, *Egypt in Revolution, an Economic Analysis* (London, 1963) pp. 18–31; see also P. M. Holt, *Egypt and the Fertile Crescent 1516–1922* (Ithaca and London, 1966) esp. pp. 176 ff.

43. The fact that the Napoleonic Expedition had a positive effect on the development of the Middle East cannot be generalised to include the European colonial conquests. Napoleon's colonial intentions were clear enough, however much French apologists for colonialism attempted to present the Expedition as a 'mission civilisatrice de la France'.

44. C. Brockelmann, *GAL*, II, p. 622.

45. W. Braune, *Der islamische Orient zwischen Vergangenheit und Zukunft*, p. 41.

46. *Ibid.*, p. 42.

47. *Ibid.* In Egyptian national historiography the progressive character of Muhammad 'Ali's regime is denied, and Muhammad 'Ali himself dismissed as a foreigner (he was Albanian). The progressive Egyptian historian 'Ammara has attacked this point of view, which although understandable from a nationalist standpoint, is not academically acceptable. See Muhammad 'Ammara, *al-'Uruba fi'l-'Asr al-Hadith* (Arabism in Modern History) (Cairo, 1967) pp. 29 ff., esp. 61 ff. See also the original and extensive research of A. Abdel-Malek, *Idéologie et Renaissance Nationale; L'Egypte Moderne* (Paris, 1969), which discusses all aspects of social change in Egypt since Muhammad 'Ali's time. It has unfortunately not been possible to make detailed use of the results of this research in the main body of this study. Wherever possible reference will be made in the notes to relevant comments by Abdel-Malek.

48. Amos Perlmutter, 'Egypt and the Myth of the New Middle Class: A Comparative Analysis', *Comparative Studies in Society and History*, X (1967/8) 46–65; here p. 50; see also note 57 below.

49. For the Muhammad 'Ali period in general, see the monograph by Henry Dodwell, *The Founder of Modern Egypt. A Study of Muhammad 'Ali* (Cambridge, 1931); Arnold Toynbee, *op. cit.*, pp. 239 ff.; as well as M. Rifaat, *op. cit.*, pp. 16 ff.; Helen Anne B. Rivlin, *The Agricultural Policy of Muhammad 'Ali in Egypt* (Cambridge, Mass., 1961).

50. See Gabriel Baer, 'The Evolution of Private Landownership in Egypt and the Fertile Crescent', in C. Issawi (ed.), *The Economic History of the Middle East, 1800–1914*, pp. 80–90, esp. p. 80 f,; see also G. Baer, *A History of Landownership in Modern Egypt 1800–1950* (London, 1962) pp. 1 ff.; Z. Y. Hershlag, *op. cit.*, pp. 78 ff.; H. A. B. Rivlin, *op. cit.*

51. For Muhammad 'Ali's attempts to industrialise see Z. Y. Hershlag, *op. cit.*, pp. 85 ff.

52. See A. Perlmutter, *op. cit.*, pp. 49 ff., and G. Baer, *op. cit.*, on which the following is based.

53. For details of British policy towards Muhammad 'Ali, see J. Marlowe, *Anglo-Egyptian Relations 1800-1953*, pp. 30–61.

54. For details see H. Dodwell, *op. cit.*, pp. 39 ff., 94 ff., 125 ff., 154 ff.

55. Cf. C. H. Becker, 'England und der vordere Orient', in *Islamstudien*, vol. II, pp. 383 ff. Becker comments on Cromer as follows: 'For him, oriental culture was fundamentally humbug . . . He totally ignored the strenuous efforts

which the Egyptians had made to assimilate themselves to Europe. Instead, he and his staff waged a bitter campaign against French culture in Egypt.' (p. 399) On the nature of British colonial policy in Egypt, see A. Perlmutter, *op. cit.*, p. 51. For references to the British colonisation of Egypt, see Chapter 9, note 5, and 'Abd al-Fattah Haikal, 'Die Auswirkung der Britischen Kolonialpolitik auf die Wirtschaft Ägyptens', in Walter Markov (ed.), *Kolonialismus und Neokolonialismus in Nordafrika und Nahost* (Berlin, 1964) pp. 226–48.

56. For Muhammad 'Ali's educational policy, see J. Heyworth-Dunne's valuable *Introduction to the History of Education in Modern Egypt*, 2nd ed. (London, 1968) (1st ed. London, 1939) pp. 96 ff.

57. See M. 'Ammara, *op. cit.*, pp. 129 ff.

58. It is remarkable that in spite of al-Tahtawi's considerable importance no detailed study of his work exists. Apart from J. Shayyal's inadequate *Rifa'a R. al-Tahtawi 1801–1873* (Cairo, 1958), the following are useful: J. Heyworth-Dunne, 'Rifa'a Bey Rafi' al-Tahtawi: The Egyptian Revivalist', *Bulletin of the School of Oriental and African Studies*, IX (1937/39) 961–7, and X (1940/42) 399–415. The first part is biographical, and second deals with al-Tahtawi's writings. Heyworth-Dunne's article includes some corrections of M. Chemoul's article on al-Tahtawi in the *Encyclopedia of Islam*. See also Ibraham Abu-Lughod, *The Arab Rediscovery of Europe* (Princeton, 1963) *passim*; Albert Hourani, *Arabic Thought* . . . , pp. 68–83; also Khaldun S. Husry, *Three Reformers, A Study in Modern Arab Political Thought* (Beirut, 1966) pp. 11–32; also W. Braune, 'Beiträge zur Geschichte des neuarabischen Schrifttums', *Mitteilungen des Seminars für orientalische Sprachen*, XXXVI (1933) No. 2, 117–40.

59. A. Hourani, *Arabic Thought* . . . , p. 69, and J. M. Ahmed, *op. cit.*, p. 12.

60. Rifa'a R. al-Tahtawi, *Takhlis al-ibriz ila talkhis Paris* (Paris Diary) (Cairo, 1834). There is a German translation: Karl Stowasser, *Al-Tahtawi in Paris, ein Dokument des arabischen Modernismus aus dem frühen 19. Jahrhundert*, unpubl. thesis (Münster, 1966), which has already been quoted. It is a reliable translation of the first edition with unimportant abridgements. Later editions are not authentic. For further material on al-Tahtawi's Paris diary see Wiebke Hermann, 'Rifa'a Beys Beschreibung seiner Reise nach Paris, ein Werk der Frühzeit des islamischen Modernismus', *Wissenschaftliche Zeitschrift der Martin-Luther-Universität Halle*, XII (1963) Nos. 3/4, 221–8, which is an analysis of the diary, including extensive quotations; Khaldun S. Husry, *op. cit.*, pp. 13–22; J. Heyworth-Dunne; 'Rifa'a Bey Rafi' al-Tahtawi: The Egyptian Revivalist', *op. cit.*, part two; I. Abu-Lughod, *op. cit.*, *passim*; A. Hourani, *Arabic Thought* . . . , pp. 70 ff.; B. Tibi, 'Akkulturationsprozesse im modernen Orient', *Neue Politische Literatur*, XV (1970) 77 ff.

61. al-Tahtawi in Stowasser, *op. cit.*, pp. 151 ff, 158 ff, 162 ff.

62. Ibid., p. 66. W. Braune, *Der islamische Orient zwischen Vergangenheit und Zukunft*, p. 43 writes: 'The book . . . did in fact fulfil the hopes of its author, who wished to awaken all the peoples of Islam from the sleep of indifference'.

63. al-Tahtawi in Stowasser, *op. cit.*, p. 69.

64. *Ibid.*, p. 70.

65. *Ibid.*

66. *Ibid.*, p. 72.

67. Sharabi discusses the change in the Arab intellectual's concept of the West since al-Tahtawi in 'Die Entstehung einer revolutionären Ideologie in der arabischen Welt', *Bustan*, x (1969) Nos. 2/3, 3–11.

68. al-Tahtawi in Stowasser, *op. cit.*, p. 65.

69. For the Saint-Simonians in Egypt see A. Hourani, *Arabic Thought . . .*, pp. 53 f. On the 'Mission de l'Orient' of the Saint-Simonians, see G. Solomon-Delatour (ed.), *Die Lehre Saint-Simons* (Neuwied, 1962), especially the introduction, p. 23. There is no detailed study of the activities of the Saint-Simonians in Egypt. See the comments by A. Abdel-Malek, *op. cit.*, pp. 189–98.

70. See J. Heyworth-Dunne, 'Rifa'a Bey Rafi' Tahtawi: The Egyptian Revivalist', *op. cit.*, first part, where al-Tahtawi's role in the dispute between Clot Bey and the Saint-Simonians is discussed.

71. See I. Abu-Lughod, *op. cit.*, and A. Hourani, *Arabic Thought . . .*, p. 71.

72. Both J. M. Ahmed, *op. cit.*, p. 10, and Khaldun S. Husry, *op. cit.*, give the figure of 2000, which is difficult to verify. J. Heyworth-Dunne, 'Printing and Translations under Muhammad 'Ali of Egypt', *op. cit.*, tabulates 243 translations, although this only covers the period 1822–42.

73. See A. Hourani, *Arabic Thought . . .*, p. 73 f.

74. *Ibid.*, p. 73; see also K. Stowasser, *op. cit.*, p. 25, and B. Tibi, 'Akkulturationsprozesse im modernen Orient', *op. cit.*, pp. 78 ff.

75. For the *Shari'a* see note 19 above.

76. A. Hourani, *Arabic Thought . . .*, p. 76; see also the texts in Shayyal's appendix.

77. See A. Hourani, *Arabic Thought . . .*, pp. 70, 76.

78. R. R. al-Tahtawi, *al-Murshid al-Amin fi Ta'lim li'l-Banat wa'l-Banin* (Guiding Truths for Girls and Youths) (Cairo, 1875). To call for female education is fairly revolutionary even in the contemporary Middle East, and was even more so in al-Tahtawi's day.

79. See J. M. Ahmed, *op. cit.*, pp. 13 f., as well as A. Hourani, *Arabic Thought . . .*, pp. 68 f., and Khaldun Husry, *op. cit.*, pp. 29 ff.

80. See al-Tahtawi's texts in J. Shayyal, *op. cit.*, pp. 57 ff., A. Hourani, *Arabic Thought . . .*, pp. 71 f., and Khaldun Husry, *op. cit.*, pp. 29 ff.

81. See Khaldun Husry, *op. cit.*, pp. 29 ff.

82. See J. Heyworth-Dunne, 'Rifa'a Bey Rafi' al-Tahtawi: The Egyptian Revivalist', *op. cit.*, Part 2, pp. 399 ff.

83. R. R. al-Tahtawi, *Kitab Manahij al-Albab al-Misriyya fi Mabahij al-Adab al-'Asriyya* (Cairo, 1912). For an interpretation, see J. M. Ahmed, *op. cit.*, p. 13–15, and Khaldun Husry, *op. cit.*, pp. 23 ff.

84. K. Stowasser, *op. cit.*, p. 26; see also B. Tibi, *op. cit.* (see note 74), pp. 78 f.

85. K. Stowasser, *op. cit.*, pp. 26 ff; see also J. Heyworth-Dunne, *op. cit.*, Part Two, pp. 406 ff., as well as W. Braune, *Der islamische Orient zwischen Vergangenheit und Zukunft*, pp. 43 f.

86. See Khaldun S. Husry, *op. cit.*, p. 18, who mistakenly claims that al-Tahtawi was aware of a dichotomy between politics and religion.

87. J. Heyworth-Dunne, *op. cit.*, Part Two, pp. 406 f., says of al-Tahtawi with justice: 'He was the only writer of this period to have produced anything readable', al-Tahtawi was the founder of modern Arabic writing, 'especially in its technical and educational needs'.

88. See R. Hartmann, 'Die Wahhabiten', *Zeitschrift der Deutschen Morgen-ländischen Gesellschaft*, LXXVIII (1924) No. 2, 176–213: see also W. C. Smith, *Islam in Modern History* (Princeton, 1957), and M. Rifaat, *al-Tawjih al-Siyasi li'l-Fikra al-'Arabiyya al-Haditha* (Political Trends in Modern Arabic Thought) (Cairo, 1964) pp. 11–31.
89. R. Hartmann, *op. cit.*, p. 178.
90. *Ibid.*, p. 177. Hans Bräker also emphasises that the Wahhabi movement 'radically rejected any foreign intellectualism in philosophy as well as in theology. It insisted on the original law, whose sources were the Qur'an and the pure Sunna alone, and it wanted these to cleanse Islam of its inner decay by calling Muslim society to its original purity and order'. Hans Bräker, *Islam-Sozialismus-Kommunismus: zur ideengeschichtlichen Grundlage der Sozialismus-und Kommunismus-Diskussion innerhalb des Islams* (Cologne, 1968) Privatdruck des Bundesinstitut für Ostwissenschaftliche und internationale Studien, p. 14.
91. Quotation from R. Hartmann, *op. cit.*, p. 182. These criticisms are primarily directed against the Ottomans; see p. 196.
92. R. Hartmann, *op. cit.*, p. 186.
93. Of Muhammad 'Ali's victory over the Wahhabis, R. Hartmann writes: 'The money and the perfidy of the Egyptians triumphed over Ibn Sa'ud's bravery' (*ibid.*, p. 198). However, the victory was due to Muhammad 'Ali's new army, which was trained and equipped on modern lines and was generally superior to that of the Wahhabis. Hartmann continues: 'Once again the old chaotic conditions replaced temperate order in Arabia' (p. 198). Hartmann laid great emphasis on this 'temperate order' because he believed: 'Even today it is only the simple puritanical, temperate belief which will discipline the unruly Arabs and convert them into fighters for the faith who do not fear death.' (p. 211) Fifteen years later, however, Hartmann describes the 'reactionary puritanism of Wahhabism'. See R. Hartmann, 'Gegenwartsfragen und-strömungen des Islam', *Koloniale Rundschau*, XXXIII (1942) No. 2, 57–71, here p. 59. See also note 113 below.
94. See C. C. Adams, *Islam and Modernism in Egypt* (London, 1933); see also A. Abdel-Malek, *op. cit.*, pp. 371 ff.
95. E.g. the highly prejudiced work of Elie Kedourie, *Afghani and 'Abduh, An Essay on Religious Unbelief and Political Activism in Modern Islam* (London, 1966); see also the introduction to Sylvia Haim (ed.), *Arab Nationalism (Berkeley and Los Angeles, 1962); also Nikki Keddie's introduction to her (ed.), *An Islamic Response to Imperialism, Political and Religious Writings of Sayyid Jamal al-Din 'al-Afghani'* (Berkeley and Los Angeles, 1968).
96. See A. Hourani, *op. cit.*, pp. 114 ff.
97. al-Afghani's reply to Renan appeared in the *Journal des Débats* in 1883. There is an English translation in N. Keddie, *op. cit.*, pp. 181–187.
98. For details, see Chapter 8 below, and *al-Afghani: al-A'mal al-Kamila* (al-Afghani: Complete Works), ed. M. 'Ammara (Cairo, 1968) *passim*.
99. For islamic universalism, see note 20 above, and 'Ammara, *op. cit.*, *passim*. The supersession of Islamic universalism by nationalism is discussed by Hassan Saab, *The Arab Federalists of the Ottoman Empire* (Amsterdam, 1958) pp. 131 ff. Saab also shows how Pan-Islamism, the irredentist interpretation of Islamic universalism, gave way to nationalism; see *ibid.*, pp. 213 ff.

100. W. Braune, *op. cit.*, p. 65.

101. For references see Chapter 8.

102. 'Abduh was introduced to Herbert Spencer by Wilfrid Blunt, an English aristocrat who sympathised with Islam. For the meeting between 'Abduh and Spencer see W. S. Blunt, *My Diaries, Being a Personal Narrative of Events 1888–1914*, 4th ed. (New York, 1934) (first published in 1921 in 2 vols) pp. 480 f. See also Charles C. Adams, *Islam and Modernism in Egypt, A Study of the Modern Reform Movement Inaugurated by Muhammad 'Abduh* (London, 1933); also Max Horten, 'Muhammad 'Abduh, sein Leben und seine theologisch-philosophische Gedankenwelt, eine Studie zu den Reformbestrebungen im modernen Ägypten', *Beiträge zur Kenntnis des Orients, Jahrbuch der Deutschen Vorderasiengesellschaft*, XIII (1916) 83–114, and XIV (1917) 74–128.

103. In 1882 'Abduh was forced into exile for three years, after the failure of 'Urabi's rebellion. This was the first national uprising in modern Arab history (see Chapter 9, note 4). 'Abduh later distances himself from the 'Urabi rebellion; see A. Hourani, *Arabic Thought* . . ., pp. 159 f. In 1882 he went to Syria and subsequently followed Afghani to Paris where they both published the shortlived periodical *al-'Urwa al-Wuthqa*. See also Chapter 8, note 33.

104. English translation *The Theology of Unity*, transl. Isaq Mus'ad and Kenneth Cragg (London, 1966).

105. P. J. Vatikiotis, 'Muhammad 'Abduh and the Quest for a Muslim Humanism', *Arabica*, IV (1957) 55–72, here p. 55.

106. Here and on the following see Malcolm Kerr, *Islamic Reform, The Political and Legal Theories of Muhammad 'Abduh and Rashid Ridha* (Berkeley and Los Angeles, 1966) pp. 103 ff.

107. See Fritz Steppat, 'Nationalismus und Islam bei Mustafa Kamil', *Die Welt des Islams*, n.s. IV (1956) 241–341, and Chapter 9 below.

108. 'Abduh, quoted by Muhammad al-Bahay, *Muhammad 'Abduh, Eine Untersuchung seiner Erziehungsmethode zum Nationalbewußtsein und zur nationalen Erhebung in Ägypten*, unpubl. Ph.D. thesis (Hamburg, 1936) p. 36. For 'Abduh's views on nationalism, see P. J. Vatikiotis, *op. cit.*, p. 63: 'Although 'Abduh begins by rejecting the idea of national units in Islam, his own attempt at a "religious patriotism" leads him to a befuddled concept of religious Nationalism'. See also J. M. Ahmed, *op. cit.*, pp. 35 ff., 44 ff.

109. W. Braune, op. cit., p. 132 f. The reference to the similarities between 'Abduh's and Spencer's views is not accidental.

110. *Ibid.*, p. 134.

111. R. Hartmann, *Islam und Nationalismus* (Berlin, 1948) p. 25; *idem*; 'Gegenwartsfragen und -strömungen des Islam', *op. cit.*, pp. 59 ff. Hartmann refers to the term 'cultural Wahhabism', which Goldziher uses to describe the followers of 'Abduh.

112. In *ibid.*, p. 62, Hartmann writes: 'While Muhammad 'Abduh as a son of the liberal age had a profoundly optimistic belief in progress, a more strongly conservative tendency is apparent with his pupil, Rashid Ridha, due to the increase in secularisation in his day.' For Rashid Ridha, see Chapter 8, note 56. For modern Islam see also A. M. Goichon, 'Le Panislamisme d'hier et d'aujourd'hui', *Afrique et l'Asie* (1950) 18–44; Kenneth Cragg, 'Religious

Developments in Islam in the 20th Century', *Journal of World History*, III (1956) No. 2, 504–24.

113. In a publication of the Nazi period, Arthur Rock's *Ibn Saud gründet das Gottesreich Arabien* (Berlin, 1935) pp. 9 ff. Saudi Arabia is favourably referred to as 'The Third Reich of Islam'.

114. On this movement see the following works: J. Heyworth-Dunne, *Religious and Political Trends in Modern Egypt* (Washington, 1950); Zvi Kaplinsky, 'The Muslim Brotherhood', *Middle Eastern Affairs*, V (1954) 377–85; I. M. Husayni, *The Moslem Brethren* (Beirut, 1956); Christina Phelps Harris, *Nationalism and Revolution in Egypt, The Role of the Muslim Brotherhood* (The Hague, 1964); and the extensive study by Richard P. Mitchell, *The Society of the Muslim Brothers* (London, 1969). For the Muslim Brothers' attitude to Pan-Arab nationalism, see Erwin I. J. Rosenthal, *Islam in the Modern National State* (Cambridge, 1965) pp. 103–24. In *Rußland und der Messianismus des Orients* (Tübingen, 1955) pp. 281–96, Emanuel Sarkisyanz, somewhat incongruously labels right-wing radical movements, such as the Muslim Brotherhood, as 'Islamic modernism' and at the same time attempts to prove their relationship to 'Bolshevism'.

115. For al-Kawakibi, see Chapter 8, and the sources quoted in notes 48–50.

116. See Chapter 8 below, which also gives references to the Caliphate movement.

117. W. Braune, 'Die Entwicklung des Nationalismus bei den Arabern', *op. cit.*, here pp. 431 f.

118. For a long time Islamic modernism remained the only political current uniting the Arab Middle East with the Maghrib. Ben Badis, one of the most influential pioneers of Algerian nationalism was strongly influenced by 'Abduh. For the political significance of Ben Badis, see the references to him in Wolfgang Ohneck, *Die französiche Algerienpolitik von 1919–1939* (Cologne and Opladen, 1967), and the monograph by Mahmud Qasim, *'Abd al-Hamid ben Badis, al-Za'im al-Ruhi li-Harb al-Tahrir al-Jaza'iriyya* (Ben Badis, the spiritual leader of the Algerian war of liberation) (Cairo, 1968).

119. On the failure of the attempt to save Islam by a reformist-modernist interpretation which would not affect the core of the religion see Manfred Halpern, *op. cit.*, pp. 119 ff. On the triumph of secularism see *ibid.*, pp. 129 ff. In this context the interpretation of H. Bräker, *op. cit.*, pp. 17 f, according to which Arab nationalism has developed within Islam itself, is incorrect. Islam today has generally been degraded into an instrument of state propaganda: in Saudi-Arabia and in the other Arab feudal states, the rulers declare themselves to be the legitimate representatives of Islam and engage in military alliances in order to hinder movements for social change, all in the name of religion. In contrast, Bonapartist regimes like that of Nasser claim that they rather than the feudal states know how to interpret Islam correctly. In fact, Islam performs a stabilising function for both systems. For the Islamic pact, see Axel Steden's somewhat uncritical 'Islampakt und Nassers Opposition', *Orient*, VII (1966) No. 3, 79–83. For Islam under Nasser, see Martin Grzeskowiak, 'Islam und Sozialismus in der VAR', *Mitteilungen des Instituts für Orientforschung*, XIV (1968) No. 1, 28–44

120. H. O. Ziegler, *Die moderne Nation, ein Beitrag zur politischen Soziologie* (Tübingen, 1931) p. 137.

121. *Ibid.*, p. 138.

Notes to Chapter 5

1. See G. Baer, 'Land Tenure in Egypt and the Fertile Crescent, 1800–1950', in Charles Issawi (ed.), *The Economic History of the Middle East 1800–1914* (Chicago and London, 1966) pp. 79–90, here p. 82.
2. *Ibid.*, see also P. M. Holt, *Egypt and the Fertile Crescent 1516–1922* (London and New York, 1966) pp. 102 ff.; A. N. Poliak, *Feudalism in Egypt, Syria, Palestine, and the Lebanon 1250–1900* (London, 1939); Abdul-Latif Tibawi, *A Modern History of Syria including Lebanon and Palestine* (London and New York, 1969).
3. See Chapter 4 above.
4. See K. Steinhaus, *Soziologie der türkischen Revolution* (Frankfurt/Main, 1969) pp. 35 f.
5. Moshe Ma'oz, *Ottoman Reform in Syria and Palestine 1840–1861, The Impact of the Tanzimat on Politics and Society* (London, 1968) pp. 4 ff.
6. *Ibid.*, p. 8; see also C. Issawi (ed.) *op. cit.*, pp. 205 f.
7. See Philip K. Hitti, 'The Impact of the West on Syria and Lebanon in the Nineteenth Century', *Journal of World History*, II (1955) No. 3, 608–33; P. M. Holt, *op. cit.*, pp. 112 ff.; Albert Hourani, *Syria and Lebanon, A Political Essay*, 4th ed. (Beirut and London, 1968); on Westernisation, see pp. 59 ff. See also Hans Kohn, *Nationalism and Imperialism in the Hither East*, 2nd ed. (New York, 1959); and *idem, Die Europäisierung des Orients* (Berlin, 1934).
8. In spite of the fact that there is an abundance of secondary writing on the Arab national movement and Arab nationalism, the primary sources have not so far been satisfactorily researched. It is even more regrettable that most of the secondary literature has been produced by Western historians and social scientists. Apart from Arab authors educated at Western universities, most of the work that has appeared in Arabic is journalistic, superficial and uncritical. Arab authors educated abroad have tended to publish their work in European languages, e.g. H. Z. Nuseibeh, *The Ideas of Arab Nationalism* (Ithaca and New York, 1956) (2nd ed., 1959); H. Saab, *The Arab Federalists of the Ottoman Empire* (Amsterdam, 1958); see also the extremely comprehensive work by Albert Hourani, *Arabic Thought. . . . The* classic account of the early Arab national movement by an Arab author, still unsurpassed, is George Antonius, *The Arab Awakening: The Story of the Arab National Movement*, 2nd ed. (London, 1938) (4th ed., New York 1965). Sylvia Haim has stated her objections to Antonius in '"The Arab Awakening": A Source for the Historian?', *Die Welt des Islams*, n.s., II, (1953) 237–50, which are however not particularly convincing. R. Hartmann evidently valued Antonius' work, describing it as 'Antonius' particularly valuable book', and 'reliable'. See R. Hartmann, 'Arabische Gesellschaften bis 1914', in *idem* (ed.), *BASI* (Leipzig, 1944) pp. 439–67. Antonius' work has proved invaluable for the present study. The following are typical examples of Arabic secondary literature which are more or less valueless for academic purposes: 'Abd al-'Aziz al-Duri, *al-Judhur al-Tarikhiyya li'l-Qawmiyya al-'Arabiyya* (The Historical Roots of Arab Nationalism) (Beirut, 1960); 'Abd al-Hadi Dakiki, *al-Shu'ubiyya wa'l-Qaumiyya al-'Arabiyya* (Xenophilia and Arab Nationalism) (Beirut, n.d. [about 1962]); 'Abd al-Latif Sharara, *al-Janib al-Thaqafi min al-Qawmiyya al-'Arabiyya* (The Cultural Dimension of Arab Nationalism)

(Beirut, 1961); finally Muhammad Maghzub, *al-Qawmiyya al-'Arabiyya* (Arab Nationalism) (Beirut, 1960). The few useful studies of Arab nationalism in Arabic will be discussed below.

9. See Henry Dodwell, *The Founder of Modern Egypt, A Study of Muhammad 'Ali* (Cambridge, 1931) pp. 41 ff., and G. Antonius, *op. cit.*, pp. 21 ff.

10. Mehmet Şinasi, 'Studien zur Geschichte der syrischen Politik Mehmed Alis von Ägypten', unpubl. Ph.D. thesis (Göttingen, 1936) p. 1. Şinasi, who disapproves of Muhammad 'Ali's policy in Syria, dismisses the enthusiastic reception given to the Egyptian troops by the local population, as the result of 'preparatory work by Muhammad 'Ali's spies'!

11. *Ibid.*, p. 8.

12. Albert Hourani, Arabic Thought . . . pp. 261 ff.; see also H. Dodwell, *op. cit.*, pp. 94 ff., 125 ff., 154 ff., and G. Antonius, *op. cit.*, pp. 25 ff.

13. M. Şinasi, *op.cit.*, p. 66; also Moshe Ma'oz, *op. cit.*, pp. 17 ff., and A. L. Tibawi, *op. cit.*, pp. 63 ff.

14. Moshe Ma'oz, *op. cit.*, pp. 12 ff.

15. *Ibid.*, pp. 14 ff., and G. Baer, *op. cit.*, p. 82.

16. Moshe Ma'oz, *op. cit.*, pp. 14 f.

17. *Ibid.*, p. 12.

18. *Ibid.*, pp. 15 f.

19. *Ibid.*, pp. 18 f., and M. Şinasi, *op. cit.*, *passim*.

19a. G. Antonius, *op. cit.*, pp. 40 f.

20. Moshe Ma'oz, *op. cit.*, p. 17 and A. L. Tibawi, *British Interests in Palestine 1800–1901* (London, 1961) pp. 13 ff.

21. Contrary to what is generally believed, the printing press of the American mission to Malta, which was taken to Beirut after the conquest of Syria by Muhammad 'Ali's troops, was not in fact an Arabic press. It was first set up with Arabic type in 1835–6. See A. L. Tibawi, *American Interests in Syria 1800–1901, A Study of Educational, Literary, and Religious Work* (London, 1966) p. 306.

22. M. Şinasi, *op. cit.*, p. 65.

23. *Ibid.*, p. 41.

24. Moshe Ma'oz, *op. cit.*, p. 19.

25. The activities of the missions will be more extensively discussed below. On this, see also B. Tibi, Introduction to Muhammad Kischli, *Kapitalismus und Linke im Libanon* (Frankfurt/Main, 1970).

26. al-Husri also distinguishes between the roles of the different missions. al-Husri, IV, pp. 198 ff. See also Chapter 8 below.

27. Jürgen Brandt, 'Zum Charakter der französischen Mandatspolitik in Syrien nach dem ersten Weltkrieg', in Walter Markov (ed.), *Kolonialismus und Neokolonialismus in Nordafrika und Nahost* (Berlin, 1964) pp. 197–225; here p. 200. This study is however not always reliable.

28. *Ibid.*, see also references to literature.

28a. For the activities of the American missions, see especially A. L. Tibawi, *American Interests in Syria 1800–1901, op. cit.*, and David H. Finnie, *Pioneers East, The Early American Experience in the Middle East* (Cambridge, Mass., 1967).

29. For the competition of the missions among themselves see A. L. Tabawi, *American Interests in Syria 1800–1901*, pp. 150 ff., and also G. Antonius,

op. cit., pp. 37 ff.

30. See especially Derek Hopwood, *The Russian Presence in Syria and Palestine 1843–1914: Church and Politics in the Near East* (London, 1969) pp. 159 ff. For the interrelationship between political and ecclesiastical interests in the Russian Orthodox missions in the Middle East, see Igor Smolitsch, 'Zur Geschichte der Beziehungen zwischen der russischen Kirche und dem orthodoxen Osten: die russische kirchliche Mission in Jerusalem', *Ostkirchliche Studien*, v (1956) No. 1, 33–51, Nos. 2/3, 89–136.

31. D. Hopwood, *op. cit.*, p. 80.

32. A. L. Tibawi, *American Interests in Syria 1800–1901*, p. 307.

33. *Ibid.*, p. 308.

34. W. Braune, 'Die Entwicklung des Nationalismus bei den Arabern', in R. Hartmann (ed.), *BASI* (Leipzig, 1944) pp. 425–38; here p. 429. See also W. Braune, 'Beitrage zur Geschichte des neuarabischen Schrifttums', *Mitteilungen des Seminars für orientalische Sprachen*, XXXVI (1933) No. 2, 117–40.

35. On Nasif al-Yaziji, see Hanna Fakhuri, *Tarikh al-Adab al-'Arabi* (History of Arab literature), 3rd ed. (Beirut, 1960) pp. 941–57; A. Hourani, *Arabic Thought* . . . , pp. 95 f. W. Braune, 'Beiträge zur Geschichte des neuarabischen Schrifttums', *op. cit.*, p. 127; and G. Antonius, *op. cit.*, pp. 45 ff.

36. An annotated bibliography has been provided by Hanna Fakhuri, *op. cit.*, pp. 945 ff.

37. A. Hourani, *Arabic Thought* . . . , p. 95.

38. On Faris Shidyaq see Hanna Fakhuri, *op. cit.*, pp. 1039–46, and A. Hourani, *Arabic Thought* . . . , pp. 97 ff; also Ibrahim Abu-Lughod, *The Arab Rediscovery of Europe* (Princeton, 1963) *passim*.

39. Faris al-Shidyaq, *Kashf al-Mukhabba' 'an Funnun Urubba* (The Discovery of the Arts of Europe) 2nd ed. (Istanbul, 1881); see also I. Abu-Lughod, *op. cit.*

40. Faris al-Shidyaq, *al-Saq'ala al-Saq fi ma huwa al-Faryaq* (Cairo, n.d.); French transl. *La vie et les aventures de Fariac* (Paris, 1855).

41. A. Hourani, *Arabic Thought* . . . , p. 98.

42. H. Fakhuri, *op. cit.*, p. 1045.

43. *Ibid.*, p. 1044.

44. A. Hourani, *Arabic Thought* . . . , p. 98.

45. On Butrus al-Bustani, see H. Fakhuri, *op. cit.*, pp. 1033–8; A. Hourani, *Arabic Thought* . . . , pp. 10 ff.; G. Antonius, *op. cit.*, pp. 47 ff.

46. That is, several decades before al-Tahtawi wrote his much more systematic work on the education of boys and girls. See Chapter 4, note 78.

46a. See Butrus al-Bustani, *Khitab fi al-Hai'a al-Ijtima'iyya wa al-Muqabala bain al-'Awa'id al-'Arabiyya wa al-Ifranjiyya* (A speech on social organisation and the points of contact and contrast between Arab and European Customs) (Beirut, 1869).

47. A. Hourani, *Arabic Thought* . . . , pp. 100 f.

48. G. Antonius, *op. cit.*, pp. 51 ff.

49. See Muhammad Kischli, *Kapitalismus und Linke im Libanon*, ed. B. Tibi, *op. cit.*, Part 3, pp. 88 ff., and notes 10, 12, 13.

50. H. Fakhuri, *op. cit.*, p. 944, and G. Antonius, *op. cit.*, p. 50.

51. For the history of the Syrian Protestant College, see A. L. Tibawi, 'The Genesis and Early History of the Syrian Protestant College', *Middle East Journal*, XXI (1967) No. 1, 1–15 and No. 2, 199–212.

52. The most important parts of the ode have been reproduced in: 'Abd al-Rahman al-Bazzaz, *Hadhihi Qawmiyyatuna* (This is our Nationalism), 2nd ed. (Cairo, 1964) pp. 374 f., and in Muhammad 'Ammara, *al-'Urubah fi al-'Asr al-Hadith* (Arabism in the Modern Age) (Cairo, 1967) pp. 316 ff.
53. See W. Braune, *Der islamische Orient zwischen Vergangenheit und Zukunft* (Berne and Munich, 1960) p. 59.
54. *Ibid.*
55. G. Antonius, *op. cit.*, p. 54.
56. Adib Ishaq, *al-Durar*, ed. 'Auni Ishaq (Beirut, 1909).
57. *Ibid.*, pp. 200–3; The English translation is to be found in H. Z. Nuseibeh, *op. cit.*, p. 142.
58. Adib Ishaq, *op. cit.*, p. 194, and H. Z. Nuseibeh, *op. cit.*, p. 144. Adib Ishaq was one of the first Western-educated Arab intellectuals to adopt the French idea of elective nationality. He sees the nation not in the sense of a cultural community speaking the same language, but, like Renan, as the practical expression of the *volonté générale*, the will to live together. See Naji 'Allush, 'Tatawwurat al-Haraka al-'Arabiyya mundhu ba'd al-Nahdha' (The Development of the Arab Movement after the Nahdha), *Dirasat 'Arabiyya*, II (1965) No. 1, 57–73.
59. See H. Z. Nuseibeh, *op. cit.*, p. 144.
60. See C. Ernest Dawn, 'From Ottomanism to Arabism: The Origin of an Ideology', in C. Ernest Dawn, *From Ottomanism to Arabism: Essays on the Origins of Arab Nationalism* (Urbana and London, 1973) pp. 122–47, as well as H. Z. Nuseibeh, *op. cit.*, p. 142, note 45.
61. G. Antonius, *op. cit.*, pp. 79 ff., and A. Hourani, *Arabic Thought* . . . , p. 275.
62. The source material shows that C. E. Dawn, *op. cit.*, is incorrect in saying that the secular nationalism of the Arab Christians had little influence and that they were only marginal to the Arab national movement. In fact, they had been the real originators of Arab nationalism before the First World War and since that time they have continued to play a far from insignificant role. However, it should be noted that Lebanese nationalism, which was long supported by France and is generally anti-Arab in character has gained the support of many Lebanese Christians.
63. K. Steinhaus, *op. cit.*, pp. 37 ff.
64. *Ibid.*, p. 37.
65. *Ibid.*, p. 38.
66. *Ibid.*, pp. 38 f.
67. See E. Be'eri, *Army Officers in Arab Politics and Society* (London and New York, 1970) pp. 286 ff, 300. The 'Urabi revolt, which was the first Arab military rebellion, must be distinguished from this, since the development of the modern army in Egypt had followed an entirely different course. For information and source material on the 'Urabi revolt, see Chapter 9, note 4.
68. Bernard Lewis, *The Middle East and the West*, 2nd ed. (Bloomington, 1965) p. 40; see also B. Tibi, 'Zum Verhältnis von Militär und kolonialem Nationalismus am Beispiel der arabischen Länder', *Sozialistische Politik*, I (1969) No. 4, 4–19.
69. Moshe Ma'oz, *op. cit.*, passim, and A. L. Tibawi, *A Modern History of Syria including Lebanon and Palestine*, pp. 94 ff.
70. Moshe Ma'oz, *op. cit.*, pp. 19 f.

71. *Ibid.*, pp. 30 ff.
72. *Ibid.*, p. 44 ff.
73. See K. Steinhaus, *op. cit.*, pp. 40 f. On Abdul Hamid II, see also the rather journalistic and heavily 'psychological' biography by Joan Haslip, *The Sultan, the Life of Abdul Hamid* (London, 1958).
74. See Şerif Mardin, *The Genesis of Young Ottoman Thought, A Study in the Modernization of Turkish Political Ideas* (Princeton, 1962).
75. See Feroz Ahmad, *The Young Turks, The Committee of Union and Progress in Turkish Politics 1908–1914* (London, 1969).
76. *Ibid.*, pp. 47 ff.
77. R. Hartmann, 'Die arabische Frage und das türkische Reich', *Beiträge zur Kenntnis des Orients, Jahrbücher der deutschen Vorderasiengesellschaft*, XV (1918) 1–31; here p. 17.
78. G. Antonius, *op. cit.*, pp. 101 ff.; see also F. Ahmad, *op. cit., passim.*
79. G. Antonius, *op. cit.*, pp. 102 f.
80. *Ibid.*, pp. 108 f.; see also Z. N. Zeine, *The Emergence of Arab Nationalism, With a Background Study of Arab–Turkish Relations in the Near East*, 2nd ed. (Beirut, 1966). Although this source is rich in material it should be used with caution. In his presentation of Arab nationalism and its relationship with the Ottoman Empire, the author tends to mould the material to fit his own interpretation. For a critique of Z. N. Zeine's work see the essay by W. Sharaf al-Din in *Dirasat 'Arabiyya*, VI (1970) No. 7, 113–24.
81. See G. Jäschke, 'Der Turanismus der Jungtürken', *Die Welt des Islams*, XXIII (1941) Nos. 1/2, 1–55.
82. W. Braune, *Der islamische Orient zwischen Vergangenheit und Zukunft*, p. 140.
83. G. Antonius, *op. cit.*, pp. 107 ff, and Z. N. Zeine, *op. cit.*, pp. 83 ff.
84. G. Antonius, *op. cit.*, p. 110 ff.
85. In addition to R. Hartmann's so far unsurpassed essay 'Arabische Gesellschaften bis 1914', *op. cit.*, the following works on the Arab national secret societies may also be consulted: Muhammad 'Ammara, *op. cit.*, pp. 313 ff., and Muhammad 'Izzat Darwaza, *Hawl al-Haraka al-'Arabiyya al-Haditha* (The Arab Movement in Modern Times), 6 vols (Beirut and Sidon, 1950), here vol. I, pp. 22 ff. The last of these is particularly useful, since the author was secretary of *Jam'iyyat al-Fatat* in 1919, and thus had intimate acquaintance with his subject matter.
86. M. 'I. Darwaza, *op. cit.*, pp. 27–32; and G. Antonius, *op. cit.*, p. 111.
87. R. Hartmann, 'Arabische Gesellschaft bis 1914', *op. cit.*, p. 461. On al-Misri, see E. Be 'eri, *op. cit.*, pp. 41–8; G. Antonius, *op. cit.*, pp. 118 f., and Chapter 9 below and note 31 to that Chapter. For *Jam'iyyat al-'Ahd*, see M. 'I. Darwaza, *op. cit.*, pp. 32 f.
88. M. 'I. Darwaza, who gives this figure, *op. cit.*, p. 33, feels that it might be exaggerated.
89. On Shibli Shumayyil see B. Tibi (ed.), *Die Arabische Linke* (Frankfurt/Main, 1969) pp. 16 f.
90. On Rashid Ridha, see Chapter 8, note 56.
91. The Ottoman Decentralisation Party, which played a major part in the Congress, published the protocols of the Congress in book form in Cairo in 1913. Since this publication has been unobtainable, information about it has been taken from secondary sources. See also al-Husri, VI, pp. 225 ff.,

G. Antonius, *op. cit.*, pp. 114 ff., and M. 'Ammara, *op. cit.*, pp. 323 ff.

92. Khairalla also published in Paris: *Les régions Arabes libérées*, 1919, and earlier 'La Syrie', *Révue du Monde Musulman*, XIX (1912) p. 1–143.
93. R. Hartmann, 'Die arabische Frage und das türkische Reich', *op. cit.*, pp. 16 f.
94. G. Antonius, *op. cit.*, pp. 98 f. Hartmann comes to the same conclusion; see 'Arabische Gesellschaften bis 1914', *op. cit.*, pp. 446 f., as well as his other works. In a course of lectures at the Institute for Advanced Arab Studies at the Arab League, Emir Mustafa Shihabi also cast doubt on the influence of Azouri's work. He showed that none of the members of the Arab nationalist secret societies before the first World War were familiar with or owned a copy of *La Réveil de la Nation Arabe*, which Azouri published in Paris in 1905. See also Naji 'Allush, *Tatawwurat al-Haraka al-'Arabiyya mundhu ba'd al-Nahdha, op. cit.*, p. 62.
95. Quoted from M. 'Ammara, *op. cit.*, p. 331, note 1.
96. See M. 'Ammara, *op. cit.*, p. 331, note 2.
97. Quoted from al-Husri, VI, pp. 228 f. 25 Arabs took part in the Congress, of whom 11 were Muslims and 14 Christians; see M. 'Ammara, *op. cit.*, p. 323.
98. al-Husri, VI, p. 229.
99. *Ibid.*
100. M. 'Ammara, *op. cit.*, p. 325.
101. *Ibid.*
102. *Ibid.*, pp. 326 f., and al-Husri, VI, p. 235.
103. M. 'Ammara, *op. cit.*, pp. 327 f.
104. Quoted verbatim in M. Ammara, *op. cit.*, pp. 328 f., and al-Husri, VI, pp. 226 f.
105. M. 'Ammara, *op. cit.*, p. 329.
106. *Ibid.*, pp. 331 f., and al-Husri, VI, p. 238.
107. Helmut Ritter, 'Die Abschaffung des Kalifats', *Archiv für Politik und Geschichte*, II (1924) part I, 343–68; here p. 346.
108. *Ibid.*, p. 351.
109. R. Hartmann, *Islam und Nationalismus* (Berlin, 1948) p. 35; and *idem*, 'Arabische Gesellschaften bis 1914', *op. cit.*, p. 460.
110. G. Antonius, *op. cit.*, pp. 115 ff.; and al-Husri, VI, pp. 240 ff.
111. R. Hartmann, *Islam und Nationalismus*, p. 35.
112. The records and documents of the trials were published by the Ottomans in 1916. See *La Vérité sur la Question Syrienne* (Constantinople, 1916). The author was not able to consult this document.
113. R. Hartmann, 'Arabische Gesellschaften bis 1914', *op. cit.*, p. 441; see also H. Ritter, *op. cit.*, p. 346.
114. See C. E. Dawn, 'The Rise of Arabism in Syria; *From Ottomanism to Arabism*, pp. 148–79. Here the table in the Appendix, pp. 166 ff.
115. See Chapter 5.
116. See the excellent study by Anis al-Sayigh, *al-Hashimiyyun w'- al-Thawra al-'Arabiyya al-Kubra* (The Hashimites and the Great Arab Revolt) (Beirut, 1966), in which the background of the Revolt of 1916 and the role of the Hashimite dynasty has been properly investigated for the first time, with the aid of valuable source material. See also the rather less brilliant but more popular work of Anis al-Sayigh, *Tatawwur al-Mafhum al-Qawmi'inda al-'Arab* (The Development of Arab National Thought) (Beirut, 1961).
117. See G. Antonius, *op. cit.*, Chaps. VII, VIII and IX.

118. *Ibid.*, Chap. XIII, pp. 243 ff.
119. Rudolf Sellheim, *Der zweite Bürgerkrieg im Islam 680–692, Das Ende der Mekkanisch-Medinensischen Vorherrschaft* (Wiesbaden, 1970) p. 30.
120. See C. E. Dawn, 'Ideological Influences in the Arab Revolt', in J. Kritzeck and R. Bayly Winder (eds), *The World of Islam, Studies in Honor of Philip K. Hitti* (New York, 1960) pp. 233–48; here p. 244; *idem*, 'The Amir of Mecca, al-Husayn ibn- 'Ali and the Origin of the Arab Revolt', *From Ottomanism to Arabism*, pp. 1–53.
121. G. Antonius, *op. cit.*, p. 281.
122. See M. Kischli, *Kapitalismus und Linke im Libanon*, ed. B. Tibi (Frankfurt/Main, 1970) pp. 99 f.
123. The development of the Arab regions of the Ottoman Empire since the First World War has been documented by Erich Topf, *Die Staatenbildung in den arabischen Teilen der Türkei seit dem Weltkriege nach Entstehung, Bedeutung und Lebensfähigkeit* (Hamburg, 1929); this also includes original documents. See also Naji 'Allush, 'al-Haraka al-'Arabiyya ba'd al-Harb al-'Alamiyya al-Ula' (The Arab Movement after the First World War) *Dirasat 'Arabiyya*, II (1965) No. 3, 54–75; Jürgen Brandt, *op. cit.*; Ann Williams, *Britain and France in the Middle East and North Africa 1914–1967* (London and New York, 1968); and Lothar Rathmann, *Araber Stehen auf* (Berlin, 1960) pp. 126 ff. See also Heinrich Kaesewieter, *Syrien und Libanon als A-Mandate* (Darmstadt, 1935).
124. Anis al-Sayigh, *al-Hashimiyyun wa al-Thawra al-'Arabiyya al-Kubra*, *passim*, as well as Naji 'Allush, 'al-Thawra al-'Arabiyya al-Kubra: Muhawalat Taqyim' (The Great Arab Revolt: an Attempt at an Evaluation), *Dirasat Arabiyya*, II (1966) No. 8, 4–12.
125. Anis al-Sayigh, *al-Hashimiyyun . . .*, pp. 277 f.; see also R. Hartmann, 'Die arabische Frage und das türkische Reich', *op. cit.*, pp. 24 f.
126. See Hisham B. Sharabi, *Governments and Politics in the Middle East in the Twentieth Century* (Princeton, New York, 1962) pp. 27 f.
127. Hans Kohn, *Nationalism and Imperialism in the Hither East*, 2nd ed. (New York, 1959) p. 64.
128. See Chapter 1, note 48.
129. E. Be'eri, *op. cit.*, p. 41.
130. *Ibid.*, p. 42; For German cultural influences in the Ottoman Empire see Otto Kley, 'Der deutsche Bildungseinfluß in der Türkei', *Beiträge zur Kenntnis des Orients, Jahrbücher der Deutschen Vorderasiengesellschaft*, XIV (1917) 1–73.
131. E. Be'eri, *op. cit.*, pp. 326 ff., and R. Hartmann, *Islam und Nationalismus*, pp. 37 f.
132. For a more detailed discussion, see Chapter 6 below.
133. See B. Tibi, 'Zum Verhältnis von Militär und kolonialem Nationalismus am Beispiel der arabischen Länder', *op. cit.* For Arab nationalists of the post-colonial era the coup d'état has become a normal method of seizing power. See also H. B. Sharabi, *Nationalism and Revolution in the Arab World* (Princeton, 1966) pp. 56 ff. S. A. Morrison, 'Arab Nationalism and Islam', *Middle East Journal*, II (1948) No. 2, 147–59, explains the 'totalitarian' character of Arab Nationalism in its later phase by claiming that Islam as a totalitarian-theocratic dogma has been synthesised with nationalism. According to Morrison, who was a missionary, this synthesis came about because post-war

Arab nationalism was no longer dominated by Arab Christians. Of course this notion is far-fetched, because fanatical Arab nationalism is strongly secular, and one of its intellectual founders, Michel 'Aflaq, is an Arab Christian.

134. See C. F. Gallagher, 'Language, Culture, and Ideology: The Arab World', in K. H. Silvert (ed.), *Expectant Peoples, Nationalism and Development* (New York, 1963) pp. 199–231; here p. 214.

135. *Ibid.*, p. 215. W. Braune comes to the same conclusion. On the relationship of Arab nationalists to the West he writes:

> There are still people alive who have fought enthusiastically for Europeanisation. But because of the threat of colonialism the relationship with the West has turned to rejection and hatred over the last years. No one either wishes or can afford to do without some aspects of Western culture. But a form of alienation which comes near to hatred only seeks this culture to the extent that it can be an instrument in the struggle against the West. (*Der islamische Orient Zwischen* . . ., p. 160)

136. The biographical data which follow are taken from M. A. Khalafallah, 'Sati' al-Husri: Qissat Hayatihi' (Sati' al-Husri: a Biography) *al-Majalla* (1969) No. 146, 24–31, as well as the anonymous obituary in *al-Tali'a*, v (1969) No. 2, 158–61. For Husri's biography see also *Oriente Moderno*, XXXVI (1956) 204; the foreword by Ralph Costi (transl.), 'Qu'est'ce que le Nationalisme? par Abou Khaldun Sati' al-Husri', *Orient* (Paris), VII (1959) 215–26, and A. Hourani, *Arabic Thought* . . ., pp. 312 ff.; see also notes 137 and 138 below.

137. L. M. Kenny, 'Sati' al-Husri's view on Arab Nationalism', *Middle East Journal*, XVII (1963) No. 3, 231–56; here p. 232.

138. See Kemal H. Karpat (ed.), *Political and Social Thought in the Contemporary Middle East* (London, 1968) pp. 55 ff. Karpat also shows the structural similarities between al-Husri's and Gökalp's organic theory of the nation. He regrets that scholars have neglected al-Husri's activities in the Ottoman Empire and his political and educational writing in Ottoman Turkish newspapers. For Ziya Gökalp as the theoretician of the Young Turks and the Kemalists see the selection of texts edited by Niyazi Berkes, *Turkish Nationalism and Western Civilisation* (New York, 1959); also Uriel Heyd, *The Foundations of Turkish Nationalism, The Life and Teachings of Ziya Gökalp* (London, 1950).

139. See Chapter 7 below.

140. See al-Husri, V, Eng. transl. (S. Glazer), *The Day of Mayasalun* (Washington, 1966).

141. See M. A. Khalafallah, *op. cit.*, pp. 26 f.

142. See Chapter 6 below.

143. See Chapter 9 below, where al-Husri's controversy with Taha Husain is discussed.

144. The controversy between al-Husri and Salama Musa has been omitted here. al-Husri's views may be found in vol. XVIII. As far as is known Musa did not reply to this. His various changes of viewpoint can be found in his autobiography *Tarbiya Salama Musa* (Cairo, 1947); Eng. transl. *The Education of Salama Musa*, ed. and intro. by L. O. Schuman (Leiden, 1961). For secondary literature, see Sylvia Haim, 'Salama Musa, An Appreciation of

his Autobiography', *Die Welt des Islams*, n.s. II, (1953) 10–24, and B. Tibi (ed.), *Die arabische Linke* (Frankfurt/Main, 1969) pp. 17–21.
145. i.e. the Sykes-Picot agreement.
146. al-Husri, *op. cit.* (note 140), and G. Antonius, *op. cit.*, Chapter XIV, pp. 276 ff. where this is discussed in detail.
147. See al-Husri, XX and XXI, which includes autobiographical notes on his activities in Iraq.
148. See 'U. K. Haddad, *Harakat Rashid 'Ali al-Gailani Sannat 1941* (The Rashid 'Ali al-Gailani Movement of 1941) (Sidon, c. 1950) pp. 83 f. Apart from the rather scanty information provided here it is difficult to find other evidence about the party.
149. The leadership of the Hashimites and that of Mufti al-Husaini has been analysed within the framework of a general examination of political leadership in modern Arab history by Anis al-Sayigh, *Fi Mafhum al-Za 'ama al-Siyasiyya, Min Faisal al-Awwal ila Jamal 'Abd al-Nasir* (The Concept of Political Leadership, from Faisal I to Jamal 'Abd al-Nasir) (Beirut, 1965). There is an abundance of literature on Mufti Amin al-Husaini of which only a few examples will be cited: M. P. Waters, *Mufti over the Middle East* (London, 1942); Maurice Pearlman, *Mufti of Jerusalem, The Story of Haj Amin el-Huseini* (London, 1947); Joseph B. Schechtmann, *The Mufti and the Führer, The Rise and Fall of Haj Amin el-Huseini* (New York and London, 1965). Fritz Grobba has written on the relationship between the Mufti and the Third Reich from his own experience as a diplomat: *Männer und Mächte im Orient, 25 Jahre diplomatischer Tätigkeit im Orient* (Göttingen, 1967).
150. 'U. K. Haddad, *op. cit.*, passim. Also F. Grobba, who was then negotiating with Haddad, reports on these relations in his memoirs, *op. cit.*, pp. 192 ff, 206 ff.
151. For al-Gailani's coup d'état see also Lukasz Hirszowicz, *The Third Reich and the Arab East* (London, 1966); Heintz Tillmann, *Deutschlands Araberpolitik im zweiten Weltkrieg* (Berlin, 1965); Majid Khadduri, *Independent Iraq*, 2nd ed. (London, 1960).
152. al-Husri makes little mention of the coup in his memoirs, see XXI, p. 596. In general he claims to have kept out of politics during his time in Iraq, see *ibid.*, pp. 525 f. He mentions his deportation and extradition after the al-Gailani coup without giving the reasons for it. See *ibid.*, pp. 518 ff.
153. L. M. Kenny, *op. cit.*, pp. 231 ff, discusses al-Husri's views on national education.
154. On the dustjacket of his books, which are constantly republished, and also when he is quoted in other works in Arabic.
155. See Shibli 'Aisami, *Haul al-Wahda al-Arabiyya* (On Arab Unity) (Damascus, 1957) pp. 4 f.
156. See Shibli 'Aisami, *op. cit.*, pp. 4 f.

Notes to Chapter 6

1. W. Sulzbach, *Imperialismus und Nationalbewußtsein* (Frankfurt/Main, 1959).
2. Charles F. Gallagher, 'Language, Culture and Ideology, The Arab World', in

K. H. Silvert (ed.), *Expectant Peoples, Nationalism and Development* (New York, 1963) pp. 199–231.
3. Hans Kohn, *The Idea of Nationalism*, p. 4.
4. *Ibid.*, p. 249.
5. Helmut Plessner, *Die verspätete Nation* (Stuttgart 1959), esp. pp. 47 ff.
6. Hans Kohn, *op. cit.*, p. 249. H. O. Ziegler, *Die moderne Nation*, also makes this distinction, but blurs it by not making it more central. He believes that the idea of the nation in Germany and in the advanced countries of Europe have a common structure, because both are animated by the fundamental principle of the sovereignty of the nation.

There is no transcendent moment in the socio-historical world for the nation based on the idea of the *Volksgeist* nor for that based on the *volonté générale*. Each nation obtains its own particular sovereignty, which in the long run remains the spiritual basis for the various forms of political sovereignty. This is the source of the important differences between the French democratic idea of the nation and the German idea of the nation (p. 223)

Ziegler prefers the German idea of the nation since he considers it 'less rigid—less dogmatic' (p. 226).
7. See H. Tillmann, *Deutschlands Araberpolitik im Zweiten Weltkrieg* (Berlin, 1965).
8. al-Husri, IV, p. 12.
9. *Ibid.*, p. 35.
10. Ibid., p. 3.
11. Ibid., p. 64.
12. See for instance *ibid.*, pp. 87 f. For the fascistoid content of the political thought of von Schönerer see H. Arendt, *The Origins of Totalitarianism*, rev. ed. (London, 1967) pp. 43 ff.
13. Hans Kohn, *Prophets and Peoples: Studies in Nineteenth Century Nationalism* (New York, 1946) pp. 77–104.
14. Robert Ergang, *Herder and the Foundations of German Nationalism* (New York, 1931) pp. 102 ff.
15. H. Kohn, *The Idea of Nationalism*, pp. 427 ff. For Herder's general impact see F. M. Barnard, *Herder's Social and Political Thought: From Enlightenment to Nationalism* (Oxford, 1965). For his influence in Germany, see pp. 153–67: outside Germany, see pp. 167–77. See also Konrad Bittner, *Herders Geschichtsphilosophie und die Slaven* (Reichenberg, 1929).
16. R. Ergang, *op. cit.*, pp. 249 ff.
17. Hans Kohn, *The Idea of Nationalism*, pp. 352 ff.
18. J. G. Herder, *Auch eine Philosophie der Geschichte zur Bildung der Menschheit*, with a postscript by H. G. Gadamer (Frankfurt/Main, 1967) esp. pp. 75 ff and *passim*. Herder dismisses the philosophy of the Enlightenment as the 'philosophy of Paris' (p. 83). He speaks of the 'French fashion books' (p. 88), and says that it has had only a limited impact. 'The so called *enlightenment* and *civilisation* of the world has only *touched and held onto a narrow strip of the globe*' (p. 110). See also pp. 126, 134.
19. See R. Ergang, *op. cit.*, p. 101, and H. Kohn, *The Idea of Nationalism*, pp. 431

ff; see also pp. 433 ff. See also F. M. Barnard, *op. cit.*
20. Quotations from Herder here and below are taken from the edition by W. Dobbek, *J. G. Herder, Werke*, 3rd ed., 5 vols (Berlin and Weimar, 1964), here *Idee zur Philosophie der Geschichte der Menschheit*, vol. IV, pp. 178 ff and 163 ff., where Herder develops his climatic theory. See here R. Ergang, *op. cit.*, pp. 89 f. and C. J. H. Hayes, 'Contributions of Herder to the Doctrine of Nationalism', *American Historical Review*, XXXII (1927) No. 4, 719–36. Herder admits than man is capable of affecting his physical environment by cultivating the area in which he lives. Thus Europe was changed from a 'damp forest' into 'cultivated areas'; see *op. cit.*, vol. IV, p. 168 f.
21. J. G. Herder, *op. cit.*, vol. IV, p. 159.
22. *Ibid.*, p. 160.
23. *Ibid.*, p. 196.
24. *Ibid.*, p. 156; see here C. J. H. Hayes, *op. cit.*, p. 723, and R. Ergang, *op. cit.*, pp. 88 f., p. 99 f, p. 101.
25. J. G. Herder, *op. cit.*, vol. IV, p. 238.
26. *Ibid.*, pp. 255 ff.
27. *Ibid.*, p. 197.
28. *Ibid.*, p. 242.
29. *Ibid.*, p. 246 f. On Herder's philosophy of language, see the selection by Erich Heintel, *Herder, Sprachphilosophische Schriften*, 2nd ed. (Hamburg, 1964).
30. J. G. Herder, *op. cit.*, vol. IV, p. 252.
31. J. G. Herder, *Sprache als Werzeug der Literatur einer Nation, Fragment*, in Herder, *op. cit.*, vol. II, p. 68.
32. *Ibid.*
33. J. G. Herder, *Idee zum ersten patriotischen Institut für den Allgemeingeist Deutschland*, in Herder, *op. cit.*, vol. III, pp. 359 ff, here p. 364.
34. *Ibid.*, p. 365.
35. This can be illustrated by the French colonial policy of assimilation. By frenchifying the indigenous élites in the French colonies, the authorities hoped to destroy resistance to colonialism. Algeria is a good example of this; here anti-colonialism began as an anti-assimilationist movement, particularly among the followers of Ben Badis. Ben Badis believed that the revival of the Arabic language would be one of the most important means of achieving his aims. For the whole problem of assimilation see Wolfgang Ohnbeck, *Die französiche Algerienpolitik von 1919–1939* (Cologne and Opladen, 1967).
36. R. Ergang, *op. cit.*, pp. 43 ff.
37. *Ibid.*, pp. 239, 240 f.
38. See H. Kohn, *The Idea of Nationalism, op. cit.*, pp. 429 ff.
39. See R. Ergang, *op. cit.*, pp. 89 ff and J. G. Herder, *Über das Wort und den Begriff der Humanität*, in Herder, *op. cit.*, vol. V, pp. 102 ff. See also F. M. Barnard, *op. cit.*, pp. 88–108.
40. R. Ergang, *op. cit.*, pp. 85, 87, and H. Kohn, *op. cit.*, pp. 434 ff, and C. J. H. Hayes, *op. cit.*, p. 726.
41. See C. J. H. Hayes, *op. cit.*, p. 725; R. Ergang, *op. cit.*, *passim*, and H. Kohn, *op. cit.*, pp. 435 ff.
42. H. D. Werner, *Klassenstruktur und Nationalcharakter* (Tübingen, n.d.), and see the review by B. Tibi in *Das Argument*, XII (1970) No. 56, 58 ff. It is clear that Herder's analysis of nationalism is purely speculative, and it is surprising

that Eugen Lemberg should present the speculative features in Herder in an even more mystical fashion. E. Lemberg, *Geschichte des Nationalismus in Europa* (Stuttgart 1950) pp. 192 ff.

43. Hans Reiss, *The Political Thought of the German Romantics* (Oxford, 1955) p. 3. 'In one respect, however, Herder did not differ from the Aufklärung; he was a cosmopolitan, a European. He laid the foundations for German nationalism when he demanded a German national literature, and by emphasising the common bond woven by a common language, and considered cultural achievements impossible without nationalistic roots, but he himself never advocated nationalist aims.'

44. See Klaus Epstein, *The Genesis of German Conservatism* (Princeton, 1966).

45. *Ibid.*, pp. 434 ff. Epstein distinguishes between two intellectual currents in Germany at the time of the French Revolution, represented by the German Jacobins and the German patriots (p. 440). See also Hans Kohn, 'The Eve of German Nationalism', *Journal of the History of Ideas*, XII (1951) 256–84, where Kohn shows that even those who had supported the French Revolution in Germany went over to the nationalist camp when the Napoleonic wars of conquest began.

46. See H. Kohn, 'Arndt and the Character of German Nationalism', *American Historical Review*, LIV (1949) No. 4, 787–803; here p. 789.

47. I. Geiss, *Der Panafrikanismus, Zur Geschichte der Dekolonisation* (Frankfurt/Main, 1968) *passim*. Eng. trans., *The Pan-African Movement* (London, 1974).

48. Hermann Simon, *Geschichte der deutschen Nation* (Mainz, 1968) p. 326.

49. On the German Romantics see e.g. Hans Kohn, 'Romanticism and the Rise of German Nationalism', *Review of Politics*, XII (1950) No. 4, 443–72; Louis L. Snyder, *German Nationalism, The Tragedy of a People: Extremism contra-Liberalism in Modern German History* (Harrisburg, 1952); Hans Reiss, *The Political Thought of the German Romantics*, *op. cit.*; A. D. Verschoor, *Die ältere deutsche Romantik und die Nationsidee* (Amsterdam, n.d. [1929]); Paul Kluckhohn, *Die deutsche Romantik* (Bielefeld and Leipzig, 1924); *idem, Persönlichkeit und Gemeinschaft, Studien zur Staatsauffassung der deutschen Romantik* (Halle, 1925); *idem, Das Ideengut der Romantik*, 3rd ed. (Tübingen, 1953); Georg Mehlis, *Die deutsche Romantik* (Munich, 1922); L. A. Willoughby, *The Romantic Movement in Germany*, 2nd ed. (New York, 1966), (first publ. 1930).

50. For contemporary German writers' views of Napoleon see Friedrich Stählin, *Napoleons Glanz und Fall im deutschen Urteil* (Brunswick, 1952).

51. Marx implicitly applied the situation in Germany during the Napoleonic conquests and its significance for world history to the colonial countries and thus arrived at the misconception that colonialism would thus participate in the dissolution of feudal and pre-capitalist structures in the territories which it conquered. See Horace B. Davis, *Nationalism and Socialism* (New York, 1967), and the review by B. Tibi, 'Marxismus und Nationalismusanalyse', *Neue Politische Literatur*, XIV (1969) No. 4, 560 f. and Chapter 3, note 1 above.

52. Hans Reiss, *op. cit.*, p. 9; Otto Wolff comes to a similar conclusion in the context of Gandhi's conservatism, which is revolutionary to the extent that it opposes foreign rule and the status quo of the colonial situation. 'It is his deep conservatism, clinging absolutely to that which is peculiar to him, which has a

profoundly revolutionary effect on the outside worlds'. O. Wolff, *Mahatma Gandhi, Politik und Gewaltlosigkeit* (Göttingen, 1963) p. 20.
53. Hans Reiss, *op. cit.*, pp. 5 f.
54. *Ibid.*, p. 9. The literary interest in the Middle Ages of the German Romantics within the framework of a backward-looking utopia is discussed by A. D. Verschoor, *Die ältere deutsche Romantik*, pp. 57 ff. Marx has interpreted the bourgeois philosophical tendency to hark back to the past in the context of the 'alienation of the individual from himself and from others' which resulted from the development of commodity production and relations of commodity exchange.

In earlier stages of development the single individual seems to be developed more fully, because he has not yet worked out his relationships in their fullness, or erected them as independent social powers and relations opposite himself. It is as ridiculous to yearn for a return to that original fullness as it is to believe that with this complete emptiness history has come to a standstill. The bourgeois viewpoint has never advanced beyond this antithesis between itself and this romantic viewpoint and therefore the latter will accompany it as a legitimate antithesis up to its blessed end. K. Marx, *Grundrisse der Kritik der politischen Ökonomie* (Berlin, 1953) p. 80. Eng. transl., *Grundrisse: Introduction to the Critique of Political Economy* (London, 1973) p. 162.

54a. See Rudolf Sellheim, 'Prophet, Chalif und Geschichte, Die Muhammed-Biographie des Ibn Isaq', *Oriens*, XVIII/XIX (1965/66) 33–91. Sellheim shows that during the 'Abbasid period (750–1258), when non-Arab Muslims, especially Persians, occupied commanding positions in the governmental system, the Arabs were forced to forge a cultural identity of their own. The Persians disparaged the Arabs as uncivilised Beduin, so that the Arab 'Abbasids employed historians and scholars to research into pre-Islamic and early Islamic history.
55. For the relationship of the later Fichte to the nation and to nationalism, see H. C. Engelbrecht, *Johann Gottleib Fichte, A Study of his Political Writings with Special Reference to his Nationalism* (New York, 1933); Hans Kohn, 'The Paradox of Fichte's Nationalism', *Journal of the History of Ideas*, X (1949) No. 3, 319–43; F. Haymann, *Weltbürgertum und Vaterlandsliebe in der Staatslehre Rousseaus und Fichtes* (Berlin, 1924); A. D. Verschoor, *op. cit.*, pp. 116–37; Hans Reiss, *op. cit.*, pp. 18 ff; J. Binder, 'Fichte und die Nation', *Logos*, X (1921) No. 3, 275–315; D. Bergner, *Neue Bemerkungen zu J. G. Fichtes Stellungsnahme zur nationalen Frage* (Berlin, 1957); H. Mehnert, 'Fichte und die Bedeutung der nationalen Frage in seinem Werk', unpubl. Ph.D. thesis (Leipzig, 1955).
56. Bernhard Willms, *Die totale Freiheit, Fichtes politische Philosophie* (Cologne and Opladen, 1967) *passim*. Richard Saage's article: 'Aspekte der politischen Philosophie Fichtes', *Neue Politische Literatur*, XV (1970) No. 3, 354–76, contains a critical survey of recent work on Fichte, including Willms' book.
57. Willms, *op. cit.*, p. 128.
58. *Ibid.*, pp. 138 f.
59. *Ibid.*, p. 144.

60. See *ibid.*, p. 134.
61. *Ibid.*, p. 146. Willms comes to the conclusion that the definition of mankind central to the early Fichte is gradually dropped. In the early Fichte mankind is realised in concrete form in the nation, while in the later Fichte the notion of mankind is completely passed over in favour of 'Germanness'; see *ibid.*, p. 151.
62. See references in Chapter 4, note 55 above.
63. J. G. Fichte, *Reden an die deutsche Nation*, ed. F. Medicus, with an intr. by A. Diemer (Hamburg, 1955) p. 26. Eng. transl., *Addresses to the German Nation* (London, 1922 and New York, 1968). References are to the pages in the German text.
64. *Ibid.*, pp. 18 f.
65. *Ibid.*, p. 21.
66. J. Binder, *Fichte und die Nation*.
67. See B. Willms, *op. cit.*, pp. 153 ff., and G. H. Turnbull, *The Educational Theory of Fichte* (London, 1926).
68. See al-Husri, vols XX and XXI, *passim*. Yusif Khalil Yusif's *al-Qawmiyya al-'Arabiyya wa Dawr al-Tarbiyya fi Tahqiqiha* (The Role of Education in the Realisation of Arab Nationalism) (Cairo, 1967), was clearly inspired by al-Husri's notion of national education.
69. This was in 1949; see P. Seale, *The Struggle for Syria, A Study of Post-War Arab Politics 1945–1958* (London, 1965) p. 77.
70. J. G. Fichte, *op. cit.*, p. 60.
71. *Ibid.*, p. 61.
72. *Ibid.*, p. 62.
73. *Ibid.*, p. 63.
74. *Ibid.*, p. 66.
75. *Ibid.*, p. 68.
76. *Ibid.*, p. 72.
77. *Ibid.*, see also p. 106 and p. 125.
78. *Ibid.*, p. 107.
79. *Ibid.*, p. 96.
80. *Ibid.*, p. 13.
81. *Ibid.*, p. 242.
82. *Ibid.*, p. 131.
83. *Ibid.*
84. *Ibid.*, p. 130.
85. *Ibid.*, p. 199.
86. *Ibid.*
87. See the selection entitled E. M. Arndt, *Deutsche Volkswerdung* (Breslau, n.d. [1934]) Parts I and II, pp. 46 ff. For Arndt's nationalism, see H. Kohn, 'Arndt and the Character of German Nationalism', *op. cit.* (note 46 above); Alfred G. Pundt, *Arndt and the Nationalist Awakening in Germany*, 2nd ed. (New York, 1968) (first publ. 1935).
88. Quoted by Hermann Simon, *Geschichte der deutschen Nation*, p. 298.
89. *Ibid.*, p. 299.
90. H. Simon, *op. cit.*, pp. 328 f.
91. *Ibid.*, p. 300.
92. The following publications on Fichte and Arndt alone appeared after 1933: the selection of texts by Fichte entitled: 'Fichte, Worte über Nation und

Menschheit, Fichtes Kampf um Deutschlands innere und äußere Befreiung',
Nationalsozialistische Monatshefte, VIII (1937) No. 86, 418–25, as well as the
writings by Ernst Bergmann, *Fichte und der Nationalsozialismus* (Breslau, n.d.
[1933]), and Alfred Baeumler, 'Fichte und Wir', *Nationalsozialistische
Monatshefte*, VIII (1937) No. 87, 482–9. Both authors consider the Third
Reich to be the realisation of Fichte's ideas. Even during the Second World
War the National-Socialist interpretation of Fichte was attacked by a German
in exile: see W. Kaufmann, 'Fichte and National Socialism', *The American
Political Science Review*, XXXVI (1942) No. 3, 460–70. On Arndt see the
selection ed. by C. Petersen and P. H. Ruth: *E. M. Arndt, Deutsche
Volkswerdung, Sein politisches Vermächtnis an die deutsche Gegenwart*
(Breslau, n.d. [1934]), and the Frankfurt dissertation by Hans Polog,
*E. M. Arndts Weg zum Deutschen, Studien zur Entwicklung des frühen Arndt
1769–1812* (Leipzig, 1936); see also H. J. Kuhn, *Arndt und Jahn als völkisch-
politische Denker* (Langensalza, 1936).

93. See Walther Euchner, 'Demokratietheoretische Aspekte der politischen
Ideengeschichte', in D. Senghaas and G. Kress (eds), *Politikwissenschaft*
(Frankfurt/Main, 1969) pp. 38 ff; here p. 38.

94. It is beyond the scope of this work to give a comprehensive outline of this
material. It is sufficient to refer to the English-language monographs on
German nationalism quoted above, most of which appeared either during or
shortly after the Second World War. It is interesting to note that some of these
works have been reprinted in recent years.

95. See Chapter 2 above.

96. Ibn Khaldun, *al-Muqaddima* (Cairo, n.d.). There is a complete English
translation: *The Muqaddima, an Introduction to History*, ed. F. Rosenthal
(New York, 1958) 3 vols.

97. F. Rosenthal, *op. cit.*, p. lxxxvii.

98. Arnold Toynbee, *A Study of History*, 6th edn, vol. III, (London, 1951) p. 322.

99. For a survey of these works see the bibliographical appendix by W. Fischel to
Rosenthal's translation of the *Muqaddima*, vol. III, pp. 485–512.

100. The *Muqaddima* was translated into Turkish in 1749, and was highly valued
by the Ottomans as an introduction to the art of politics. Hammer-Purgsthal,
who carried out research in the Ottoman Empire at the beginning of the
nineteenth century, was surprised at the extent to which the *Muqaddima* was
known within the state bureaucracy and how frequently it was referred to; he
described Ibn Khaldun as the 'Arab Montesquieu'. al-Husri also discusses the
Ottomans' high appreciation of the *Muqaddima* in his work on Ibn Khaldun.
See al-Husri, vol. II, pp. 140 f., p. 615 ff.

101. al-Husri, vol. II.

102. Heinrich Simon gives a summary of this discussion in his Berlin habilitation
dissertation: *Ibn Khalduns Wissenschaft von der menschlichen Kultur* (Leipzig,
1959) pp. 48 ff.

103. Erwin Rosenthal, *Ibn Khalduns Gedanken über den Staat* (Berlin, 1932).

104. H. Ritter, 'Irrational Solidarity Groups, a Socio-psychological Study in
Connection with Ibn Khaldun', *Oriens*, I (1948), 1–44.

105. K. Ayad, *Die Geschichts-und Gesellschaftslehre Ibn Khalduns* (Stuttgart,
1930).

106. See Heinrich Simon, *op. cit.*, p. 51.

107. A. von Kremer, *Ibn Haldun und seine Kulturgeschichte der islamischen Reiche*, Sitzungsberichte der Akademie der Wissenschaften zu Wien (1878).

108. T. Khemiri, 'Der 'Asabiyya-Begriff in der Muqadimma des Ibn Haldun', *Der Islam*, XXII (1936) 163–88.

109. Ibn Khaldun, *al-Muqaddima* (Arabic edn), p. 129.

110. *Ibid.*, see K. Ayad, *op. cit.*, p. 109.

111. See here Heinrich Simon, *op. cit.*, pp. 110 ff.; see also *al-Muqadima*, p. 44.

112. 'Ibn Khaldun knows ideology in the form of religion. A common religious faith would be capable of strengthening the *'asabiyya'*, H. Ritter, *op. cit.*, p. 31.

113. For the doctrine of Islamic universalism, see W. M. Watt, *Islam and the Integration of Society* (London, 1961) pp. 273 ff. Today Islamic universalism has been abandoned even by the leading representatives of Islam, who have joined the national current in order to save Islam by means of a synthesis with nationalism. Thus the well-known Syrian Islamic scholar Muhammad Mubarak thinks that Arab nationalism is only an outward form in need of an ideological content, and postulates that Islam should be this content, see M. Mubarak, *al-Umma al-'Arabiyya fi Ma'rakat Tahqiq al-Dhat* (The Arab Nation and its Struggle for an Identity) (Damascus, 1959) pp. 55 ff. This demand is entirely in the spirit of Ibn Khaldun. There are traces of the nationalisation of Islam in the works of almost all Islamic modernists. See B. Tibi, 'Akkulturationsprozesse in modernen Orient', *Neue Politische Literatur*, XV (1970) No. 1, 77–84.

114. A. von Kremer, *op. cit.*, pp. 10 ff.

115. In the same way P. Sorokin is confused and bewildered by 'the peculiar mixture of what we term "real science" and magico-religious topics and problems', P. Sorokin, *Social and Cultural Dynamics*, vol. II (New York, 1937) p. 155.

116. See also Husri, vol. II, p. 39, and 'Ali al-Wardi, *Mantiq Ibn Khaldun* (Ibn Khaldun's Logic) (Cairo, 1962) pp. 14 f.

117. Heinrich Simon, *op. cit.*, pp. 110 ff.

118. H. A. R. Gibb puts forward the controversial claim that in the long run Ibn Khaldun's theory is 'a moral and religious, not a sociological [one]'. However, he overlooks the marginal role played by religion in Ibn Khaldun's work; see H. A. R. Gibb, 'The Islamic Background of Ibn Khaldun's Political Theory', in *Studies on the Civilisation of Islam*, (London, 1962) pp. 166–75.

119. It is well known that European ideologists of racialism accuse the 'Semites' of being incapable of creative work. The French philosopher Renan seems to have been the originator of this idea, when he suggested that Arab and Jewish philosophers had merely written commentaries on Plato and Aristotle rather than formulating their own theories. Ernst Bloch has vigorously criticised this theory. In his introduction he emphasises:

> Everything intelligent might well have been thought seven times. But if it is thought again in another time and in another place, it is no longer the same. It is not only the one who thought it originally who has changed, but more importantly, that which is thought about has changed as well. The intelligent (idea) must prove itself to that which is thought about anew and prove its own originality. This was to have particularly important consequences for the great thinkers of the Orient, who both saved and

transformed the light of Greece.' Ernst Bloch, *Avicenna und die Aristotelische Linke* (Frankfurt/Main, 1963) p. 9.

Notes to Chapter 7

1. al-Husri, vol. III, p. 118. On this myth see Eckart Paterich, *Götter und Helden der Griechen*, 5th ed. (Frankfurt/Main, 1965) pp. 64 f.; for an interpretation, see Ernst Bloch, *Das Prinzip Hoffnung*, 2nd ed., vol. I (Frankfurt/Main, 1967) pp. 387 ff.

2. al-Husri, vol. III. Thus when reference is made to al-Husri's early political works this volume is indicated; pp. 9–22 are from 1923 and pp. 23–50 are from 1928. The rest of the text was written some time between 1928 and 1944, the year in which the book was first published. The first two texts contain the core of al-Husri's theory, to which he adhered throughout his life.

3. See on this Elias Murqus, *Naqd al-Fikr al-Qawmi* (Critique of Nationalist Thought), vol. I, *Sati' al-Husri* (Beirut, 1966). In this monograph, the first study of al-Husri, Murqus shows that al-Husri formulated his ideas in his first political writings (vol. III), which were merely explained, extended and refined in his later works.

4. al-Husri, vol. VI.

5. al-Husri, vol. III, p. 14 and p. 23; see also vol. VI, pp. 14 f.

6. The process of nation formation had already begun before the nineteenth century in the advanced Western European countries, but al-Husri does not take this into account. He was almost exclusively interested in the irredentists who struggled for national unity in Germany and Italy in the nineteenth century. al-Husri brings these European experiences to bear on the Arab irredentist movement of the twentieth century.

7. al-Husri, vol. III, pp. 14 f.

8. al-Husri, vol. VI, pp. 19 ff.

9. al-Husri, vol. IV, p. 35.

10. *Ibid.*, pp. 193 ff.

11. al-Husri, vol. IV, p. 28.

12. *Ibid.*, pp. 26 f. The emergence of Japan and her victory over the Russian fleet in 1904 played an extremely important role in encouraging the emergence of a Pan-Asiatic nationalism. The Asian nationalists took Japan as an example, until the Second World War, when Japan misused 'Pan-Asianism' for its own expansionist designs. Nationalists in the Arab world were also encouraged by the rise of Japan, though less so than their Chinese and South East Asian counterparts. The subject requires detailed investigation which cannot be attempted here.

13. al-Husri, vol. III, pp. 44 ff., 84 ff.

14. al-Husri, vol. IV. This was written between 1944 and 1947, although not published until 1959.

15. For Islamic modernism see Chapter 4 above. al-Husri's criticism of Pan-Islamism will be discussed in Chapter 8.

16. al-Husri, vol. IV, pp. 31 ff.

17. Cf. Elias Murqus, *op. cit.*, pp. 559 ff.

18. al-Husri, vol. III, p. 21.

19. *Ibid.*, pp. 21 ff.
20. *Ibid.*, p. 109. It is clear that the idea of national character is derived from Herder.
21. *Ibid.*, p. 20.
22. *Ibid.*, p. 109.
23. *Ibid.*, p. 32.
24. *Ibid.*, p. 30.
25. *Ibid.*, p. 31.
26. *Ibid.*, p. 32.
27. al-Husri, vol. IV, pp. 53 ff.
28. *Ibid.*, p. 35.
29. *Ibid.*, pp. 56 ff.
30. *Ibid.*, p. 57.
31. *Ibid.*, p. 60. al-Husri considers that the adherence of Fichte and most of the German cosmopolitans to nationalism after the defeat of Jena in 1806 was the identification of the correct path to follow: see al-Husri, vol. III, pp. 80 ff.
32. al-Husri, vol. IV, p. 69: see also the informative work of Hans Kohn, *Pan-Slavism: its History and Ideology* (Notre Dame, 1953).
33. al-Husri, vol. III, pp. 30, 33, 111 f.
34. *Ibid.*, p. 114.
35. *Ibid.*, pp. 110 f.
36. *Ibid.*, p. 33. Fanon considers that the rehabilitation of the pre-colonial culture fulfils a progressive function: see Fanon, *op. cit.*, and Chapter 2 above.
37. For Mazzini's nationalism, see Hans Kohn, *Prophets and Peoples, Studies in Nineteenth Century Nationalism* (New York, 1946) pp. 77–104.
38. al-Husri, vol. IV, pp. 39 ff.
39. al-Husri, vol. IV, pp. 42 ff., and vol. III, pp. 25 ff, 29, 61, 66.
40. al-Husri, vol. III, p. 29.
41. *Ibid.*, pp. 38, 42 ff.
42. *Ibid.*, p. 40.
43. *Ibid.*, p. 36.
44. al-Husri, vol. IV, pp. 259 ff.
45. *Ibid.*, pp. 75 ff., and vol. XII, pp. 151 ff.
46. al-Husri, vol. IV, p. 106.
47. *Ibid.*, pp. 45 ff.
48. al-Husri, vol. III, pp. 147 ff., 159 ff.
49. *Ibid.*, p. 57. The application of religious terminology to the 'secularised' language of nationalism has been a feature of the history of nationalism since the time of the French Revolution. See B. C. Shafer, *Nationalism, Myth and Reality* (New York, 1955).
50. al-Husri, vol. XVIII, p. 45.
51. *Ibid.*, pp. 44–50.
52. E. Renan, *Qu'est-ce qu'une nation?*, Eng. transl., 'What is a Nation?' in Alfred Zimmern, *Modern Political Doctrines* (London, 1939) pp. 186–205.
53. *Ibid.*, pp. 186 f.
54. *Ibid.*, p. 189.
55. *Ibid.*, p. 190.
56. *Ibid.*, p. 191.
57. *Ibid.*, pp. 194 ff.

58. *Ibid.*, p. 195.
59. *Ibid.*, p. 196.
60. *Ibid.*, p. 198.
61. *Ibid.*, p. 199.
62. *Ibid.*, p. 200.
63. *Ibid.*
64. *Ibid.*, p. 201.
65. *Ibid.*, pp. 201 ff.
66. *Ibid.*, pp. 202 ff.
67. *Ibid.*, p. 203.
68. *Ibid.*, p. 204.
69. *Ibid.*
70. *Ibid.*
71. al-Husri, vol. IV, p. 119.
72. *Ibid.*, p. 142.
73. al-Husri, vol. IV, pp. 33–81.
74. *Ibid.*, p. 34.
75. *Ibid.*, p. 40.
76. *Ibid.*, p. 59.
77. *Ibid.*, p. 65.
78. *Ibid.*, pp. 65 ff.
79. *Ibid.*, pp. 66 ff.
80. See Fustel de Coulanges, 'De la manière d'écrire l'histoire en France et en Allemagne depuis cinquante ans: la politique d'envahissement: Louvois et M. de Bismarck: L'Alsace, est-elle allemande ou francaise? Réponse à M. Mommsen', *Questions Contemporaines* (Paris, 1916).
81. al-Husri, vol. IV, pp. 123–32.
82. *Ibid.*, pp. 133 ff., and vol. III, p. 45. al-Husri implies that elective national affiliation would mean the equation of nations with political parties, which he considers to be a travesty of the idea of the nation.
83. al-Husri, vol. IV, p. 135.
84. *Ibid.*, pp. 136 ff.
85. *Ibid.*, pp. 140 f.
86. See Henri Hauser, *Le principe des nationalités, ses origines historiques* (Paris, 1916).
87. al-Husri, vol. IV, pp. 147 ff, and vol. XVI, pp. 295 ff.
88. See Chapter 2 above, and H. B. Davis, *Nationalism and Socialism, Marxist and Labor Theories of Nationalism to 1917* (New York, 1967); also B. Tibi, 'Marxismus und Nationalismus-Analyse', *Neue Politische Literatur*, XIV (1969) No. 4, 560 ff. See further I. Fetscher, *Der Marxismus und seine Geschichte in Dokumenten, vol. III, Politik* (Munich, 1965) pp. 91 ff.
89. al-Husri, vol. III, pp. 77 ff.
90. *Ibid.*, p. 78. See also I. Fetscher, *Rousseaus politische Philosophie, zur Geschichte des demokratischen Freiheitsbegriffe* (Neuwied and Berlin, 1960) pp. 63 f. It is clear that Rousseau had a strong influence on Herder: See Hans Kohn, *The Idea of Nationalism*, pp. 354 ff. It is possible that al-Husri was made aware of Rousseau through the works of Herder. He was particularly influenced by Rousseau's educational theories, although he only actually acknowledges German influences. On the 150th anniversary of Rousseau's

death in 1928, a special issue of the Baghdad periodical *Majallat al-Tarbiya wa'l-Ta'lim* was devoted to Rousseau, and al-Husri himself made the major contributions. These articles, which are an appreciation of Rousseau's political and educational theories, have been reprinted in al-Husri, vol. XVIII, pp. 219–82. For Rousseau's educational theories, see also I. Fetscher, *Rousseaus politische Philosophie*, pp. 194 ff. In this context it is worth mentioning that Rousseau's philosophy has generally had a profound influence upon 'Third World' nationalists: see C. B. Macpherson, *The Real World of Democracy*, pp. 22 ff.

91. G. Lukács, 'Über einige Eigentumlichkeiten der geschichtlichen Entwicklung Deutschlands', in *idem, Die Zerstörung der Vernuft* (Berlin, 1962), *Werke*, vol. IX, pp. 37 ff.

92. al-Husri, vol. III, pp. 79 ff.

93. *Ibid.*, p. 88.

94. See Marx' criticism of the cosmopolitanism of the Free Traders in 'Rede über die Frage des Freihandels', in *Marx-Engels-Werke*, 3rd ed., vol. IV (Berlin, 1964) pp. 444–58; Eng. transl. 'Speech on the Question of Free Trade', in *Collected Works*, vol. VI (London, 1976) pp. 450–65; see also H. B. Davis, *op. cit.*

95. al-Husri, vol. III, p. 89.

96. *Ibid.*, p. 91.

97. The first two parts of al-Husri, vol. III (Pt. I, pp. 9–22, Pt. II, pp. 23–50), consist of newspaper articles which appeared between 1923 and 1928, and the rest of the volume consists of articles which appeared between 1928 and 1944. The postscript quoted here must have been written between 1941 and 1942, since it mentions the dissolution of the Comintern, which took place in 1941.

98. al-Husri, vol. III, pp. 91 ff. See also I. Fetscher, *Von Marx zur Sowjetideologie*, 11th ed. (Frankfurt/Main, 1965) pp. 134 ff. Fetscher points out that a clear distinction must be made between Soviet patriotism and Great Russian nationalism. The former is related to 'the achievements of the Soviet Union', while the latter relates to the 'vanguard role' of the Russian people in the October Revolution. Fetscher considers that Great Russian nationalism is an integral part of Soviet patriotism. In his opinion the revival of nationalism took place under Stalin in 1932.

99. al-Husri, vol. III, pp. 91 ff.

100. *Ibid.*, p. 93. al-Husri believes that a socialist can also be a nationalist, since he does not consider that proletarian internationalism is an integral part of socialism.

101. *Ibid.*, p. 94.

102. al-Husri, vol. IV.

103. al-Husri, vol. XVI, p. 133.

104. Elias Murqus, *Naqd al-Fikr al-Qawmi* (A Critique of Nationalist Thought), vol. I: *Sati' al-Husri* (Beirut, 1966), pp. 223 ff. Here Murqus deals with al-Husri's views on Marxism in great detail, and formulates his own critique of them (pp. 227–97). In spite of its many weaknesses, Murqus' work is an important landmark, since it is the first non-Stalinist Arab Marxist critique of Arab nationalism. However, the work as a whole does not meet the required scholarly standards. Murqus is also the first critic of the Stalinist Arab Communist Parties who is not himself an anti-Communist. See Elias Murqus,

'Die Lehren der Erfahrung', in B. Tibi, (ed.), *Die arabische Linke* (Frankfurt/Main, 1969) pp. 46–67.

105. After the fall of the Iraqi monarchy on 14 July 1958, as the result of a military coup d'état, the leader of the Free Officers, 'Abd al-Karim Qasim, attempted to play off the various competing political factions against one another in order to consolidate his own rule (see Majid Khadduri, *Republican Iraq, A Study in Iraqi Politics since the Revolution of 1958* (London, 1969), and Uriel Dann, *Iraq Under Qassem, a Political History 1958–1963* (London, 1969)) In 1959 Qasim gave the Iraqi Communist Party a free hand to begin 'mopping-up' operations against various Arab nationalist groups, which led to a rising by nationalist officers in Mosul. These officers were supported by Arab nationalists from other countries, several of whom came to Mosul to take part in the rising against Qasim and the Communists, which in fact ended with a bloody victory for Qasim. However, once he had got rid of the Arab nationalist opposition, Qasim turned against the Communists. He was soon able to strip them of power, since they had not taken the opportunity to consolidate themselves, as the Soviet Union, whose line the ICP followed, was opposed to a Communist takeover, for a series of complicated reasons which cannot be discussed here. The Pan-Arabists took brutal revenge for the dead of Mosul after the Ba'thist–Nationalist combination came to power in February 1963. Following the coup, the Communists became the victims of an abominable public massacre.

106. See al-Husri, vol. IV. The volume contains 262 pages but only pp. 161–94 discuss Marxism.

107. al-Husri, vol. VIII, p. 78. This text was written in 1950 and published in 1951.

108. *Ibid.*, p. 83.

109. al-Husri, vol. IV, pp. 162 ff.

110. *Ibid.*, p. 164.

111. On this see B. Tibi, (ed.), *Die arabische Linke, op. cit.*, pp. 21 ff., 43 ff.

112. al-Husri, vol. IV, p. 166.

113. *Ibid.*, p. 169.

114. See here I. Fetscher, *Der Marxismus und seine Geschichte in Dokumenten*, vol. III, pp. 91 ff.

115. J. V. Stalin, 'Marxism and the National Question', in *Collected Works* (Eng. transl.) vol. II (London and Moscow, 1953) pp. 300–81; here p. 307.

116. al-Husri, vol. IV, p. 181.

117. al-Husri's knowledge of Lenin's writing was confined to 'The Right of Nations to Self-Determination'. See *Collected Works* (London and Moscow, 1964) vol. XX, pp. 393–454.

118. al-Husri, vol. IV, pp. 193 ff.

119. Kamel Abu Jaber, 'Kleines Glossar zum arabischen Sozialismus', *Bustan* (1969) Nos. 23, 61–5; here p. 65.

Notes to Chapter 8

1. al-Husri, vol. XIII.
2. *Ibid.*, pp. 37 ff.
3. *Ibid.*, pp. 47 ff.

4. *Ibid.*, pp. 72 ff, especially 87 ff. For the Tanzimat period, see K. Steinhaus, *op. cit.*, pp. 26 ff.; for its impact in Syria and Palestine, see Moshe Ma'oz, *op. cit.*, and Chapter 5 above.

5. On Turanianism, see Gotthard Jäschke, 'Der Turanismus der Jungtürken', in *Die Welt des Islams*, XXIII (1941) Nos. 1–2, 1–54.

6. al-Husri, vol. v. There is a complete English translation by S. Glazer: *The Day of Maysalun, a Page from the Modern History of the Arabs* (Washington, 1966).

7. *Ibid.* (Arabic edn) p. 17.

8. See al-Husri, vol. VI, pp. 201 ff.

9. *Ibid.*, p. 192.

10. *Ibid.*; for modernisation under Muhammad 'Ali, see Chapter 4 above.

11. *Ibid.*, pp. 198 ff; see also Chapter 5 above.

12. On al-Kawakibi, see Albert Hourani, *Arabic Thought in the Liberal Age*, pp. 271 ff., and notes 48–50 below.

13. For instance at the Arab Nationalist Congress in Paris in 1913; see Chapter 5 above.

14. The Orthodox Patriarchate of Antioch was the first Christian Church in the modern Middle East to be Arabised; al-Husri describes this as 'the first real victory for Arab nationalism'. On the Russian Orthodox Church in the Middle East, see Derek Hopwood, *op. cit.*, especially pp. 159 ff.

15. al-Husri, vol. VI, pp. 200 ff. For the American Protestant missions in the Middle East, see A. L. Tibawi, *American Interests in Syria 1800–1901, a Study of Educational, Literary and Religious Work* (Oxford and London, 1966), and David H. Finnie, *Pioneers East, The Early American Experience in the Middle East* (Cambridge, Mass., 1967). For a general survey of the work of the missionaries in Greater Syria, see B. Tibi, introduction to Muhammad Kischli, *Kapitalismus und Linke im Libanon*.

16. al-Husri, vol. VI, pp. 239 ff: see also Chapter 5 above.

17. al-Husri, vol. XI, p. 7 (his emphasis).

18. al-Husri, vols. XIV, XV, XVII (on Arab culture).

19. See here Gerhard Höpp, 'Zur Rolle internationaler panislamischer Organisationen in der Befreiungsbewegung der arabischen Völker', in Werner Loch (ed.), *Asien, Afrika, Lateinamerika, 1969* (Berlin, 1969) pp. 159–76; Sylvia Haim, 'The Abolition of the Caliphate and its Aftermath', postscript to the second edition of Sir Thomas Arnold, *The Caliphate* (London, 1965) pp. 205–44; Anwar G. Chejne, 'Pan-Islamism and the Caliphal Controversy', *Islamic Literature* (1955) 679–97. These works give a useful survey of the Pan-Islamic movement and the whole question of the Caliphate since its dissolution. Arnold's work (to which Haim has contributed a postscript) is still useful on the question of the Caliphate since the beginning of Islam. It was first published in 1925 and was reprinted without alterations in 1965. On the question of the Caliphate, see also E. I. J. Rosenthal, *Islam in the Modern National State* (Cambridge, 1965) pp. 64 ff. Franz Taeschner provides a survey of the development of Islam after the dissolution of the Ottoman Caliphate, 'Der Islam im Banne des Nationalismus der Zwischen weltkriegszeit', in R. Hartmann (ed.), *BASI* (Leipzig, 1944) pp. 484–513. Even some contemporary Arab authors mourn the passing of the Caliphate. Thus the Pan-Islamist

Salah Munajjid criticises the Arab nationalists because the call for nationalism has had

two results. In the first place, it has destroyed the Islamic Caliphate of the Ottomans. In the second place, it has brought neither independence nor freedom to the Arabs. After the Turks were defeated, and the Ottoman Empire had fallen, the Arab countries became mandates, protectorates and colonies. But the Arab nationalists castigated the Ottoman Turks, who were of course Muslims themselves, as "colonists", as the Europeans had taught them to do. (S. Munajjid, *Wohin treibt die arabische Welt?* (Munich, 1968) p. 19)

For the Muslim Brethren, see the study of R. P. Mitchell, *The Society of the Muslin Brothers* (London, 1969).

20. Jamal al-Din al-Afghani, *al-A'mal al-Kamila* (Complete Works), ed. Muhammad 'Ammara (Cairo, 1968) p. 303. al-Afghani's conservative views on social questions will not be discussed here. See also B. Tibi, *Die arabische Linke, op. cit.*, pp. 13 ff., 26.

21. Jamal al-Din al-Afghani, *op. cit.*, pp. 349 ff; see also pp. 304, 310.

22. *Ibid.*, pp. 305 ff.

23. See here the biographical information by Nikki Keddie in her introduction to N. Keddie (ed.), *An Islamic Response to Imperialism: Political and Religious Writings of Sayyid Jamal al-Din 'al-Afghani'* (Berkeley and Los Angeles, 1968).

24. As soon as al-Afghani came to understand the role that he himself and Pan-Islamism were performing for 'Abd al-Hamid II, his relationship to the Sultan began to cool. For instance, during an audience with 'Abd al-Hamid, whose reign of terror was constantly claiming new victims, al-Afghani had the audacity to indicate his boredom by playing with his beads. When an official admonished him for this later, he replied: 'If His Majesty the Sultan can play with the fate of millions of the *umma*, as it pleases him, without anyone daring to object, then Jamal al-Din may play with his beads if he wishes'. Quoted by M. 'Ammara in the introduction to his Arabic edition of *al-Afghani: al-A'mal al-Kamila*, p. 53. During another audience he asked the Sultan to release him from his obligations towards him. The extent of al-Afghani's influence and of his following is clear from the fact that the Sultan never dared to order his execution, the usual fate of those who opposed him. The rumour that al-Afghani was poisoned by 'Abd al-Hamid's agents remains unproven. On 'Abd al-Hamid, see the popular biography by Joan Haslip, *The Sultan*. It is curious that C. H. Becker's article on Pan-Islamism, 'Panislamismus', *Archiv für Religionswissenschaft*, VII (1904) 169–92, which is widely known in Germany and has recently been reprinted for the third time (*Islamstudien*, vol. II (1934) pp. 231–51, reprinted 1967), contains no evaluation of al-Afghani. The articles in *Islamstudien* are generally rather dated.

25. al-Afghani, Arabic text, *op. cit.*, p. 345 (my emphasis).

26. *Ibid.*, p. 447.

27. *Ibid.*, p. 49.

28. *Ibid.*, pp. 207 ff., English translation in N. Keddie, *op. cit.*, pp. 181 ff. See Ernst Bloch's critique of this racialist thesis in Chapter 6, note 119 above.

29. N. Keddie, *op. cit.*, p. 59.
30. M. 'Ammara, *op. cit.*, pp. 58 ff.
31. *Ibid.*, p. 51.
32. N. Keddie, *op. cit.*, p. 97.
33. An original copy of this journal is available in the Public Record Office, London (FO 78/3682). al-Afghani's articles are included in 'Ammara, *op. cit.*, and in a number of different Arabic publications with the same title which have appeared in Cairo and Beirut. Some of these have appeared in *Orient* (Paris), in French translations by Marcel Colombe during 1962 and 1963. N. Keddie's selection only includes one article from *al-'Urwa al-Wuthqa* (pp. 175 ff). The following Arabic edition has been used: Jamal al-Din al-Afghani and Muhammad 'Abduh, *al-'Urwa al-Wuthqa* (Cairo, 1958).
34. al-Husri, vol. IV, p. 221.
35. *Ibid.*, p. 223.
36. *Ibid.*, p. 229.
37. al-Afghani, Arabic text, ed. 'Ammara, *op. cit.*, p. 221: al-Husri, vol. IV, p. 235.
38. See al-Afghani (transl. Mehdi Hendessi), 'Philosophie de l'union nationale basée sur la race et l'unité linguistique', *Orient*, VI (1958) 123–8. This text is not included in the 'complete works' (!) of al-Afghani edited by M. 'Ammara.
39. *Ibid.*, and al-Husri, vol. IV, pp. 233 ff.
40. *Ibid.*, pp. 237 f.
41. *Ibid.*, pp. 238 ff.
42. Sylvia Haim, 'Islam and the Theory of Arab Nationalism', *Die Welt des Islams*, n.s. IV (1955) Nos. 2–3, 124–49; here p. 130.
43. *Ibid.*, p. 128.
44. *Ibid.*, p. 130 ff.
45. *Ibid.*, p. 129.
46. *Ibid.*, p. 137; see also p. 146 (my emphasis).
47. *Ibid.*, p. 139.
48. On al-Kawakibi see Sylvia Haim, *The Ideas of a Precursor: 'Abd al-Rahman al-Kawakibi (1849–1902), in Relation to the Trend of Muslim Arab Political Thought*, unpublished Ph.D. thesis (Edinburgh, 1953); *idem.*, 'Alfieri and al-Kawakibi', *Oriente Moderno*, XXXIV (1954) No. 2, 321–34; *idem*, 'Blunt and al-Kawakibi', *Oriente Moderno*, XXXV (1955) No. 3, 132–43. See also the dissertations of G. Roth, *al-Kawakibi, ein arabischer Nationalist* (Berlin, 1942), and C. Kessler, *'Abd al-Rahman al-Kawakibis Reform des Islam* (Berlin, 1956), and Norbert Tapiéro, *Les idées réformistes d'al-Kawakibi* (Paris, 1956). See also the chapter on al-Kawakibi in the book by al-Husri's son; Khaldun Sati Husry, *Three Reformers, a Study in Modern Arab Political Thought* (Beirut, 1966) pp. 55–112.
49. al-Kawakibi, *Umm al-Qura* (Aleppo, 1959); partial translation in G. Roth, *op. cit.*, pp. 87–110. *Umm al-Qura* (Mother of the Villages), is one of the names of Mecca. According to al-Kawakibi, Mecca must become the seat of the Arab Caliphate which he demands. In her essay 'Blunt and al-Kawakibi', Sylvia Haim suggests that *Umm al-Qura* was inspired by ideas taken from W. S. Blunt's book *The Future of Islam* (London, 1882). Blunt was certainly a personal friend of Muhammad 'Abduh: he lived in Cairo for a time and took part in the anti-colonial movement there (See his memoirs: *My Diaries, Being a Personal Narrative of Events 1888–1914*, 4th ed. (New York, 1932)). For

Haim this explains how al-Kawakibi was able to absorb the contents of Blunt's book, since he knew no European language, and the book was not translated into Arabic. K. S. Husry, *op. cit.*, pp. 94 ff. attacks this thesis, and proves with quotations that Blunt did not himself call for an Arab Caliphate, but simply commented on what he had heard during a journey in the Arabian Peninsula. Husry also proves quite convincingly that *Umm al-Qura* was written in Aleppo, before al-Kawakibi's flight to Egypt, and hence before he joined Muhammad 'Abduh's circle where he met Blunt for the first time.

50. In 'Alfieri and al-Kawakibi', Sylvia Haim suggests that *Taba'i' al-Istibdad* (Features of Tyranny) was strongly influenced by *Della Tirannide*, by the Italian writer Vittorio Alfieri, which appeared in 1800, since the two works are almost identical. Alfieri's ideas are borrowed from Voltaire, Rousseau and Montesquieu. al-Kawakibi was probably familiar with the Turkish translation of this work which had been carried out by the Young Ottomans in Geneva in 1897, since he himself knew no European language. E. Rossi discovered the Turkish text of this work as a result of Haim's research. See E. Rossi, 'Una Traduzione Turca dell'Opera "Della Tirannide" di V. Alfieri Probabilmente Conosciuta da al-Kawakibi', *Oriente Moderno*, XXXIV (1954) No. 7, 335-7. Husry, *op. cit.*, pp. 72 ff. contests Haim's thesis, but in contradistinction to his objections to her essay on Blunt, he cannot put forward any valid evidence against this claim.

51. Using similar arguments to those of his father, Khaldun Husry makes al-Kawakibi into the founder of Arabism: 'He transforms Arabism into Arab Nationalism, and with this transformation he establishes himself clearly as the forerunner of the doctrine of modern Arab nationalism', *op. cit.*, p. 102. This interpretation is inadequate: it is more accurate to consider al-Kawakibi as an Islamic revivalist, whose revivalism generally worked in a direction favourable to Arab nationalism. The two tendencies are of course in no way identical.

52. S. Haim, 'Blunt and al-Kawakibi', *op. cit.*, p. 136.

53. *Ibid.*, p. 143.

54. al-Kawakibi, *Taba'i' al-Istibdad, passim*, and S. Haim, 'Alfieri and al-Kawakibi', *op. cit.*

55. al-Husri, vol. IV, pp. 214 ff.

56. al-Husri, vol. IV, pp. 214 ff.; although al-Husri says that al-Kawakibi wanted an Arab instead of an Ottoman Caliphate he does not give sufficient emphasis to this, and tends to make al-Kawakibi into an Arab nationalist in the modern sense, which is inaccurate. For both al-Kawakibi and al-Afghani, Islam was the guiding principle, the main difference between them being that al-Afghani assigned a special place to the Arabs within Islam, since they were allegedly its dignitaries. It is also wrong to suggest that Rashid Ridha shared al-Kawakibi's views, even though he published his writings. Like al-Kawakibi, Ridha was a pupil of 'Abduh, and he held an orthodox view of the Caliphate. He considered Islam not simply as a religion but also as a system of government, and held that the two could not be divided. Like 'Abduh, Ridha considered that an Arab revivalist movement was essential, but only because he believed that this would be identical to a restoration of Islam, in which the Arabs would have pride of place. For Ridha, therefore, Islam is never subordinated to Arabism, although this emerges as an unintended consequence of al-Kawakibi's theory. Ridha's support for the Arab Revolt of 1916

does not contradict this. The Arab Revolt was not backed up by secular nationalist arguments from its nominal leader Sharif Husain of Mecca, but by the argument that the Turks had abandoned Islamic orthodoxy (see here C. E. Dawn, 'Ideological Influences in the Arab Revolt', in J. Kritzeck and R. Bayly Winder (eds) *The World of Islam* (New York, 1960) pp. 233–48). When Ridha became aware of the nationalist features of the Revolt, he turned away from it and gave his support to the archaic Wahhabi movement, and its representatives, the House of Sa'ud, who had taken over the Arabian Peninsula in 1924 and declared the area an 'Islamic State' (see A. Hourani, *op. cit.*, p. 231, and the account in Chapter 4 above). For his ideas on the Caliphate see Rashid Ridha, *al-Khalifa aw al-Imama ul-'Udhma* (The Caliphate, or the Great Imamate) (Cairo, 1923), originally a series of essays in the periodical *al-Manar*, XXIII–XXIV. There is a French translation by Henri Laoust, *Le Califat dans le Doctrine de Rashid Ridha* (Beirut, 1938). See the Arabic text pp. 62 ff., and the French text pp. 105 ff., where Ridha criticises the Arab nationalists, and refers to them disparagingly as *mutafarnijin* (Westernised). There is a partial English translation by Sylvia Haim, 'Rashid Ridha: Islam and the National Idea', in *idem* (ed.), *Arab Nationalism, an Anthology*, 2nd ed. (Berkeley and Los Angeles, 1976) pp. 75–7. See also Malcolm Kerr, *Islamic Reform, The Political and Legal Theories of Muhammad 'Abduh and Rashid Ridha* (Berkeley and Los Angeles, 1966) pp. 153 ff., 187 ff. The difference between Ridha and al-Kawakibi emerges clearly in H. Z. Nuseibeh's *The Ideas of Arab Nationalism* (Ithaca and New York, 1956) when the author ends his analysis of Ridha's ideas, and then turns to those of al-Kawakibi: 'It is with a sense of relief that one comes to the works of 'Abd al-Rahman al-Kawakibi . . .' (p. 129). However, Nuseibeh avoids falling into the trap of describing al-Kawakibi as an Arab nationalist, and describes him accurately as an 'Islamic revivalist', whose ideas had an important influence on Arab nationalism.

57. al-Husri, vol. III, pp. 169 ff., 99 ff., 104.
58. *Ibid.*, p. 102.
59. *Ibid.*, pp. 100 ff.
60. *Ibid.*
61. *Ibid.*, pp. 103 ff.
62. Quoted in al-Husri, vol. III, p. 169. Maraghi was not only one of the most militant opponents of the Arab national movement, but also one of the leading Egyptian members of the Pan-Islamic Caliphate movement. For further information on his activities, see E. Kedourie, 'Egypt and the Caliphate', *Journal of the Royal Asiatic Society* (1963) 208–48. Kedourie points out that Maraghi was supported by King Fu'ad, since the latter had ambitions to become Caliph himself, and to revive the Pan-Islamic Caliphate movement after the dissolution of the Caliphate by the Kemalists. See also M. Colombe, *L'évolution de l'Égypte 1924–1950* (Paris, 1951) pp. 171 ff.
63. al-Husri, vol. III, pp. 169 ff.
64. al-Husri, vol. IV, pp. 207 ff.
65. al-Husri, vol. XIII, pp. 42 ff. After the fall of the 'Abbasid dynasty in Baghdad in 1258, the Mamluke rulers of Egypt made use of one of the surviving members of the family, whom they installed as Caliph and successor to the 'Abbasids in Cairo in 1261. This 'Caliphate' was clearly a fictional veneer for

Mamluke rule, but it lasted until the Ottoman conquest of Egypt under Selim I in 1517 (Sir Thomas Arnold, *The Caliphate*, pp. 89 ff., R. Hartmann, *Zur Vorgeschichte des 'abbasidischen Schein-Chalifats von Cairo* (Berlin, 1950)). The Ottoman court historians claim that al-Mutawakkil, the last 'Abbasid Caliph in Egypt, surrendered the Caliphate to Selim I, although ' . . . of the alleged transfer of the dignity of the Khalifat there is no contemporary evidence at all' (Sir Thomas Arnold, *op. cit.*, p. 143). In *Islamstudien*, vol. II, p. 244, C. H. Becker dismisses the view that the Ottomans were the lawful heirs of the Caliphate as an 'anecdote', and says that the Ottoman 'flatterers and court historians' also invented a 'fabulous Arab family tree', which would prove the 'legitimacy' of the Ottomans' claim to the Caliphate by tracing their descent back to the Prophet Muhammad himself.

66. al-Husri, vol. XIII, p. 46.

67. *al-Islam wa Usul al-Hukm*, ed. M. Dasuqi (Beirut, 1966), first ed., Cairo, 1925; French translation by L. Bercher, 'L'Islam et les bases du pouvoir', *Révue des Etudes Islamiques*, VII (1933) 353–91, and VIII (1934) 163–222. References below are to Dasuqi's edition.

68. 'Ali 'Abd al-Raziq, *op. cit.*, pp. 76 ff. al-Kawakibi had already used similar arguments: see S. Haim, 'Alfieri and al-Kawakibi', *op. cit.*, pp. 324 ff.

69. For the *fatwa* of the *'ulama'* of al-Azhar against 'Abd al-Raziq, see L. Bercher, 'De la brochure intitulée "sentence des grands Uléma" (d'al-Azhar) sur le livre "L'Islam et les bases du pouvoir"', *Révue des Études Islamiques*, IX (1935) 75–86. See also G. E. von Grunebaum, *Modern Islam*, p. 132. The Arab nationalist Sanhoury has also criticised 'Abd al-Raziq: *Le Califat, son évolution vers une Société des Nations Orientales* (Paris, 1926) pp. 37 ff. For a criticism of Sanhoury's thesis see R. Hartmann, 'Ein moderner Ägypter über die Chalifatsfrage', *Der Islam*, XVI (1927) 274–6. Hartmann proves that in spite of all his assurances to the contrary, Sanhoury has himself departed from true orthodoxy in his criticism of 'Abd al-Raziq.

70. 'Abd al-Raziq, *op. cit.*, pp. 71 ff. On Ibn Khaldun see Chapter 6 above and the secondary literature quoted in the notes to that Chapter.

71. *Ibid.*, p. 70. 'Abd al-Raziq's interpretation is in line with the Sunni tradition in which the Caliphate only lasted for 30 years, and was then transformed into a kingdom (mulk). Independently of 'Abd al-Raziq, Horovitz wrote that contemporary Arab thinkers were also seeking a division between a religious and secular authority, basing their claims on the same Sunni tradition. See J. Horovitz, 'Neuere Literatur über das Kalifat', *Der Islam*, XV (1926) 79–82, especially p. 81.

72. 'Abd al-Raziq, *op. cit.*, p. 73. Ibn Taimiyya's interpretation of Islam denies this: see here G. von Grunebaum, 'Problems of Muslim Nationalism', in R. N. Frye (ed.), *Islam and the West* ('s Gravenhage, 1957) pp. 7–29. von Grunebaum shows that Ibn Taimiyya considers that the exercise of power is an integral part of the Islamic religion, an interpretation accepted by Rashid Ridha and the Wahhabis.

73. 'Abd al-Raziq, *op. cit.*, p. 73.

74. *Ibid.*, pp. 181 ff., here p. 182.

75. *Ibid.*, p. 184.

76. *Ibid.*, p. 201.

77. al-Husri, vol. IV, pp. 242 ff.

78. *Ibid.*, p. 252.
79. G. E. von Grunebaum, 'Nationalism and Cultural Trends in the Arab Near East', *op. cit.*, p. 126, writes 'It is much more difficult to identify the cause of Islam with any of the actually existing Arab states; and where 'Pan-Arabism' and Islam may be considered complementary aspects of the same cultural and political manifestation, the local nationalism cannot as readily be reconciled with the Islamic aspiration'. This essay and 'Problems of Muslim Nationalism' have been reprinted in Grunebaum's *Modern Islam, The Search for Cultural Identity* (Berkeley and Los Angeles, 1962). This collection is an interesting survey of contemporary Islam, though the interpretation is somewhat ethno-centric and is thus not always reliable. Other standard works on contemporary Islam include: R. N. Frye (ed.), *Islam and the West*; E. I. J. Rosenthal, *Islam in the Modern National State* (Cambridge, 1965); Bernard Lewis, *The Middle East and the West* (Bloomington, 1965); R. Hartmann, *Islam und Nationalismus* (Berlin, 1948), and the essays in R. Hartmann (ed.), *BASI*, vol. III (Leipzig, 1944) pp. 425–530. See also the references in Chapter 4 above.
80. In *Auflösung der Kolonialreiche* (Munich, 1966), Franz Ansprenger claims: 'Pan-Islamism went back to the original values of Islam and based itself upon them, and in fact became more strongly directed towards Pan-Arabism. . . . The First World War politicised Pan-Islamism and transformed it into Pan-Arabism' (p. 134). In general his three pages of explanation of Pan-Islamism as a supra-regional anti-colonial movement are somewhat vague. This is also true of the chapter entitled 'The Confining of Arab Nationalism', (pp. 74 ff.), where Egyptian, that is regional, nationalism, is confused with Pan-Arab nationalism. See my review in *Berliner Zeitschrift für Politologie*, IX (1968) No. 4, 79–81.
81. Thus Elie Salem, 'Nationalism and Islam', *The Muslim World*, lii (1962) 277–87. Salem claims that 'Arab nationalism was . . . the synthesis between universal Pan-Islamism and the local nationalism' (p. 277). The examples that he gives are almost entirely irrelevant, and are taken from unimportant authors.

Notes to Chapter 9

1. Negib Azoury, *La Réveil de la Nation Arabe dans l'Asie Turque* (Paris, 1905).
2. On Muhammad 'Ali's policy in Syria see Mehmet Şinasi, *Studien zur Geschichte der syrischen Politik Mehmed Alis von Ägypten*, unpublished Ph.D. thesis (Göttingen, 1936), and George Antonius, *The Arab Awakening*, 2nd ed. (London, 1938) Chapter II, and the introduction to Chapter 5 above.
3. See H. Dodwell, *The Founder of Modern Egypt, A Study of Muhammad 'Ali* (Cambridge, 1931) *passim.*, and Chapter 4 above.
4. On the 'Urabi Revolt, see L. Rathmann, *Neue Aspekte des 'Arabi-Aufstandes 1879 bis 1882 in Ägypten* (Berlin, 1968); Ibrahim Abu Lughod, 'The Transformation of the Egyptian Elite: Prelude to the 'Urabi Revolt', *Middle East Journal*, XXI (1967) No. 3, 325–44; R. Tignor, 'Some Materials for a History of the 'Arabi Revolution', *Middle East Journal*, XVI (1962) 239–48; also B. Tibi, 'Zum Verhältnis von Militär und kolonialem Nationalismus am

Beispiel der arabischen Länder', *Sozialistische Politik*, I (1969) No. 4, 4-19. The 'Urabi revolt was in fact directed simultaneously against the ruling alien feudal caste and the beginnings of British colonial hegemony in Egypt. It was the occasion of the first participation by middle ranking officers in the national progressive movement: 'Urabi himself was a colonel. M. Rifaat is merely repeating colonial propaganda when he says that the Revolt was the *reason* for the British occupation of Egypt, without understanding that it provided the perfect *pretext* for the occupation: see M. Rifaat, *The Awakening of Modern Egypt* (London, 1947) pp. 172 ff.

5. On British colonial rule in Egypt see Theodore Rothstein, *Die Engländer in Ägypten*, Ergänzungsheft zur *Neuen Zeit*, No. 10 (Stuttgart, 1911); John Marlowe, *Anglo-Egyptian Relations 1800-1953* (London, 1954) pp. 112 ff.; R. L. Tignor, *Modernisation and British Colonial Rule in Egypt 1882-1914* (Princeton, 1966), and Afaf Lutfi al-Sayyid, *Egypt and Cromer, a Study in Anglo-Egyptian Relations* (New York and London, 1968).

6. For the relations between Britain and the Pan-Arab nationalists, see G. Antonius, *op. cit.*, Chapters VII and IX.

7. Fritz Steppat, 'Nationalismus und Islam bei Mustafa Kamil, ein Beitrag zur Ideengeschichte des ägyptischen Nationalismus', *Die Welt des Islams*, n.s. IV (1956) 241-341; here p. 258.

8. Walther Braune, 'Die Entwicklung des Nationalismus bei den Arabern', in R. Hartmann (ed.), *BASI* (Leipzing, 1944) pp. 425-38; here p. 434. The changes in Egyptian attitudes towards Pan-Arabism have been studied by Anwar Chejne, 'Egyptian Attitudes Towards Pan-Arabism', *Middle East Journal*, XI (1957) 253-67. See also M. Colombe, *L'Évolution de l'Égypte 1924-1950* (Paris, 1951) pp. 160 ff.

9. See N. Safran, *Egypt in Search of a Political Community, an Analysis of the Intellectual and Political Evolution of Egypt, 1804-1952* (Cambridge, Mass., 1961) pp. 62 ff., and J. M. Ahmed, *The Intellectual Origins of Egyptian Nationalism* (London, 1960).

10. See Albert Hourani's foreword to J. M. Ahmed, *op. cit.*, p. x.

11. F. Steppat, *op. cit.*, p. 267.

12. *Ibid.*, p. 266.

13. *Ibid.*, p. 269 ff.

14. *Ibid.*, pp. 268, 271, 334 ff.

15. *Ibid.*, p. 277.

16. *Ibid.*, pp. 258 ff.

17. *Ibid.*, p. 282.

18. *Ibid.*, p. 288.

19. *Ibid.*, p. 289.

20. *Ibid.*, p. 287 ff.

21. *Ibid.*, p. 284.

22. *Ibid.*, pp. 300 ff. If Kamil is considered a Europeanised liberal nationalist, it must also be emphasised, following Steppat, that his thought included elements of integral nationalism as well as liberalism. *op. cit.*, pp. 334 ff.

23. F. Steppat, *op. cit.*, pp. 304 ff. Before his disillusionment, Kamil remarked: 'Egypt cannot exist without Europe' (*ibid.*, p. 305), but later added 'until today we believed that the goal of European civilisation was total equality and true justice . . . but we have been betrayed . . .' (*ibid.*, p. 306). On the *entente*

cordiale, see Erhard Richter, 'Lord Cromer, Ägypten und die Entstehung der französich-englischen Entente von 1904', Ph.D. dissertation (Leipzig, 1931). On Mustafa Kamil see also N. Safran, *op. cit.*, pp. 85–90, Albert Hourani, *Arabic Thought in the Liberal Age*, pp. 199 ff., and Lothar Rathmann, 'Mustafa Kamil, Politisches Denken und Handeln eines ägyptischen Patrioten', *Zeitschrift für Geschichtswissenschaft*, IV (1961) supplementary volume, pp. 102–22. Rathmann relies heavily on Steppat, but has also used new material, and places Kamil in the context of the Egyptian national movement as a whole.

24. See L. Rathmann, *op. cit.*, p. 121.
25. *Ibid.*, p. 120.
26. N. Safran, *op. cit.*, p. 85.
27. *Ibid.*, pp. 90–97; on Lutfi al-Sayyid, see J. M. Ahmed, *op. cit.*, pp. 85–112, and A. Hourani, *Arabic Thought* . . ., pp. 170–82.
28. N. Safran, *op. cit.*, pp. 92 ff.
29. For the crisis of Egyptian liberalism see N. Safran, *op. cit.*, pp. 181 ff., especially pp. 187 ff. Safran also shows how the liberal-democratic intelligentsia were forced to bow to archaic and conservative forces; see pp. 209 ff. There was also a change from democratic liberalism to archaic religious thought within the Egyptian middle class, which is documented in the life and work of Muhammad Husain Haikal. The development of his thought has been traced in Baber Johansen's *Muhammad Husain Haikal, Europa und der Orient im Weltbild eines ägyptischen Liberalen* (Beirut and Wiesbaden, 1967). Haikal was one of the founders of the Liberal Constitutional Party and a pupil of Ahmad Lutfi al-Sayyid.
30. As the liberalism of the Westernised bourgeois intelligentsia became weaker, fundamentalist Islamic tendencies became stronger. This is reflected in the strength of the Muslim Brotherhood, founded in Egypt in 1929, which was very powerful until the Free Officers' coup in 1952. Christina Phelps Harris has studied this phenomenon in *Nationalism and Revolution in Egypt, The Role of the Muslim Brotherhood* (The Hague and London, 1964) especially pp. 111–42. See also E. I. J. Rosenthal, *Islam in the Modern National State*, (Cambridge, 1965) p. 103, which presents the Muslim Brotherhood's critique of all varieties of nationalism.
31. See the various references to al-Misri's role in the early Pan-Arab movement in G. Antonius, *op. cit.*, and Richard Hartmann (ed.), *BASI* (Leipzig, 1944) pp. 439–67, especially pp. 461 ff. For a more detailed treatment, see Majid Khadduri, ''Aziz 'Ali al-Misri and the Arab Nationalist Movement', *St. Antony's Papers*, (1960) 140–63, and the well-documented but somewhat prejudiced work of E. Be'eri, *Army Officers in Arab Politics and Society* (London and New York, 1970) pp. 41–8, 78 ff., which also discusses al-Misri's influence on the Free Officers. Of course Pan-Arabism had emerged before the Free Officers, although it was not particularly influential: see here Anwar Chejne, *op. cit.*, pp. 257 ff. Chejne shows that Pan-Arabism was first able to take root in Egypt with the advent to power of the Free Officers, *ibid.*, pp. 262 ff.
32. One of the Free Officers has recorded details of these contacts: see Anwar El-Sadat, *Revolt on the Nile* (London, 1957). On the Free Officers, see Jean Ziegler, *Politische Soziologie des neuen Afrika* (Munich, 1966) pp. 216 ff. The

group was formally founded in 1938, with only three members, Nasser, Sadat, and Muhi al-Din; see here el-Sadat, *op. cit.*, and in a wider context, Lothar Rathmann, 'Uber die Rolle der Armee in der ägyptischen Revolution', *Zeitschrift für Militärgeschichte*, VII (1968) No. 2, 167–82, especially pp. 172 ff.; also E. Be'eri, *op. cit.*, pp. 76 ff. Fritz Steppat has given a profile of Nasser, the leader of the Free Officers, and an outline of his political ideas in 'Gamal 'Abdannasir', in R. Kerschagl (ed.), *Die geistig politischen Profile der Gegenwart in Asien* (Vienna, 1964, on behalf of the Austrian Commission to UNESCO) pp. 32–50; see also *idem.*, 'Nassers Revolution', *Europa Archiv*, XVII (1962) No. 5, 163–73.

33. See Chapter 5 above. It is important to note that the Iraqi officers who took part in this coup d'état had been associates of al-Misri from their days together in *al-'Ahd.*

34. El-Sadat, *op. cit.* In the same way that the francophile and anglophile nationalists were unable to distinguish between the emancipating and colonising aspects of British and French activity in the early stages of the national movement, the germanophile Arab nationalists failed to see that Germany had colonial interests just as much as Britain and France, and had pursued a colonial policy since the time of Bismarck. See here Hans-Ulrich Wehler, *Bismarck und der deutsche Imperialismus* (Cologne, 1969) pp. 227 ff., and Lothar Rathmann, 'Zur Ägyptenpolitik des deutschen Imperialismus vor dem Ersten Weltkrieg', in Walter Markov (ed.), *Geschichte und Geschichtsbild Afrikas* (Berlin, 1960) pp. 73–99; *idem.*, 'Zur Legende vom "antikolonialen" Charakter der Baghdadbahnpolitik in der wilhelminischen Ära', *Zeitschrift für Geschichtswissenschaft*, IX, supplementary volume (1961) 246–70. Wehler's work is superior to Rathmann's in that it is factual and not polemical: Rathmann occasionally has difficulty in distinguishing between analysis and propaganda.

35. El-Sadat, *op. cit.*

36. Nasser, *The Philosophy of the Revolution*, Eng. transl. (Cairo, n.d.).

37. Quoted by al-Husri, vol. VIII, p. 7.

38. *Ibid.*, p. 7. He considered the constitution to be 'a great step forward, indeed a miraculous leap towards Arabism', ibid., p. 12.

39. *Ibid.*, p. 11.

40. *Ibid.*, p. 8.

41. See Chapter 4 above.

42. See here A. Hourani, *Arabic Thought* . . ., pp. 95 ff., and the introduction to Chapter 5 above.

42a. See J. Heyworth-Dunne, 'Printing and Translations under Muhammad 'Ali of Egypt, The Foundation of Modern Arabic', *Journal of the Royal Asiatic Society*, (1940) 325–49, and Walther Braune, 'Beiträge zur Geschichte des neuarabischen Schrifttums', *Mitteilungen des Seminars für orientalische Sprachen*, XXXVI (1933) No. 2, 117–40.

43. al-Husri, vol. VIII, p. 15.

44. See *ibid.*, pp. 17 ff.

45. *Ibid.*, pp. 19 ff.

46. *Ibid.*, p. 21, and vol. XI, p. 81.

47. al-Husri, vol. III, p. 143. For the importance of Egypt in al-Husri's ideas, see A. G. Chejne, *op. cit.*, p. 257.

48. On 'Urabi see note 4 to this chapter.
49. On Muhammad Farid see the useful material now available in *al-Katib*, IX (1969) Nos. 104 and 105.
50. al-Husri, vol. IV, p. 209.
51. *Ibid.*, p. 211. It is well-known that 'Abd al-Hamid engineered the deposition of Khedive Isma'il with the help of Britain, since the latter accepted the demands put forward by 'Urabi and his associates: see here L. Rathmann, 'Uber die Rolle der Armee in der ägyptischen Revolution', *op. cit.*, p. 168.
52. On Lutfi al-Sayyid see note 27 of this chapter.
53. A. Lutfi al-Sayyid in *al-Musawwar* (5 May 1950), quoted by al-Husri, vol. VIII, pp. 103 ff.
54. al-Husri, vol. VIII, p. 110.
55. On Taha Husain see A. Hourani, *op. cit.*, pp. 324–40, N. Safran, *op. cit.*, pp. 129–31, and the wide-ranging study by Pierre Cachia, *Taha Husayn, his Place in the Egyptian Literary Renaissance* (London, 1956). Husain had an immense influence on cultural life in Egypt, largely because of the posts he held. He combined the positions of Dean of the Faculty of Philosophy at Cairo University and Minister of Education.
56. 'al-Duktur Taha Husain yatahaddath 'an al-'uruba', (Dr Taha Husain speaks on Arabism) in *al-Makshuf* (Beirut, 1938) No. 175, quoted by al-Husri, vol. III, p. 119.
57. Taha Husain in *al-Hilal* (1939), quoted by al-Husri, vol. III, pp. 136 ff.
58. al-Husri, *op. cit.*, p. 125.
59. *Ibid.*, p. 139.
60. Taha Husain, *Mustaqbal al-Thaqafa fi Misr* (Cairo, 1938), Eng. transl., *The Future of Culture in Egypt*, (Washington, 1950). Page references below are to the Arabic text.
61. A. Hourani, *Arabic Thought . . .*, p. 327.
62. Taha Husain, *op. cit.*, p. 28 ff. It is interesting that al-Tahtawi had commented on the similarities between the Arabs and the Europeans long before Taha Husain, although from a completely different point of view: he did not simply compare Arabs and Europeans, but more specifically the Egyptians and the French. See Karl Stowasser, *op. cit.*, pp. 304 ff. al-Tahtawi writes: 'After mature reflection on the customs and political relationships of the French, it seems to me that they are closer to the Arabs than the Turks and other peoples . . .' (p. 304).
63. This attitude is not unique to Taha Husain: it was common among Europeanised bourgeois intellectuals in Egypt, who wanted to become more European than the Europeans.
64. Taha Husain, *op. cit.*, p. 16.
65. *Ibid.*, pp. 281, 292, ff.
66. al-Husri, vol. XVIII, p. 383 ff.
67. *Ibid.*, p. 352.
68. al-Husri, vol. VIII, p. 25.
69. *Ibid.*, pp. 35 ff.
70. *Ibid.*, pp. 41 ff.
71. *Ibid.*, pp. 42, 66 ff.; see also Chapter 7 above.
72. *Ibid.*, p. 66.
73. *Ibid.*, p. 64.

74. *Ibid.,* pp. 65 ff. According to al-Husri, the Egyptians have four possible affiliations besides the Arab one: (1) the African, (2) the Mediterranean, (3) the Pharaonic, and (4) the Islamic. al-Husri debates these four forms of affiliation with a number of Egyptian writers who have asked to which sphere Egypt belongs (see al-Husri, vol. XI, pp. 77–138). al-Husri rejects the affiliation with Africa, since belonging to a continent cannot be a political act (pp. 91, 93, 95). Belonging to the Mediterranean cultural area is simply a myth perpetrated by the French to enable them to establish their hegemony on the ideological pretext of this non-existent cultural sphere (pp. 96, 99). Belonging to Pharaonic culture is also untenable, since this is part of classical history: there is nothing left of the Pharaohs besides the Pyramids and other monuments, while modern Egyptian culture is quite clearly Arab (pp. 113 ff., and al-Husri, vol. VIII, p. 90). Finally, al-Husri rejects the idea that Egypt is a Muslim country, since some two million Christians live there as well as Muslims: a weighty argument, when one considers that al-Husri does not consider religion to be a political bond (see al-Husri, vol. XI, pp. 100, 107). Thus the Arab bond emerges as the only viable variety of cultural affiliation (pp. 108, 110). The whole question of whether in fact Egypt is Arab is a central problem for Pan-Arab authors, who have to oppose the Egyptian nationalists as well as the Pan-Syrian nationalists, who disparage the Egyptians as the successors of the Pharaohs. Among a large number of works on this topic is the influential study by the Pan-Arab historian Muhammad 'Izzat Darwaza, *'Uruba Misr fi'l-Qadim wa'l-Hadith, aw Qabl al-Islam wa Ba'dahu* (Arabism in Egypt Past and Present, or Before and After Islam), 2nd ed. (Beirut, 1963); see also Anis al Sayigh, *al-Fikra al-'Arabiyya fi Misr* (Arabic Thought in Egypt) (Beirut, 1959), and the relevant chapter in 'Abd al-Rahman al-Bazzaz, *Hadhihi Qawmiyyatuna* (This is our Nationalism), 2nd ed. (Cairo, 1964) pp. 397 ff.
75. B. Johansen, *op. cit.,* p. 63, also pp. 69 ff.
76. Quoted *ibid.,* p. 70.
77. On the Wafd Party see the monograph by Zaheer M. Quraishi, *Liberal Nationalism in Egypt, The Rise and Fall of the Wafd Party* (Delhi, 1967), and Ernst Klingmüller, 'Geschichte der Wafd-Partei im Rahmen der gesamtpolitischen Läge Ägyptens, Ph.D. thesis (Berlin, 1937); Marcel Colombe, *L'Évolution de l'Égypte, 1924–1950,* pp. 53 ff., and Jacob M. Landau, *Parliaments and Parties in Egypt* (Tel Aviv, 1953) pp. 148 ff.
78. See here B. Tibi (ed.), *Die arabische Linke* (Frankfurt/Main, 1969) pp. 31 ff., with references and bibliography in the appendix: see also the Postscript below.

Notes to Chapter 10

1. After the failure of the coup which it had organiseu in 1961, SSNP writings were banned in Lebanon until the middle of 1969. Long before this, however, the writings of Sa'ada and his followers were proscribed in other Arab countries. Since the German public libraries, which in any case have little in the way of modern Arabic political literature, possess none of the original writings of Sa'ada or any other representative of Syrian nationalism, recourse must be made to the following, which are accessible: three long extracts from

Sa'ada's writings in English translation in K. H. Karpat (ed.), *Political and Social Thought in the Contemporary Middle East* (London, 1968) pp. 72 ff., 87 ff., 95 ff. In his annotated bibliography *Inside The Arab Mind* (Arlington, 1960) pp. 45–8, F. I. Qubain gives a survey of the party literature; see also the bibliography of L. Z. Yamak, *The Syrian Social Nationalist Party*, 2nd ed. (Cambridge, Mass., 1969) pp. 149 ff. The latter has been used extensively in the section which follows; it is a doctoral dissertation by a former member of the SSNP, and shows an intimate knowledge of the party's writings. The useful chapter on the SSNP in Patrick Seale, *The Struggle for Syria* (London, 1965) pp. 64–72, has also been used. See also J. Sawaya, 'The Genesis of the Syrian Social Nationalist Party', in K. H. Karpat, *op. cit.*, pp. 98 ff., and K. Jumblatt, 'Spiritual Materiality is a False Theory . . .', in *ibid.*, pp. 102 ff.

2. It is interesting that the French Jesuit Lammens makes Syria out to be neither Arab nor Islamic in his *La Syrie* (Beirut, 1921). Lammens is well known for his 'Christian' anti-Arab and anti-Islamic attitudes. The same theme may also be found in the short history of Syria by the American Lebanese writer Philip K. Hitti, *Surya w'al-Suriyyun min Nafidha al-Tarikh* (A Historical View of Syria and the Syrians) (New York, 1926). Presumably Sa'ada was familiar with both these works, although Yamak, *op. cit.*, p. 54, considers this unlikely. Sa'ada's idea of the 'Syrian nation' seems to be a synthesis of Lammens' notions and those of German and Italian populist nationalism.

3. Yamak, *op. cit.*, pp. 56 ff.; P. Seale, *op. cit.*, p. 68; see also A. Hourani, *op. cit.*, pp. 317 ff.

4. See note 1 to this chapter.

5. al-Husri is aware of the difference between the first and the second editions: al-Husri, vol. IX, pp. 115, where the two texts are exhaustively compared.

6. Yamak, *op. cit.*, pp. 67; P. Seale, *op. cit.*, p. 70.

7. Yamak, *op. cit.*, pp. 72 ff., 146.

8. *Ibid.*, p. 68 ff.

9. A Hourani, *op. cit.*, p. 318; P. Seale, *op. cit.*, p. 72.

10. See here F. I. Qubain, *Crisis in Lebanon* (Washington, 1961), and M. S. Agwani (ed.), *The Lebanese Crisis of 1958, a Documentary Study* (London, 1965).

11. See e.g. the series of articles by a leading SSNP member, Asad Ashqar, under the pseudonym Sab' Bulos Humaidan in the Lebanese daily *al-Nahar*. These articles have been reprinted in book form: Asad Ashqar, *Nadharat fi Tarikhna wa Awda'na al-Hadira: Min Mafahim al-Insan al-Jadid* (A View of Our Contemporary History and Our Present Relationships: On the Concept of the New Man) (Beirut, n.d. [ca. 1969]); Henri Hamati, *Jamahir wa Kawarith* (Masses and Disasters) (Beirut, 1968). See also the new SSNP journal, *al-Fikr* (Beirut). For a critique of recent publications and activities of the SSNP, see 'Afif Farraj, 'al-Qawmiyyun al-Ijtima'iyyun w'al-hujum 'ala al-Marksiyya' (The Social Nationalists and the Assault on Marxism), *al-Hurriyya*, x (1969) No. 466, 12–13, and No. 467, 12–14; *idem.*, 'al-Qawmiyyun al-Suriyyun fi Tab'a Munaqqaha' (A Revised Edition of the Syrian Nationalists), *al-Hurriyya*, x (1969) No. 480, 10–11, and No. 482, 10–11; see also Zahi Sharfan, 'Abna' al-Hayat wa Shajarat al-Fikr al-Yabisa' (The Sons of Life and the Dried Up Tree of Thought), *Dirasat 'Arabiyya*, VI (1970) No. 3, 114–28,

whose title is a parody of the romantic political terminology used by the SSNP.

12. See Yamak, *op. cit.*, p. 59: Seale, *op. cit.*, p. 69.
13. Yamak, *op. cit.*, p. 59: 'While the SSNP was decidedly a dictatorial organisation with strong fascistic tendencies, there was apparently no tangible evidence to prove its subservience to Germany and Italy.' See also Seale, *op. cit.*, p. 69.
14. Yamak, *op. cit.*, p. 76.
15. *Ibid.*, p. 77.
16. Sa'ada, quoted by Yamak, *op. cit.*, p. 79.
17. Quoted by Yamak, *op. cit.*, pp. 79 ff.
18. Quoted Yamak, *op. cit.*, p. 80.
19. Quoted in H. Sharabi, 'Die Enstehung einer revolutionären Ideologie in der arabischen Welt', *Bustan*, x (1969) Nos. 2–3, 3–11; here p. 8.
20. H. B. Sharabi, *op. cit.*, shows the great influence exerted on Sa'ada by the irredentist movement in Italy: see note 2 to this chapter.
21. See Antun Sa'ada, 'The Teaching Book of the Syrian Social Nationalist Party', in K. H. Karpat, *op. cit.*, pp. 95 ff: Yamak, *op. cit.*, pp. 82 ff.; al-Husri, vol. IX, pp. 104 ff.; P. Seale, *op. cit.*, pp. 65 ff.
22. See Antun Sa'ada, 'The Principles of Syrian Nationalism and its Party', in K. H. Karpat, *op. cit.*, pp. 88 ff.; Yamak, *op. cit.*, pp. 89 ff.; al-Husri, vol. IX, pp. 106 ff.; P. Seale, *op. cit.*, pp. 65 ff.
23. On this question generally see Muhammad Kischli, *Kapitalismus und Linke im Libanon*, ed. B. Tibi, *op. cit.*, pp. 88 ff., and the editor's introduction; also Wilhelm Kewenig, *Die Koexistenz der Religionsgemeinschaften im Libanon* (Berlin, 1965). For information on the francophone Lebanese particularism propagated by the semi-fascist 'Phalanges Libanaises' see the text by the founder and ideologue of the party, Pierre Gemayel, 'Lebanese Nationalism and Its Foundations: the Phalangist Viewpoint', in K. H. Karpat, *op. cit.*, pp. 107 ff. al-Husri also crossed swords with the 'Phalanges Libanaises': see al-Husri, vol. IX, pp. 34–68, where he answers criticisms in the party organ *al-A'mal* (Beirut). In 1951 (23, 24, 25, 26, 30 Aug., 2 Sep.), *al-A'mal* ran a series entitled 'al-Wahda al-'Arabiyya Bainana wa Bain Failsufiha Sati' al-Husri' (Pan-Arabism: our View and the View of its Philosopher Sati' al-Husri). This controversy is too complicated to be discussed here.
24. Translated from the Arabic: quoted by al-Husri, vol. XII, p. 23, English translation in Yamak, *op. cit.*, p. 111.
25. P. Seale, *op. cit.*, p. 67.
26. al-Husri, vol. IX, p. 70.
27. *Ibid.*; Yamak, *op. cit.*, *passim*.
28. al-Husri, vol. IX, p. 70.
29. *Ibid.*, p. 74 ff.
30. *Ibid.*, pp. 71 ff.
31. *Ibid.*, pp. 89 ff.
32. *Ibid.*, pp. 136 ff.
33. *Ibid.*, pp. 79 ff., 97 ff., etc.
34. *Ibid.*, p. 71.
35. *Ibid.*, p. 73.
36. *Ibid.*

37. *Ibid.*, p. 72.
38. *Ibid.*, pp. 74 ff.
39. al-Husri, vol. IX.
40. al-Husri, vol. XII.
41. Quoted al-Husri, vol. XII, p. 34.
42. Quoted in *ibid.*, p. 37.
43. *Ibid.*, p. 30.
44. *Ibid.*, pp. 13 ff.
45. Sami Khuri, *al-Radd 'ala Sati' al-Husri* (Reply to Sati' al-Husri) (Beirut, n.d.).

Notes to the Postscript

1. On the Ba'th Party, see the monograph by Kamel Abu Jaber, *The Arab Ba'th Socialist Party, History, Ideology, and Organization* (Syracuse, 1966), and B. Tibi, *Die arabische Linke, op. cit.*, pp. 26 ff. Both sources contain further reference material.
2. Eric Rouleau 'The Syrian Enigma; What is the Ba'th?' *New Left Review* (1967) No. 45, 53–65; here p. 57.
3. *Ibid.*
4. *Ibid.*, p. 56.
5. Gordon H. Torrey's *Syrian Politics and the Military* (Columbus, Ohio, 1964), deals with Syrian history since the achievement of independence in 1945. Although useful, it contains a number of mistakes and inaccuracies: see the review by Fritz Steppat in *Oriens*, XVIII–XIX (1965/66). See also Patrick Seale, *op. cit.*, and A. L. Tibawi, *A Modern History of Syria* (London, 1969).
6. Fanon's thesis is discussed in B. Tibi, 'Zum Verhältnis von Militär und kolonialem Nationalismus am Beispiel der arabischen Länder', *Sozialistische Politik*, I (1969) No. 4, 4–19. See also Chapter 2 above.
7. The difference between al-Husri and 'Aflaq has been analysed by Muhammad Kishli: 'al-Idiolojiyya w'al-Jamahir f'il-Thawra al-'Arabiyya' (Ideology and the Masses in the Arab Revolution), *Mawaqif*, I (1969) No. 6, 60–71, especially pp. 69 ff.
8. Michel 'Aflaq, *Fi Sabil al-Ba'th* (Towards the Renaissance), 3rd ed. (Beirut, 1963) p. 48.
9. *Ibid.*, p. 85.
10. *Ibid.*, p. 26.
11. *Ibid.*, p. 224. Parts of 'Aflaq's writings have been translated into English, e.g. 'The Socialist Ideology of the Ba'th', in K. H. Karpat, *op. cit.*, pp. 185–97: 'Nationalism and Revolution', in Sylvia Haim (ed.), *Arab Nationalism, an Anthology*, 2nd ed. (Berkeley and London, 1976), pp. 242–50. For an interpretation of 'Aflaq's ideas within the general context of the Ba'th Party, see B. Tibi (ed.), *Die arabische Linke, op. cit.*, pp. 26 ff.; K. Abu Jaber, *op. cit.*; L. Binder, *The Ideological Revolution in the Middle East* (New York, 1964) pp. 154–97; Gordon H. Torrey, 'Ba'th Ideology and Practice', *Middle East Journal*, XXIII (1969) No. 4, 445–70.
12. For a discussion of the Bonapartist nationalism of the petite bourgeoisie, see B. Tibi (ed.) *Die arabische Linke, op. cit.*, pp. 69 ff., 87 ff., and *idem.*, 'Zum Verhältnis von Militär und kolonialem Nationalismus am Beispiel der

arabischen Länder', *op. cit.*, *idem.*, 'Die Krise der Burgibismus, Entstehung und Verfall des "konstitutionellen Sozialismus" in Tunesien', *Das Argument*, XII (1970) No. 59, 530–55.

13. al-Husri, vol. XIX, p. 241.
14. *Ibid.*, *passim.*
15. Malcolm Kerr, *The Arab Cold War, 1958–1967*, 2nd ed. (London and New York, 1967). See also Fritz Steppat, 'Die arabischen Staaten zwischen Ost und West', in Wilhelm Cornides (ed.), *Die internationale Politik* (Munich, 1961) pp. 671–752.
16. For an ideological critique of the Nasserist variety of 'Arab Socialism' see the reference to Tibi in Note 12 to this chapter, and B. Tibi, 'Der arabische Sozialismus', in Iring Fetscher (ed.), *Der Sozialismus* (Munich, 1968) pp. 378–87. See also the documentation in S. Hanna and G. Gardner (eds), *Arab Socialism, a Documentary Survey* (Leiden, 1969). W. Ule's *Der arabische Sozialismus* (Opladen, 1969), is unreliable.
17. For the organisational structure of the Ba'th Party, see K. Abu Jaber, *op. cit.*, *passim.*, especially the diagram on page 145.
18. *Nidal al-Ba'th* (The Struggle of the Ba'th), 7 vols (Beirut, 1963–5).
19. See the bibliography in Abu Jaber, *op. cit.*
20. al-Hakam Darwaza and Hamid Jabburi, *Ma' al-Qawmiyya al-'Arabiyya* (With Arab Nationalism), 4th extended edition (Beirut, 1960). Darwaza is the son of the historian Muhammad 'Izzat Darwaza (see Chapter 5, note 85), one of the leading members of the early Arab national movement.
21. See John P. Halstead, *Rebirth of a Nation: The Origins and Rise of Moroccan Nationalism* (Cambridge, Mass., 1967); D. E. Ashford, *Political Change in Morocco* (Princeton, 1961), and the review article by John Damis, 'Developments in Morocco under French Protectorate 1925–1943', *Middle East Journal*, XXIV (1970) No. 1, 74–86. See also B. Tibi, (ed.), *Mehdi Ben Barka, Revolutionäre Alternative* (Munich, 1969).
22. See T. Oppermann, *Die algerische Frage* (Stuttgart, 1959); Wolfgang Ohneck, *Die französische Algerien politik, 1919–1939* (Cologne and Opladen, 1967); David C. Gordon, *The Passing of French Algeria* (London, 1965); Frantz Fanon, *Studies in a Dying Colonialism* (London, 1970).
23. W. Ruf, *Burgibismus und der Außenpolitik des unabhängigen Tunesien* (Bielefeld, 1969); C. H. Moore, *Tunisia Since Independence* (Berkeley and Los Angeles, 1965); D. L. Ling, *Tunisia, from Protectorate to Republic* (Bloomington, 1967). On the Maghrib in general see Roger Le Tourneau, *L'Évolution Politique de l'Afrique du Nord Musulmane 1920–1961* (Paris, 1962).
24. See note 22 to this chapter.
25. This document is reproduced in *al-Hurriyya*, VII (Beirut, 1966) No. 305, 16–17, the source which is quoted here.
26. Yasin Hafiz, 'Zu einigen kleinbürgerlichen Begriffen über die nationale Frage', in B. Tibi (ed.), *Die arabische Linke*, *op. cit.*, pp. 72 ff., here pp. 74 ff.
27. *Ibid.*, pp. 84 ff.
28. *Perspectives* group, 'Allgemeine Charakteristika der gegenwärtigen Entwicklungsphase Tunesiens', in B. Tibi, *op. cit.*, pp. 90 ff. This shows that the objective of Arab unity need not necessarily be a petty bourgeois ideology, but can also function within the framework of a progressive strategy. On the

relationship between Pan-Arabism and the Arab labour movement, see Willard A. Beling, *Pan-Arabism and Labor* (Cambridge, Mass., 1960).

29. Elias Murqus, *Naqd al-Fikr al-Qawmi* (A Critique of Nationalist Thought), vol. I, *Sati' al-Husri* (Beirut, 1966) p. 578.

30. This process is documented in detail in B. Tibi (ed.), *Die arabische Linke, op. cit., passim.*

31. See the criticism of Nasserism in A. Abdel-Malek, *Egypt, Military Society* (New York, 1968); H. Riad, *L'Egypte Nassérienne* (Paris, 1964), and Mahmoud Hussein, *Class Conflict in Egypt 1945–1970* (New York and London, 1973).

32. See Muhsin Ibrahim (ed.), *Limadha Munadhdhamat al-Ishtirakiyyin al-Lubnaniyyin* (Why the Organisation of Lebanese Socialists?) (Beirut, 1970) *passim.*

Bibliography

For greater convenience the Bibliography has been divided into the following seven sections:

1. General surveys and monographs on nationalism in Western Europe and theoretical works.
2. Works on German, Pan-Slav and Irish nationalism and their historical context.
3. Works on nationalism in the Third World (excluding the Arab World).
4. The works of Sati' al-Husri, including translations and secondary literature.
5. Arabic primary sources.
6. Works on Arab nationalism, modern Islam and the modern history of the Arab Middle East.
7. Other works cited.

1. General surveys and monographs on nationalism in Western Europe and theoretical works

Arendt, Hannah, *The Origins of Totalitarianism*, revised ed. (London, 1967).

Baron, Salo Wittmayer, *Modern Nationalism and Religion* (New York, 1947).

Bauer, Otto, *Die Nationalitätenfrage und die Sozialdemokratie, Marx-Studien*, vol. II, eds Adler, M. and Hilferding, R., 2nd ed. (Vienna, 1924).

Bloom, Solomon Frank, *The World of Nations: A Study of the National Implications in the Work of Karl Marx*, unpublished Ph.D. dissertation (New York, 1941).

Bracher, Karl D., 'Der Nationalstaat', in K. D. Bracher and E. Fraenkel (eds), *Staat und Politik, Das Fischer Lexikon* (Frankfurt/Main, 1962) pp. 198–204.

Buthmann, William, C., *The Rise of Integral Nationalism in France with Special Reference to the Ideas and Activities of Charles Maurras*, unpublished Ph.D. dissertation (New York, 1939).

Chadwick, H. Munro, *The Nationalities of Europe and the Growth of National Ideologies*, 2nd ed. (Cambridge, 1966).

Davis, Horace B., *Nationalism and Socialism: Marxist and Labor Theories of Nationalism to 1917* (New York and London, 1967).

Deutsch, Karl W., *An Interdisciplinary Bibliography on Nationalism 1935–1953* (Cambridge, 1956).

——, *Nationalism and Social Communication: An Inquiry into the Foundations of Nationality*, 2nd ed. (Cambridge, Mass., 1966).

Deutsch, Karl W. and Foltz, W. J. (eds), *Nation-Building* (New York, 1963).

Dreitzel, Hans Peter (ed.), *Sozialer Wandel* (Neuwied, 1967).

Engels, Friedrich, 'Das Fest der Nationen in London', in *Marx-Engels-Werke*, vol. II (Berlin, 1962) pp. 611–24; Eng. transl., 'The Festival of Nations in London', in *Collected Works*, vol. VI (London, 1976) pp. 3–14.

——, 'Über den Verfall des Feudalismus und das Aufkommen der Bourgeoisie', in *Marx-Engels-Werke*, vol. XXI (Berlin, 1962) pp. 392 ff.

——, 'Po und Rhein', in *Marx-Engels-Werke*, vol. XIII, 2nd ed. (Berlin, 1964) pp. 225–68.

Euchner, Walter, *Naturrecht und Politik bei John Locke* (Frankfurt/Main, 1969).

Fetscher, Iring, *Rousseaus politische Philosophie: Zur Geschichte des demokratischen Freiheitsbegriffs* (Neuwied-Berlin, 1960), 3rd ed. (Frankfurt/Main, 1975).

——, *Der Marxismus und seine Geschichte in Dokumenten*, vol. III, *Politik* (Munich, 1965) pp. 91–128.

——, *Von Marx zur Sowjetideologie*, 11th ed. (Frankfurt/Main, 1965).

——, *Karl Marx und der Marxismus* (Munich, 1967).

Fetscher, Iring, *et al.*, *Rechtsradikalismus*, 2nd ed. (Frankfurt/Main, 1967).

Habermas, J., *Theorie und Praxis: Sozialphilosophische Studien* (Berlin, 1963); Eng. transl., *Theory and Practice* (London, 1974).

——, *Strukturwandel der Öffentlichkeit: Untersuchungen zur einer Kategorie der bürgerlichen Gesellschaft*, 2nd ed. (Berlin, 1965).

——, *Erkenntnis und Interesse* (Frankfurt/Main, 1968); Eng. transl., *Knowledge and Human Interests* (London, 1972).

Hayes, C. J. H., *The Historical Evolution of Modern Nationalism* (New York, 1950).

Hobsbawn, Eric, *Primitive Rebels: Studies in Archaic Forms of Social Movement in the 19th and 20th Centuries* (Manchester, 1959).

Hoffmann-Linke, Eva, *Zwischen Nationalismus und Demokratie, Gestalten der französischen Vorrevolution*, Beiheft 9 der *Historischen Zeitschrift* (Munich and Berlin, 1927).

Kautsky, Karl, *Sozialismus und Kolonialpolitik* (Berlin, 1907); Eng. transl., *Socialism and Colonial Policy: An Analysis* (Belfast, 1975).

——, 'Nationalität und Internationalität', Erganzungshefte zur *Neue Zeit*, No. 1 (Stuttgart, 18 January 1908).

Kohn, Hans, *The Idea of Nationalism: A Study in its Orgins and Background* (New York, 1945).

——, *Prophets and Peoples: Studies in Nineteenth Century Nationalism* (New York, (1946).

——, 'Napoleon and the Age of Nationalism', *Journal of Modern History*, XXII (1950), No. 1, 21–37.

——, *The Age of Nationalism: The First Era of Global History* (New York, 1962).

——, *Von Machiavelli zu Nehru: Zur Problemgeschichte des Nationalismus* (Freiburg, 1964).

Lemberg, Eugen, *Geschichte des Nationalismus in Europa* (Stuttgart, 1950).

——, Nationalismus: definition, Tendenzen, Theorie', *Moderne Welt*, VIII (1967) No. 3, 317–33.

Lenk, Kurt (ed.), *Ideologie, Ideologiekritik und Wissenssoziologie*, 2nd ed. (Neuwied and Berlin, (1964).

Lévi-Strauss, Claude, *The Savage Mind* (London, 1966).

Lübbe, Hermann, *Säkularisierung, Geschichte eines ideenpolitischen Begriffs* (Freiburg and Munich, 1965).

Mannheim, Karl, *Ideologie und Utopie*, 4th ed. (Frankfurt/Main, 1965); Eng. transl., *Ideology and Utopia*, 7th ed. (London, 1954).

Marcuse, H., *One-Dimensional Man* (London, 1964).

Marx, K., *Grundrisse der Kritik der politischen Ökonomie* (Berlin, 1953); Eng. transl., *Grundrisse: Introduction to the Critique of Political Economy* (London, 1973).

Marx, K. and Engels, F., 'Rede über die Frage des Freihandels', in *Marx-Engels-Werke*, vol. IV., 3rd ed. (Berlin, 1964) pp. 444–58; Eng. transl., 'Speech on the Question of Free Trade', in *Collected Works*, vol. VI (London, 1976) pp. 450–65.

——, 'Die Deutsche Ideologie', in *Marx-Engels-Werke*, vol. III (Berlin, 1962); Eng. transl., 'The German Ideology', in Marx and Engels, *Selected Works*, vol. II (London, 1965).

——, 'Manifest des kommunistischen Partei', in *Marx-Engels-Werke*, vol. VI, 3rd ed. (Berlin, 1964) pp. 459–93; Eng. transl., 'The Communist Manifesto', in L. S. Feuer (ed.), *Karl Marx and Friedrich Engels: Basic Writings on Politics and Philosophy* (London, 1969) pp. 43–82.

Neusüss, Arnhelm, *Utopisches Bewußtsein und Freischwebende Intelligenz: Zur Wissenssoziologie Karl Mannheims* (Meisenheim am Glan, 1968).

Nolte, E., *Der Faschismus in seiner Epoche*, 2nd ed. (Munich, 1965); Eng. transl., *Three Faces of Fascism* (New York and Toronto, 1969).

Pinson, Koppel S., *A Bibliographical Introduction to Nationalism* (New York, 1935).

Pollard A. F., *Factors in Modern History* (London, 1907).

Salomon-Delatour, G. (ed.), *Die Lehre Saint-Simons* (Berlin and Neuwied, 1962).

Schmidt, Alfred, 'Der strukturalische Angriff auf die Geschichte', in A. Schmidt (ed.), *Beiträge zur marxistischen Erkenntnistheorie* (Frankfurt/Main, 1969) pp. 194–265.

Schuon, Karl Theodor, 'Typologie und kritische Theorie', *Das Argument*, XI (1969) No. 50, 93–124.

Shafer, B. C., *Nationalism: Myth and Reality* (London and New York, 1955).

Sieyès, Emmanuel, *Qu'est-ce que le Tiers État?*, ed. R. Zapperi (Geneva, 1970); Eng. transl., *What is the Third Estate?* (London, 1963).

Snyder, Louis, L., *The Meaning of Nationalism* (New Brunswick, 1954).

Stalin, J. V., 'Marxism and the National Question', (1913) in *Collected Works*, vol. 2 (London and Moscow, 1953) pp. 300–81.

Sulzbach, Walther, 'Zur Definition und psychologie von "Nation" und "Nationalbewußtsein"', *Politische Vierteljahresschrift*, III (1962) No. 2, 139–58.

Tibi, Bassam, 'Marxismus und Nationalismus-Analyse', *Neue Politische Literatur*, XIV (1969) No. 4, 560–61.

Viefhaus, Erwin, *Die Minderheitsfrage und die Entstehung der Minderheitsschutzverträge auf der Pariser Friedenskonferenz*

1919: Eine Studie zur Geschichte des Nationalitätenproblems im 19. und 20. Jahrhundert (Würzburg, 1960).

Vogt, Hannah (ed.), *Nationalismus Gestern und Heute* (Opladen, 1967).

Werner, Hans Detlef, *Klassenstruktur und Nationalcharakter* (Tübingen, n.d. [1968]).

Wirth, L., 'Types of Nationalism', *American Journal of Sociology*, XLI (1936) No. 6, 723–37.

Zapf, Wolfgang, *Theorien des sozialen Wandels*, 2nd ed. (Cologne and Berlin, 1970).

Ziegler, Heinz O., *Die moderne Nation* (Tübingen, 1931).

2. Works on German, Pan-Slav and Irish nationalism and their historical context

Anderson, Eugene Newton, *Nationalism and the Cultural Crisis in Prussia, 1806–1815* (New York, 1939).

von Aretin, K. O., 'Über die Notwendigkeit kritischer Distanzierung vom Nationsbegriff in Deutschland nach 1945', in H. Bolewski (ed.), *Nation und Nationalismus* (Stuttgart, 1967) pp. 26–45.

Arndt, Ernst Moritz, *Deutsche Volkswerdung, Sein politisches Vermächtnis an die deutsche Gegenwart, Kernstellen aus seinen Schriften und Briefen,* eds Carl Petersen and Paul H. Ruth (Breslau, n.d. [1934]).

Baeumler, A., 'Fichte und Wir', *Nazionalsozialistische Monatshefte*, VIII (1937) No. 87, 482–9.

Barnard, Frederick, *Herder's Social and Political Thought: From Enlightenment to Nationalism* (Oxford, 1965).

Bergmann, Ernst, *Fichte und der Nationalsozialismus* (Breslau, n.d. [1933]).

Bergner, Dieter, *Neue Bemerkungen zu J. G. Fichte: Fichtes Stellungsnahme zur nationalen Frage* (Berlin, 1957).

Binder, Julius, 'Fichte und die Nation', *Logos*, x (1921) No. 3, 275–315.

Bittner, Konrad, *Herders Geschichtsphilosophie und die Slaven* (Reichenberg, 1929).

Engelbrecht, H. C., *Johann Gottlieb Fichte, A Study of His Political Writings with Special Reference to His Nationalism* (New York, 1933).

Engels, F., 'The State of Germany', *The Northern Star* (25 October 1845); Karl Marx and Friedrich Engels, *Collected Works*, vol. VI (London, 1976) pp. 19 ff.

——, 'Was hat die Arbeiterklasse mit Polen zu Tun?', in *Marx-Engels-Werke*, vol. XVI (Berlin, 1962) pp. 153–63.

——, 'Eine polnische Proklamation', in *Marx-Engels-Werke*, vol. XVIII, 2nd ed. (Berlin, 1964) pp. 521–7.

Epstein, Klaus, *The Genesis of German Conservatism* (Princeton, 1966).

Ergang, Robert, *Herder and the Foundations of German Nationalism* (New York, 1931).

Fichte, J. G., *Reden an die Deutsche Nation* (Hamburg, 1955); Eng. transl., *Addresses to the German Nation* (London, 1922, and New York, 1968).

——, 'Fichte-Worte über Nation und Menschheit, Fichtes Kampf um Deutschlands innere und äußere Befreiung', (Auszüge) *Nationalsozialistische Monatshefte*, VIII (1937) 418–25.

Grebing, Helga, 'Nationalismus und Demokratie in Deutschland', in I. Fetscher (ed.), *Rechtsradikalismus*, 2nd ed. (Frankfurt/Main, 1967) pp. 31–66.

Hayes, C. J. H., 'The Contributions of Herder to the Doctrine of Nationalism', *American Historical Review*, XXXII (1927) No. 4, 719–36.

Haymann, Franz, *Weltbürgertum und Vaterlandsliebe in der Staatslehre Rousseaus und Fichtes* (Berlin, 1924).

Herder, Johann Gottfried, *Sprachphilosophische Schriften*, ed. and introd. by E. Heintel, 2nd ed. (Hamburg, 1964).

——, *Werke*, 5 vols, ed. and introd. by W. Dobbek (Berlin and Weimar, 1964).

——, *Auch eine Philosophie der Geschichte zur Bildung der Menschheit*, with a postscript by H. Gadamer (Frankfurt/Main, 1967).

Hroch, Miroslav, *Die Vorkämpfer der nationalen Bewegung bei den kleinen Völkern Europas, eine vergleichende Analyse zur Gesellschaftlichen Schichtung der patriotischen Bewegungen* (Prague, 1968).

Kaufmann, F., 'Fichte and National Socialism', *American Political Science Review*, XXXVI (1942), No. 3, 460–70.

Kluckhohn, Paul, *Die deutsche Romantik* (Bielefeld and Leipzig, 1924).

——, *Persönlichkeit und Gemeinschaft, Studien zur Staatsauffassung der deutschen Romantik* (Halle, 1925).

——, *Das Ideengut der deutschen Romantik*, 3rd ed. (Tübingen, 1953).

Kohn, Hans, 'Arndt and the Character of German Nationalism', *American Historical Review*, LIV (1949) No. 4, 783–803.

——, 'The Paradox of Fichte's Nationalism', *Journal of the History of Ideas*, X (1949) No. 3, 319–43.

——, 'Romanticism and the Rise of German Nationalism', *Review of Politics*, XII (1950) No. 4, 443–72.

——, 'The Eve of German Nationalism', *Journal of the History of Ideas*, XII (1951) 256–84.

——, *Pan-Slavism: Its History and Ideology* (Notre Dame, 1953).

——, *Prelude to Nation States, the French and German Experience, 1789–1815* (Princeton, 1967).

Kuhn, H. J., *Arndt und Jahn als völkisch-politische Denker* (Langensalza, 1936).

Marx, Karl, *Manuskripte über die polnische Frage*, ed. Werner Conze ('sGravenhage, 1961).

——, 'Entwurf eines Vertrages zur irischen Frage gehalten im Deutscher Bildungsverein für Arbeiter in London am 16 Dez. 1867', in *Marx-Engels-Werke*, vol. XVI (Berlin, 1962) pp. 445–59.

——, 'Entwurf einer nicht gehaltenen Rede zur irischen Frage', in *Marx-Engels-Werke*, vol. XVI (Berlin, 1962) pp. 439–44.

——, 'Die englische Regierung und die eingekerkerten Fenier', in *Marx-Engels-Werke*, vol. XVI (Berlin, 1962) pp. 401–6.

Marx, Karl, and Engels, Friedrich, 'Rede über Polen', in *Marx-Engels-Werke*, vol. IV, 3rd ed. (Berlin, 1964) pp. 416–18; Eng. transl., 'On Poland', in *Collected Works*, vol. VI (London, 1976) pp. 388–9.

Matl, Josef, *Europa und die Slaven* (Wiesbaden, 1964).

McCaffrey, Lawrence, *The Irish Question, 1800–1922* (Lexington, 1968).

Mehlis, Georg, *Die deutsche Romantik* (Munich, 1922).

Mehnert, Helmut, *Fichte und die Bedeutung der nationaler Frage in seinem Werk*, unpub. Ph.D. thesis (Leipzig, 1955).

Pinson, K. S., *Pietism as a Factor in the Rise of German Nationalism* (New York, 1934).

Plessner, Helmuth, *Die verspätete Nation; über die politische Verführbarkeit bürgerlichen Geistes* (Stuttgart, 1959).

Polog, Hans, *E. M. Arndts Weg zum Deutschen, Studien zur Entwicklung des frühen Arndt 1769–1812* (Leipzig, 1936).

Pundt, Alfred G., *Arndt and the Nationalist Awakening in Germany*, 2nd ed. (New York, 1968).

Reiss, Hans, *The Political Thought of the German Romantics* (Oxford, 1955).

Saage, Richard, 'Aspekte der politischen Philosophie Fichtes', *Neue Politische Literatur*, xv (1970) No. 3, 354–76.

Sauer, Wolfgang, 'Das Problem des deutschen Nationalstaates', *Politische Vierteljahresschrift*, iii (1962) No. 2, 159–86.

Simon, Hermann, *Geschichte der deutschen Nation* (Mainz, 1968).

Snyder, Louis L., *German Nationalism, the Tragedy of a People: Extremism contra Liberalism in Modern German History* (Harrisburg, 1952).

Stählin, Friedrich, *Napoleons Glanz und Fall im deutschen Urteil* (Brunswick, 1952).

Turnbull, J. G., *The Educational Theory of Fichte, A Critical Account Together with Translations* (London, 1926).

Verschoor, A. D., *Die ältere deutsche Romantik und die Nationalidee* (Amsterdam, n.d. [1929]).

Willms, Bernhard, *Die totale Freiheit, Fichtes politische Philosophie* (Cologne and Opladen, 1967).

Willoughby, L. A., *The Romantic Movement in Germany*, 1st ed. (New York, 1930), 2nd ed. (New York, 1966).

3. Works on nationalism in the Third World (excluding the Arab World)

Adam, Heribert, 'Die afrikanische Misere', in *idem.*, *Südafrika, Soziologie einer Rassengesellschaft* (Frankfurt/Main, 1969) pp. 110–19.

Apter, David, *The Politics of Modernisation* (Chicago, 1965).

Behrendt, Richard F., *Soziale Strategie für Entwicklungsländer* (Frankfurt/Main, 1965), (2nd ed. with postscript, 1968).

Bottomore, T. B., *Elites and Society*, 2nd ed. (London, 1966).

Césaire, Aimé, *Discourse on Colonialism* (New York and London, 1972).

Chesneaux, J., *Le Vietnam: Études de Politique et d'Histoire* (Paris, 1968).

Clausen, Lars, *Industrialisierung in Schwarzafrika, eine soziologische Lotstudie zweier Großbetriebe in Sambia* (Bielefeld, 1968).

De Graft-Johnson, J. C., *African Glory, The Story of Vanished*

Negro Civilisations, 2nd ed. (New York, 1966).

Emerson, Rupert, *From Empire to Nation, The Rise of Self-Assertion of Asian and African Peoples*, 3rd ed. (Boston, 1964).

Fanon, F., *Black Skin, White Masks* (New York, 1967).

——, *The Wretched of the Earth* (London, 1967).

——, *Studies in a Dying Colonialism* (London, 1970).

Feltrinelli, Giangiacomo, *Lateinamerika—ein zweites Vietnam?* (Reinbek, 1968).

Gandhi, M., *Sarvodaya, the Welfare of All* (Ahmedabad, 1954).

——, *Freiheit ohne Gewalt*, ed. and introd. K. Klostermeier (Cologne, 1968).

Geismar, Peter, 'Frantz Fanon, Evolution of a Revolutionary, a Biographical Sketch', *Monthly Review*, xxi (1969–70) No. 1, 22–30.

Geiss, I., *The Pan-African Movement* (London, 1974).

Grohs, Gerhard, 'Frantz Fanon, ein Theoretiker der afrikanischen Revolution', *Kölner Zeitschrift für Soziologie und Sozialpsychologie*, xvi (1964) No. 3, 457–80.

——, *Stufen afrikanischer Emanzipation: Studien zum Selbstverständnis afrikanischer Eliten* (Stuttgart, 1967).

Heintz, Peter (ed.), *Soziologie der Entwicklungsländer, eine systematische Anthologie* (Cologne and Berlin, 1962).

Kautsky, John H., *Political Change in Underdeveloped Countries, Nationalism and Communism*, 7th ed. (New York, 1967).

König, Réné, *Aspekte der Entwicklungssoziologie*, Special issue of No. xiii of *Kölner Zeitschrift für Soziologie und Sozialpsychologie* (Cologne and Opladen, 1970).

Lenin, V. I., 'Socialism and War' (Eng. transl.), in *Collected Works*, vol. xviii (London, n.d.), pp. 215–58.

——, 'The Peace Question' (Eng. transl.), in *Collected Works*, vol. xviii (London, n.d.), pp. 264–8.

——, 'The Right of Nations to Self-Determination' (Eng. transl.), in *Collected Works*, vol. xx (Moscow and London, 1964) pp. 393–454.

——, 'The Socialist Revolution and the Right of Nations to Self-Determination' (Eng. transl.), in *Collected Works*, vol. xxii (Moscow and London, 1964) pp. 143–56.

Luxemburg, Rosa, *Die russische Revolution*, ed. O. K. Flechtheim (Frankfurt/Main, 1963); Eng. transl. *The Russian Revolution* (Ann Arbor, 1961).

Macpherson, C. B., *The Real World of Democracy* (Oxford, 1966).

Matossian, Mary, 'Ideologies of Delayed Industrialisation: Some Tensions and Ambiguities', *Economic Development and Cultural Change*, VI (1958) No. 3, 217–28.

Matus, G. L., 'Der Status der Nation und das internationale Schichtungssystem', in Peter Heintz (ed.), *Soziologie der Entwicklungsländer, eine systematische Anthologie* (Cologne and Berlin, 1962) pp. 45–69.

Mehnert, Klaus, 'The Social and Political Role of the Intelligentsia in the New Countries', in Kurt London (ed.), *New Nations in a Divided World* (New York, 1963) pp. 121–33.

Millikan, M. F., and Blackmer, D. (eds), *The Emerging Nations* (Boston and Toronto, 1961).

Moneta, Jakob, *Die Kolonialpolitik der französischen KP* (Hannover, 1968).

Mühlmann, W. E., *Rassen, Ethnien, Kulturen, Moderne Ethnologie* (Neuwied and Berlin, 1964).

Mühlmann, W. E. (ed.), *Chiliasmus und Nativismus, Studien zur Psychologie, Soziologie und historischen Kasuistik der Umsturzbewegungen* (Berlin, 1961).

Plamenatz, J., *On Alien Rule and Self-Government* (London, 1960).

Sartre, Jean-Paul, *Colonialisme et Néocolonialisme* (Paris, 1964).

Schuhler, Conrad, *zur politischen Ökonomie der Armen Welt* (Munich, 1968).

Senghaas, Dieter, 'Politische Innovation, versuch über den Pan-Afrikanismus', *Zeitschrift für Politik*, n.s. XII (1965) No. 4, 333–55.

Senghor, L. S., *Négritude et Humanisme* (Paris, 1964).

Serauky, Christa, 'Das philosophisch-literarische System der Négritude bei Senghor', *Mitteilungen des Instituts für Orient-Forschung*, XV (1969) No. 3, 425–39.

Shils, Edward, *Political Development in the New States* (The Hague, 1965).

Sigmund, Paul E. (ed.), *The Ideologies of the Developing Nations*, 2nd ed. (New York, 1967).

Silvert, K. H., *Expectant Peoples, Nationalism and Development* (New York, 1963).

Sulzbach, Walter, *Imperialismus und Nationalbewußtsein* (Frankfurt/Main, 1959).

Thiam, Doudou, *The Foreign Policy of African States: Ideological Bases, Present Realities, Future Prospects* (London, 1965).

Tibi, Bassam, 'Léopold Senghors "Négritude" ', *Das Argument*, IX (1967) No. 45, 422–5.

——, 'Fanons Gewalttheorie und Hegel-Rezeption', *Sozialistische Politik*, I (1969) No. 2, 84–7.

——, 'Aspekte der vietnamesischen Emanzipationsbewegung', *Neue Politische Literatur*, XV (1970) No. 3, 396–402.

——, 'Kolonialherrschaft, Antikolonialismus und Dekolonisation, Das afrikanische Exempel', *Neue Politische Literatur*, XVI (1970) No. 4, 507–32.

Trappe, Paul, *Die Entwicklungsfunktion des Genossenschaftwesens am Beispiel ostafrikanischer Stämme* (Neuwied and Berlin, 1966).

Trotsky, L., *The Permanent Revolution*, Eng. transl. (London, 1962).

Wallace, A. F. C., 'Die Revitalisierungsbewegungen', in P. Heintz (ed.), *Soziologie der Entwicklungsländer, eine systematische Anthologie* (Cologne and Berlin, 1962) pp. 431–54.

Wittfogel, Karl, *Oriental Despotism: a Comparative Study of Total Power*, 5th ed. (London and New Haven, 1964).

Wolff, Otto, *Mahatma Gandhi, Politik und Gewaltlosigkeit* (Göttingen, 1963).

Worsley, Peter, 'Frantz Fanon, Evolution of a Revolutionary, Revolutionary Theories', *Monthly Review*, XXI (1969–70) No. 1, 30–49.

Zeller, Claus, *Elfenbeinküste, ein Entwicklungsland auf dem Wege zur Nation* (Rombach, 1969).

Ziegler, Jean, *Politische Soziologie des neuen Afrika* (Munich, 1966).

4. The works of Sati' al-Husri, including translations into European languages and secondary literature

This bibliography includes only al-Husri's political writings, and not his works on archaeology, education etc. There is a comprehensive bibliography in:

'Awwad, Jurjis, *Mi'jam al-Mu'allifin al-'Iraqiyyin 1800–1969* (Handbook of Iraqi authors 1800–1969) (Baghdad, 1969). al-Husri's works are listed in vol. II, pp. 16–19.

(A) SATI' AL-HUSRI'S WRITINGS (The Roman Numerals are used in the Notes to indicate the works cited in full here)

I. *Ara' wa Ahadith fi'l-Tarbiyya wa'l-Ta'lim* (Speeches and

Reflections upon Education and Culture) (Cairo, 1944); Newspaper articles 1928–38.

II. *Dirasat 'an Muqaddimat Ibn Khaldun* (Studies on the *Muqaddima* of Ibn Khaldun), 2nd ed. (Cairo, 1961) 655 pp.; 1st ed., 2 vols, 1943–4.

III. *Ara' wa Ahadith fi'l-Wataniyya wa'l-Qawmiyya* (Speeches and Reflections on Patriotism and Nationalism), 4th ed. (Beirut, 1961) 173 pp.; Newspaper articles 1928–39, first published in book form in 1944.

IV. *Ma hiya al-Qawmiyya? Abhath wa Dirasat 'ala Dhaw' al-Ahdath wa 'l-Nadhariyyat* (What is Nationalism? Empirical and Theoretical Studies and Researches), 3rd ed. (Beirut, 1963) 262 pp.; lectures given at the Institute for Advanced Arab Studies at the Arab League between 1944 and 1947, first published in 1959.

V. *Yawm Maisalun* (The Day of Maisalun) (Beirut, n. d.) 443pp.; written in 1945 and first published in 1947.

VI. *Muhadharat fi Nushu' al-Fikra al-Qawmiyya* (Lectures on the Emergence of the National Idea), 5th ed. (Beirut, 1964) 276 pp.; a series of lectures given at the Cairo Geographical Society in 1948, first published in 1951.

VII. *Safahat min al-Madi al-Qarib* (Pages from the Recent Past) (Beirut, 1948).

VIII. *Ara' wa Ahadith fi'l-Qawmiyya al-'Arabiyya* (Speeches and Reflections upon Arab Nationalism), 4th ed. (Beirut, 1964) 175pp.; first published in 1951.

IX. *al-'Uruba baina Du'atiha wa Mu'aridhiha* (Arabism between its Supporters and its Opponents), 4th ed. (Beirut, 1961) 175pp.; first published in 1952.

X. *Ara' wa Ahadith fi 'l-Tarikh wa 'l-Ijtima'* (Reflections on History and Sociology), 2nd ed. (Beirut, 1960).

XI. *al-'Uruba Awwalan!* (Arabism First!), 5th ed. (Beirut, 1965) 192 pp.; first published in 1955.

XII. *Difa' 'an al-'Uruba* (The Defence of Arabism), 3rd ed. (Beirut, 1961) 191 pp.; first published in 1956.

XIII. *al-Bilad al-'Arabiyya wa 'l-Dawla al- 'Uthmaniyya* (The Arab Countries and the Ottoman Empire), 3rd ed. (Beirut, 1965) 287pp.; first published in 1957.

XIV. *al-Lugha wa'l-Adab wa 'Alaqatuhuma bi'l-Qawmiyya* (Language and Literature and their Relationships to Nationalism), 2nd ed. (Beirut, 1966) 255pp.; first published in 1958.

XV. *Hawl al-Wahda al-Thaqafiyya al-'Arabiyya* (On Arab Cultural Unity) (Beirut, 1959) 134 pp.

XVI. *Hawl al-Qawmiyya al-'Arabiyya* (On Arab Nationalism) (Beirut, 1961) 392 pp.; written between 1959 and 1961.

XVII. *Thaqafatuna fi Jami 'at al-Duwal al-'Arabiyya* (Our Culture in the Arab League) (Beirut, 1962) 176 pp.

XVIII. *Ahadith fi'l-Tarbiyya wa 'l-Ijtima'* (Speeches on Education and Society) (Beirut, 1962) 414 pp.

XIX. *al-Iqlimiyya, Judhuruha wa Budhuruha* (Regionalism, Its Roots and Its Seeds), 2nd ed. (Beirut, 1964) 255 pp.; first published in 1963.

XX. *Mudhakkarati fi 'l-'Iraq 1921–1927 (vol. I)* (My Memoirs in Iraq 1921–1927) (Beirut, 1927) 627 pp.

XXI. *Mudhakkarati fi 'l-'Iraq 1927–1941 (vol. II)* (Beirut, 1968) 629 pp.

(B) TRANSLATIONS OF AL-HUSRI'S WORKS
IN EUROPEAN LANGUAGES

al-Husri, S., 'Qu'est ce-que le Nationalisme?', transl. R. Costi, *Orient*, VII (1959) 215–26.

——, 'Muslim Unity and Arab Unity', in Sylvia Haim (ed.), *Arab Nationalism, an Anthology*, 2nd ed. (Berkeley and Los Angeles, 1976) pp. 147–54.

——, 'Primauté de l'Arabisme', in A. Abdel-Malek (ed.), *Anthologie de la Littérature Arabe Contemporaine* (Paris, 1965) pp. 154–6.

——, *The Day of Maysalun*, transl. S. Glazer (Washington, 1966).

——, 'The Historical Factor in the Formation of Nationalism', in K. H. Karpat (ed.), *Political and Social Thought in the Contemporary Middle East* (London, 1968) pp. 56–58.

(C) SECONDARY LITERATURE ON SATI' AL-HUSRI

Anon., 'Sati' al-Husri, al-Mufakkir al-Munadhil' (Sati' al-Husri, The Militant Thinker), *al-Tali'a*, v (1969) No. 2, 158–61.

Ahmad, 'Abd al-Karim, 'Sati' al-Husri', *al-Katib*, IX (1969) No. 95, 11–18.

Cleveland, W. L., *The Making of an Arab Nationalist: Ottomanism and Arabism in the Life and Thought of Sati' al-Husri* (Princeton, 1971).

Hourani, Albert, *Arabic Thought in the Liberal Age, 1798–1939* (London, 1962) pp. 311–16.

Kenny, L. M., 'Sati' al-Husri's views on Arab Nationalism', *Middle*

East Journal, XVII (1963) No. 3. 231–56.

Khalafalla, M. A., `Sati` al-Husri: Qissat Hayatihi' (Sati` al-Husri: a Biography), *al-Majalla* (1969) No. 146, 24–31.

Khuhaila, `Abbada, `Sati` al-Husri: al-Fikra wa'l-Tarikh' (Sati` al-Husri: Thought and History), *al-Fikr al-Mu'asir* (1969) No. 48, 20–26.

Murqus, Elias, *Naqd al-Fikr al-Qawmi: vol. I, Sati` al-Husri* (A Critique of Nationalist Thought: vol. I, Sati` al-Husri) (Beirut, 1966).

5. Arabic Primary Sources

The following is a list of the most important Arabic primary sources used in this book, with translations into European languages where available. The list does not claim to be exhaustive, and the reader should also consult the work of Hourani, Qubain and Safran in Section 6 below. There are four anthologies of modern Arabic political writing in English, German and French, which also include bibliographies and introductory material. These are:

Abdel-Malek, Anouar (ed.), *Anthologie de la littérature arabe contemporaine* (Paris, 1965).

Haim, Sylvia (ed.), *Arab Nationalism, an Anthology*, 2nd ed. (Berkeley and Los Angeles, 1976).

Karpat K. H. (ed.), *Political and Social Thought in the Contemporary Middle East* (London, 1968).

Tibi, Bassam (ed.), *Die arabische Linke* (Frankfurt/Main, 1969).

*   *   *   *

`Abd al-Raziq, `Ali, *al-Islam wa Usul al-Hukm* (Islam and the Foundations of Rule) (Cairo, 1925); ed. M. Dasuqi (Beirut, 1966).

——,'L'Islam et les bases du pouvoir', transl. L. Bercher, *Révue des Études Islamiques*, VII (1933) 353–91, and VIII (1934) 163–222.

`Abduh, Muhammad, *Risalat al-Tawhid* (Discourse on the Unity of God), 6th ed. (Cairo, 1942).

——, various writings in A. Abdel-Malek (ed.), *Anthologie de la littérature arabe contemporaine* (Paris, 1965) pp. 54 ff., 57 ff., 75 ff., 79 ff.

——, *The Theology of Unity*, transl. Isaq Mus`ad and Kenneth Cragg (London, 1966).

al-Afghani, Jamal al-Din, *al-A'mal al-Kamila* (Complete Works), ed. M. 'Ammara (Cairo, 1968).

———, 'Philosophie de l'union nationale basée sur la race et l'unité linguistique' (transl. M. Hendessi), in *Orient*, vi (1958) 123–28.

———, various writings in N. R. Keddie, (ed.), *An Islamic Response to Imperialism: Political and Religious Writings of Sayyid Jamal al-Din 'al-Afghani'* (Berkeley and Los Angeles, 1968).

al-Afghani, Jamal al-Din and 'Abduh, Muhammad, *al-'Urwa al-Wuthqa* (The Unbreakable Bond), 2nd ed. (Cairo, 1958); first printed 1884.

'Aflaq, Michel, *Fi Sabil al-Ba'th* (Towards the Renaissance), 3rd ed. (Beirut, 1963).

———, 'The Socialist Ideology of the Ba'th', in K. H. Karpat, (ed.) *Political and Social Thought in the Contemporary Middle East* (London, 1968), pp. 185–97.

———, 'Nationalism and Revolution', in Sylvia Haim (ed.) *Arab Nationalism, an Anthology*, 2nd ed. (Berkeley and Los Angeles, 1976), pp. 242–50.

al-Bustani, Butrus, *Khitab fi 'l-Hai 'a al-Ijtima'iyya wa 'l-Muqabala bain al-Awa'id al-'Arabiyya wa 'l-Ifranjiyya* (Speech on Social Organisation and on the Points of Contrast and Contact between Arab and European Customs) (Beirut, 1869).

Gemayel, Pierre, 'Lebanese Nationalism and its Foundations: the Phalangist Viewpoint', in K. H. Karpat (ed.), *Political and Social Thought in the Contemporary Middle East* (London, 1968) pp. 107–14.

Husain, Taha, *Mustaqbal al-Thaqafa fi Misr* (Cairo, 1938); Engl. transl., *The Future of Culture in Egypt* (Washington, 1950).

Ishaq, Adib, *al-Durar* (The Pearls) (Beirut, 1909).

al-Kawakibi, 'Abd al-Rahman, *Umm al-Qura* (Mother of the Villages) (reprinted Aleppo, 1959).

———, incomplete German translation in Gerhard Roth, *Kawakibi, ein arabischer Nationalist*, unpub. Dr. Phil. (Berlin, 1942) pp. 87–110.

———, extract in English in Sylvia Haim (ed.), Arab Nationalism, an Anthology, 2nd ed. (Berkeley and Los Angeles, 1976) pp. 78–80.

———, *Taba 'i' al-Istibdad,* (Features of Tyranny) (reprinted Aleppo, 1957).

———, incomplete translation in Gerhard Roth, *op. cit.*, pp. 20–86.

———, extract in French in A. Abdel-Malek (ed.) *Anthologie de la littérature arabe contemporaine* (Paris, 1965), pp. 66 ff.

Musa, Salama, *Tarbiya Salama Musa*, (Cairo, 1947).

——, *The Education of Salama Musa*, ed. and transl. L. O. Schuman (Leiden, 1961).

Ridha, Rashid, *al-Khilafa aw al-Imama al-'Udhma* (The Caliphate or the Great Imamate) (Cairo, 1923); originally a series of articles in *al-Manar*, XXIII, XXIV.

——, *Le Califat dans la Doctrine de R. Rida*, transl. H. Laoust, (Beirut, 1938).

——, 'Islam and the National Idea', in Sylvia Haim, (ed.), *Arab Nationalism, an Anthology*, 2nd ed. (Berkeley and Los Angeles, 1976) pp. 75–7.

Sa'ada, Antun; see the bibliography in L. Z. Yamak, *The Syrian Social Nationalist Party, an Analysis*, (Cambridge, Mass., 1969).

——, 'Genuine and False Arabism', in K. H. Karpat (ed.), *Political and Social Thought in the Contemporary Middle East* (London, 1968) pp. 72–9.

——, 'The Principles of Syrian Nationalism and its Party', in *ibid.*, pp. 87–94.

——, 'The Teaching Book of the Syrian Social Nationalist Party', in *ibid.*, pp. 95–98.

al-Shidyaq, Faris, *Kashf al-Mukhabba' 'an Funun Urubba* (The Discovery of the Arts of Europe), 2nd ed. (Istanbul, 1881).

——, *al-Saq 'ala al-Saq fi ma huwa 'l-Faryaq*, 2 vols, (Cairo, n.d.); French Transl., *La Vie et les Aventures de Firyaq* (Paris, 1855).

al-Tahtawi, Rifa'a Rafi', *Takhlis al-Ibriz ila Talkhis Paris* (Paris Diary) (Cairo, 1834).

——, Abridged German translation in Karl Stowasser, *at-Tahtawi in Paris, ein Dokument des arabischen Modernismus aus dem frühen 19. Jahrhundert*, unpubl. Dr. Phil. (Münster, 1966).

——, *al-Murshid al-Amin fi Ta'lim al-Banat wa'l-Banin* (Guiding Truths for Girls and Youths)[1] (Cairo, 1875).

——, *Kitab Manahij al-Albab al-Misriyya Mabahij al-Adab al-'Asriyya* (The Paths of Egyptian Hearts in the Joys of the Contemporary Arts)[1], 2nd ed. (Cairo, 1912).

On Egyptian nationalism, and its theoreticians Mustafa Kamil, Ahmad Lutfi al-Sayyid, Muhammad Haikal, Taha Husain, etc., see Safran's bibliography, and the works of Cachia, Hourani, Johansen and Steppat below. For translations, see A. Abdel-Malek (ed.) *Anthologie de la littérature arabe contemporaine* (Paris, 1965).

---

[1] The translations of these titles are taken from A. H. Hourani, *Arabic Thought in the Liberal Age, 1798–1939* (London, 1962) p. 72.

6. Works on Arab Nationalism, Modern Islam and the Modern History of the Arab Middle East

Abdel-Malek, A., *Egypt, Military Society* (New York, 1968).

——, *Idéologie et Renaissance Nationale; L'Egypte Moderne* (Paris, 1969).

Abu Jaber, Kamel, *The Arab Ba'th Socialist Party, History, Ideology, and Organization* (Syracuse, 1966).

Abu-Lughod, Ibrahim, *The Arab Rediscovery of Europe: A Study in Cultural Encounters* (Princeton, 1963).

——, 'The Transformation of the Egyptian Elite: Prelude to the 'Urabi Revolt', *Middle East Journal*, XXI (1967) No. 3, 325–44.

Adams, C. C., *Islam and Modernism in Egypt: A Study of the Modern Reform Movement Inaugurated by Muhammad 'Abduh* (London, 1933).

Ahmad, Feroz, *The Young Turks: The Committee of Union and Progress in Turkish Politics 1908–1914* (London, 1969).

Ahmed, J. M., *The Intellectual Origins of Egyptian Nationalism* (London, 1960).

Amin, Osman, 'The Modernist Movement in Egypt', in R. N. Frye (ed.), *Islam and the West* ('sGravenhage, 1957) pp. 165–78.

Amin, Samir, *The Arab Nation* (London, 1978).

'Ammara, Muhammad, *al-'Uruba fi'l-'Asr al-Hadith* (Arabism in the Modern Period) (Cairo, 1967).

Antonius, George, *The Arab Awakening: The Story of the Arab National Movement*, 2nd ed. (London, 1938); 4th ed., New York, 1965.

Arnold, Sir Thomas, *The Caliphate*, with a postscript by Sylvia Haim, 2nd ed. (London, 1965); first published 1924.

Ayalon, David, 'The Historian al-Jabarti and his Background', *Bulletin of the School of Oriental and African Studies*, XXIII (1960) 217–49.

al-Azm, Sadiq Jalal, *al-Naqd al-Dhati ba'd al-Hazima*, (Self-Criticism after the Defeat) (Beirut, 1968).

——, *Naqd al-Fikr al-Dini* (Critique of Religious Thought) (Beirut, 1969).

Azoury, Négib, *Le Réveil de la Nation Arabe dans L'Asie Turque*, (Paris, 1905).

Baer, Gabriel, *A History of Land Ownership in Modern Egypt, 1800–1950* (London, 1962).

al-Bahay, Muhammad, *Muhammad 'Abduh, Eine Untersuchung*

seiner Erziehungsmethode zum Nationalbewußtsein und zur nationalen Erhebung in Ägypte unpubl. Ph.D. thesis (Hamburg,1936).

al-Bazzaz, 'Abd al-Rahman, 'Islam and Arab Nationalism', transl. Sylvia Haim, *Die Welt des Islams*, III (1954) 201–18.

——, *Hadhihi Qawmiyyatuna* (This is our Nationalism), 2nd ed. (Cairo, 1964).

Becker, C. H., *Islamstudien, vom Werden und Wesen der islamischen Welt*, 2nd ed. (Hildesheim, 1967).

Be'eri, E., *Army Officers in Arab Politics and Society* (London and New York, 1970).

Beling, Willard A., *Pan-Arabism and Labor* (Cambridge, Mass., 1960).

Bercher, L., 'De la Brochure intitulée "sentence des grands Uléma" (d'al-Azhar) sur le livre *L'Islam et les Bases du Pouvoir'*, *Révue des Études Islamiques*, IX (1935) 75–86.

Berkes, N. (ed.), *Turkish Nationalism and Western Civilisation* (New York, 1959).

Blunt, Wilfrid S., *The Future of Islam* (London, 1882).

——, *My Diaries, being a Personal Narrative of Events 1888–1914*, 4th ed. (New York, 1932).

Bräker, Hans, *Islam-Sozialismus-Kommunismus: zur ideengeschichtlichen Grundlage der Sozialismus- und Kommunismus-Diskussion Innerhalb des Islams* (Cologne, 1968); privately printed for the Bundesinstitut für ostwissenschaftliche und internationale Studien.

Brandt, Jürgen, 'Zum Charakter der französischen Mandatspolitik in Syrien nach dem ersten Weltkrieg' in Walter Markov (ed.), *Kolonialismus und Neokolonialismus in Nordafrika und Nahost* (Berlin, 1964) pp. 197–225.

Braune, Walther, 'Beiträge zur Geschichte des neuarabischen Schrifttums', *Mitteilungen des Seminars für orientalische Sprachen*, XXXVI (1933) No. 2, 117–40.

—— 'El-Azhar, die älteste Universität der Welt', *Der Nahe Osten* (1943) 53–6.

——, 'Die Entwicklung des Nationalismus bei den Arabern', in R. Hartmann (ed.), *BASI* (Leipzig, 1944) pp. 425–38.

——, *Der islamische Orient zwischen Vergangenheit und Zukunft* (Berne and Munich, 1960).

Brockelmann, Carl, *Geschichte der arabischen Literatur (GAL)*, vol. II, 2, and *Supplements* 2 and 3 (Leiden, 1938, 1942 and 1949).

Cachia, Pierre, *Taha Husayn, His Place in the Egyptian Literary Renaissance* (London, 1956).

Charles-Roux, François, *Bonaparte, Gouverneur d'Egypte*, 2nd ed. (Paris, 1946).

Chejne Anwar, 'Pan-Islamism and the Caliphal Controversy', *Islamic Literature* (1955) 679–97.

——, 'Some Aspects of Islamic Nationalism', *Islamic Literature* (1956) 435–45.

——, 'Egyptian Attitudes Towards Pan-Arabism', *Middle East Journal*, xi (1957) 253–68.

——, 'The Use of History by Modern Arab Writers', *Middle East Journal*, xiv (1960) No. 4, 382–97.

Colombe, Marcel, *L'Évolution de l'Égypte, 1924–1950* (Paris, 1951).

Coon, Carleton S., 'The Impact of the West on Middle Eastern Social Institutions', *Proceedings of the Academy of Political Science*, xxiv (1952) No. 4, 443–66.

Cragg, Kenneth, 'Religious Developments in Islam in the 20th Century', *Journal of World History*, iii (1956) No. 2, 504–24.

Dann, Uriel, *Iraq under Qassem, a Political History, 1958–1963* (London, 1969).

Dawn, C. Ernest, 'Ideological Influences in the Arab Revolt', in J. Kritzeck and R. Bayly Winder (eds), *The World of Islam, Studies in Honor of Philip K. Hitti* (New York, 1960) pp. 233–48. Reprinted in C. E. Dawn, *From Ottomanism to Arabism, op. cit.*, pp. 69–86.

——, 'From Ottomanism to Arabism: The Origin of an Ideology', *ibid., From Ottomanism to Arabism* (London and Urbana, 1973) pp. 122–47.

——, 'The Rise of Arabism in Syria', in *ibid., From Ottomanism to Arabism, op. cit.* pp. 148–79.

——, 'The Emir of Mecca, al-Husayn ibn 'Ali and the Origin of the Arab Revolt', in *From Ottomanism to Arabism*, pp. 1–53.

Dodwell, Henry, *The Founder of Modern Egypt, A Study of Muhammad 'Ali* (Cambridge, 1931).

al-Duri, 'Abd al- 'Aziz, *al-Judhur al-Tarikhiyya li'l-Qawmiyya al-'Arabiyya* (The Historical Roots of Arab Nationalism) (Beirut, 1960).

al-Fakiki, 'Abd al-Hadi, *al-Shu'ubiyya wa'l-Qawmiyya al-'Arabiyya* (Xenophilia and Arab Nationalism) (Beirut, n.d., ca. 1962).

Farraj, 'Afif, 'al-Qawmiyyun al-Ijtima'iyyun w'al-Hujum 'ala Marksiyya' (The Social Nationalists and the Assault on Marxism), *al-Hurriyya*, x (1969), No. 466, 12–13, and No. 467, 12–14.

——, 'al-Qawmiyyun al-Suriyyun fi Tab'a Munaqqaha' (a revised edition of the Syrian Nationalists), *al-Hurriyya*, x (1969) No. 480, 10–11, and No. 482, 10–11.

Finnie, David H., *Pioneers East, The Early American Experience in the Middle East* (Cambridge, Mass., 1967).

Frye, R. N. (ed.), *Islam and the West* ('sGravenhage, 1957).

Fu'ad, Nu'mat, *A'idu Kitabat al-Tarikh* (Rewrite the History Books!) (Cairo, 1974).

Gallagher, Charles F., 'Language, Culture and Ideology: The Arab World', in K. H. Silvert (ed.), *Expectant Peoples, Nationalism and Development* (New York, 1963) pp. 199–231.

Gibb, H. A. R., *Modern Trends in Islam* (Chicago, 1947).

——, *Mohammedanism, an Historical Survey*, 2nd ed. (London, 1950).

Gibb, H. A. R. and Bowen, H., *Islamic Society and the West, A Study of the Impact of Western Civilisation on Moslem Culture in the Near East*, 2 vols (London, 1950, 1957).

Goichon, A. M., 'Le Panislamisme d'hier et d'aujourd'hui', *Afrique et l'Asie* (1950) 18–44.

Goitein, S. D., 'The Rise of the Near Eastern Bourgeoisie in Early Islamic Times', *Journal of World History*, III (1957) No. 3, 583–604.

von Grunebaum, G., *Modern Islam, the Search for Cultural Identity* (Berkeley and Los Angeles, 1962).

Grzeskowiak, Martin, 'Islam und Sozialismus in der VAR', *Mitteilungen des Instituts für Orientforschung*, XIV (1968) No. 1, 28–44.

Haikal, 'Abd al-Fattah, 'Die Auswirkungen der britischen Kolonialpolitik auf die Wirtschaft Ägyptens', in Walter Markov (ed.), *Kolonialismus und Neokolonialismus in Nordafrika und Nahost* (Berlin, 1964) pp. 226–48.

Haim, Sylvia, 'Salama Musa, an Appreciation of his Autobiography', *Die Welt des Islams*, n.s., II (1953) 10–24.

——, ' "The Arab Awakening": a Source for the Historian?', *Die Welt des Islams*, n.s., II (1953) 237–50.

——, 'Alfieri and al-Kawakibi', *Oriente Moderno*, XXXIV (1954) No. 7, 321–34.

——, 'Blunt and al-Kawakibi', *Oriente Moderno*, xxxv (1955) No. 3, 132–43.

——, 'Islam and the Theory of Arab Nationalism', *Die Welt des Islams*, n.s., iv (1955) Nos. 2–3, 124–49.

——, 'The Abolition of the Caliphate and its Aftermath', postscript to Sir Thomas Arnold, *The Caliphate*, 2nd ed. (London, 1965) pp. 205–44.

Halpern, Manfred, 'Middle Eastern Studies, a Review of the State of the Field with a few Examples', *World Politics*, xv (1962) No. 1, 108–22.

——, *The Politics of Social Change in the Middle East and North Africa* (Princeton, 1963).

Hamui, Mamun, *Die Geschichte der arabischen Nationalbewegung bis zum Ende des Ersten Weltkrieges*, unpub. Dr. Phil. thesis (Jena, 1943).

Hanna, Sami and Gardner, George (eds), *Arab Socialism, a Documentary Survey* (Leiden, 1969).

Harris, Christina Phelps, *Nationalism and Revolution in Egypt: the Role of the Muslim Brotherhood* (The Hague, 1964).

Hartmann, Richard, 'Die arabische Frage und das türkische Reich', *Beiträge zur Kenntnis des Orients, Jahrbücher der Deutschen Vorderasiengesellschaft*, xv (1918) 1–31.

——, 'Die Wahhabiten', *Zeitschrift der Deutschen Morgenländischen Gesellschaft*, lxxviii (1924) No. 2, 176–213.

——, 'Ein moderner Ägypter über die Chalifatsfrage', *Der Islam*, xvi (1927) 274–6.

——, 'Gegenwartsfragen und -strömungen des Islam', *Koloniale Rundschau*, xxxiii (1942) No. 2, 57–71.

——, (ed.), *Beiträge zur Arabistik, Semistik und Islamwissenschaft* (*BASI*) (Leipzig, 1944).

——, *Islam und Nationalismus*, Abhandlungen der Deutschen Akademie der Wissenschaften zu berlin, 1945–46, Philosophisch-historische Klasse, No. 5 (Berlin, 1948).

Haslip, Joan, *The Sultan* (London, 1958).

Henle, Hans, *Der neue Nahe Osten* (Hamburg, 1966).

Hermann, Wiebke, 'Rifa 'a Beys Beschreibung seiner Reise nach Paris, ein Werk der Frühzeit des islamischen Modernismus', *Wissenschaftliche Zeitschrift der Martin-Luther-Universität Halle*, xii (1963) Nos. 3–4, 221–8.

Heyd, U., *The Foundations of Turkish Nationalism, The Life and Teachings of Ziya Gökalp* (London, 1950).

Hershlag, Z. Y., *Introduction to the Modern Economic History of the Middle East* (Leiden, 1964).

Heyworth-Dunne, James, 'Arabic Literature in Egypt in the Eighteenth Century', *Bulletin of the School of Oriental and African Studies*, IX (1937–39) 675–89.

——, 'Rifa'a Bey Rafi 'al-Tahtawi: The Egyptian Revivalist', *Bulletin of the School of Oriental and African Studies*, IX (1937–39) 961–7, and X (1940–42) 399–415.

——, 'Printing and Translations under Muhammad 'Ali of Egypt; the Foundations of Modern Arabic', *Journal of the Royal Asiatic Society* (1940) 325–49.

——, *Religious and Political Trends in Modern Egypt* (Washington, 1950).

——, *An Introduction to the History of Education in Modern Egypt*, 2nd ed. (London, 1968); first published 1939.

Hitti, Philip K., 'The Impact of the West on Syria and Lebanon in the Nineteenth Century', *Journal of World History*, II (1955) No. 3, 608–33.

Höpp, Gerhard, 'Zur Rolle internationaler panislamischer Organisationen in der Befreiungsbewegung der arabischen Völker', in Werner Loch (ed.), *Asien, Afrika, Lateinamerika* (Berlin, 1969) pp. 159–76.

Holt, P. M., *Egypt and the Fertile Crescent, 1516–1922* (London and New York, 1966).

Hopwood, Derek, *The Russian Presence in Syria and Palestine 1843–1914: Church and Politics in the Near East* (London, 1969).

Horten, Max, 'Muhammad 'Abduh, sein Leben und seine theologisch-philosophische Gedankenwelt, eine Studie zu den Reformbestrebungen im modernen Agypten', *Beiträge zur Kenntnis des Orient, Jahrbuch der Deutschen Vorderasiengesellschaft*, XIII (1916) 83–114, and XIV (1917) 74–128.

Hourani, Albert, *Arabic Thought in the Liberal Age, 1798–1939* (London, 1962).

——, *Syria and Lebanon, a Political Essay*, 4th ed. (Beirut and London, 1968).

Husayni, Ishaq Musa, *The Muslim Brethren, The Greatest of Modern Islamic Movements* (Beirut, 1966).

Husry, Khaldun S., *Three Reformers, A Study in Modern Arab Political Thought* (Beirut, 1966).

Hussein, Mahmoud, *Class Conflict in Egypt, 1945–1970* (New York and London, 1973).

Issawi, Charles *Egypt in Revolution, an Economic Analysis'* (London, 1963).

Issawi, Charles (ed.) *The Economic History of the Middle East 1800–1914* (Chicago and London, 1966).

Jäschke, Gotthard, 'Der Turanismus der Jungtürken', *Die Welt des Islams*, XXIII (1941) Nos. 1–2, 1–55.

Johansen, Baber, *Muhammad Husain Haikal, Europa und der Orient im Weltbild eines ägyptischen Liberalen* (Beirut and Wiesbaden, 1967).

Kaesewieter, H., *Syrien und Libanon als A-Mandate* (Darmstadt, 1935).

Kaplinsky, Zvi, 'The Muslim Brotherhood', *Middle Eastern Affairs*, V (1954) 377–85.

Kedourie, E., 'Egypt and the Caliphate, 1915–1946', *Journal of the Royal Asiatic Society*, (1963) 208–48.

——, *Afghani and 'Abduh, an Essay on Religious Unbelief and Political Activism in Modern Islam* (London, 1966).

Kendall, Patricia, 'Der ambivalent Charakter des Nationalismus bei ägyptischen Akademikern', in P. Heintz (ed.), *Soziologie der Entwicklungsländer* (Cologne and Berlin, 1962) pp. 490–504.

Kerr, Malcolm, *Islamic Reform, The Political and Legal Theories of Muhammad 'Abduh and Rashid Ridha* (Berkeley and Los Angeles, 1966).

——, *The Arab Cold War 1958–1967*, 2nd ed, (London, 1967).

Kessler, Christel, *'Abd al-Rahman al-Kawakibis Reform des Islam*, unpub. Dr. Phil. (FU Berlin, 1956).

Khadduri, Majid, *Independent Iraq*, 2nd ed. (London, 1960).

——, *Republican Iraq, a Study in Iraqi Politics since the Revolution of 1958* (London, 1969).

Kischli, Muhammad, *Kapitalismus und Linke im Libanon* (Frankfurt/Main, 1970).

——, 'al-Idiolojiyya w'al-Jamahir fi'l-Thawra al-'Arabiyya' (Ideology and the Masses in the Arab Revolution), *Mawaqif*, I (1969) No. 6, 60–71.

Kley, Otto, 'Der deutsche Bildungseinfluß in der Türkei', *Beiträge zur Kenntnis des Orients, Jahrbücher des Deutschen Vorderasiengesellschaft*, XIV (1917) 1–73.

Klingmüller, Ernst, *Geschichte der Wafd-Partie im Rahmen des gesamtpolitischen Läge Ägyptens*, Ph.D thesis (Berlin, 1937).

Kohn, Hans, *Nationalism and Imperialism in the Hither East* (London, 1932).

——, *Die Europäisierung des Orients* (Berlin, 1934).

Kuzbari, Rashad, *Die Politik Englands und Frankreichs in Syrien*, Auslandswissenschaftliche Dissertation (Berlin, 1943).

Leiden, Carl (ed.), *The Conflict of Traditionalism and Modernism in the Muslim Middle East* (Austin, 1966).

Lerner, Daniel, *The Passing of Traditional Society, Modernising the Middle East*, 2nd ed. (Glencoe, 1962).

Lewis, Bernard, *The Middle East and the West*, 2nd ed. (Bloomington, 1965).

Lutfi al-Sayyid, Afaf, *Egypt and Cromer, A Study in Anglo-Egyptian Relations* (New York, 1968).

Lutfi al-Sayyid, Afaf (Lutfi al-Sayyid-Marsot), *Egypt's Liberal Experiment, 1922–1936* (Berkeley and Los Angeles, 1977).

Maghzub, Muhammad, *al-Qawmiyya al-'Arabiyya* (Arab Nationalism) (Beirut, 1960).

Ma'oz, Moshe, *Ottoman Reform in Syria and Palestine, 1840–1861: The Impact of the Tanzimat on politics and Society* (London, 1968).

Mardin, Şerif, *The Genesis of Young Ottoman Thought, A Study in the Modernization of Turkish Political Ideas* (Princeton, 1962).

Marlowe, John, *Anglo-Egyptian Relations, 1800–1953* (London, 1954).

——, *Arab Nationalism and British Imperialism, a Study in Power Politics* (London, 1961).

Mitchell, R. P., *The Society of the Muslim Brothers* (London, 1969).

Morrison, S. A., 'Arab Nationalism and Islam', *Middle East Journal*, II (1948) No. 2, 147–59.

Nuseibeh, H. Z., *The Ideas of Arab Nationalism*, 2nd ed. (Ithaca, 1959).

Ohneck, Wolfgang, *Die französiche Algerienpolitik von 1919–1939* (Cologne and Opladen, 1967).

Pérès, Henri, 'L'Institut d'Egypte et l'oeuvre de Bonaparte jugés par deux historiens arabes contemporains', *Arabica*, IV (1957) 113–30.

Perlmutter, Amos, 'Egypt and the Myth of the New Middle Class: A Comparative Analysis', *Comparative Studies in Society and History*, X (1967–68) 46–65.

Poliak, A. N., *Feudalism in Egypt, Syria, Palestine and the Lebanon 1250–1900* (London, 1939).

Qubain, Fahim, *Inside the Arab Mind, a Bibliographical Survey of Literature in Arabic* (Arlington, 1960).

——, *Crisis in Lebanon* (Washington, 1961).

Quraishi, Zaheer Masood, *Liberal Nationalism in Egypt, The Rise and Fall of the Wafd Party* (Delhi, 1967).

Rathmann, Lothar, *Araber stehen auf, über den Befreiungskampf der arabischen Völker bis zum Ausbruch des zweiten Weltkrieges* (Berlin, 1960).

——, 'Zur Ägyptenpolitik des deutschen Imperialismus vor dem Ersten Weltkrieg', in Walter Markov (ed.), *Geschichte und Geschichtsbild Afrikas* (Berlin, 1960) pp. 73–99.

——, 'Mustafa Kamil, Politisches Denken und Handeln eines ägyptischen Patrioten', *Zeitschrift für Geschichtswissenschaft*, IX, (1961) suppl, vol., 102–22.

——, 'Zur Legende vom "antikolonialen" Charakter der Baghdadbahnpolitik in der wilhelminische Ära', *Zeitschrift für Geschichtswissenschaft*, IX (1961) 246–70.

——, *Neue Aspekte des 'Arabi-Aufstandes 1879 bis 1882*, Sitzungsberichte der deutschen Akademie der Wissenschaften zu Berlin, Klasse Philosophie, Geschichte, No. 10 (Berlin, 1968).

——, 'Über die Rolle der Armee in der ägyptischen Revolution', *Zeitschrift für Militärgeschichte*, VII (1968) No. 2, 167–82.

Riad, Hassan, *L'Égypte Nassérienne* (Paris, 1964).

Richter, Erhard, *Lord Cromer, Ägypten und die Entstehung der französischen-englischen Entente von 1904*, Ph.D. thesis (Leipzig, 1931).

Rifaat, Muhammad, *The Awakening of Modern Egypt* (London, 1947).

——, *al-Tawjih al-Siyasi li'l-Fikra al-'Arabiyya al-Haditha* (Political Trends in Modern Arabic Thought) (Cairo, 1964).

Rivlin, Helen Anne B., *The Agricultural Policy of Muhammad 'Ali in Egypt* (Cambridge, Mass., 1961).

Rosenthal, E. I. J., *Islam in the Modern National State* (Cambridge, 1965).

Rossi, Ettore, 'Una Traduzione Turca dell' Opera "Della Tirannide" di V. Alfieri Probabilmente Conosciuta da al-Kawakibi', *Oriente Moderno*, XXXIV (1954) No. 7, 335–7.

Rothstein, Theodor, *Die Engländer in 'Agypten*, Ergänzungsheft zur Neuen Zeit, No. 10 (Stuttgart, 1911).

Rouleau, Eric, 'The Syrian Enigma, What is the Ba'th?', *New Left Review* (1967) No. 45, 53–65.

Ruf, Werner, *Der Burgibismus und die Außenpolitik des unabhängigen Tunesien* (Bielefeld, 1969).

Saab, Hassan, *The Arab Federalists of the Ottoman Empire* (Amsterdam, 1958).

el-Sadat, A., *Revolt on the Nile* (London, 1957).

Safran, Nadav, *Egypt in Search of a Political Community, an Analysis of the Intellectual and Political Evolution of Egypt, 1804–1952* (Cambridge, Mass., 1961).

Salem, Elie, 'Nationalism and Islam', *The Muslim World*, lii (1962) 277–87.

Sarkisyanz, Emanuel, *Rußland und der Messianismus des Orients, Sendungsbewußtsein und politischer Chiliasmus des Ostens* (Tübingen, 1955).

Schechtman, Joseph B., *The Mufti and the Führer, The Rise and Fall of Haj Amin el-Husseini* (New York and London, 1965).

Seale, Patrick, *The Struggle for Syria, a Study of Post-War Arab Politics 1945–1958* (London, 1965).

Sellheim, Rudolf, 'Prophet, Chalif und Geschichte, die Muhammad-Biographie des Ibn Ishaq', *Oriens*, xviii-xix (1965–66) 33–91.

——, 'Neue Materialen zur Biographie des Yaqut', in R. Sellheim *et al.*, *Schriften und Bilder, Drei orientalische Untersuchungen* (Wiesbaden, 1967) pp. 41–72.

——, *Der zweite Bürgerkrieg im Islam (680–692)* (Wiesbaden, 1970).

Sharabi, Hisham B., *Governments and Politics of the Middle East in the Twentieth Century* (Princeton, 1962).

——, *Nationalism and Revolution in the Arab World* (Princeton, 1966).

——, 'Die Entstehung einer revolutionären Ideologie in der arabischen Welt', *Bustan*, x (1969) Nos. 2–3, 3–11.

Sharara, 'Abd al-Latif, *al-Janib al-Thaqafi min al-Qawmiyya al-'Arabiyya* (The Cultural Dimension of Arab nationalism) (Beirut, 1961).

Shaw, Stanford J., *The Financial and Administrative Organization and Development of Ottoman Egypt, 1517–1798* (Princeton, 1962).

Shaw, Stanford J. (ed. and transl.), *Ottoman Egypt in the Eighteenth Century, the Nizāmnāme-i-Misr of Cezzār Ahmed Pasha* (Cambridge, Mass., 1962).

Shayyal, Jamal al-Din, *Rifa'a R. al-Tahtawi, 1801–1873* (Cairo, 1958).

Şinasi, Mehmet, *Studien zur Geschichte der syrischen Politik*

Mehmed Alis von Ägypten, unpub. Ph.D. thesis (Göttingen, 1936).

Smith, W. C., *Islam in Modern History* (Princeton, 1957).

Smolitsch, Igor, 'Zur Geschichte der Beziehungen zwischen der russischen Kirche und dem orthodoxen Osten: Die russische kirchliche Mission in Jerusalem', *Ostkirchliche Studien*, v (1956) No. 1, 33–51, and Nos. 2–3, 89–136.

Spillmann, Georges, *Napoléon et l'Islam* (Paris, 1969).

Steden, Axel, 'Islampakt und Nassers Opposition', *Orient*, VII (1966) No. 3, 79–83.

Steinhaus, Kurt, *Soziologie der türkischen Revolution, zum Problem der Entfaltung der bürgerlichen Gesellschaft in sozioökonomisch schwach entwickelten Ländern* (Frankfurt/Main, 1969).

Steppat, Fritz, 'Nationalismus und Islam bei Mustafa Kamil, ein Beitrag zur Ideengeschichte der ägyptischen Nationalbewegung', in *Die Welt des Islams*, n.s., IV (1956) 241–341.

——, 'Die arabischen Staaten zwischen Ost und West', in Wilhelm Cornides (ed.), *Die Internationale Politik* (Munich, 1961) pp. 671–752.

——, 'Nassers Revolution', *Europa-Archiv*, XVII (1962) No. 5, 163–73.

——, 'Die arabische Welt in der Epoche des Nationalismus', postscript to Franz Taeschner, *Geschichte der arabischen Welt* (Stuttgart, 1964) pp. 178–236.

——, 'Gamal 'Abdannasir', in R. Kerschagl (ed. for the Austrian Commission to UNESCO), *Die geistig-politischen Profile der Gegenwart in Asien* (Vienna, 1964) pp. 32–50.

——, 'Der Muslim und die Obrigkeit', in *Zeitschrift für Politik*, n.s., XII (1965) No. 4, 319–32.

Taeschner, F., 'Der Islam im Banne des Nationalismus der Zwischen weltkriegszeit', in *BASI* (ed. R. Hartmann, q.v.,) (Leipzig, 1944) pp. 484–513.

Tapiéro, Norbert, *Les idées réformistes d'al-Kawakibi 1849–1902, contribution à l'étude de l'Islam moderne* (Paris, 1956).

Tibawi, A. L. *British Interests in Palestine, 1800–1901, a Study of Religious and Educational Enterprise* (London and Oxford, 1961).

——, *American Interests in Syria 1800–1901, A Study of Educational, Literary and Religious Work* (London and Oxford, 1966).

——, 'The Genesis and Early History of the Syrian Protestant College', *Middle East Journal*, XXI (1967) No. 1, 1–15, and No. 2, 199–212.

——, *A Modern History of Syria including Lebanon and Palestine* (London, 1969).

Tibi, Bassam, 'Der arabische Sozialismus', in I. Fetscher (ed.), *Der Sozialismus* (Munich, 1968) pp. 378–87.

——, 'Skizze einer Geschichte des Sozialismus in den arabischen Ländern', in B. Tibi (ed.), *Die arabische Linke* (Frankfurt/Main, 1969) pp. 7–41.

——, 'Zum Verhältnis von Militär und kolonialem Nationalismus am Beispiel der arabischen Länder', *Sozialistische Politik*, I (1969) No. 4, 4–19.

——, 'Akkulturationsprozesse im modernen Orient', *Neue Politische Literatur*, XV (1970) No. 1, 77–84.

——, 'Die Krise des Burgibismus, Entstehung und Verfall des "Konstitutionellen Sozialismus" in Tunesien', *Das Argument*, XII (1970) No. 59, 530–55.

——, 'Sprachentwicklung und sozialer Wandel. Die Diskussion über Sprache und Kultur im arabischen Orient', *Die Dritte Welt*, I (1972) 518–48.

——, 'Von der Selbstverherrlichung zur Selbstkritik. Zur Kritik des politischen Schrifttums der zeitgenössischen arabischen Intelligenz', *Die Dritte Welt*, I (1972) No. 2, 158–84.

——, *Militär und Sozialismus in der Dritten Welt. Allgemeine Theorie und Regionalstudien über arabischen Länder* (Frankfurt/Main, 1973).

——, 'Die Wiederentdeckung des ägyptischnationalen, kulturellen Identität. Ägyptens Loslösung vom Panarabismus unter Sadat', *Die Dritte Welt*, VII (1978) No. 2, 253–65.

——, 'Der arabische Nationalismus als Forschungsgegenstand', in B. Tibi, *Internationale Politik und Entwicklungsländerforschung* (Frankfurt/Main, 1979).

——, 'Der Islam als politsche Ideologie', *Die Neue Gesellschaft*, XXVI (1979) No. 3, 212–17.

Tibi, Bassam (ed.), Mehdi Ben Barka, *Revolutionäre Alternative* (Munich, 1969).

Tignor, Robert L., *Modernisation and British Colonial Rule in Egypt, 1882–1914* (Princeton, 1966).

Tillmann, Heinz, *Deutschlands Araberpolitik im zweiten Weltkrieg* (Berlin, 1965).

Topf, Erich, *Die Staatenbildung in den arabischen Teilen der Türkei seit dem Weltkriege nach Entstehung, Bedeutung und Lebensfähigkeit* (Hamburg, 1929).

Toynbee, Arnold, *A Study of History*, vol. VIII (London, 1954); esp. 'The Modern West and the Islamic World', pp. 216 ff.

Vatikiotis, P. J., 'Muhammad 'Abduh and the Quest for a Muslim Humanism', *Arabica*, IV (1957) 55–72.

Volney, C. F., *Voyage en Égypte et en Syrie les années 1783–1785* (repr. Paris, 1959); Eng. transl., *Travels through Syria and Egypt in the years 1783, 1784, and 1785*, 2 vols (London, 1787); facsimile reproduction, Farnborough, 1972.

Watt, W. M., *Islam and the Integration of Society* (London, 1961).

Williams, Ann, *Britain and France in the Middle East and North Africa, 1914–1967* (London and New York, 1968).

Yamak, Labib Zuwiyya, *The Syrian Social Nationalist Party, An Ideological Analysis*, 2nd ed. (Cambridge, Mass., 1969).

Yusuf, Yusuf Khalil, *al-Qawmiyya al-'Arabiyya wa Dawr al-Tarbiyya fi Tahqiqiha* (The Role of Education in the Realisation of Arab Nationalism) (Cairo, 1967).

Zeine, Z. N., *The Emergence of Arab Nationalism, With a Background Study of Arab-Turkish Relations in the Near East*, 2nd ed. (Beirut, 1966).

7. Other Works Cited

Abu Jaber, K. S., 'Kleines Glossar zum arabischen Sozialismus', *Bustan* (1969) Nos. 2–3, 61–5.

Agwani, M. S., *The Lebanese Crisis of 1958, a Documentary Study* (London, 1965).

'Aisami, Shibli, *Hawl al-Wahda al-'Arabiyya* (On Arab Unity) (Damascus, 1967).

'Allush, Naji, 'Tatawwutar al-Haraka al-'Arabiyya mundhu ba'd al-Nahdha' (The Development of the Arab Movement after the *Nahdha*) *Dirasat 'Arabiyya*, II (1965) No. 1, 57–73.

——, 'al-Haraka al-'Arabiyya ba'd al-Harb al-'Alamiyya al-Ula' (The Arab Movement after the First World War), *Dirasat 'Arabiyya*, II (1965) No. 3, 54–75.

——, 'al-Thawra al-'Arabiyya al-Kubra: Muhawalat Taqyim' (The Great Arab Revolt: an Attempt at an Evaluation), *Dirasat 'Arabiyya*, II (1966) No. 8, 4–12.

Ansprenger, F., *Auflösung der Kolonialreiche* (Munich, 1966).

Ashford, D. E., *Political Change in Morocco* (Princeton, 1961).

Ashqar, Asad, *Nadhara fi Tarikhna wa Awda'na al-Hadira: min*

Mafahim al-Insan al-Jadid (A View of our Contemporary History and our Present Relationships: on the Concept of the New Man) (Beirut, c. 1969).

Ayad, K., *Die Geschichts- und Gesellschaftslehre Ibn Khalduns* (Stuttgart, 1930).

Binder, L., *The Ideological Revolution in the Middle East* (New York, 1964).

Bloch, Ernst, *Avicenna und die Aristotelische Linke* (Frankfurt/Main, 1963).

——, *Das Prinzip Hoffnung*, vol. I, 2nd ed. (Frankfurt/Main, 1967).

Bonn, Gisela, *Léopold S. Senghor, Wegbereiter der Culture Universelle* (Düsseldorf, 1968).

de Coulanges, Fustel, 'De la manière d'écrire l'histoire en France et en Allemagne depuis cinquante ans: la politique d'envahissement: Louvois et M.de Bismarck: L'Alsace, est-elle allemande ou francais? Réponse à M. Mommesen,' *Questions Contemporaines* (Paris, 1916).

Damis, John, 'Political Developments in Morocco under French Protectorate 1925–1943', *Middle East Journal*, xxiv (1970) No. 1, 74–86.

Darwaza, al-Hakam and Jabburi, Hamid, *Ma'al-Qawmiyya al-'arabiyya* (With Arab Nationalism), 4th ed. (Beirut, 1960).

Darwaza, M. 'I., *'Uruba Misr fi'l-Qadim wa'l-Hadith, aw Qabl al-Islam wa Ba'dahu* (Arabism in Egypt Past and Present, or Before and After Islam) 2nd ed. (Beirut, 1963).

Euchner, Walther, 'Demokratietheoretische Aspekte der politische Ideengeschichte', in D. Senghaas and G. Kress (eds), *Politikwissenschaft* (Frankfurt/Main, 1969).

Fakhuri, Hanna, *Tarikh al-Adab al-'Arabi* (History of Arabic Literature), 3rd ed. (Beirut, 1960).

Fishman, Joshua A., *Language and Nationalism* (Rowley, Mass., 1972).

Gibb, H. A. R., 'The Islamic Background of Ibn Khaldun's Political Theory', in *Studies in the Civilisation of Islam* (London, 1962) pp. 166–75.

Gordon, D. C., *The Passing of French Algeria* (London, 1965).

Grobba, Fritz, *Männer und Mächte im Orient: 25 Jahre diplomatischer Tätigkeit im Orient* (Göttingen, 1967).

Grohs, Gerhard and Tibi, Bassam (eds), *Zur Soziologie der Dekolonisation in Afrika* (Frankfurt/Main, 1973).

Haddad, 'Uthman Kamil, *Harakat Rashid 'Ali al-Gailani Sannat*

1941 (The Movement of Rashid 'Ali al-Gailani in 1941) (Sidon, c. 1950).

Haim, Sylvia, *The Ideas of a Precursor; 'Abd al-Rahman al-Kawakibi (1849–1902) in Relation to the Trend of Muslim Arab Political Thought*, unpub. Ph.D. thesis (Edinburgh, 1953).

Halstead, John P., *Rebirth of a Nation: The Origins and Rise of Moroccan Nationalism* (Cambridge, Mass., 1967).

Hamati, Henri, *Jamahir wa Kawarith* (Masses and Disasters) (Beirut, 1968).

Hartmann, R., *Zur Vorgeschichte des 'abbasidischen Schein-Chalifats von Cairo* (Berlin, 1950).

Hauser, Henri, *Le principe des nationalités, ses origins historiques* (Paris, 1916).

Hirszowicz, Lukasz, *The Third Reich and the Arab East* (London, 1966).

Hitti, Philip K., *Surya wa'l-Suriyyun min Nafidha al-Tarikh* (A Historical View of Syria and the Syrians) (New York, 1926).

Horovitz, J., 'Neuere Literatur über das Kalifat', *Der Islam*, xv (1926), 79–82.

Ibn Khaldun, *al-Muqaddima* (Prolegomena to History) (Cairo, n.d.).

——, *The Muqaddima, an Introduction to History*, ed. and transl. F. Rosenthal (New York, 1958).

Ibrahim, Muhsin, *Limadha Munadhdhama al-Ishtirakiyyin al-Lubnaniyyin?* (Why the Organisation of Lebanese Socialists?) (Beirut, 1970).

al-Jabarti, 'Abd al-Rahman, *'Aja'ib al-Athar, fi'l-Tarajim w',al-Akhbar*, 4 vols (Cairo, 1904–5). French transl., *Merveilles Biographiques et historiques ou chroniques du Cheikh Abd El-Rahman El-Jabarti*, 8 vols (Cairo, 1888–96).

Kewenig, Wilhelm, *Die Koexistenz der Religionsgemeinschaften in Libanon* (Berlin, 1965).

Khadduri, Majid, 'The Nature and Sources of the *shari'a*', *George Washington Law Review*, xx (1953) 3–23.

——, ''Aziz 'Ali al-Misri and the Arab Nationalist Movement', *St Antony's Papers* (1960) 140–63.

Khemiri, T., 'Der 'Asabiyya-Begriff in der Muqaddima des Ibn Haldun', *Der Islam*, xxii (1936) 163–88.

Khuri, Sami, *al-Radd 'ala Sati' al-Husri* (Reply to Sati' al-Husri) (Beirut, n.d.).

von Kramer, A., *Ibn Haldun und seine Kulturgeschichte der islamis-*

chen Reiche, Sitzungsberichte der Akademie der Wissenschaften zu Wien (Vienna, 1878).

Lammens, Henri, *La Syrie* (Beirut, 1921).

Landau, J. M., *Parliaments and Parties in Egypt* (Tel Aviv, 1953).

Le Tourneau, Roger, *L'évolution politique de l'Afrique du Nord Musulmane 1920–1961* (Paris, 1962).

Ling, D. L., *Tunisia from Protectorate to Republic* (Bloomington, 1967).

Lukács, G., 'Über einige Eigentumlichkeiten der geschichtlichen Entwicklung Deutschlands' in *idem.*, *Die Zerstörung der Vernunft* (Berlin, 1962), *Werke*, vol. IX, pp. 37 ff.

Moore, C. H., *Tunisia since Independence* (Berkeley and Los Angeles, 1965).

Mubarak, M., *al-Umma al-'Arabiyya fi Ma'rakat Tahqiq al-Dhat* (The Arab Nation in its Struggle for an Identity) (Damascus, 1959).

Munajjid, Salah, *Wohin treibt die arabische Welt?* (Munich, 1968).

Nasser, G. A., *The Philosophy of the Revolution* (Cairo, n.d.).

Oppermann, T., *Die algerische Frage* (Stuttgart, 1959).

Paterich, Eckart, *Götter and Helden der Griechen*, 5th ed. (Frankfurt/Main, 1965).

Pearlman, Maurice, *Mufti of Jerusalem, The Story of Haj Amin el-Huseini* (London, 1947).

Qasim, Mahmud, '*Abd al-Hamid bin Badis, al-Za'im al-Ruhi li-Harb al-Tahrir al-Jaza'iriyya* ('Abd al-Hamid ben Badis, The Spiritual Leader of the Algerian War of Liberation) (Cairo, 1968).

Renan, E., *Qu'est-ce qu'une nation?*, Eng. transl., 'What is a Nation?', in Alfred Zimmern (ed.), *Modern Political Doctrines* (London, 1939).

Ritter, H., 'Die Abschaffung des Kalifats', *Archiv für Politik und Geschichte*, II (1924), Part I, 343–68.

——, 'Irrational Solidarity Groups, a socio-psychological study in connection with Ibn Khaldun', *Oriens*, I (1948), 1–44.

Rodinson, Maxime, *Islam and Capitalism* (London, 1974).

Rosenthal, E. I. J., *Ibn Khalduns Gedanken über den Staat* (Berlin, 1932).

Sanhoury, A., *Le Califat, son Évolution vers une Société des Nations Orientales* (Paris, 1926).

al-Sayigh, Anis, *al-Fikra al-'Arabiyya fi Misr* (Arabic Thought in Egypt) (Beirut, 1959).

——, *Tatawwur al-Mafhum al-Qawmi'inda al-'Arab* (The

Development of Arab National Thought) (Beirut, 1961).

——, *Fi Mafhum al-Za'ama al-Siyasiyya, min Faisal al-Awwal ila Jamal 'Abd al-Nasir*, (On the Significance of Political Leadership: from Faisal I to Jamal 'Abd al-Nasir) (Beirut, 1965).

——, *al-Hashimiyyun wa'l-Thawra al-'Arabiyya al-Kubra* (The Hashimites and the Great Arab Revolt) (Beirut, 1966).

Sharfan, Zahi, 'Abna' al-Hayat wa Shajara al-Fikr al-Yabisa' (The Sons of Life and the Dried Up Tree of Thought), *Dirasat 'Arabiyya* VI (1970) No. 3, 114–28.

Simon, H., *Ibn Khalduns Wissenschaft von der menschlichen Kultur* (Leipzig, 1959).

Smith, Anthony D., *Theories of Nationalism* (New York, 1972).

Sorokin, P., *Social and Cultural Dynamics*, vol. II (New York, 1937).

Stokes, Gale, 'The Undeveloped Theory of Nationalism', *World Politics*, XXXI (1978) No. 1, 150–160.

Talmon, J. L., *The Origins of Totalitarian Democracy* (London, 1952).

Tignor, R., 'Some Materials for a History of the 'Arabi Revolution', *Middle East Journal*, XVI (1962) 239–48.

Torrey, Gordon, H., *Syrian Politics and the Military* (Columbus, Ohio, 1964).

——, 'Ba'th Ideology and Practice', *Middle East Journal*, XXIII (1969) No. 4, 445–70.

Ule, W., *Der arabische Sozialismus* (Opladen, 1969).

al-Wardi, 'Ali, *Mantiq Ibn Khaldun* (Ibn Khaldun's Logic) (Cairo, 1962).

Waters, M. P., *Mufti over the Middle East* (London, 1942).

Weber, Max, *Wirtschaft und Gesellschaft: Grundriß der verstehenden Soziologie*, 2 vols (Cologne and Berlin, 1962); Eng. transl. *Economy and Society*, 3 vols (New York, 1968).

Wehler, Hans-Ulrich, *Bismarck und der deutsche Imperialismus* (Cologne, 1969).

Zahar, Renate, *Kolonialismus und Entfremdung: zur politischen Theorie Frantz Fanons* (Frankfurt/Main, 1969).

Index

This index does not cover material in the new Introduction to the Second Edition